the risk society
and
beyond

the risk society
and
beyond

critical issues for social theory

edited by
barbara adam, ulrich beck
and joost van loon

SAGE Publications
London • Thousand Oaks • New Delhi

SAGE Publications Ltd
6 Bonhill Street
London EC2A 4PU

SAGE Publications Inc
2455 Teller Road
Thousand Oaks, California 91320

SAGE Publications India Pvt Ltd
32, M-Block Market
Greater Kailash - I
New Delhi 110 048

British Library Cataloguing in Publication data

A catalogue record for this book is
available from the British Library

ISBN 0 7619 6468 1
ISBN 0 7619 6469 X (pbk)

Library of Congress catalog card number available

Typeset by SIVA Math Setters, Chennai, India.
Printed in Great Britain by Athenaeum Press, Gateshead

Contents

Notes on contributors   vi

Acknowledgements   viii

Introduction: Repositioning Risk; the Challenge for Social Theory   1
Barbara Adam and Joost van Loon

PART I   Recasting Risk Culture

1 Risk Society or Angst Society?
   Two Views of Risk, Consciousness and Community   33
   Alan Scott

2 Risk Culture   47
   Scott Lash

3 Risk, Trust and Scepticism in the Age of the New Genetics   63
   Hilary Rose

PART II   Challenging Big Science

4 Nuclear Risks: Three Problematics   78
   Alan Irwin, Stuart Allan and Ian Welsh

5 Genotechnology: Three Challenges to Risk Legitimation   105
   Lindsay Prior, Peter Glasner and Ruth McNally

6 Health and Responsibility: From Social Change to
   Technological Change and Vice Versa   122
   Elisabeth Beck-Gernsheim

PART III   Mediating Technologies of Risk

7 Child Organ Stealing Stories: Risk, Rumour and
   Reproductive Technologies   136
   Claudia Castañeda

8 Liturgies of Fear: Biotechnology and Culture   155
   Howard Caygill

9 Virtual Risks in an Age of Cybernetic Reproduction   165
   Joost van Loon

PART IV   P(l)aying for Futures

10 Worlds in Action: Information, Instantaneity and
    Global Futures Trading   183
    Deirdre Boden

11 Discourses of Risk and Utopia   198
    Ruth Levitas

12 Risk Society Revisited: Theory, Politics and Research Programmes   211
    Ulrich Beck

Index   230

Notes on Contributors

Barbara Adam is Professor in Social Theory at the University of Wales in Cardiff and has published widely on time and social theory. Until 1999, she was the founding-editor of *Time & Society*.

Stuart Allan lectures in Cultural and Media Studies at the University of the West of England, Bristol. He has published widely in the areas of journalism, nuclear issues, cultural theory and media history. He is a series editor with the Open University Press.

Ulrich Beck is Professor of Sociology at the Maximilian Universität in München. He was previously a Distinguished Research Professor at the University of Wales in Cardiff and is now Visiting Professor at the London School of Economics.

Elisabeth Beck-Gernsheim is Professor of Sociology at the University of Erlangen-Nürnberg, Germany. Her research and publications range from the sociology of work and occupations to family studies, gender studies, demographical change and reproductive technologies. Currently, she is working on a project on 'Multicultural families and ethnic identity'.

Deirdre Boden holds the Chair in Communication at the Copenhagen Business School. Her publications encompass a wide range of topics, including ethnomethodology, conversation analysis, sociology of organizations and social theory.

Claudia Castañeda is Lecturer in Science Studies at Lancaster University. Her main area of interest is post-colonial science and technology studies.

Howard Caygill is Professor of Cultural History at Goldsmiths College, University of London. He has widely published in the areas of philosophy and cultural studies, in particular on the works of Kant and Walter Benjamin.

Peter Glasner is Research Professor in Sociology at the Centre for Social and Economic Research at the University of the West of England, Bristol, where since July 1997 he has been Executive Dean of the Faculty of Economics and Social Science. He has published extensively on science policy and the sociology of science.

Alan Irwin is Professor of Sociology at Brunel University. His recent research has focused on regulatory science, environmental sociology and the public understanding of science.

Scott Lash is Director of the Centre for Cultural Studies at Goldsmith's College, University of London. His main publications are on theories of culture and modernity.

Ruth Levitas is Reader in Sociology at the University of Bristol. She has written widely on utopianism and contemporary political ideologies.

Ruth McNally is a Research Fellow in the Centre for Research into Innovation, Culture and Technology (CRICT), Brunel University. She is a Director of Bio-Information (International) Limited, which has undertaken consultancies on policy and regulation, regarding modern genetic engineering, for the European Commission and the European Parliament. She has published on such far ranging subjects as gene therapy, the social management of genetic engineering, UK environmental policy, bioethics, European biotechnology policy, animal genetic engineering, fox rabies vaccine, patenting in biotechnology, DNA fingerprinting and abortion for risk of foetal handicap.

Lindsay Prior is Research Director of the Health and Risk Programme, at the University of Wales, College of Medicine and Cardiff University. His general research interests are in the field of medical sociology. He is currently working on issues relating to the communication of risk in medical consultations.

Hilary Rose is Visiting Research Professor in Sociology at City University, Emeritus Professor of Social Policy at the University of Bradford and Professor of Physic at Gresham College. She has researched and published extensively in the field of social studies of science. Currently she is working on a book on genomics.

Alan Scott is Professor of Sociology at the University of Innsbruck. His main areas of interest are political and cultural sociology and social theory. He has recently written on intellectuals, on politics and methods in Weber and on theories of globalization.

Joost van Loon works at the Theory, Culture & Society centre of the Nottingham Trent University. He is co-editor of *Space and Culture*. He has published extensively on issues in social and cultural theory. His current work is on risk and infectious diseases.

Ian Welsh is Lecturer in Sociology, University of Wales, Cardiff. He is author of numerous publications on nuclear power, globalization and risk.

Acknowledgements

The editors wish to thank all participants of the 'Risk, Technologies, Futures' Conference held at the University of Wales in Cardiff on 2nd and 3rd of March, 1996 for their contribution to the very high quality of stimulating debate during and after the meetings. We would also like to thank the School of Social and Administrative Studies of Cardiff University and the British Sociological Association's Theory Group, in particular Alan Scott, for their support. Moreover, we would like to thank Chris and Robert Rojek, Jackie Griffin and Seth Edwards at Sage for facilitating the publication of this edited collection. A final word of thanks goes to Dr Patricia Taraborrelli, who has been of great help with the administrative organization of this project during the early stages of development.

Introduction: Repositioning Risk; the Challenge for Social Theory

Barbara Adam and Joost van Loon

Since the first publication in Germany of Ulrich Beck's *Risikogesellschaft* (1986, translated as *Risk Society*, 1992), a book which in many ways is not only a visionary excursion into our present condition but also a prophetic perspective on the future, Beck's work has continued to challenge the social science tradition and to initiate some of the most interesting debates in contemporary social theory. This volume brings together some of these debates and it repositions perspectives on risk with reference to recent developments in nuclear, genetic, reproductive and communication technologies. It explores socio-political and socio-scientific issues associated with these technologies across the full spectrum of contemporary existence, ranging from the bodily and personal to the familial, public and global. Not a mere application of Beck's notion of risk society to various empirical domains, the chapters provide critical reappraisals of perspectives on risk in the light of past/present praxis and with an eye to future developments.

What can social theory contribute to our understanding of the nature of modern risks and to debates about how such risks may be minimized and more justly distributed? What has it to offer with respect to the indeterminate future and the potential dangers posed by techno-hazards that are largely beyond the reach of sense perception? Of course, these questions can be addressed only once there is an acceptance that social theory should be about something other than itself, and that it needs to engage with the central socio-political and economic issues of its times. This takes us to the core question about social theory, that is, the question about its role in society. Is social theory to cultivate specific ways of thinking, to foster understanding of the theoretical and conceptual universe or is it to provide not only a better understanding of the world we inhabit, but, more ambitiously, to relate this to the domains of politics, ethics and situated moralities? Is it about praxis, the bringing together of theory and practice?

Although there are obvious reasons for preferring the more limited, instrumental role of social theory, the majority of authors in this collection, strongly opt for the more inclusive one. In a risk society, we want to argue, even the most restrained and moderate–objectivist account of risk implications involves a hidden politics, ethics and morality. This does not mean that we advocate a moralizing role for social theory; it simply means that with every form of 'coming to terms' and 'making sense', we face a decision about whether to acknowledge or ignore the ethico-political implications. To acknowledge that we indeed face these options is the foundation of 'reflexive modernisation, that is, the inescapable "self-confrontation" that accompanies the contemporary industrial way of life' (Beck et al., 1994: 5).

In this book, therefore, we advocate a social theory that takes heed of the consequences of living in a risk society. This reflexivity has implications for social theory's treatment of the constellation of risks, technologies and the relationship to the future which constitutes our specific focus. We would like to highlight five of these implications:

1 The necessary involvement of a sense of 'construction' in the configuration of risk-perception;
2 the inevitability of the contested nature of these constructions as 'relations of risk-definition';
3 the need to transgress the disciplinary boundaries of knowledge and instead focus on the 'unbounded' nature of knowledge-practices which might include those of science, the media, politics and commerce;
4 the appeal to transform 'the language of risk' from the ethos of calculation (and binary logic) to the ethos of mediation; and
5 the imperative of positioning technologically induced 'risks' in relation to the future, for which we cannot but take some semblance of responsibility.

Construction

The first aspect we would like to draw attention to is the 'constructed nature' of risk. This already points to a paradox as the vernacular usage of 'nature' implies an essence that comes before all constructions. This apparent paradox, however, must be fully appreciated. It is not the question of whether risks are real or 'mere' constructions that we are pursuing here as ours is not a book on epistemology. Instead, we argue for the need to understand risk construction as a practice of manufacturing particular uncertainties that may have harmful consequences to 'life' in the broadest sense of the term. The essence of risk is not that it *is* happening, but that it *might be* happening. Risks are manufactured, not only through the application of technologies, but also in the making of sense and by the technological sensibility of a potential harm, danger or threat. One cannot, therefore, observe a risk as a thing-out-there – risks are necessarily constructed. However, they are not constructed on the basis of voluntary imagination; that is, we are not free to 'construct' risks as we please. Instead risks are being revealed in their construction. The construction of risk must obey the logic (discourse or reason) of its revelation. In order to make sense it has to incorporate the technological sensibility (know-how) of that which granted its existence. The consequences of this revealing are irreversible but not fixed.

The theory and analysis of risk therefore takes us out of both the empirically accessible world of social facts as well as the sphere of pure social construction. This is so because, on the one hand, the materiality of technologically-constituted hazards always includes the virtual domain of latency, invisibility and contingency. On the other hand, socially constructed risks are also lived as potential harm. This im/materiality constitutes a difficulty at two different levels: it forces theorists to transcend not only the choice between realism and constructivism but also the reliance on the empirically accessible world of social facts. For social theory this means a radical destabilization of two often unquestioned problematics and critical tools that lie at the very heart of the social sciences' epistemology and methodology.

For social scientists, perceptions of risk are intimately tied to understandings of what constitutes dangers, threats and hazards and for whom. Today, however, a significant number of technologically-induced hazards, such as those associated with chemical pollution, atomic radiation and genetically modified organisms, are characterized by an inaccessibility to the senses. They operate outside the capacity of (unaided) human perception. This im/materiality gives risks an air of unreality until the moment at which they materialize as symptoms. In other words, without visual presence, the hazards associated with these technologies are difficult to represent as risks, let alone sustain their 'existence' beyond their momentary emergence. Radiation from nuclear power is a case in point. It was the mass media's representation of the anti-nuclear campaign of the women at Greenham Common, for example, or the reports of continued traces of high degrees of exposure to radiation in animals and soil after the nuclear explosion at Chernobyl, that made the invisible threat tangible and kept the issues alive. Transformed into an embodied danger, the threat of radiation has engendered widespread expression of public concern and intense academic debate about the risks to people and the environment which, in turn, put it firmly on the political agenda. Today, the potential for harm from nuclear power is in no way diminished. On the contrary, ever-increasing nuclear waste, ageing nuclear power plants, the proliferation of nuclear capability and, most worryingly, the seepage and mysterious disappearance without trace of nuclear weapons and materials from the former USSR have vastly increased the threat of radiation and nuclear disaster. And yet, it is exceedingly quiet on the nuclear front. Gene technology has taken over where concern about nuclear power has been shelved.

Similar, and yet so different, the perceived and defined risks associated with gene technology are generating patterns of public concern that seem to replicate the proliferation of pressure groups, expert advisers, scientific and political debate as well as extensive media coverage that was previously associated with nuclear power and the threat of radiation. Thus, if social theory is to play a meaningful public and political role, it needs to provide analyses not only of people's perceptions, definitions and legitimations of such risks but also of the mutual constitution of implicit assumptions, technological imposition and uptake, and the mediation of otherwise inaccessible knowledge. This book takes on this challenge. It is concerned with the sociality of these and other hazards and their translation into risks. It considers their impact on the socio-natural environment and ponders some of the ensuing approaches to the future.

Contested definitions

The im/materiality and in/visibility of the threats that suffuse the 'risk society' mean that all knowledge about it is mediated and as such dependent on interpretation. This presents the second challenge for analyses of these socially constituted industrial phenomena: all interpretation is inherently a matter of perspective and hence political. In the 'risk society', the im/material in/visible nature of technologically induced hazards puts natural scientists, social theorists, news workers, business managers and members of the public in similar structural positions with respect to the truth, objectivity and certainty of knowledge. That is, the ontology of risk as such does not grant privilege to any specific form of knowledge. In practice, of course, some people have substantially better access to information and research facilities than others. In addition, there are differences in discursive competencies, in acquiring accreditations of legitimacy, in resources to divert and displace risks to other groups and, last but not least, in shielding oneself from potential harm.

In risk society, therefore, the politics and sub-politics of risk definition become extremely important. They highlight the contested nature of who is defining what as risk and how. Risks have become a considerable force of political mobilization, often replacing references to, for example, inequalities associated with class, race and gender. It is the particular reliance on both interpretation and expert systems that have made risks the object of one of the most effective discursive strategies for changing the political horizon of modern industrialized society towards what Beck (1997) calls 'sub-politicization'. Here, it seems, it is no longer 'interests' that dominate the political horizon but claims about the legitimacy of particular forms of expertise and knowledge.

The inescapability of interpretation makes risks infinitely malleable and, as Beck (1992: 23) insists, 'open to social definition and construction'. This in turn puts those in a position to define (and/or legitimate) risks – the mass media, scientists, politicians and the legal profession – in key social positions. Analogous to Marx's 'relations of production' Beck points to the importance of risk in terms of 'relations of definition'. The pervasiveness of mediation, the high level of indeterminacy and the inevitability of political involvement mean that there is no one truth, that there are no facts outside the relativizing influence of interpretations based on context, position, perspective, interest, and the power to define and colour interpretation. Therefore, there can be no such thing as innocent knowledge. As Haraway (1988) pointed out, knowledge is inevitably tied to particular locations we inhabit; we all engage in situated knowledge. The socio-cultural study of risk thus exposes disembodied information as a farce and reveals instead (a) that knowledge is principally embodied, contextual and positional and (b) that taking up a position and to be positioned is inevitably a question of ethics (Adam, 1996, 1998; Diprose, 1994; Haraway, 1988, 1990; Van Loon, 1996). Moreover, it places those in charge of theory and analysis in the position of having to insist that there are no unambiguous, objective, scientific facts to be presented. This brings with it its own problems in so far as we still live in a cultural climate of positivism, in which this message of situated knowledge is regarded to be socially unacceptable. Science, politics, the media, law and commerce by and large still operate as particular establishments of expertise and knowledge/power and consequently tend to either proceed to translate the relativist and probabilistic logic of science into statements of certainty and fact or to restrict funding and patronage to those studies and analyses that retain the socio-politically and economically acceptable focus on all that is factual and quantifiable. What is thus perpetuated is the denial of the fundamental ambivalence and indeterminacy of risk as something that has not yet happened.

Here we encounter the particular problematic of the relationship between 'risk society' and 'risk culture'. In Beck's (1992) original argument 'risk society' refers to a particular set of social, economic, political and cultural conditions that are characterized by the increasingly pervasive logic of manufactured uncertainty and entail the transformation of existing social structures, institutions and relationships towards an incorporation of more complexity, contingency and fragmentation. On the basis of this analysis, it could be argued that risk society informs a particular mode of organization as a response to new challenges enforced upon the world by technologies and practices. 'Risk culture', in contrast, could be seen as a radicalization of such a response. From the perspective of 'risk culture' we can no longer speak of a new form of 'organization' since this perspective emphasizes a far less coherent ensemble of sensibilities and practices informed by uncertainty, contingency, complexity, fragmentation and turbulence. In this volume, Scott Lash points out that whereas risk society would always entail a sense of institutional domination (hence 'society'), risk culture embraces all kinds of residual and marginal forms of sense-making practices. However, in his reply (Chapter 12, this volume), Beck argues that the lack of institutional integration of the organization of manufactured uncertainty marks the essence of his risk society thesis, and concludes that there is no fundamental difference between risk society and risk culture. If there is a difference between the two terms, it is a matter of degree and not principle. One way to clarify the confusion is perhaps to point to the unmentioned counterparts of both: which would be risk-aversion society and risk-aversion culture. These seem to point to the currently dominant institutional forms and sensibilities of our western world. However, as all institutions and sensibilities can only be articulated as forms of rationalization, it is here that we must locate 'domination'. That is, they are not dominant in their immanent materiality, but more in the stranglehold they have placed on discursive constructions of uncertainty, complexity, contingency and turbulence. Hence, risk cultures are marginal counter-discursive articulations against the dominant risk-aversion culture of the sub-politics of expertise and commerce. Likewise risk society constitutes an institutional articulation against the main institutional forms of risk-aversion society that we currently live in. There is no point in defining risk culture and risk society as opposites, nor is there much to be gained by seeing them as one and the same; they refer to different modalities of sense-making. It is in their supplementary relationship that we may begin to make sense out of their effect on everyday life in the contemporary world.

The porosity of boundaries

A third difficulty for social theory relates to the porosity of disciplinary boundaries. To conceive of the risk technology-future relation as social practices requires that social theorists engage, to some extent at least, with the knowledge spheres of experts in a variety of fields: science and engineering, politics and financial markets, industry and insurance. It means that we need go beyond the conception of risk and technology as mere social constructs and grasp instead how specific technologies are lived as future-creating social praxis and in what way particular risks are experienced, perceived, defined, mediated, legitimated, and/or ignored. Such extended social science understanding, we suggest, is a precondition to thinking in meaningful ways about the perceived and defined risks – for human life, the existence of other species, even life as we know it to date – from hazards associated with Big Science that affect us now and for the long-term future. This is not easy in a discipline such as sociology, for example, that owes its existence to the explicit and tight delimitations of its subject matter (but not its methodology) with reference to other academic fields such as psychology, history and the natural sciences. Beck's 'risk society' is a society that makes a mockery of such boundaries: when the hazards that constitute an integral part of contemporary existence know no boundaries in time and space then analyses of their understanding and translation into risk have to be similarly 'unbounded' in their enquiries. Ulrich Beck is one of the leading exponents of this approach and this book as a whole is consistent with this essential insight.

Critical of disciplinary boundaries and the attendant dualistic choices between culture and nature, space and time, local and global, public and private, realist and constructivist epistemology, positivist and interpretative methodology, we can focus more freely on the chosen subject matter and pursue ways of seeing that were previously out of bounds. The products of Big Science are a case in point. Created for specific functions and without cognizance of the networked inter-connectivity of life, technological products enter the living world as 'foreign bodies' (Adam, 1998). Once inserted into the ecology of life, they begin to interact with their networked environments and from that point onwards scientists and engineers have inescapably lost control over the effects of their creations. Beck (1992) and Giddens (1991, 1995) refer to this phenomenon as 'manufactured uncertainty'; Wynne (1992) stresses its inescapable indeterminacy. Effects of the prized 'foreign bodies' suffuse our earth in uneven intensity, the resulting hazards dispersed not only over space but also time. Innovative, disembedded technologies whose impacts are temporally and spatially unbounded, yet affect some areas and beings more than others, render traditional assumptions about planning and managing the future inappropriate and consequently the language of prediction and control loses its pertinence. Moreover, notions of predictability, often taken as extrapolations of 'the present' or based on knowledge of 'the past', have indeed been overtaken by their own failures to secure any calculable future. With the disciplinary boundaries transgressed, we are able to appreciate how the current speed of technological change has warped the very notion of risk into an entirely different orbit.

The language of risk

This takes us directly to the fourth issue of relevance for social theorists intent on engaging with risk issues; this is the need for changing the prevalent genre of articulating risks and hazards from one based on calculation to one imbricated in meditation. We need a new symbolic ordering of risk perceptions and articulations as the nature of some of the contemporary hazards and their social risk relations of definition are being transformed at an implied structural level. The language of risk is traditionally associated with the economic world of trade and insurance, the medical world of health professionals and their clients, as well as dangerous sports and individuals 'risking' their lives for others. In these traditional risk situations, people assessed the risk potential of certain actions and made decisions and choices in the light of their appraisal. Specific risks were conceived with reference to the person, the family, the company, the nation and their physical, mental, social and/or economic welfare. This language of risk, therefore, was deeply, even inescapably, social. The perception of risk entailed a particular relationship to an essentially unknown future whose likelihood of coming about could nevertheless be calculated on the basis of extrapolating from past occurrences: a calculated socio-cultural response to potential anticipated happenings. Risk assessment and behaviour of this kind is a question of mathematics irrespective of whether the risk is explicitly or implicitly calculated (Adams, 1995). As such, this world of risk assessment belongs to the realm of rational action and scientific certainty, a realm of clear distinctions between safety and danger, truth and falsity, past and future.

The world of risk discussed in this book, however, is not of this kind. Instead of the realm of predictability and demystified futures, this book delineates a world of hazards and risks that is both more messy and more insidious, a world that can be encompassed neither by the traditional conceptions of risk nor their underlying dualistic assumptions. 'Risk society', argues Beck (1996: 28) 'is *not an option* which could be chosen or rejected in the course of political debate.' Instead it is an inescapable *structural* condition of advanced industrialization where the produced hazards of that system, in Beck's (1996: 31) words, *'undermine and/or cancel the established safety systems of the provident state's existing risk calculation'*. Beck contrasts contemporary hazards associated with nuclear power, chemical pollution and genetic engineering with the traditional problems in which the language of risk originated when he suggests that risks associated with the former cannot be limited in time and space, cannot be grasped through the rules of causality, and cannot be safeguarded, compensated or insured against. 'Industrial society, which has involuntarily mutated into risk society through its own systematically produced hazards', he thus suggests, 'balances *beyond the insurance limit*' (Beck, 1996: 31).

In other words, if reflexivity as self-confrontation is to mean anything in this context it is not a confrontation between two sets of calculations. Risk society has already taken us beyond the security of mathematics; we have to acknowledge that in this sense of constituting a new sort of reality, risk is not reducible to the product of probability of occurrence multiplied with the intensity and scope of potential harm. Instead, reflexivity requires us to be meditative, that is, looking back upon that which allows us to reflect in the first place. In the context of technologically-induced hazards, this means that we appropriate technology in a Heideggerian sense as 'that which reveals'. For Heidegger, modern technology implies a highly specific form of revelation. 'The revealing that rules in modern technology is a challenging which puts to nature the unreasonable demand that it supply energy that can be extracted and stored as such' (Heidegger, 1977: 14). It is this 'storage' of energy, unlocked from 'nature' that transforms itself into a 'standing-reserve'. In the risk society, what stands-in-reserve is revealing itself to us as our destiny, which we can no longer 'enframe' (organize) ourselves. Following Heidegger, it would mean the possibility of a new revealing because enframing implies concealment, hence loss of enframing implies unconcealment. Indeed, only in the risk society, we are perhaps enabled to 'unconceal the essence of technology'. It is this meditative insight that might be the saving power emerging with the growing danger (Heidegger, 1977: 28–9).

Ulrich Beck's 'risk society' is the backcloth against which most of the arguments presented in this book are developed and from which they take their critical departure. Many of the chapters are concerned with risks that are not just taken by individuals but imposed on entire societies, risks that escape detection by sense perception and safeguarding by public means, that elude not just calculation but even the powers of the conventional imagination. In the analyses presented in this book, technologically-constituted hazards and their associated social relations of risk definition turn out to be source, medium and outcome in unspecified time and space, at once globally dispersed, locally specific, contextual and personal, constructed and lived now into an open future. Consequently, most contributors search for ways to engage with the complexity and paradoxical nature of contemporary risks as they are lived, perceived, conceptualized, defined, mediated, legitimized, and/or institutionalized. An integral part of this effort is the endeavour to deconstruct bipolar oppositions by aligning themselves neither with the realist–absolutist stance nor with the constructionist–relativist position, transgressing instead (either pragmatically or synthetically) the borders between them. This involves shifting the plane of discussion from epistemological and metaphysical preoccupations to socially embedded analyses of risks, technologies and ways of relating to the future.

Futures

Finally, and closely allied to the issues above, are the difficulties associated with causal analysis and our relationship to the future. The connections between risks, technologies and futures are neither of a singular determination nor governed by linear causal connections. Certainly, perceptions of risk are likely to lead to new technologies as a key means to alleviate the threat. This in turn opens up an array of possible futures. Likewise, innovative technologies engender unexpected alternative futures which in turn cast new shadows of risk; and, of course, imagined futures condition perceptions and assessments of risk by setting into work particular technologies. Thus, connections between risks, technologies and futures might be understood as triangular and as mutually implicating, with no particular privileged node or relationship. This clearly takes social theorists outside conventional causal analysis and the traditional social science engagement with the future. In other words, technologically induced hazards problematize the relationship to the future not just for those charged with public protection but for those seeking to offer social analyses of the complex interdependencies between socio-political, socio-scientific/technological, socio-economic, media and every-day social spheres.

In the face of hazards that escape the logic of control, the pressure is on for everyone to find new ways of relating to risks associated with the impact of past/present decisions and practices. Where mastery fails, moreover, there arises the need to take responsibility for that which outlives us and creates futures for contemporaries and presents for future generations. Not in the material past, how-ever, but in the realm of embodied imagination do we need to seek the source of that responsible projection. Counterfactual thought and utopias, embodied per-formance art and the creation of (electronic) virtual realities, as we suggest in the latter part of the book, are some of the means at our disposal to take account of such largely unknowable futures.

The role of social theory in risk society/culture

> Only when insight brings itself disclosingly to pass, only when the coming to presence of technology lights up as Enframing, do we discern how, in the ordering of the standing-reserve, the truth of Being remains denied as world. (Heidegger, 1977: 48)

Traditionally, social theory has taken on three roles:

1 Social engineering: through functionalist perspectives to assist in the social construction of order, control and regulation;
2 political mobilization: through Marxist, critical and feminist theories to estab-lish a base for critique and emancipation; and
3 sense-making: through interpretative approaches to facilitate understanding of how socio-cultural intelligibility is achieved.

Co-existing as traditions of (applied) social science, the articulations of each of these three roles could develop in relative isolation from each other, constituting their own problematics, methodologies and accumulated knowledge (Gouldner, 1970; Ritzer, 1975). Consequently, little attention has been paid to the interde-pendencies between the three. However, social engineering, political mobiliza-tion and sense-making cannot really accomplish anything on their own; that is, they never exist in 'pure forms'. For example, social engineering without some form of sense-making is clearly impossible; sense-making is a form of political mobilization and every form of political mobilization implies social engineering. In isolation, these three traditions engendered the assumption that there could be 'innocent' or 'pure' knowledge, that was to be developed on the presumption of the autonomy of rationality and the acceptance of an external, objective, world (nature) into which knowledgeable, rational beings, informed by accredited logic, could enact their will to transform and cultivate nature. Irrespective of their dif-ferences, these three theoretical traditions considered socio-cultural interactions, institutions and structures to be distinct and separate from their natural environ-ment and to a lesser extent from the material, technological context within which human actions take place and knowledge is created. All three to varying degrees assume the primacy of rationality, valorize science and its knowledge base and rely on the intransgressible distinctiveness of fact versus value, object (structure) versus subject (agency), means versus ends, reality versus fiction, eternity versus history and generality versus particularity.

From this external knowledge base, social scientists have tended to take a number of perspectives on risk. Thus, risk is studied, understood and theorized with reference to risk behaviour, risk awareness, and risk perception or, in a more realist mode, with reference to 'risks themselves' (whatever this might mean) in which case they are classified according to the different principles that underpin them such as natural or manufactured risks. Manufactured risks are further distinguished by the degree to which they can be delimited in time and space or divisible into, for example, economic, political, professional and personal risks and similar categories are imposed on the various responses to risks. Irrespective of these distinctions, however, risk is conventionally associated with calculability, with the weighing-off of pros and cons, dangers and gains, the likelihood of coming to grief; that is, calculated risk is the product of the probability and intensity of harm.

However, in the previous section we have argued that there is a need for a repositioning of risk. This is marked by a particular turning in the social and cultural conditions under which particular risks are being unconcealed. This turning is not exclusively the domain of the 'physical' technosciences; it implies the social sciences as well (in particular social engineering). In this book, we aim to make a start with this turning, by unlocking the disciplinary entrapment of social theory that has been assigned, by its own tradition, to legislate by means of a self-grounding, the conditions of what counts as 'truth' and 'justice'. There are therefore two related questions which provide the overall problematic of the chapters in this volume: (1) 'What are the implications of the repositioning of risks for social theory?' and (2) 'What is the role of social theory in risk society and risk culture?' With social theory we refer to an organized abstraction of sense-making practices. It is obvious that whether we use the term 'risk society' or shift our attention to the perhaps more radical notion of 'risk culture', the implications of the repositioning of risk for social theory are unsettling. They are discomforting because the tools with which we used to 'handle' the social world in theoretical reflections seem no longer adequate to 'contain' the viroid turbulence of risk society/culture. This need for conceptual 're-tooling' is certainly not a new requirement. Ever since the crisis in sociology during the late 1960s (Gouldner, 1970), social scientists have urged for new concepts and new ways of thinking beyond the triad of functionalism, Marxism and interactionism. Despite these repeated calls for change, however, the vast majority of social scientists continue to use the traditional tried-and-tested language of the disciplines, conceptualizing their domains in terms of 'society', 'the individual', 'markets', 'the nation state', 'politics' or 'culture' without explicit acknowledgement that such terms have become almost entirely self-referential (Luhmann, 1990). Moreover, this repositioning of risk not only affects a repositioning of concepts, but also the very act of repositioning itself. The erosion of the authority of the scientific establishment leaves all knowledge-creating practices in a state of permanent instability and all certainties as necessarily contingent, particular and thus temporary. We cannot, therefore, claim new conceptual tools as ready-to-hand, because their very tool-ness already discloses their obsoleteness. In the ambivalent context of risk society/culture, social theory has the central task of re-inventing itself in an ongoing process if it is to be more than a self-referential activity.

The implications for social theory are thus first and foremost unsettling without granting us any sense of resolution. What is required is a different way of working. Instead of fragmenting, taking apart, scrutinizing, focusing, particular-izing, social theory needs to reinvent itself as an art of connecting, unfolding, disclosing, broadening and universalizing concepts. It needs to be speculative, without being teleological. Social theorists are only likely to accomplish this if they abandon their narrow-minded disciplinary interests and open up to the unknowable that resides in all forms of knowledge. However, this does not mean an abandonment of a concern for matters/energies of being, that is, the materiality of life. On the contrary, we want to argue that social theorists cannot but take into account the unfolding of events to which they must bear witness if they are to make sense of 'our' predicament.

This brings us to the second question, which is reflexively constituted by the first: 'What could the role of social theory be in a world marked by a reposition-ing of risk?' In modern thought, the traditional role of theory was to create structures in which knowledge could be developed; for example by providing abstractions, general laws, deductions or testable hypotheses (Foucault, 1970; Lyotard, 1984). In this sense, social theory is a particular practice of ordering knowledge. However, in the face of risk society/culture, and after a few decades in which first chaos theory and now complexity theory have undermined the very assumption of the normality of predictable order, such a role may seem rather inadequate to deal with the challenges of making sense. This inadequacy concerns, on the one hand, the insensitivity to singularity (the irreducibility of the concept), complexity and contingency (the multiplicity of the concept) that is inherent in any ordering-framework that tries to establish general laws; in other words, it is too indiscriminative. On the other hand, however, the logic of struc-turing is inappropriately limited to the ring-fencing of its own categorical imper-atives which engender the objects and objectives of this ordering of knowledge. Hence, traditional modern social theory is both too particular and too general. In order to overcome this double-flaw, social theory needs to become at once, more sensitive to the contingent and the specific, and more open to the unthinkable and undisciplined possibilities of ambivalence (Genosko, 1998). It is this paradoxical role in which social theorists find themselves when repositioning risk.

Within modern thought, however, ordering knowledge has never been the only concern of social theorists. Apart from granting better understanding, more insight and 'illuminating' the world, which is the more generally established and most widely accepted role of social theory, theory has – from its earliest reconstitution in modern thought – been charged with an almost as important responsibility of 'challenging' common sense. On the one hand, and in its more generally acclaimed epistemology, this challenging refers to the adequacy of 'reason' and 'logic' (in terms of truth); on the other hand, however, it also engendered a function of a more political and normative challenge, whereby theory becomes a different form of critique, not of Untruth, but of Injustice. Perhaps both forms of critique were already inscribed in Kant's threefold philosophical project; however, with the arrival of, for example, Marxism, feminism and post-colonialism, critical social theory has been established very effectively as a countervailing practice against instrumental positivist and neutral 'objective' science. We need to question however whether or not this specific role of challenging dominant modes of thinking by means of theoretically informed but normatively charged critique is still possible in the face of risk society/culture. The language of risk is not a language that easily accommodates itself to the language of injustice. This is because risks have been predominantly identified in relations of risk definition that are to a large extent oriented towards epistemologies of facticity and truth. The essence of the 'badness' of risk is not differentiated in terms of, for example, class, gender or race, but in more generalistic terms such as 'quality of life', which are primarily understood in medico-biological and economic terms rather than social-cultural ones. It is against the backdrop of this homogenizing, undifferentiated understanding of risk society that the chapters in the first section are being presented.

Recasting risk culture

In his lectures in the early 1970s, Niklas Luhmann distinguished between hazards and risks and later devoted an entire volume to the issue of risk in 1995. During the 1980s Mary Douglas and Aaron Wildavsky wrote *Risk and Culture* (1983). Yet despite these pertinent analyses, the theme of risk has not been taken up by the mainstream of social science but has remained instead the preserve of insurance experts and a range of specialists in the diverse field of risk assessment. Beck's *Risk Society*, in contrast, not only opened up the issue of risk for wider social science debate but also captured the public imagination: Chernobyl, Bhopal, Exxon Valdez, and more recently the risks associated with Bovine Spongiform Encephalopathy (BSE) (Ford, 1996; Lacey, 1994; Ratzan, 1998) and hormone-disrupting chemicals (Colborn et al., 1996) are prime exemplars for the book's thesis. Beck's work speaks to the contemporary western experience of the industrial way of life, and it touches deep fears about the shadow side of the successes of industrialization, scientific progress and technological innovation. Moreover, it depicts the socio-cultural and institutional nature of the environmental crisis which means that solutions too have to be sought in the socio-cultural sphere and the social institutions of that way of life.

Central to Beck's risk society thesis is the idea that a new system of articulations has emerged between capitalism, media, science and politics. This system manifests itself at the institutional level, for example, in the form of the uninsurability of major projects in the (bio)chemical, genetic and nuclear industries and their associated paradoxical co-articulations of in/calculability and un/decidability. Risk society operates on what Dillon (1996) has termed 'the politics of (in)security'. These paradoxes are intricately connected to the increased complexity of risk in contemporary society. That is to say, in 'risk society', technological innovations have attained such a high level of transformative capacity that the catastrophic potential of an increasing number of our (military) industrial activities has magnified beyond the comprehensible (e.g. Chernobyl, biochemical warfare, genetics). The established institutionalization of 'risk' in terms of 'insurance' (coupling risk with money and the future) has collapsed because it has become clear that this catastrophic potential can no longer be grasped in the form of the commodity fetish to which money is related. The probability/magnitude nexus of this catastrophic potential thus becomes incalculable in so far as it has lost its ultimate point of reference. Hence, as the need for more complex and more precise calculations rises with the increased complexity of risk, so does the impossibility to establish such calculations (Adam, 1998; Colborn et al., 1996; Lang and Clutterbuck, 1991; Ratzan, 1998).

This difficulty is tied to a simultaneous process which concerns scientific knowledge and political action. In risk society, we have developed greater knowledge and sensitivity towards the unintended consequences of our actions, which includes an awareness of an 'open' rest-category, that is, the inevitability of other unintended consequences we do not and cannot yet know. This last category is necessary for the inclusion of the aforementioned catastrophic potential which in turn disables the calculability of risk, but it also has profound political consequences. As Beck emphasizes, risk implies decision-making. In the face of this catastrophic potential, political action is absolutely vital as it might include life-or-death decisions. However, in the face of risk-complexity and the unknown factor of catastrophic potential, these decisions are increasingly disabled. Hence, as the need for decidability increases, so does the pertinence of undecidability. In such a context, theory operates in the political realm of interpretative choice.

The double paradox of un/calculability and un/decidability generates anxieties that are pervasive in the risk society as it moves from crisis to crisis. In between these crises there is a build up of displacement strategies which project a sense of security onto the dense complexity of risks by inhibiting their articulation in public discourses – in particular those of the mass media – by, for example, institutionalizing silence or denial (as in the case of 'mad cow disease' in Britain), or by asserting that full calculability and decidability is possible and attainable, if not already accomplished, by 'scientific experts' (as is, for example, often claimed by representatives of the nuclear industry) (Adam, 1998; Welsh, 2000; Wynne, 1996). In Beck's risk society, therefore, risk management is intricately connected with strategies of risk displacement.

Environmental hazards and the risks they pose for society are often unintended consequences of the industrial production process, a rest-product. As surplus, they are in excess of the utility of goods and services that have been intentionally produced. This residual character provides an anchoring point for the socio-cultural dimension of risk perception and risk management. Not merely a technical or organizational problem, the issue of risk has important cultural implications. It involves practices of sense-making and, as such, operates as a cover for all that cannot be 'named'. The chapters in the first section focus specifically on the cultural dimension of risk and stress the need for any discussion on the subject matter to take account of the cultural and historical context. Risk cultures, the authors argue, differ from one country to the next, even within Northern Europe, and it is the culturally specific they want to recover for studies that follow Beck's more structural, ideal-typical analysis of the risk society and its institutionally anchored processes. The work of Douglas and Wildavsky (1983) on the one hand and the social studies of science on the other are invoked as reminders for the need not to lose sight of the empirically specific culture in the case of the former, scientific and technological activity in the case of the latter. As a heuristic device, a label, 'risk culture' enables the discursive fixture of the fluidity of signification for the time being. The question is thus not what risk culture *is*, but what it *does*. By stressing the high value of risk, the contributors to this first part of the book highlight its investments in symbolic exchange relations. Too often, the authors suggest, the cultural aspects of environmental problems have been ignored as have been the material effects of symbolic exchange. This dual neglect contributes significantly to conceptually confused and ineffective strategies and policies associated with the issue of contemporary socio-environmental risk.

In Chapter 1, Alan Scott examines Beck's analysis of the risk society in the light of the rival theory by Mary Douglas and Aaron Wildavsky (1983) and, more specifically, Mary Douglas' (1992) *Risk and Blame: Essays in Cultural Theory*. He makes a distinction between the novel content of Beck's work and its traditional rhetorical structure. It is the conventional form – the periodization of the analysis and its narrative of discontinuity – that Scott takes to task in this chapter. Carefully and systematically he unpacks the cluster of before-and-after characteristics of Beck's analysis and shows each to be present throughout the entire period of industrialization from its very earliest beginnings to the present. As Scott takes us through these distinctions, Beck's respective characteristics of class and risk society disintegrate as markers of specific phases of history. Collectivization and individualization, the distribution of 'goods' and 'bads', hunger and fear, class and risk consciousness – the characteristics of the two phases of industrial society – are shown instead to be interpenetrating features of the entire history of industrialization. 'Is insecurity not merely the flip side of scarcity?' Scott asks, 'Or, more strongly, is insecurity not a function of scarcity?' Should we not rather look at insecurity, he asks further, as 'the inability to control those events which impact directly on life chance?' Insecurity and poverty, hunger and scarcity, the mobility of the wealthy, individualization and reflexivity get reassembled in Scott's discourse of continuity into new and fluid constellations.

This chapter is interesting not only for its scholarly weaving together of Beck and Douglas' very different analyses of risk but also for the effect it has on the innovative dimension of Beck's work: under Scott's recovery of the cultural relativism of the historical context, the dualistic framework crumbles but so also does that which makes the *Risk Society* and Beck's later publications such powerful social theory. Scott's chapter shows that when we focus on the conventional in Beck's work, the innovative disappears from view: we lose Beck's point that nuclear, chemical and genetic hazards are not only invisible but inaccessible to the senses and that this poses difficulty at every level of risk conception and social organization. We lose track of the time–space distantiation of the technologies' effects, of the fact that their impact may appear as symptom in some other, indeterminate time and space. Dropped from Scott's frame of reference, some of Beck's key issues simply vanish. His embracing of paradoxes, his reformation of contradictions and dis/continuities, his conscious play with the previously unthinkable, all fade into the background, become invisible and inaccessible. Thus, it seems, new thoughts, when analysed through their own inevitably traditional rhetoric, get re-embedded and imprisoned in the conceptual conventions they seek to transcend.

In the next chapter, Scott Lash is developing the notion of 'risk culture' in preference to both Beck's 'risk society' and Douglas and Wildavsky's (1983) 'risk and culture' in order to insert his analysis between the apparent realism of the former and constructivism of the latter. He considers the role of the open body as an antidote against the reductionism of both the traditional alternatives to respectively either a solid, external reality or free-floating internalized, solipsism. Appropriating Kant's third critique (the critique of judgement) he considers the implications of aesthetic reflexivity as a starting point for forms of socio-political action that are more responsive to social processes at the margins. The argument of the chapter is grounded in the Kantian distinction between determinate and reflexive judgement – the former associated with closed, prepositional truths, the latter with open estimations based on bodily feeling and the imagination. Our relation to contemporary environmental hazards such as nuclear power, chemical pollution and genetic engineering, Lash suggests, is not and cannot be grounded in determinate judgement; instead, it is inescapably tied to the world of imagination and emotions. This reflexive mode is then broken down further into a distinction between judgements of beauty which rely on the eye and judgement of the sublime which are not visual but 'more tactile, immediate and sensuous'. Faced with such hazards, the judgement of the sublime confronts us with our own finitude and mobilizes action from sources other than the (Cartesian) I, the eye, and the rational self. If we fail to acknowledge the 'lack' and indeterminacy of the contemporary risk context we remain wedded to the logic of determinate judgement: our analysis will inevitably be flawed and, worse still, we would forgo the capacity to act in a meaningful way. As an anti-rationalist and anti-reductionist perspective that mobilizes bodily powers, Lash's plea for an aesthetic of the sublime is a much needed antidote to the overly scientific and rationalist approaches to social knowledge in general and risk management in particular. While Beck points to the incalculability of the techno-hazards mentioned above at the same time as seeking solutions in the conventional realm of science and politics, Lash stresses the public need to mobilize resources that were hitherto considered personal, private and subjective. It is these 'subinstitutional' resources we depend on, he argues, if we are to engage effectively with contemporary risk situations where the continuously increasing risk potential disables traditional decision-making processes and actions rooted in the logic of determinate judgement.

Hilary Rose enters the subject of risks from a sociology of science perspective and explores the complex interconnectedness of scientific, political and economic realities and interests. She too considers how society can better manage the 'risks posed by incessant technological change'. Like Alan Scott she thinks that contemporary social theory needs to be grounded in the shifting and contradictory context of lived risks. First, however, social theory needs to take seriously the issue of risk which has been of concern to natural scientists, politicians and the business community and found expression in art, literature and popular culture for a substantial part of the century. Secondly, it needs to connect this concern with risk to an epistemological critique of the rationalist, scientific and economistic basis of the risk discourse. She focuses on the new genetics – the science of difference – to illustrate how new forms of techno-science not only 'reach into our most intimate lives, disturbing our created narratives of self …' but also produce a new form of 'cultural terror' that 'works to mobilize fear and to deny space for scepticism and social trust'. With the new genetics comes a new form of eugenics: the old state eugenics is displaced by a consumer eugenics based on enforced individual choice. The eugenics' new clothes, however, have not diminished its racism: the new alliance between science and the market 'reground both violence and race once more in nature'. Social theory, Rose suggests, is still blind to the implications that arise from this new configuration of interests and its neo-reductionist discourse. It needs to come to terms not only with its political role but also with the enormity of the conceptual task involved. It has to achieve the transcendence of dualistic frames of reference: nature or culture, public or private, truth or falsity, risk or safety, free choice or enforced decision in a theoretical context of realist or constructivist epistemology.

The three defences of 'risk culture' are clearly not theoretical alternatives to analyses of the 'risk society'. Instead 'risk society' and 'risk culture' are supplementary approaches that may not be totally compatible, but each have their own crucial role to play in the effective theorizing of contemporary socio-cultural relations of risk and risk definition. Each offer an important theoretical contribution to socio-institutional decisions and actions in the face of new constellations and logics of risk re/production. Collectively they are part of the spirit that motivated the writing of the *Risk Society* in the first place:

> we are the heirs of a cultural criticism that has become rigid, and can thus no longer be satisfied with the diagnoses of cultural criticism, which was always meant more as a kind of admonitory pessimism. An entire epoch cannot slide into a space beyond the previous defining categories without that 'beyond' being recognized and cast off for what it is: the artificially prolonged authority claim of a past which has seen the present and the future slip out of its hands. (Beck, 1992: 12)

As we have argued above, in the section on 'contested definitions', the point is not to choose between definitions and approaches but to stress the sign value of risk on the one hand and the collective concern with praxis, with the critical powers of theory in a socio-cultural context of complexity, indeterminacy and ambivalence on the other.

Challenging Big Science

The question of what the role of social theory should be in the face of a risk society/culture is thus first answered in terms of a refinement of how relations of risk definition cultivate particular risk perceptions and thereby not only affect the institutional forms that organize late-modern society, but also the more embedded and situated moralities of those who live in such risk societies/cultures. Hence, the first role of social theory which we could identify as being of paramount importance in a risk society/culture is to broaden our perspective. This can be accomplished through a recontextualization of risks by shifting our focus to the turbulent and dynamic social, cultural, political and economic conditions under which they emerge. To challenge established knowledge has always been a particular role assigned to social theory, whether in the form of undermining common sense or dominant assumptions about how the social world works. This role of challenging marks the sub-political dimension of social theory. The sub-political refers to a domain of society in which political issues are transformed into issues of expertise (Beck, 1997). Big Science refers to a particularly strong and hegemonic notion of the sub-polity of expertise. In the first instance, Big refers to the intensive involvement of capital. Big Science is characterized by large amounts of incoming economic capital, for example in the form of government funds and business sponsorship as well as high amounts of political, social and symbolic capital. These forms of capital grant authority, status and significance to scientific projects. Thus, in the second instance, Big refers to the prominence and prestige accredited to particular scientific programmes which tend to negate questions of legitimation and societal impact.

In this book, we engage with two examples of such Big Science: nuclear physics and genetics. Whereas nuclear science could be seen as the prototype of Big Science in the first three decades since the Second World War, in the 1980s, it was overtaken by genetics. Chapter 4, 'Nuclear Risks: Three Problematics' by Alan Irwin, Stuart Allan and Ian Welsh, gives us three short analyses of theoretical concepts in relation to which nuclear risks have been cast: modernity, discourse and desire. Whereas there may be large differences between the three analyses in terms of approach and perspective, all three revolve around the fundamental claim that nuclear risks have never been defined in a singular way, neither by science, nor media or government, and have always operated to some degree in contested relations of risk-definition. The analyses consider three related but analytically distinct problematic domains of science: the sub-politics of expertise, the mediation of social impact, and the libidinal economy of motivation. All three suggest that in these domains nuclear technologies are reconfigured within discursive formations that enable the enforcement of particular closures of risk perceptions and articulations. That is, what we call nuclear technology is the enframing of relations of risk definition in which unintended side-effects are the object of 'management', not 'public' debate or ethical engagement. The point to stress here is that the contestations and disagreements between experts have become increasingly visible. In such a context we need to establish the role of social theory and consider how it is to mount a challenge to such a Big Science; after all, even now operating in relative silence, the nuclear industry still exists and attracts state and private capital, despite all the criticisms that have been accumulated against it.

Alan Irwin starts this triple challenge of nuclear Big Science with an analysis of the attempts within sociological theory to encapsulate our understanding of nuclear power in terms of 'modernity'. He emphasizes that such conceptual acrobatics are relatively pointless if they do not articulate 'the flexibility and responsiveness of current systems of knowledge and social practice' of which nuclear technologies provide one example. Irwin's analysis contains a critique of monolithic notions of modernity, science and technology. He argues that many social theorists use the term 'modernity' in a very loose way often by reducing science and technology to black boxes and subordinating their intrinsic complexities to an overly speculative and generalist framework. What is problematic about such generalist theorizing, he suggests, is its inability to conceive of the relationship between technology (e.g. nuclear power) and social form (modern society) outside of an abstract opposition between technological and social determinism. In order to escape this, Irwin argues for more detailed observations of science and technology as social practices, as well as a more 'open' concept of modernity: one which emphasizes its dynamic and constructed character. This latter point clearly echoes Beck's (1992, 1997) and Beck et al. (1994) own political commitment to offer a theoretical framework that engages 'another', more reflexive modernity. Furthermore, the call for more detailed empirical studies of science and technology resonates with similar ones made by, for example, Latour (1987) and Haraway (1988, 1989).

Evidently, Irwin sees the challenge for social theory in terms of providing better understanding. However, as risks evade the principle of empirical observation, we need to be cautious not to be seduced into thinking that risk-manufacturing technologies can be accessed via direct observations or indirect 'accounting' (interviews for example). Studies of science and technology that want to engage 'nuclear risks' must therefore acknowledge their entrance into the sub-political realm of expertise and counter-expertise, as well as their implicit evasion of moral and ethical issues since these are incompatible with such sub-politics. That is, only by opening themselves to the political can such studies imply a sense of situated morality and thus inform a challenge that is more than a provision for a better understanding. The strength of Irwin's analysis, is that it does allow for such an engagement, by concerning himself directly with the struggles over the nuclear industry, which, in particular when related to the issues of risk, have become firmly grounded in a language dominated by scientific notions of harm and probability. In this sense, the nuclear industry is not unique as such struggles have also taken place in relation to other industries that are heavily endowed with the pedigree of Big Science (for example, the biochemical industry). What is highly significant in this account is that such struggles and challenges also take place 'within' science; that is, the notion of Big Science is a construct that fails to acknowledge that the enclosures which its capital seemingly affords have been far from complete. The question remains why such images of Big Science as a monolithic, dangerous, but highly successful enterprise have successfully persisted in public discourse. It seems that empirical studies of science and technology are unable to affect the way in which nuclear risks have been managed in public discourse.

Stuart Allan focuses his attention on opposite tendencies. Whereas Irwin emphasizes the incompleteness of closure, even in generalistic and all-inclusive notions such as modernity, science and technology, Allan points to the role of news media in providing textual closures of meaning by which risks become pacified and regulated as modalities of discourse that serve particular interests to sustain existing relations of domination. Of course, the very notion of closure already presupposes a notion of openness. Indeed, the Big Science of nuclear power has always encountered challenges from the inside and outside of its institutionalized establishment. However, as Irwin points out, the type of challenge was more directed against the feasibility of the nuclear industry (including its ecological impact), than the rationality of nuclear technology *per se*. That is, most opposition was already enframed within the language of risk inherent to nuclear science and technology. Opposition that did challenge nuclear rationality, for example in moral terms, has been much less effective in acquiring public visibility and a place on the political agenda. Hence, when we consider the 'effects' of the main challenges to nuclearism, we have to acknowledge that the balance between openness and closure is quite biased towards the latter.

Here we encounter a second mode of 'challenging' that social theory needs to engage in. Not only does it require a more critical stance towards its own subpolitics and lack of ethical engagement thereof, social theory also needs to challenge the dominant forms of mediation with which particular forms of risk are endowed. The sub-politics of risk management not only imply a particular enframing of relations of risk-definition, but also particular discursive strategies which neutralize the neurosis that accompanies Big Science. It is the role of mass media to devise such strategies and allow them to circulate more widely, inducing a particular logic-of-sense as the norm, while reducing others to deviations of obscurity. This is not to say that media serve particular dominant interests, although it is quite obvious that as every closure implies a selection and imposition of particular interpretations, there should be little surprise in findings that suggest that media more often than not do endorse the dominant views and thus closures that support existing relations of domination. What stands out most from Allan's analysis is that obviousness is expressed when it is not articulated, that is, in the silence of the text. Hence, the mediation of risk allows for particular risk perceptions to be endowed with common sense and is most effective where and when it is seemingly absent. In this sense, it takes the form of risk itself. Like radiation, DNA or viruses, it is the apparent invisibility of risk-mediation which makes it so effective in enframing public debate in terms of expertise. Indeed, nuclear modernity 'contains' a multiplicity of contested sites, in its commonsensical form, it also conceals those contestations. After all, containment is a form of covering-up. This in turn can be seen as an indication that the involvement of mass-mediation in this concealment shows that mass media too are a riskmanufacturing technology.

For Ian Welsh, Big Science is a discursive construction based on a negation of uncertainty. This negation, he suggests, is rooted in a desire that compensates for the gaps in knowledge that any internal challenge to nuclear physics would expose. Such challenges have always been part of nuclear physics, but never really stopped the formation of the Big Science project that informed the application of nuclear technology. Welsh's analysis extends the specific focus on the science and technology of nuclearism in media representations to their wider cultural embedding in post-war western societies, in which the understanding of 'risks' was developed in particular sensibilities of historical fatality and destiny. Desire, which in this cultural climate is diametrically oppositional to cognitive logic, involves an appreciation of risk in which a risk culture takes an ironic playful turn on risk society by exploiting a marginal contradiction of manufactured uncertainties. This marginal contradiction is that science as such only proceeds through an irrational desire for rational completion, thereby displacing uncertainty with faith and thus failing to incorporate the basic principle of modern thought: suspicion.

This deep-seated desire has rather unsettling implications for how we are to confront Big Science. Within the confines of the logical, rational and cognitive, as empirical studies of science and technology tell us time and time again, there is plenty of scope for internal critique and recognition that the scientific premises are far less certain than they are perceived to be. Indeed, as in all Big Science projects, there are many uncertainties and loose ends in need of clarification. However, this in itself has not stopped the fixation on technocratic solutions that characterize Big Science. Immanent critique of scientific rationality is ineffective because it fails to address the desire that motivates it: such critique, it seems, exacerbates the technofixation. Indeed, it would seem that the exposition of 'gaps' only intensifies the desire to find closures. It should come as no surprise then that not only Big Science but more mundane science too closes ranks as soon as outsiders, such as social and cultural analysts, engage scientists in critical debates, because the production of science is not exclusively a question of knowledge, not even of epistemology, but of desire and faith: desire emerges in embodied, material and spontaneous forms, whereas faith is cultivated, idealized and simulated. Conversely, whereas desire remains unaccountable and concealed, faith can be constituted more explicitly in the form of for example dogma, canon or script.

Chapter 5, 'Genotechnology: Three Challenges to Risk Legitimation' is a compilation of three shorter essays by Lindsay Prior, Peter Glasner and Ruth McNally. As the analysis of nuclear Big Science has already shown, what is noteworthy is not the absence of challenges to Big Science but their lack of impact. Reasons for that are, on the one hand, an effective inter-institutional regulation of the discursive domain upon which Big Science operates and through which it gains privileges and legitimacy and secures access to scarce resources. On the other hand, the challenges mounted against Big Science projects never really addressed the wider cultural embedding of the libidinal economy which constitutes the silence and concealment of Big Science technologies.

Nuclear and gene technologies have much in common. Both engage with the order of things on a sub-molecular level at which the primary principles of natural order are to be found. The gene is to biology what the atom has been to physics: the monadic principle that organizes the complexity of the entire cosmos. It would be too simplistic, however, to extrapolate this analysis to the field of genetics, if only because the latter form of Big Science has taken shape in a rather different socio-historical and cultural context. Most important for our purposes here is that, in contrast to nuclearism, the genetic sciences have been discursively regulated with a much higher public and critical sensibility to notions of risk and probability.

Lindsay Prior's contribution to the chapter focuses on the mathematical concept of probability. He places probability-perception in a historical context which he pairs with the development of mathematics and statistics. He shows that probability belongs to an entire series, not an individual event. Genetic risks are, therefore, the probability of populations rather than individuals. He briefly extrapolates this observation to a critique of population management and eugenics which, on the basis of pure mathematical logic, fail to understand the logic of probability that underscores gene technology in the first place. Mathematical models have little relevance to analyses that attempt to relate risk perception to individual biographies. Consequently, mathematical models of risk and probability lack a sensitivity to the virtual catastrophic potential that such new risk technologies entail. Once the logical distortions in probability-assessment are established, theory can shift to critique and challenge risk-assessment on the socio-cultural ground of equity and justice.

Peter Glasner argues that the lack of public involvement in debating the implications of gene technologies does not stem from ignorance, but from a framing of the debate in terms of medical expertise of risk perception. He argues that in the construction of a public debate around the Human Genome Project (HGP), the approach to the question of how to deal with its ethical implications (read: risks) was basically framed upon the assumption that genetics as such did not pose new ethical dilemmas. Consequently, the main line of ethical debate was taken to be a traditional one, in which medical expertise was considered to be the infrastructure upon which debates were to take place. For Glasner, genetic risks are not so much a question of accuracy but of democracy. However, what is less clear is whether such democratic input, provided for example by public forums, would lead to less distorted risk perceptions. What is needed in addition to otherwise undeniably strong claims for more public scrutiny is a recasting of the question of distortion itself. This means that the debate needs to shift from its purely calculative and cognitive embedding in probability-thinking and statistics, to engagement with the meditative and subjective aspects of risk perception that constitute particular risk cultures.

What is necessary then, is an understanding of the social and cultural implications of particular challenges to risk. Ruth McNally's detailed and insightful account of the use of gene technology in the European Rabies Eradication Programme highlights how risk-assessment operates in the enclosure of a technologically-induced hazard that was created to replace a 'natural risk'. She appropriates 'Actor-Network Theory' to account for the 'enrolment' of different actors, including 'the public at large', to transform their identities to that of the newly establishing actor-network of the anti-rabies programme. However, she questions whether fox rabies itself has been enrolled and raises serious doubts about the assumptions behind the programme. Her analysis clearly shows the risk of risk management. Under the banner of expertise, a programme has been devised to genetically re-engineer a particular risk in order to make it more manageable. Yet, the unknown variables that are left unexplored are larger than the technologies of control allow to take into account. The closures of such unknown variables and their exclusion from enrolment are part of the risk management itself. Indeed, whereas such closures are not exclusive to Big Science projects, it is the latter's conjunction with economic, political and moral implications (and capital) that make such closures and concealment the more probable. Distortion is thus central to risk management and concerns not only issues of 'truth' and 'facts', but also of legitimation and justification. This makes the question of distortion a profoundly ethical and political issue. Not only does it address questions of risk perception, but also that of the risks of risk management. Locked in their containers of expertise, the institutional linking between science and politics can indeed pose far greater threats to society as a whole than the risks they are aiming to tackle.

Elisabeth Beck-Gernsheim's chapter, 'Health and Responsibility', deals more directly with the moral and therefore also social, political and cultural embedding of implications of risk-assessment for individual biographies and subjective experiences. It provides a sweeping account of how 'the imperative of health' can be understood as a cultivation of individualization that in turn affects the public perception of gene technology and has generated a hitherto completely unknown terrain of personalized political and ethical dilemmas. Of course, such dilemmas are differentiated between age groups, gender, race and class, but the point to make is that gene technologies radicalize the inherent individualization of the risk society. What is important to note here is that risks may be termed as manufactured uncertainties, but the social embedding of the risk perceptions which constitute their becoming-real have a knock-on effect as well. That is, people appropriate risk perceptions in their everyday lives which may further generate 'hazards' that may be turned into risks.

To summarize, whereas the first role of social theory is to broaden the scope of articulation of relations of risk-definitions in terms of their socio-cultural embedding, its second role is to challenge taken-for-granted assumptions and established conventions, such as those ruling the rationalization, accreditation and legitimation of Big Science. On the basis of the chapters in this section of the book, we could argue that the challenge to science is therefore a double charge. The first charge emanates from within, in the form of immanent critique. The second comes from without in the form of a genealogical critique of the metaphysical tradition upon which modern science rests. In both cases it leads to the formation of what Foucault (1971) called a counter-discourse. Social theory, however, does not need to 'invent' this counter-discourse. As Irwin, Welsh and Glasner for example show, many forms of critique to Big Science already have a strong public footing, even within scientific establishments themselves. Instead, social theorists are well placed to identify these critical moments and movements, and work through the logics they are engaged in. The specific function of social theory in the formation of a counter-discourse would be that of providing connections between the various sub-political realms, organizing the accounts that are being rendered and presenting them in their ambivalent complexity as a collage, rather than a linear narrative.

The avoidance of narrative imposition is important. Narrative implies a singular perspective to which the setting, the plot, the main characters and the storyline are related. The unfolding and resolution of the story line always require a meta-perspective, one that organizes all the other perspectives into a singular fold (Barthes, 1990; Todorov, 1990). Social theory is not a religion and thus is incapable of providing such a meta-narrative. The role of social theory is thus not to lead the charge, as radical intellectuals, for social theory cannot provide any superior moral basis to any other form of political and ethical thought. However, its focus on abstraction does allow it to render an explicit account of particular accounts and explore and un-conceal their implicit accountability. The challenge to taken-for-granted assumptions and the scientific establishment of expertise is therefore, first of all, a political affair. Social theory is politics by other means. The potential to politicize the sub-polity to which so many decisions are displaced in a risk society is there to be actualized. This re-politicization emerges from abstracting the connections between the various segments of the sub-political realm. Social theory thus has a role to play in subverting the depoliticization of risks, by mobilizing their implications for the concern over 'our' and other forms of being, here and there, now and in the future.

In short, social theory is perhaps not as much engaged in establishing aims and objectives, a telos-oriented abstraction, but much more pragmatic. Its is a means-oriented form of abstraction. Similar to the contributions of the first part of this book, the chapters in this second part point out that the narrowing down of perspectives by the sub-polity of expertise that provides the social infrastructure of Big Science requires a counter-discourse that reverses this process by broadening the perspectives. Linking nuclearism to modernity, discourse and desire, and tying genetics to democracy, risk management, probability calculations, individualization and the future, allows us to make connections between the various concerns involved that are effectively fragmented by the specific operational logic of expertise in modern societies. As such, social theory has the capacity to connect science, technology, engineering and risk management to politics, media and economics. The critical function of social theory therefore does not stop with immanent critique, with criticizing inconsistencies, empirical inadequacies, illogical conclusions and unverifiable hypotheses that constitute 'common sense', nor does it end with placing the full moral weight of informed political correctness behind the analysis. In the face of the risk society, social theory needs to redefine itself as an art of bridging, connecting, formatting as well as abstracting. This form of 'knowledge' allows political mobilization to team up with informed and sustained immanent critique, to broaden perspectives and articulate alternative interpretations; work on the multiplicity (collage) rather than the unity (narrative) of perspectives.

The accounts of Elisabeth Beck-Gernsheim, Peter Glasner and Hilary Rose provide striking examples, of the way in which genetic risks are modified by mediations aimed at enhancing public knowledge about the technologies and their risk-implications. The 'distortion' that this implies is relatively straightforward as most of what is publicly-produced about the Human Genome Project (which is not very much) can be classified as plain propaganda. There is a need therefore to locate such propaganda in relation to the struggle to obtain scarce funding for research in a highly competitive environment. That 'risks' related to the unknown and uncertain aspects of such large gene-technological projects are underplayed should come as no surprise. When such mediations, however, are the only publicly obtainable information about this Big Science then demands for more public scrutiny seem warranted. Hence, whereas scientists may publicly claim that they are not involved in some sinister *Jurassic Park* type of project, it is exactly such films that dominate the publicly mediated image of gene technology. This will be further explored in the third part of this book which explicitly deals with the mediation of risk technologies.

Mediating technologies of risk

Having defined the first function of social theory as contextualization, and the second function as that of challenging, we would now like to point out a third function: that of disclosure. As has been stated, risk mobilizes concern. However, all risks are mediated and entail relations of information, communication and regulation that constitute the definition of their particular contingent reality. It has also been stated that such definitions are themselves operationalized, for example, in the form of risk management. It is therefore nonsensical to suggest that risk perceptions are 'merely' social constructions if this is used in contrast to 'being real'. As Beck argues in his contribution to this book, the question of construction/real is irrelevant; what matters is the actualization of risk, as lived, responded to and acted upon. If particular risk perceptions regulate the relations of risk definition, then it is quite logical to assume that they also exercise some influence over the particular modes of risk management; if only in the form of post-hoc rationalizations. The focus on risk mediation concerns a hitherto under-explored dimension of the risk society thesis, namely the role of 'mass media'. The media are instrumental, of course, in the creation of 'a' public (audience) and their function in the enrolment of actors is undoubtedly of huge importance.

Claudia Castañeda's contribution perhaps gives the most clear example of the material force of mediating technologies of risk. Her chapter discusses the role of rumour in the reproduction of stories over child-abductions for the purpose of obtaining organ donations. Such stories have a particularly potent resonance in countries such as Guatemala, where Americans are thought to be using such stolen organs for highly lucrative donor-organ markets in the US. What allows for the reproduction of such stories is that as rumours, they have no identifiable origin and are therefore unaccountable in terms of, for example, libel or defamation. Castañeda's analysis also shows that such mediated processes have to be understood in a wider political, economic, social and cultural context which makes the referent of these rumours, the violent and illegal confiscation of donor organs, seem quite realistic.

The rumour of child organ stealing is related to the risks of reproductive technologies in a multiplicity of ways; what counts here above all, however, is the effectiveness of rumours in relation to the authorization of risk (What counts as risk? What constitutes 'a' risk?). In the political-economic context and the global–local dynamics of Guatemala as a country in the 'backyard' of the USA, such authorizations are highly contested. The relations of risk definition thus remain open for contestation as there is no single actor-network in which they can be enrolled. By constructing rumour as a technology of reproduction, Castañeda is providing the first step towards rethinking 'media technology' before applying this to a repositioning of risks. Here as elsewhere, it is the mass-mediated nature of risk definition and risk management which itself engenders new risks (see also Chapter 4 in this volume). It is important to stress that this does not primarily take place in the form of conscious knowledge or other cognitive faculties, but in a far more immediate matter of concern for being in the world. To counter the rumour with 'pure logic' is therefore hardly effective, because rumours are not operating on that level of articulation. Such a media dissemination of risk therefore shows, again, that the distinction between reality and construct is irrelevant; what matters is the becoming-real of risks. Repositioning risk in this context means that theorizing risk is no longer a question of epistemology but of ontology.

In contrast to Castañeda's more politicized discussion of unconcealment, Howard Caygill's concern is far more detached from the immediate implications of media technologies. He presents a comparative analysis of two textual mediations of risks associated with gene technology: the 1995 encyclical letter of Pope John Paul II, and a 1992 report by a working party of the British Medical Association (BMA). He shows that whereas the papal letter is obviously hostile to genetic technology as it represents the forces of death which threaten the forces of life, the BMA's report is more ambiguous towards the issue as it distinguishes between impacts of a genotypical (individual members of a species) and phenotypical (the species as a whole) kind. Whereas it is cautiously positive about the first (as changes at the level of genotype relate only to modifying somatic cells), the BMA's report shares with the encyclical letter a disapproval of phenotypical modifications to germ lines. To contrast these two accounts, Caygill reflects on the work of the Australian performance artist Stelarc, whose work is specifically targeted at changing the germ line of the human species, by changing his own body. These three cultural strategies highlight that there is never simply a mediation of risk; the media which are being appropriated to make sense of risk, provide risk sensibility and are thus involved both in the engendering and manipulation of risks, as well as in their negotiation and displacement. The type of disclosure he points towards has less to do with *de-mythification*, which is the leading mode of the counter-offensive against child organ stealing rumours, but with the *translation* of risk perceptions between and across the domains of religion, medicine and performance art. These three genres can be understood as particular ways of translating the heterogeneous contingency of genetic risks. Each regulated by their own ethical imperatives, these risk-mediations are thus forms of constructing meaning out of a seemingly infinite heterogeneity, in order to reconstitute religious morality, medical ethics and transgressive aesthetics. Weaving a web of heterogeneous discourses, Caygill is able to point out that the particular disclosures that they entail are in turn a concealment of these imperatives. Far from being transparent then, mediating technologies of risk contribute to the increased confusion that marks risk society/culture in the world of today.

In concordance with the preceding chapters in this section, Joost van Loon's chapter suggests that mediations of risk materialize as risk. He appropriates the term 'virtual risk' to highlight that risks are never 'real' as such, but always imply a 'becoming-real'. He argues that the becoming-real of virtual risks has acquired particular potency in an age where electronic media have displaced the emphasis on mechanical reproduction (mass produced instant copies of the same) and entered an age of cybernetic reproduction, in which our very own central nervous systems are being externalized in a world-wide-web of connected media-technologies (McLuhan, 1964). The case of the media accounts of a possible relationship between BSE and CJD is used as an illustration of the materialization of such mediations of virtual risks. The 'madness' is no longer contained by cow-brains, but circulates in the very nervous system of society.

Here we touch upon the essence of the mediated techno-logic of risk. The media do not simply 'pass on' particular relations of risk definition, but constitute them. Media are hence part of the mode of risk production. The role of social theory therefore becomes not exclusively marked by the continued need for challenging established knowledge under the newly appropriated banner of contingency and complexity. Instead, social theory bears witness to the unfolding of events. The unsettling consequences of risk affect not just Big Science but the human condition itself. Caygill, for example, points towards the transformative aspects of risk embodiment. He questions the validity of the distinction between the somatic and the genetic. When applied to mediating technologies in general, and we may include both 'rumours' and 'digital virtuality', the distinction between the discursive and the performative simply implodes. Discourses, including counter-discourses, never merely 'represent', rather representations are practices and already imply a principle of performativity and thus transformation.

Although 'disclosure' may seem at first hand to be far less political than 'challenging', Castañeda, Caygill and Van Loon all embrace a need for ethical sensibility, which in their case is an affirmation of the heterogeneity, rather than the unity of counter-discourse. What marks their concern with mediating technologies of risk is a postponement of judgement, a suspense of revelation in order to generate an interval for contemplation and meditation. What such a postponement and suspense enables is an acute sensitivity towards the performative of discourse, that is, the materiality of mediation or what Deleuze and Guattari (1988) called *modulation*. Mediations transform risks themselves and in doing so open up an ethical moment which is not an opinion but an acceptance of our own vulnerability and mortality. Disclosure, in this sense, is more than an exhibition of 'knowledge of' and 'understanding'. Unconcealment transgresses the distinctions between the discursive and the performative and implies an essence of risk as a becoming-real. The modulation of risk is the transformation of potential into kinetic energy/matter: it is a setting-into-motion of the actual, an actualization. This actualization is direct and material, it operates upon bodies. For Castañeda it is through rumour and violence; for Caygill it is through the aesthetics of performativity; for Van Loon it is through the diseased/infected protein of the prion. All three forces are a setting-into-work of 'truth' (Vattimo, 1988), that is revealed as 'concern for being'. This setting-into-work is an appropriation of the modulation of risk and its unconcealment of an emergent ethical moment. Because it is emergent, it is unfoundational and its weakness is that this emphasis on emergent ethics makes it vulnerable to all kinds of political mobilization. It leaves no ground for judgement. The disabling of a notion of directly accessible reality, the postponement of judgement and the suspension of truth harbour a rather problematic prospect for social theory as it is no longer able to politicize human concerns by connecting truth and justice on a firm ground of universal rationality and legislative morality.

P(l)aying for futures

The concern to sustain a link between social theory and political interests emerges out of a sense of urgency to act in the 'here-and-now', to not lose sight of the inevitability of modulation, as social theory too is a technology of mediation. The quest for the present/presence however must not return to a self- valorizing blindness that informed the link between social theory and practices of political (in)correctness, which by the sheer force of their self-righteous intolerance, have turned into oppressive forms of politics and censorship. Instead, we need to appreciate that modern thought, of which social theory is inevitably a part, thrives much better in a climate of liberal pluralism and a relative absence of imposed regulation than in a climate ruled by anxieties over political correctness.

What may inform a political orientation for social theory without sliding into political correctness is a concern for our future. The future, which as an open, multiple, contested, undefineable site, never exists in general, but is always pluralized in singularities – each future being different. The challenge to the sub-politics that thrive in a risk society, then, could be formed more effectively if we were to find ways of actualizing particular connections between technologies and their futures. The fourth and final part therefore deals directly with how we can perceive our relationship to the future. The chapters present us alternative visions of the future by appropriating the concept of risk as a predicament of human being towards the twenty-first century.

Deirdre Boden's chapter engages us, on a very grounded and ethnographic plane, with the rising popularity of futures markets trading. On futures markets, 'traders are trading in time itself'. Drawing on Simmel's theory of money as the most abstract expression of the relativity of valuation, and framing this more broadly within an ethnomethodological orientation, her account presents 'the fragile rather than fragmented nature of work and technology in the late modern age'. The world of futures markets illustrates Beck's thesis that in a risk society, increased calculability generates increased uncertainty. Boden's concern is not with moralizing questions that stem from a politics of urgency, but with providing a detailed description of the actuality of the future as a particular market. Her disclosure of the commodification of the future is then focused on the pragmatics of how technology (including machinery as well as know-how) 'works'. The technological transformation of global communications has affected the ways in which futures markets operate, not only by the intensification of the speed and scope of transactions, but also by the transformation of intimacy and sense-making practices that inform the way in which stockbrokers operate on such markets. Boden's analysis furthermore provides an account of how risks are not only paired with ontological insecurities and anxieties, but also with 'opportunities'. From this, we could deduce that the political role of social theory extends from challenging the taken-for-granted and providing alternative perspectives, to repairing, enforcing and making sense of breakdowns in social order. Hence, whereas some accounts of risk and risk culture are framed under the assumption of a total collapse of sociality, Boden's account highlights that the signifying role of risk as potential breakdowns is quite regulated and institutionalized, and indeed an integral part of the operating technologies of dealing with particular futures.

Whereas Boden's analysis is deeply informed by her insistence on an eth-nomethodological grounding of 'the world as it happens' in the present, Ruth Levitas argues for a perspective drawn from the future. In her chapter, Levitas endorses 'the necessity of (transformative) utopian thinking' against the ethos of 'resignation' which she associates with theories of reflexive modernity. She distinguishes between the discourses of risk and of risk society. Whereas the 'discourse of risk brings the future into a calculative relation to the present', the discourse of risk society refers to 'a theoretical discourse of sociologists'. As such, the discourse of risk society represents for Levitas a dystopian ethos, which is preoccupied with the legitimation of risks, rather than inequality. Her critique of this discourse is threefold, it is:

1   too utopian about current (present) society;
2   too dystopian about alternatives, and
3   inadequately idealist in its political agenda.

In response she argues that the question 'what is to be done' should be at the heart of social theory and suggests that analyses of risk and risk society need to be 'allied to a rigorous analysis of capitalism', even though she admits that such an alliance may be difficult to sustain.

The differences between Boden's hesitant politics and Levitas' politics of urgency are obvious. For Boden, the separation between the ethical implications and actual operations of the transformation of the future into capital is the starting point of her analysis. Her concern is with the role of technology in intensifying the fragile state of existence in a risk society, but also with the residual resilience of the social itself. Her focus is therefore on how breakdowns are made ready-to-hand and incorporated into institutional practices, which in turn enable the transformation of risks into opportunities, and those who are involved in these markets to capitalize on such uncertainties. Levitas, in contrast, is concerned with social inequalities. She does not pair risks with capital and opportunities, but with issues of choice and decision-making. In that sense, her politics of urgency are against the sort of pragmatics which focus on actualization as these are more bent towards social engineering than social change. For Levitas, the future is a political weapon against injustice; it holds the possibility of utopian thinking as the a priori grounding of ethics. In such an account the role of social theory has much less to do with a repair, or even a making sense of breakdowns, but with a radical exploitation of them. Still, Levitas couples utopian thinking with a rigorous analysis of social actualities. It is this analysis that would allow us to appropriate 'risk' as a mobilizing force, and a (Leninist) 'weak moment' in the established order, hence posing an opportunity for radical change.

Reflecting on these very different analyses of relations to the future, we note interesting parallels between the contributions of Boden and Levitas. Both analyses require a distinction between the actual and the possible. The role of social theory in relation to the actual is that of making sense, the role of social theory in relation to the possible is an articulation of a future singularity that is thought of as being desirable. Boden and Levitas may differ strongly in the means and route of getting from the actual to the possible as well as what they consider as the necessary articulations of ethics, desire and rationality that are required if such politics are to become operational; yet they share a commitment to practical reason and an acceptance of both the unavoidability of understanding and the appropriation of pragmatics.

In some way we may read Ulrich Beck's concluding contribution as providing a bridge between Boden's pragmatic and Levitas' utopian thinking. In this final chapter, Beck replies to critiques such as those given by Alan Scott, Scott Lash, Hilary Rose and Ruth Levitas, by pointing out that 'risks and manufactured uncertainties set off a dynamic of cultural and political change that undermines state bureaucracies, challenges the dominance of science and redraws the boundaries and battle lines of contemporary politics'. There are clear, future-oriented utopian moments in his analysis of the potential of the risk society to become 'an other modernity'. However, he strongly opposes any form of dogmatism, whether ontological or epistemological. He emphasizes 'relations of definition' to provide a materialist basis for theorizing the ontology of risk in terms of 'impact'. This pragmatic stance allows him to maintain a sense of 'materialism' without having to confess to any a priori, metaphysical belief. Far from being an idealist, he thus perceives this pragmatic position not as a matter of individual, calculated, rational (reflective) judgement but as the logical consequence of reflexive modernization. Only reflexivity can help us avoid the double bind 'risk trap' of 'doing nothing and demanding too much'.

Hence, Beck's politcal-ethical moment is highly pragmatic; at the same time his pragmatics are very political and concerned with ethics. His main objective is to bring further clarity to what he means by 'another modernity' on the one hand, and to what the role of social theory could and even should be in relation to the question of our possible futures, on the other hand. Hence, not only does he accommodate Deirdre Boden's insistence on the need to provide an understanding of what is actualized, he also incorporates Ruth Levitas' twofold critical utopianism which identifies the difference between the actual and the possible as well as desired futures. Beck, however, goes further than this when he identifies both the way(s) to get there, including the obstacles we may face, and the means to change course if necessary. Hence, Beck does not place the political role of social theory under a banner of some fixed utopian thought. Instead he aims to incorporate a notion of reflexivity. His ethics are therefore situated and also concerned with the aesthetics of self-confrontation. This, he suggests, might be a better way to understand 'risk'. Rather than a culture of risk-taking (which, after all, is nothing more than a Freudian death drive), risk culture is better conceived as a loose ensemble of sense-making and sensibilities, that constitute a reflexive-ethics of contextualization, challenging, disclosure and politicization. Risk cultures in Beck's work are reflexively transgressive, situated, pragmatic and responsive.

To summarize, then, we have argued that the relevance of social theory in the face of risk culture is fourfold:

1 to provide a contextualized understanding of the social and cultural, political and economic implications of risks and risk technologies on society;
2 to challenge the established codes and assumptions that constitute the vast majority of institutionalized risk technologies (Big Science);
3 to effect a disclosure of the transgressive implications of the mediation of risk technologies on actual subjective and biographic experiences; and
4 to offer an imaginative account of how we may incorporate such experiences into a concern for (the) future(s), including ways to actualize desired possibilities.

Casting, connecting, providing alternatives and setting these to work are some of the modalities through which social theorists may be able to accomplish such objectives.

References

Adam, B. (1996) 'Re-vision: the Centrality of Time for an Ecological Social Science Perspective', in S. Lash, B. Szerszynski and B. Wynne (eds), *Risk, Environment and Modernity: Towards a New Ecology*. London: Sage. pp. 84–103.

Adam, B. (1998) *Timescapes of Modernity: The Environment and Invisible Hazards*. London: Routledge.

Adams, J. (1995) *Risks*. London: UCL Press.

Barthes, R. (1990) *S/Z*. Trans. R. Miller. Oxford: Blackwell.

Beck, U. (1986) *Risikogesellschaft: Auf dem Weg in eine andere Moderne*. Frankfurt am Main: Suhrkamp Verlag.

Beck, U. (1992) *Risk Society: Towards a New Modernity*. Trans. M. Ritter. London: Sage.

Beck, U. (1996) 'Risk Society and the Provident State', in S. Lash, B. Szerszynski and B. Wynne (eds), *Risk, Environment and Modernity: Towards a New Ecology*. London: Sage. pp. 27–43.

Beck, U. (1997) *The Reinvention of Politics: Rethinking Modernity in the Global Social Order*. Cambridge: Polity.

Beck, U., Giddens, A. and Lash, S. (1994) *Reflexive Modernization: Politics, Tradition and Aesthetics in the Modern Social Order*. Cambridge: Polity.

Colborn, T., Myers, J.P. and Dumanoski, D. (1996) *Our Stolen Future: How Man-made Chemicals are Threatening our Fertility, Intelligence and Survival*. Boston: Little Brown and Co.

Deleuze, G. and Guattari, F. (1988) *A Thousand Plateaus: Capitalism and Schizophrenia*. Trans. B. Massumi. London: Athlone.

Dillon, M. (1996) *The Politics of Security: Towards a Political Philosophy of Continental Thought*. London: Routledge.

Diprose, R. (1994) *The Bodies of Women: Ethics, Embodiment and Sexual Difference*. London: Routledge.

Douglas, M. (1992) *Risk and Blame: Essays in Cultural Theory.* London: Routledge.

Douglas, M. and Wildavsky, A. (1983) *Risk and Culture.* Berkeley: University of California Press.

Ford, B.J. (1996) *BSE: The Facts. Mad Cow Disease and the Risk to Mankind.* London: Corgi Books.

Foucault, M. (1970) *The Order of Things: An Archaeology of the Human Sciences.* New York: Vintage Books.

Foucault, M. (1971) *L'Ordre du Discours.* Paris: Gallimard.

Genosko, G. (1998) *Undisciplined Theory.* London: Sage.

Giddens, A. (1991) *Modernity and Self-Identity: Self and Society in the Late-Modern Age.* Cambridge: Polity.

Giddens, A. (1995) *Beyond Left and Right: The Future of Radical Politics.* Cambridge: Polity.

Gouldner, A. (1970) *The Coming Crisis in Western Sociology.* New York: Basic Books.

Haraway, D. (1988) 'Situated Knowledges: The Sciences Question in Feminism and the Privilege of Partial Perspective', *Feminist Studies*, 14 (3): 575–99.

Haraway, D. (1989) *Primate Visions: Gender, Race and Nature in the World of Modern Science.* London: Verso.

Haraway, D. (1990) 'A Manifesto for Cyborgs: Science, Technology and Socialist Feminism in the 1980s', in L.J. Nicholson (ed.), *Feminism/Postmodernism.* New York: Routledge, pp. 199–233.

Heidegger, M. (1977) *The Question Concerning Technology and Other Essays.* New York: Harper & Row.

Lacey, R.W. (1994) *Mad Cow Disease: The History of BSE in Britain.* St. Helier, Jersey (C.I.): Cypsela.

Lang, T. and Clutterbuck, C. (1991) *P is for Pesticides.* London: Ebury Press.

Lash, S., Szerszynski, B. and Wynne, B. (eds) (1996) *Risk, Environment and Modernity: Towards a New Ecology.* London: Sage.

Latour, B. (1987) *Science in Action: How to Follow Scientists and Engineers through Society.* Milton Keynes: Open University Press.

Luhmann, N. (1990) *Essays on Self-Reference.* New York: Columbia University Press.

Luhmann, N. (1995) *Die Soziologie des Risikos.* Berlin: De Gruyter.

Lyotard, J.F. (1984) *The Postmodern Condition: A Report on Knowledge.* Manchester: Manchester University Press.

McLuhan, M. (1964) *Understanding Media: The Extensions of Man.* Harmondsworth: Penguin.

Ratzan, S.C. (ed.) (1998) *The Mad Cow Crisis: Health and the Public Good.* London: UCL Press.

Ritzer, G. (1975) *Sociology: A Multiple Paradigm Science.* London: Allen & Unwin.

Todorov, T. (1990) *Genres in Discourse.* Trans. C. Porter. Cambridge: Cambridge University Press.

Van Loon, J. (1996) 'Technological Sensibilities and the Cyberpolitics of Gender: Donna Haraway's Postmodern Feminism', *Innovation: The European Journal of Social Sciences*, 9 (2): 231–43.

Vattimo, G. (1988) *The End of Modernity: Nihilism and Hermeneutics in Post-modern Culture.* Cambridge: Polity.

Welsh, I. (2000) *Mobilizing Modernity: The Nuclear Moment.* London: Routledge.

Wynne, B. (1992) 'Misunderstood Misunderstanding: Social Identities and the Public Uptake of Science', *Public Understanding of Science*, 1 (3): 281–304.

Wynne, B. (1996) 'May the Sheep Safely Graze? A Reflexive View of the Expert-Lay Knowledge Divide', in S. Lash, B. Szerszynski and B. Wynne (eds), *Risk, Environment and Modernity: Towards a New Ecology.* London: Sage. pp. 44–83.

1

Risk Society or Angst Society? Two Views of Risk, Consciousness and Community

Alan Scott

Every technology produces, provokes, programs a specific accident ... The invention of the boat was the invention of shipwrecks. The invention of the steam engine and the locomotive was the invention of derailments. The invention of the highway was the invention of three hundred cars colliding in five minutes. The invention of the airplane was the invention of the plane crash. I believe that from now on, if we wish to continue with technology (and I don't think there will be a Neolithic regression), we must think about both the substance and the accident....

(Paul Virilio, 1983: 32)

Wir [Deutschen] sind Weltmeister der Angst.

(Helmut Schmidt speech, 15 May 1996)

Since the first publication of Ulrich Beck's *Risk Society*, the intervening years have provided enough reminders, as if reminders were needed, of the centrality of risk in contemporary societies. There have been spectacular accidents, Chernobyl being the most spectacular. AIDS has initiated intense discussion of risk and personal sexual expression. Anxiety about deforestation due to acid rain or economic exploitation, holes in the ozone layer and other slow-burning issues have become a permanent background feature of normal politics occasionally pushing themselves into the foreground, sometimes through nothing more extraordinary than the arrival of summer. First glasnost, then the collapse of the Soviet Union have revealed previously hidden environmental damage on an enormous scale.

Third World populations remain no less, and are arguably more, vulnerable to natural and social catastrophes. In the still affluent West growing unemployment and declining security, even for those in employment, not least due to the decline in welfare facilities, have heightened awareness of vulnerability to contingencies such as ill health, accident and old age.

It is in this context that *Risk Society* and Beck's subsequent work represents one of two systematic attempts by social scientists to wrest the issue of risk away from specialists (the risk analysts) and place it on a wider social scientific and public agenda. The work of Mary Douglas and Aaron Wildavsky is the other (see Douglas and Wildavsky, 1903, Douglas, 1992). Although they have this common purpose, there are striking differences between the two approaches and their implication for assessing the objective 'risk of risk' are quite distinct. Since Beck's work stands at the centre of this volume, the aim of this discussion will be to examine his analysis, in part, in the light of its major 'rival' perspective.

There is a striking combination of the familiar and the novel in *Risk Society* which might be caught in the observation that the work makes an unconventional claim in a conventional guise. Since it is the novel content rather than the conventional form which has – unsurprisingly and rightly – received most attention, I would like to focus here on the latter; on the argumentative and rhetorical structure which is the medium of the argument. This structure may be considered conventional in that it assumes the shape of a narrative of discontinuity of a type familiar in sociological argument. Industrial versus post-industrial (or information) society, modernity versus post- or late-modernity, fordism versus post-fordism, nation state societies versus global networks; all these oppositions and the claims which accompany them are grist to the mill of sociological debate. The particular opposition which underpins Beck's analysis is that between a class society and a risk society, and underlying this distinction in turn is the more crucial dualism of scarcity versus insecurity (risk) through which the organizing principles and the core contentious issues of these two social forms may be identified. Since much of Beck's analysis and many of his observations, particularly in the early chapters, echo this dualistic argumentative strategy, they can be economically represented in Table 1.1.

Any critical response to this analysis would have to do more than merely show that neither of these two societies exists in pure form. Beck is well aware and keen to emphasize that, for example, issues of scarcity and of the distribution of goods are not absent within the contemporary risk society. Nor would it be sufficient to demonstrate that Beck is basing a general diagnosis of modernity on a specifically German (or even Bavarian) experience (though one does sometimes feel that 'Germany' and 'advanced contemporary society' are treated as synonyms). Although this raises problems, to which we shall return below, there is a sense in which this generalization from a specific case is neither here nor there. Much classical sociological theory is prompted by quite specific contexts or events, the key question being whether the formulation of the reflections stimulated by such events finds echoes in (and is thus generalizable to) other places and later times. Thus, while I think it might be reasonable to suggest that

TABLE 1.1   *Class society versus risk society*

	Class Society	Risk Society
Basic social organizing principle	Collectivization (into families, classes, corporations, status groups, etc.) plus tradition	Individualization plus reflexivity
Form of inequality	Social class position	Social risk position
Core contentious issues/ questions of justice and fairness focus on	Distribution of scarce goods (wealth)	Distribution of 'bads' (risks)
Experienced personally paradigmatically as	Hunger	Fear
Experienced collectively potentially as	Class consciousness	Risk consciousness
Utopian projects aimed at	Elimination of scarcity	Elimination of risk

the primary immediate contextual background of *Risk Society* was the campaign against a planned nuclear reprocessing plant in Bavaria (Wackersdorf), this is a no less legitimate starting point for theoretical reflection than the Dreyfus affair was for Durkheim's reflections on individualism, or Prussian bureaucracy and Bismarck's social policy for Weber's theory of bureaucratic domination.

So, rather than criticize Beck for ignoring the 'good old problems' of the class society or for the possible 'Bavariacentrism' of his vision, the crucial question is whether the claim that 'scarcity' and 'risk' are *qualitatively* distinct holds water. It is upon this assumption that the validity of the distinction between class and risk society ultimately rests.

One source of doubt about the distinction is raised by the simple question: is insecurity not merely the flip side of scarcity? Or, more strongly, is insecurity not a function of scarcity? In the German folk poems collected in the early nineteenth century under the generic title *Des Knaben Wunderhorn* (and still widely known through Mahler's settings) there is a pair of thematically linked poems called 'Earthly Life' and 'Heavenly Life' which illustrate the problem vividly. 'Earthly Life' is a tale of a child's hunger-induced death angst and of the mother's attempt to calm the child's fear while simultaneously disguising her own. Predictably, the child is lying on the death bier before the promised bread has arrived on the table. In contrast, in the folk vision of heaven, heaven is represented not merely by abundance, but also by release from toil and from the money economy ('the wine cost not one penny'). In 'Earthly Life' it is insecurity – in this case due to the unpredictability and slowness of supply – rather than absolute scarcity upon which fear is fixed: the crop had ripened, the harvest had been gathered, the corn threshed. In fact the poems are dotted with examples of fear induced by insecurity and, significantly, these fears are not always focused upon hunger; war and consequences of war are no less common cause of anxiety. Hunger here is not, even paradigmatically, the typical source of fear, but is merely one of many misfortunes which can befall those in insecure positions; insecurity being the inability to control those events which impact directly upon life chance. To define insecurity in these terms – i.e. in terms of environmental unpredictability rather than objective risk – is to suggest that while its sources are variable (both within and between societies) there is a necessary link to scarce resources, be they basic needs such as food and shelter, or a secure position within the 'normal employment relation'. 'I am afraid', for Beck the motto of the risk society, is no less appropriate to class societies even if the focal point of anxiety has shifted. Fear of hunger, like the risk of ecological catastrophe, is most of the time probabilistic.

But there is a further move in the *Risk Society* which may have been intended to pre-empt this objection. Beck argues that modern risks are qualitatively differ-ent from earlier scarcity because the visible, tangible and localized nature of wealth can insulate the wealthy from the misfortunes of the poor, while even those in relatively advantageous 'social risk positions' cannot be insulated from the intangible and deterritorialized (globalized) nature of contemporary risks such as pollution and general environmental deterioration. All this Beck neatly captures in the formulation 'poverty is hierarchic, smog is democratic' (1992: 36). But such a move does not of itself address doubts about the water-tightness of the scarcity/insecurity divide for two related reasons. First, particularly in agrarian societies (but to a degree in industrial societies also) the wealthy were only ever relatively insulated from the catastrophes which befell the poor. Wealth affects the level of exposure to the risk of, say, harvest failure and famine, and could certainly dampen the effects of such catastrophes, but there was rarely a completely secure position. Secondly and conversely, wealth can and does offer (relative) protection from contemporary risks. Those who can, do move away from areas of high pollution, environmental degradation and danger. That this does not offer ultimate security from environmental disaster does not thereby place them in a significantly different position from those with relative wealth in 'scarcity societies'. The crucial point here is that the assertion of a qualitative dif-ference between scarcity and risk is only plausible if ultimate catastrophe (the 'greatest theoretically possible accident') is taken as the paradigmatic form of contemporary risk; i.e. if we neglect degrees of risk by subsuming all risk cate-gories under the umbrella of total catastrophe (under the nuclear mushroom, as it were). But, as Beck is aware, the 'greatest theoretically possible accident' upon which the fears of social movement activists are, understandably, focused is a hypothetical construct. It is not, however, the form that risk takes when actors are making routine daily decisions as to where and how to live. Despite an awareness of gradations of risk, there is a slippage in the analysis in which at key points the actually existing risks – as opposed to hypothetical risk – are subsumed under ultimate catastrophe.[1] But it is no more legitimate to take maximum catastrophe as archetypal of modern risk than to take absolute harvest failure as being the archetype of scarcity. In both cases the empirical reality facing actors as they make decisions at any given point is (most of the time) sub-catastrophic, relative, and to a degree predictable. This means that in effect the wealthy were protected from scarcity and remain protected from risk; 'protection' here being understood as 'relative protection'. Smog is just as hierarchical as poverty so long as some places are less smoggy than others.[2]

Doubt about the validity of the distinction between scarcity and risk raises further, and more fundamental, doubts about the two characteristics Beck imputes to the risk society: individualization and reflexivity. One of the key arguments in *Risk Society* takes up the German debate about the decline in the so-called *Normalarbeitsverhältnis* (standard employment relation) – i.e. the secure, largely male employment patterns upon which not merely the distribution of labour (both within the labour market and the domestic division of labour) but also much of Germany's political and welfare system rests.[3] Beck's argument, briefly expressed, is that the shift towards less secure, more 'flexible' patterns of employment has undermined deeply-held assumptions about both employment-based status groupings (Germany's almost *ständisch* – estate – status consciousness) and the gender division of labour in the 'public' and 'private' spheres. As Mark Ritter, *Risk Society's* translator, indicates (Beck, 1992: 129), the term Beck uses to describe the implication of this process, *Freisetzung*, is exquisitely (and intentionally) ambiguous in that it means both liberation ('setting free') and dismissal/redundancy. For Beck – as for his later British-based co-authors – this liberation 'detraditionalizes' values and the social relations they embody. The ultimate implication of this 'individualization of risk' (see Beck et al., 1994: 100) is that 'the individual himself or herself becomes the reproduction unit of the social in the lifeworld' (ibid.: 90). Status groups, corporate entities and families lose their function in reproducing not merely culture within the lifeworld, but also, to a degree, social privilege. For the individual this floating free from (or being thrown out of) both security and tradition means being faced with choices in place of established paths with their supporting norms and expectations. We are forced to reflect where reflection was previously not required ('forced to be free'). Such reflection seeps deep into the most private recesses of our lives on a routine daily basis; into our every action as colleagues, parents, partners, children. Insecurity is thus not merely an environmental context, it is an existential state; echoing Wittgenstein, we no longer 'know how to go on' on the basis of sacred tradition. Here we are close to Habermas' analysis of the destruction of tradition through the increasing reach of instrumental rationality and 'systems' logic' (Habermas, 1987). For Beck, as for Habermas, this process means that taken-for-granted values and assumptions become, to use Habermas' term, 'virtualized', i.e. their previously implicit validity claims become thematized, problematic and thus potentially called into question and to account. 'Reflexive modernization' is the catch phrase through which Beck seeks to capture these complex processes.[4]

Although perhaps vulnerable to the accusation of exaggeration (particularly in the German case), there is much in this analysis of *Freisetzung* which is both plausible and powerful. Where the analysis becomes problematic is in the use to which it is put to support what I earlier called a 'narrative of discontinuity', i.e. to support the claim that there is some new break between a modernity which is and one which was not (or was less) 'reflexive'. The point can be made with reference to Georg Simmel to whom the credit for the term 'individualization' may be ascribed.

Central to Simmel's analysis is the argument that individualization is not a once-and-for-all 'event'; rather it occurs each time, say, an informal social relation is replaced by a monetary one. Thus, not only does individualization occur much earlier in modernity (or even pre-modernity) than can be imagined within the narrow historical vision of debates about contemporary social change but, more importantly, for Simmel, the push towards individualization is a constant feature of modern social forms, and one which furthermore is in ceaseless tension with tradition.[5] The idea that one can use the concept of 'individualization' as a tool for periodizing modernity is thus foreign to Simmel. The thought which animated his use of the notion is much closer to that which lay behind Marx's observation that the capitalist means of production are, and must be, constantly revolutionizing (though Simmel extends this insight beyond the confines of capitalism and the economic sphere). It resembles too Karl Polanyi's argument that markets become disembedded from traditional relations (Polanyi, 1957) and Weber's claim that each 'modernizing offensive' (the term is Peter Wagner's, 1994) is accompanied by a 'bureaucratic revolution' in which traditional patterns are systematically and consciously destroyed (Weber, 1968).[6] Where these accounts differ from the use Beck has made of the concepts of 'individualization' and 'reflexivity' is that the processes they describe are (to varying degrees) independent of any one narrow historical time frame. This is particularly clear in Simmel where individualized forms constitute one always available type of sociation (albeit one which is loosely associated with 'modern' relations based upon monetary exchange, labour contracts, etc.).

The point here is not that Beck has misunderstood or misused Simmel's concept of individualization, but rather that Simmel's account, though less tidy, is more plausible. Beck's argument, like Habermas', is in the line of strongly discontinuous narratives of modernity whereas – above all – Simmel and Polanyi, posit a complex and permanent struggle between those which we call 'modern' and those which we call 'traditional' forms; a struggle in which there is no permanent victor and no irreversible victory. Each *Freisetzung* can and will be met by a *Rücksetzung*; each de- by an eventual re-traditionalization.[7] It is in this context that the contrast between the account of risk offered by Beck and that offered by Mary Douglas (and Aaron Wildavsky) is significant. I shall focus upon Douglas' more recent formulations (Douglas, 1992).

Like Beck, Douglas is struck by the link between risk perception and individualism (a notion related to, but not the same as, individualization). But there is a basic move in Douglas which takes the analysis in a quite different direction. Earlier I criticized Beck for taking the hypothetical 'greatest theoretically possible accident' as the paradigm for contemporary risk. Douglas goes further by arguing that the concept of 'risk' itself is hypothetical or metaphorical: '[risk] is not a thing, it is a way of thinking, and a highly artificial contrivance at that' (1992: 46). Although Beck is highly critical of the (pseudo) objectivism of scientific risk analysis, he does not break, as Douglas does, with the notion that risk is 'out there'. Indeed, this is a second way in which the structure of *Risk Society* is sociologically conventional: risk consciousness reflects 'real risk' just as 'class consciousness' was said to reflect 'real class inequality'; 'being' still 'determines consciousness' in the risk society (despite Beck's protestations to the contrary). From the perspective of Douglas' cultural theory there is no such reification of risk: risk consciousness reflects risk perception. This cultural relativization enables us to identify two related questions which are prior to those we have so far discussed: 'how safe is safe enough for this particular culture?' (Douglas, 1992: 41) and 'why do we seek to avoid risk?'. There is nothing nat-ural about risk-aversion; it is a sociological fact demanding explanation: 'the commercial risk-averse culture has locally vanquished the risk-seeking culture, and writes off the latter as pathological or abnormal' (1992: 41).[8]

Although Douglas does not spell it out quite in these terms, one interesting implication of this relativization of risk is the suggestion that there is no simple correspondence between risk perception and, this time in very heavy quotation marks, 'real risk'. Indeed, since the risk-averse will take measures to avoid high risk situations, perhaps one could go as far as to say that there is often an inverse relationship between risk consciousness and 'social risk location'. This is perhaps the thought behind the veteran SPD politician Helmut Schmidt's provocative observation quoted at the head of the chapter: 'We [Germans] are the world champions at anxiety'. It is those in the relatively secure positions who are most risk conscious, and for reasons somewhat more subtle than that they have more to lose than the rest. What Beck characterizes as the 'risk society' may thus be more appropriately labelled the 'risk-averse society', or, polemically, the 'angst society'. I want to dwell on this point for the remaining part of the discussion to see whether it enables us to take the sociological analysis of risk further. To do so I shall sketch in a somewhat impressionistic fashion possible differences between 'British' and 'German' risk perception not in the name of national stereotyping (this task can safely be left to Britain's self-styled 'Euro-realists'), but because the difference between these two societies may constitute a weak form of the distinct social patterns which Douglas has famously identified in terms of her grid/group distinction.

Douglas makes the following methodological point about any would-be soci-ology of risk: 'There is no way of proceeding with analyzing risk perception without typifying kinds of communities according to the support their members give to authority, commitment, boundaries, and structure' (Douglas, 1992: 47). Her attempt to proceed on the basis of a typology of community in line with these criteria is cast in very broad-brush terms as the difference between western, indi-vidualist, and commercial societies and some other social type; be it Japan as a non-western, non-individualist commercial society, or, more exotic still, societies which share none of these characteristics. What I want to suggest here is that the typology she developed can be applied to some degree to differences between what we sometimes take to be rather similar commercial societies (like Britain and Germany).[9]

'What has gone wrong', Douglas writes, 'is that the public response to risk has been individualized. Public perception of risk is treated as if it were the aggregated response of millions of private individuals' (1992: 40). She traces the method-ological individualism of risk analysis to the individualism of commercial soci-eties which display low grid/low group characteristics: i.e. in which there is high frequency of social exchange, but a weak sense of common (collective) identity.[10] This sounds like Beck's individualization, but in one important respect it is not. Perceptions of high risk reinforce already existing social divisions: 'It may be a general trait of human society that fear of danger tends to strengthen the lines of division in a community' (Douglas, 1992: 34). No democratic smog here. The most lurid manifestation of this reinforcement of already existing divisions is blame; the tendency to ascribe danger and misfortune to individuals or groups in already marginalized social positions: the poor, the dangerous classes, homosexuals, unmarried mothers, foreigners, etc.:

> Since it is inherently difficult to be aware of liminal groups in a society organized under the principles of competitive individualism, it is easier to write them off as human derelicts. Hierarchy does not necessarily perform better, but it is capable of being more aware of minority interests, because it is a political system for incorporating subgroups. (Douglas, 1992: 41)

It is not quite clear from the discussion in *Risk and Blame*, with its highly essayistic style, exactly how Douglas sees the relationship between individualism, risk and blame. But one interpretation of the link between individualized risk and blame strategies may be set out as follows: in the low grid/low group (i.e. individualistic and market) society there are two types of response to the perception of high risk.[11] At the level of the collectivity there will be scapegoating and blame of already vulnerable individuals and groups. At the level of individuals, there will be personal solutions to perceived risk, e.g. individuals buying themselves out of dangerous (natural or social) environments. The two strategies are linked through what has come to be known as the 'tragedy of the commons',[12] i.e. the tendency in individualistic societies for individuals acting as rational egotists to free-ride on the maintenance of public goods, of which public space is one. Generalized free-riding *vis-à-vis* the maintenance of public space (and thus of the natural environment in general) will lead to its progressive deterioration. Given the prevalence of free-riding, the path of a collective effort to address the problem is closed and individuals will respond by seeking to enclose and protect areas of private space. Such a cycle of behaviour is a perpetuum mobile. The greater the degree of deterioration of public space, the more difficult it is to mobilize moral resources, e.g. of civic pride or citizens' responsibility, and the more inclined we will be to tend our own private spaces as oases within a hostile environment. 'Private affluence' and 'public misery' are thus constant companions.[13] The link here to a discourse of blame is not hard to see: risks are perceived as threats from outside and outsiders to the fences individuals have built for themselves in their personalized 'solutions' to the tragedy of the commons. Douglas' analysis seems to draw us towards the opposite conclusions from those of Beck: high risk consciousness decreases rather than increases the chance of solidarity.

It is striking that this scenario is, first, quite unlike the responses of ecological movements in addressing questions of environmental degradation, and second, that it is also unlike aspects of the German case. Rather than blame the weak, ecological movements ascribe blame and responsibility to powerful bodies – national and multinational corporations, the nuclear industry, governments. Rather than seek individualistic solutions they call for new forms of solidarity in which the tragedy of the commons can be addressed through collective action in a context in which free-riding is taboo. In terms of Douglas' grid-group typology this is unmysterious: social movements are societies within societies displaying strong group characteristics (political and moral solidarity) often in opposition to the individualism which surrounds them. Indeed, as they are based in collective action, have the mobilization of collective sentiments as their key resource and provide their members with a sense of super-individual purpose, social movements are all but strong social groups per-definition.

But why argue that German society as a whole is less individualistic than Douglas' general characterization of 'western' commercial society? Perhaps an example is useful here. The 1990s has been characterized not merely by the problems with which I introduced the discussion, but also by efforts – with varying degrees of sincerity and effectiveness – to address these problems. One, albeit small, effort has been the introduction by the German Government of rules governing the treatment of household waste which involve the complex and very time-consuming pre-sorting of waste by individual householders (*Mülltrennung*). What is most remarkable about this is the degree of co-operation the policy has elicited. Of course there are penalties (co-operation is rare without some element of coercion). Nevertheless, the frequent appeals to citizens' responsibility and to solidarity (not merely with other human beings, but also with nature and future generations) appears to have worked to the point where there is a degree of mutual policing among neighbours. Remembering Douglas' methodological injunction that understanding risk perception demands an examination of the support a community's members give to 'authority, commitment, boundaries, and structure', perhaps there is evidence here of cultural resources which are lacking in the even more individualistic commercial cultures of Britain or America and which can be mobilized at a general societal (in addition to localized social movement) level to address the tragedy of the commons.

The preservation of such resources might be traced to a number of structural and historical factors: in the abiding political impact of the Church through Christian Democracy; the co-socialism of Germany's economic and political institutions (the 'social market economy' model in which politicians, trade union leaders and employers are 'partners' and in which even cuts in government expenditure come in the guise (or disguise) of a 'solidarity pact'); historical memory of the *Wiederaufbau* (rebuilding after the Second World War) which was, and is, presented as a collective effort;[14] or perhaps much older historical residues, e.g. remnants of *Obrigkeitsglauben* (ingrained respect for authority demanded by authoritarian states). The suggestion here is that Germany retains elements of a 'hierarchical society' in Douglas' sense (i.e. 'a political system for incorporating subgroups') and is thus able to mobilize collective sentiments against perceived threats to the public space.

But I think we have to be careful with such explanations because they can easily take the form of an appeal to 'essential cultural difference', or even descend into exoticism. It has, for example, been much easier to persuade 'ruggedly individualistic' Americans to drive their cars at reasonable speeds than it has been to persuade 'socially conscious' Germans. The motto of the anti-speed-limit lobby – *Freie Fahrt für freie Bürger* (roughly, 'freedom of the road for free citizens') – echoes the 'rights of true-born Americans' rhetoric of the American gun lobby.

Likewise, the collective sentiments of solidarity mobilized in the face of perceived environmental risks in Germany are not always carried over into the area of perceived risk to the German welfare state where, as attacks on guest workers and asylum seekers have all too vividly illustrated, scapegoating and blame strategies are available. These examples suggest that elements of hierarchy, and the cultural resources associated with hierarchy, exist in societies (predominantly) based upon competitive individualism, and perhaps, conversely, elements of competitive individualism can and do exist within hierarchies. Thus we cannot map Douglas' high/low grid/group distinctions onto actually existing societies in a straightforward way, e.g. by contrasting commercial with non-commercial or western with non-western society, or simply by characterizing Britain and America as individualistic and Germany (or Japan) as hierarchic.[15] This raises a sociologically interesting question: do appeals to solidarity (rather than the privatized/blame strategy) work because there are cultural resources there to be tapped, or are the cultural resources more readily available because of the frequency of attempts to appeal to and mobilize them? On balance I would prefer the second answer not only because it relies less on assumed essential cultural difference but also because it suggests that the free-riding/blame strategy is not the inescapable fate of societies predominantly characterized by 'competitive individualism'.[16]

If we accept this proposition, at least for the sake of argument, a series of backward- and forward-looking implications emerge which may enable us to think sociologically about the preconditions of a *reasonable* societal discourse on risk (i.e. one in which risk is not conceived merely as an aggregate and in which scapegoating is avoided). I shall finish by simply listing some of these:

- While social movements have good reasons to adopt the 'greatest theoretically possible accident' as the paradigm of modern risk – they need to mobilize passions and have weapons in debate – this is not a satisfactory starting point for the sociological analysis of risk which must remain sensitive to the variety of risk perceptions and their links to the constitutive character of community and to the location of actors within those communities.

- The sociology of risk needs to address the question: 'what cultural resources does this particular society or social group have which may facilitate a reasonable debate about risk?'.[17] The universalizing language used by Beck (and by the more millenarian varieties of ecological movements) is not sufficiently context-sensitive to pose this question, and the 'we are all in the same boat' rhetoric distracts attention from differences both to exposure and perception of risk. As I have suggested, we even need to exercise caution when applying grid/group categories to entire societies (whether 'western' society, or more intermediate 'nation state societies'). Unless we assume that there are some cultural resources available within each society through which risk debates may be channelled, it is difficult to see how any reasonable conversation can get underway.

- Nor is an ecological utopia in the sense of the elimination of risk a suitable, obtainable or even desirable aim for such a conversation. The fully risk-averse are not only immobilized in action (this is presumably another thought behind

Schmidt's comment), but life in a society of the risk-averse would be suffocating. Neither is risk, except for the deeply conservative-minded, simply a 'bad' or its elimination unambiguously a 'good'. The question is not pleasant, but it must also be posed: 'How much mutual policing is the protection of the commons worth?' The avoidance of risk has costs too, and the issue of 'acceptable risks' – of 'how safe is safe enough for this particular culture?' – cannot simply be brushed aside (as the universalizing language of an ecological utopia again tends to do). The issue here is the one of appropriate balance between individual freedom and collective responsibility (egotism and altruism) which so occupied Emile Durkheim, and which contemporary sociologists cannot ignore however passionate they are about the preservation of the commons, or however high they believe the stakes to be. As a good Durkheimian, Douglas, rightly, argues that risk questions are matters of social negotiation and compromise – not least over the questions 'what is risk?' and 'whose risk'– not simple either/ors.

This sense of the ambivalence of risk, of its dynamism as well as its dangers; of the costs as well as the benefits of its elimination, is perhaps not a bad starting point for a sociology of risk.

Acknowledgements

I would like to thank Barbara Adam, Paul Bellaby and Angus Ross for their helpful comments on an earlier draft of this chapter.

Notes

1   This slippage can be seen in the observation that with the risk society 'the "class" of the "affected" does not confront a "class" that is not affected. It confronts at most a "class" of not-yet-affected people' (Beck, 1992: 40).

2   Or even so long as one can afford the room air filter advertised in *Brigitte*, one of Germany's best-selling women's magazines. The advert depicts a scene which can be read as a retort to a scenario in *Risk Society* (and this may be no coincidence): a child peacefully asleep in her air-filtered room, the parents' (contemporary counterparts of the mother in *Earthly Life*) anxiety about their child's asthma presumably having been stilled; the problems of the risk society having been solved here and now, for these particular people, at a particular cost. The advert thus promises an individualized and purchasable solution to modernity's 'democratic' dangers.

3   For an excellent discussion of the interdependence of these employment patterns and Germany's welfare system, see Offe (1991).

4   Beck, 1995, seeks to distinguish 'reflexive' from 'primary' modernization by defining the former as a 'rationalization of rationalization' rather than of tradition. This does not, however, alter the criticisms made below – though they are largely confined to 'primary modernization' in Beck's sense – as both usages presuppose a narrative of discontinuity.

5   The complexity of Simmel's view of individualization can be seen, for example, in his comments on monogamy and marriage where he notes that 'modern culture seems more and more to individualize the character of the given marriage, but at the same time to leave untouched, even in some respects to emphasize, its super-individuality, which is the core of its sociological form' (Simmel, 1950: 112–13). This caution about the

ambivalent nature of individualization in gender relations should still be remembered when we consider the new 'choices' opened up by the more recent developments of the type Beck discusses.

6   For a more detailed discussion of these arguments from Polanyi and Weber, see Scott (1996).

7   Beck has the category of 'reintegration', but does not work through the implication of reintegrative processes from the possibility of the narrative of discontinuity or for the very idea of a 'reflexive modernity'.

8   Thus, for example, the hoo-ha which periodically surrounds novels and films such as *Trainspotting* is often due precisely to the refusal of their authors and/or directors to write off risk-seeking cultures (in this case heroin users) as pathological and abnormal.

9   This is in line with some of Douglas' own observations, for example that risk is an important theme in American society (see Douglas, 1992: 28).

10   For a clear account and helpful discussion of Douglas' group/grid analysis, see Hargreaves Heap and Ross (1992).

11   This may not be quite the connection implicit in Douglas (or not the only one). One central implication of her analysis is that risk perception is not grounded in objective danger, but requires the presence (or imagined presence) of other human agents whom we may consider responsible for those dangers. This makes risk perception and blame an inseparable part of a single response. I am grateful to Angus Ross for suggesting this inter-pretation of Douglas' cultural theory of risk.

12   Although the argument is Aristotle's, the term and original formulation are from Garrett Hardin (1968). Hardin's concern was with the over-exploitation of scarce resources, e.g. too many sheep grazing on the common, and beyond that with the issue of over-population. The current crisis surrounding over-fishing in EU waters fits the bill. Here I have rendered Hardin's original neo-Malthusian formulation in the language of rational choice, albeit in loose and non-technical terms. It is interesting too to note specifically what Hardin means by 'tragedy'. He quotes Whitehead: 'The essence of dramatic tragedy is not unhappi-ness. It resides in the solemnity of the remorseless working of things' (Hardin, 1968: 1244). Hardin takes this notion of 'remorseless working' very literally, arguing that only the aban-donment of the commons (the enclosure of everything including what he calls 'freedom to breed') can address the tragedy. It is this claim which has drawn criticisms (see note 17). Like many such would-be general models, Hardin works with little reference to actual occasions of over-exploitation of common land. In contrast, the historian Christopher Hill argues that where over-grazing of the commons did occur it was frequently part of the strategy of larger farmers to assist the process of the primitive accumulation of common land (see Hill, 1996).

13   By linking the tragedy of the commons to individualistic and privatized strategies I am relativizing the 'tragedy' in a way quite foreign to Hardin's original analysis which makes a strong claim for its universality and which views privatization as the *solution* rather than the problem.

14   A view which Rainer Werner Fassbinder brilliantly sought to debunk in his 1978 film *Die Ehe der Maria Braun*.

15   This is another reason for preferring Simmel's argument that any categorization of social forms identifies oppositions which can be used to distinguish both boundaries between societies *and* alternative strategies available within them. In this connection O'Riordan has criticized Douglas, as I am implicitly doing here, for the suggestion that opportunist and hierarchy cultures are incompatible (see O'Riordan, 1992). This problem is however of a different order to that in Beck's analysis where the class/insecurity dis-tinction is asked to do more than act as a typology, i.e. identify categorical periodizations. The usefulness of the grid/group distinction in identifying the *predominant* characteristics of a given society or social group is not diminished by the empirical mixture of types.

16   There is no time here to develop the arguments to support such a preference, but these can be found among such diverse writers as the rational choice theorists Adam

Przeworski (especially Przeworski, 1985) and the cultural sociologist Pierre Bourdieu. Although arguing from opposing disciplines and paradigms, both Przeworski and Bourdieu criticize sociology and political science for indulging in simplistic one-way explanations in which social events are deduced from structural features of their 'context'. Such 'explanations' are frequently no more than post factum reconstructions; punditry by hindsight. Adopting alternative methodological principles has implications not merely for our understanding of the nature of the *explanation* in general, but also for the *interpretation* of specific 'social facts'. For example, the sceptical – or perhaps cynical – reading of the *Mülltrennung* policy would be that it is merely a palliative – an accusation aimed (with some justification) at the introduction of the 'green mark' (*Grüne Punkt*) on recyclable packaging as mere *Etikettschwindel* (labelling con, i.e. marketing ploy). But a less hard-nosed, more Durkheimian, reading is also possible. *Mülltrennung* is not, or not primarily, instrumentally rational, but has an additional ritualistic purpose: through collective participation a sense of common responsibility can be mobilized and thus reinforced. As Benedict Anderson has emphasized, such rituals are all the more effective due to the simultaneity, or near simultaneity, of participation in the ritual act (Anderson, 1983). Ritualized collective mobilization is in principle available to any society.

17   And in her recent and influential analysis of the tragedy of the commons, Ellen Ostrum (1990) argues (contra Hardin) precisely that real human communities *do* possess the cultural and intellectual resources to address the tragedy by instituting rules to protect common property from the destructive logic of economic exploitation. Her argument in turn echoes Karl Polanyi's classical analysis in which he claims that societies will attempt to protect themselves from the destructive force of unconstrained market activity by seeking to regulate and constrain markets (Ostrum, 1990; Polanyi, 1957).

References

Anderson, B. (1983) *Imagined Communities*. London: Verso.

Beck, U. (1992) *Risk Society: Towards a New Modernity.* Trans. M. Ritter. London: Sage.

Beck, U. (1995) *Ecological Enlightenment*. NJ: Humanities Press.

Beck, U., Giddens, A. and Lash, S. (1994) *Reflexive Modernization: Politics, Tradition and Aesthetics in the Modern Social Order*. Cambridge: Polity.

Douglas, M. (1992) *Risk and Blame: Essays in Cultural Theory.* London: Routledge.

Douglas, M. and Wildavsky, A. (1983) *Risk and Culture*. Berkeley: California University Press.

Habermas, J. (1987) *The Theory of Communicative Action*, Vol. 2. Trans. T. McCarthy. Cambridge: Polity.

Hardin, G.J. (1968) 'The Tragedy of the Commons', *Science*, 162: 1243–8.

Hargreaves Heap, S. and Ross, A. (1992) 'Introduction: Mary Douglas and the Enterprise Culture', in Hargreaves Heap, S. and Ross, A. (eds), *Understanding the Enterprise Culture*. Edinburgh: Edinburgh University Press.

Hill, C. (1996) *Liberty Against the Law: Some Seventeenth-Century Controversies*. London: Allen Lane–The Penguin Press.

Offe, C. (1991) 'Smooth Consolidation in the West German Welfare State: Structural Change, Fiscal Policies, and Populist Politics', in F. Fox Piven (ed.), *Labour Parties in Postindustrial Societies*. Cambridge: Polity.

O'Riordan, T. (1992) 'Environmental Risk Management in an Enterprise Culture', in Hargreaves Heap, S. and Ross, A. (eds), *Understanding the Enterprise Culture*. Edinburgh: Edinburgh University Press.

Ostrum, E. (1990) *Governing the Commons*. Cambridge: Cambridge University Press.

Polanyi, K. (1957 [1944]) *The Great Transformation*. Boston, MA: Beacon Press.

Przeworski, A. (1985) *Capitalism, Socialism and Democracy*. Cambridge: Cambridge University Press.

Scott, A. (1996) 'Bureaucratic Revolutions and Free Market Utopias', *Economy and Society*, 25 (1): 89–110.

Simmel, G. (1950) 'The Isolated Individual and the Dyad', in K.H. Wolff (ed.), *The Sociology of Georg Simmel*. New York: The Free Press.

Virilio, P. (1983) *Pure War*. New York: Semiotext(e).

Wagner, P. (1994) *A Sociology of Modernity: Liberty and Discipline*. London: Routledge.

Weber, M. (1968) *Economy and Society*, Vol. 2. G. Roth and C. Wittich (eds), New York: Bedminister Press.

2

Risk Culture

Scott Lash

This chapter argues that a way of positioning risk in order that it be more effective as social critique is to displace, or at least supplement, the notion of 'risk society' with an idea of 'risk culture'. I want to argue that the notion of risk society presumes a focus on society and the social. The idea of *society* presumes a determinate, institutional, normative, rule bound and necessarily hierarchical ordering of individual members in regard to their utilitarian interests. Risk *cultures*, in contrast, presume not a determinate ordering, but a reflexive or indeterminate disordering. Risk cultures lie in non-institutional and anti-institutional sociations. Their media are not procedural norms but substantive values. Their governing figurations are not rules but symbols: they are less a hierarchical ordering than a horizontal disordering. Their fluid quasi-membership is as likely to be collective as individual, and their concern is less with utilitarian interests than the fostering of the good life. This chapter will not develop these ideal types systematically. It will however touch on all of these aspects of what risk cultures, as distinct from risk societies, might be through a discussion of the work of Mary Douglas and of Kant's critique of aesthetic judgement. Risk cultures, it will be argued, are based less in cognitive than in aesthetic reflexivity. Risk cultures are reflexive communities (Beck et al., 1994).

In this context the first section of the chapter draws critically on Douglas and Wildavsky's (1983) writing on risk and culture. In particular it looks at their distinction between hierarchical institutions on the one hand and sectarian boundaries on the other. It attempts to use the idea of sect to understand the emergent non-institutional sociations of the risk culture. Here I contrast the normative institutional ordering of the risk society, with the freer, less ordered, more horizontal and sociational nature of the culture (Hetherington, 1993). The second section further develops the idea of risk culture through a discussion of aesthetic or reflexive judgement in Kant. It contrasts such aesthetic judgement with cognitive or determinate judgement. It argues that the open-ended nature of aesthetic judgement is integral to the *mentalité*, to the habitus, the background assumptions of the risk culture. The third section further develops the idea of aesthetic judgement, distinguishing between judgements of beauty and judgements of the sublime. Here we see how an open and bodily subjectivity, whose vulnerability exposes it to the sublime is part and parcel of the risk culture. The final section speculates on emergent properties of the risk culture both in the realm of techno-logical futures and the sub-politics of new sociations.

Risk and culture: institutions and sects

The notion of the 'risk society' may well be a contradiction in terms. A set of circumstances in which our mentalities, our categories are pervaded by risk think-ing, by risky forms of life, by a language increasingly coloured by risk discourse can, it seems to me, only be possible in conjunction with a certain decline in sig-nificance of 'the social'. The idea of risk society and reflexive modernization pre-sumes a three stage chronology: A movement from tradition to simple modernity and finally to reflexive modernity. Here in the shift from tradition to simple modernity the *gesellschaftliche* organizations and institutions of 'society' replace the *gemeinschaftliche* forms of sociation of the traditional order. In reflexive modernity the dominance of the social, itself displacing a *gemeinschaftliche* and traditional order, is now challenged. It is challenged by global geographies, the culturalization and informationalization of everyday life and the decline in legitimacy of social norms. It is only now that risk culture can emerge. What I am claiming is that 'risk culture' is an entity that displaces 'institutional society'. I am claiming that risk culture introduces whole areas of indeterminacy where there was previously determinacy. The problem with the idea of risk society is not that it is too modernist, but that it is not modern enough. With the remaining strength of determinate institutional norms in Beck's risk society, there is not yet full detraditionalization (Heelas, 1996a). This is only possible with displacement of risk society by risk culture.

In *Risk and Culture* (1983), Mary Douglas and Aaron Wildavsky offer tools to begin to develop this sort of notion of risk culture (see Alexander, 1996). The crux of their argument is that there is in fact no increase in risks in contemporary times. There is instead only an increase in perceived risks. They argue that there is such an increase in perceived risks because a set of very influential social actors have claimed with considerable force that there is an increase in real dangers. For Douglas and Wildavsky the point is not the reality of these risks but that the risks are constructed by this particular group of social actors that have been attracted to the environmental movements. They come, the authors maintain, from the margins, the borders of society. The groups are on the margins of society, they claim, largely due to the inability of our core institutions to integrate them into the mainstream social order.

Douglas and Wildavsky's thesis is profoundly and openly conservative. It follows very much from Douglas' earlier works, *Purity and Danger* (1966) and *Natural Symbols* (1970) and should be understood in the context of, and as a reaction against, the student and grass roots trade union radicalism of the late 1960s and early 1970s. Douglas effectively blamed this rise in radicalism on the 'softness' and putative excesses of tolerance in the dominant institutions of society. Douglas understood this in terms of her concepts of 'group' and 'grid'.

'Group' here refers to the solidity of boundaries between the inside and outside of a society, while 'grid' refers to the properties and the more or less tight or loose character of a group's classificatory categories. The weaker the boundary between inside and outside and the more ambivalent the classificatory categories, the weaker a society's group and grid. For Douglas, too much tolerance in our core institutions led to a slackening of group and grid, in turn leaving space for liminality, chaos and radicalism: in the context of risk, leaving space for a particular group of militants attached to ecological causes. These militants themselves could construct risks in their cultural and symbolic struggles against the mainstream. *Risk and Culture* thus sees (ecological) risks and dangers largely as constructed by these radicals from 'the borders' that have emerged out of the erosion of both group and grid in modern society.

Douglas and Wildavsky understand these risk constructors from the borders as 'sectarians'. The idea of sectarian is important here. In her earlier books Douglas spoke approvingly of – as opposed to sects – the institutions of the Catholic Church. She bemoaned the 'softening' in these institutions, arguing that this might well be fine for upper and middle class, well-educated Catholics, but she despaired for what she called the 'bog Irishman'? He would enter a state of anomie and become prey to the pulls of social disorganization. Note here a profound sympathy with the normatively ordered institution, the church and a profound antipathy to the informal, non-institutional and putatively chaotic sects. Other sociologists of religion influenced by Douglas such as Barker (1984) and Heelas (1996b) have also written of the excesses of sects in this context. Thus for Douglas the risk culture concerns primarily these 'sectarians from the borders' who construct these risks. Through their symbolic violence from the borders they enforce their constructions as the truth for the rest of us. For Douglas these risk constructors are doubly damned: as border inhabitants and sectarians. We will return to this below.

I think that we can easily go too far in demonizing these sects and that there may be a certain amount of mileage in the notion of sect, for a positive understanding of radical critical risk communities today. By definition, sects are anti-institutional. They are less individualist than communal. They are organizations with loose structures, even effectively 'disorganizations' (McNaughten and Urry, 1998). I want to use Douglas against herself to talk about risk cultures. Risk cultures are reasonable (though not rationalist) and reflexive communities: communities constructed in the context of institutional uncertainty of risk, and which may work to identify environmental and other risks. These are communities of risk sub-politics.

Beck and Giddens have a very strong idea of the place of institutions within their respective notions of risk society. This is not like Douglas' conservatism. Beck and Giddens are social liberals whose institutions function as both expert systems and democratic forums. They function not in the re-assertion of tradition à la Douglas, but in progressive and ordered social change. These authors' concern is not with social control of radicals, but with a measure of amelioration of environmental and identity-risks (for example in spheres of the family and biotechnology). Their idea is that modern political and economic institutions in fact led to the creation of a number of these natural and identity hazards, while at the same time, these and other institutions have also worked to deal with these hazards. In doing so they have been partly successful but also produced side effects of yet further risks. Beck and Giddens propose a set of more reflexive, democratically structured institutions to deal with these side effects and the continuous production of new risks. They are however modest in their claims about these new institutions, which will themselves create further, though possibly less noxious consequences, side effects and risks. But in the last analysis the idea of risk society in Beck and in Giddens is institutionalist. Their positioning of risk is in a risk society that is institutionally structured. The 'risk society' is normatively ordered, vertically structured and individually based. Risk cultures in contradistinction are value-disordered, horizontally destructured and communally based. Could it be that inside the risk society a set of such risk cultures are emerging, that is cultures that are less institutions or 'churches' but rather more like sects in the best sense of the word? Is it possible that we are undergoing less an institutional restructuring than a non- or anti-institutional de-structuring; that the predominant movement is from a risk society to a risk culture?

Let us enter in a bit more detail into the argument in *Risk and Culture*. Douglas and Wildavsky proffer a risk typology. This is not a typology of real risks, but instead a typology of concern with risk, a typology of risk perception. It is a typology of how different sorts of social groups select risks; of how each group's cultural characteristics have an elective affinity with particular risk perceptions. They identify three generic areas of concern with risk or 'risk selection'; these are:

1 socio-political risks: dangers to social structure, coming from internal deviants; especially risks from human violence: from crime or external military foes;
2 economic risks: threats to the economy, or risks of economic failure and;
3 natural risks: ecological threats to nature and the body; that is, 'risks from technology'.

They claim that it is the third type of perceived risk that has greatly increased, although in fact risks from technology may have decreased. Douglas and Wildavsky's explanation is cultural. To them, structural change is caused by the existence of three separate 'risk cultures':

1 a hierarchical-institutional culture which tends to select *social* risks;
2 a culture of market individualism which tends to select *economic* risks; and
3 a 'sectarian' 'border' culture which tends to select *natural* risks.

The first two of these categories, the hierarchical institutionalists and the market individualists constitute for Douglas and Wildavsky the 'centre'; while the border culture constitutes a threatening periphery. Their argument is that culture leads to disorganization of structure.

It seems to me that structural change, or largely economic change, is a basis for the growth of a risk *culture*. Moreover, it seems likely that there has been a much more general growth of indeterminacy and perceived risk than Douglas and Wildavsky admit. Not just in terms of the third category, i.e. of natural risks, but also as regards dangers to social structure, in the context of growing individualization and the decline of and threat to the nation state. And further, in regard to economic risk with the turbulence built in to increasingly globalized markets, specialized consumption and the like. Contrary to Douglas and Wildavsky, then, there is a growth, not just of natural risks due to technology but the emergence of a more general indeterminacy, a decline in ordering of world capitalism. I would further disagree with them regarding the source of this indeterminacy. Given the contemporary global market economy and its effects, this risk mentality is not just introduced, *pace* Douglas and Wildavsky, by the emergence of a 'sectarian' 'border' ranged against the centre. Thus, Douglas and Wildavsky should not exclusively blame the 'sectarians', not blame those at the margins for the creation of the risk mentality, for the disorganization of the contemporary social order.

Douglas and Wildavsky's 'culturalism' is tied to a constructivist framework much in the same sense as Beck's lack of discussion of culture, i.e. his 'societalism' is linked to realist assumptions about knowledge. Beck would seem to be a realist in terms of the growth of environmental or natural risks and especially in terms of the centrality of responsibility in his *Gegengifte: die organisierte Unverantwortlichkeit* (Beck, 1988). Discussed here is the systematic off-loading of responsibility for dangers by industry and science onto the lay public as the latter's individual responsibility (see Wynne, 1996). In contrast, Douglas and Wildavsky's view is that all risks are primarily social constructions: Risks are always a question of 'purity and danger', of some sort of ritual pollution: indeed that natural pollution is just one variety of ritual pollution. Their view is that organized irresponsibility is secondary. It is that individuals from the various risk cultures they identify do not look for the risks and then make inferences about who to blame. Instead they begin from social groups that they want to blame and from this make inferences about which risks to focus on. That is, risk cultures always start not from the risk but from the blame, start from the 'who to blame'. Thus, the danger can be understood in terms of this 'who to blame'. Studying risk and responsibility, therefore, implies that rather than looking for responsibility following from the real existence of risk, one must look first at whom risk cultures blame. Thus hierarchical-institutional cultures blame the outsiders, the criminals, the foreigners. Key here is the phenomenon of trust. The idea in this is if you first locate whom you cannot trust, then you know what the salient risks are. Starting from a distrust of outsiders or strangers, hierarchical cultures will select a particular outsider-linked list of risks – war, crime, AIDS, etc. As in Douglas' earlier work, there is a question of ritual pollution here, a question of purity and danger (Douglas, 1966). The danger or ritual pollution comes from outside of the nation, the state, the social structure to challenge its purity. One distrusts the ritual polluter, the pariah.

If Douglas and Wildavsky's first risk culture ideal type is 'hierarchical institutionalists', their second is 'market individualists'. Market individualist cultures have a different notion of the 'who to blame'. For them the main danger is economic failure. The 'who to blame' is a bit trickier here. The 'who to blame' in fact are individuals who will not blame themselves. The who to blame is the danger that threatens the purity of market individualism, of neo-liberalism. It is welfare mothers, trade unions, the unemployed, the underclass. For Douglas and Wildavsky, ritual pollution and purity is much more a problem for the third ideal–typical risk culture, the 'sectarians from the borders' than it is for either of the first two risk cultures which the authors see as somehow more tolerant. I think that this is not the case. The true believers among hierarchs, market individualists and ecologists are equally purity minded. For 'border sectarians', the centre, the military–industrial complex, understood as 'technology', is blamed. Here, like for the hierarchs, distrust plays a very important role. If Serbs blame Croats and vice versa for 'bads' inflicted in the past, in the risk culture each group blames another group whom they distrust, for future 'bads'. Douglas and Wildavsky would cast authors like Beck in the role of border sectarians. Douglas and Wildavsky think that all three risk cultures have realist notions of risk. But that the sectarians from the borders are the most realist of all. For them, commentators like Beck would be taking the position from the border and recasting it as realism.

Aesthetic judgement, reflexive judgement

Douglas and Wildavsky say that dangers or risks should not be understood as objective but instead as inscribed in forms of life. They write that risk perception is subjective and liken it literally to 'aesthetic judgements'. Let us take this notion of aesthetic judgement seriously. In *The Critique of Judgement*, Kant (1952) addresses 'aesthetic judgements of taste'. Aesthetic judgements of taste are what Kant calls 'reflective judgements'. These are understood by Kant in contraposition to determinate judgement. It seems to me that we can understand reflexivity in modernity along the lines of these reflective or what I prefer to call 'reflexive' judgements which include apart from a mental, reflective, conceptualization also affective, embodied and habitual notions of taste (see Lash, 1994: 135–9). Indeed reflexive judgement is at the core of the risk culture. Determinate judgement is the sort of judgement involved in the *Critique of Pure Reason*. These are objective judgements. They have objective validity. Their model is physics and mathematics. Their conditions of possibility are the categories of logic, the categories of what Kant calls 'the understanding'. In contrast, aesthetic, or in my own terms reflexive, judgements are not objective but subjective. Thus for Douglas and Wildavsky, judgements regarding dangers are subjective. Moreover reflexive judgements do not operate from given rules of logic as do determinate judgements. In reflexive judgement we must *find* the rule.

Thus in regard to environmental and other natural and/or bodily 'bads', we do not judge objectively. We do not subsume the event or object under a given rule. Instead we judge the (future) event subjectively. We do not have a given rule, but subjectivity must go in search of a rule to judge the object, to judge the event. There are some further properties of reflexive judgement that are consistent with

Douglas' constructivism. First unlike the propositional truths that are determinate judgements, reflexive (aesthetic) judgements are estimations that are based on 'feelings' of pleasure and displeasure but also on feelings of shock, overwhelmedness, fear, loathing as well as joy. They have less to do with predicative statements, with validity claims and rational argument supporting the validity claims, than with determinate judgements. Determinate judgements involve the subsumption of events (like an AIDS-related death or a nuclear power station explosion) under the logical categories of the understanding, under Kant's 'transcendental unity of apperception'. Reflexive judgements – which are estimations based in feelings – take place not through the understanding, but through the imagination and more immediately through sensation.

Most feelings, most everyday experiences are a matter of what Kant as well as many phenomenologists call trivial meanings or banal meanings. These are trivial or banal in comparison to the logical meanings, the propositional truths of determinate judgement (but also of the calculative rules and instrumental rationality of the marketplace). But aesthetic-reflexive judgements arise from a very special type of experience. They arise from only those trivial meanings that open up a set of existential or transcendental meanings. They thus connect everyday experiences to supra-logical meanings. These are not necessarily a matter of an ecstatic or epiphanic moment or 'now'. But they do relate to different sorts of 'duration' than those of either trivial or logical meanings. Thus the trivial, the particular in cultural artefacts that are 'aesthetic' (as distinct Kant would say from just 'empirical') must also point in the direction of such supra-logical meaning. This supra-logical (existential, transcendental) sort of meaning is what Kant saw in his 'Ideas of Reason' (freedom, infinity, the noumenon, the moral imperative). In this sense all cultures need particulars, artefacts, rituals, events which are affectively charged; that is, they point to existential meanings as those involved in the temporality of death, love, sexuality, relations with one's children, friendship. The meanings involved here are more important than logical meanings. The cognitive and non-cultural orientation of Beck's and Giddens' notions of risk and reflexivity involve important dimensions of Kantian determinate judgement while aesthetic reflexivity should be conceived very much along the lines of aesthetic–reflexive judgements, that incorporate Kant's notion of reflective judgement, but entrench it in a wider understanding of affective embodiment.

Let us bring this back to risks or 'bads'. We assign meanings to risks, to 'bads'. But these are not just, and not even primarily, logical meanings or determinate judgements. They are more than just bads or *dommages*, coming under the calculations of insurance and some sort of insurance principle. Consider for example the famous Robert Mapplethorpe photography exhibition that toured the world's art museums between 1990 and 1995 and featured violent homoerotic photos, especially of black men. A number of viewers of the exhibition no doubt thought of Mapplethorpe's death from AIDS, and about AIDS more generally as they looked through the exhibition. Surely this is a vastly different way of judging the bad, the event, the risk of AIDS, than subsuming it under a set of statistics, under probabilistic logic. It takes the particular, i.e. the photographs which can potentially open up a space of existential meaning.

To consider AIDS through probabilities and statistics is a way of looking at risks via determinate judgement. The more aesthetic consideration of AIDS through the existential meanings of Mapplethorpe's images instead involves reflexive judgement. To understand risk in terms of the monitoring, the subsumption, is to foreground the cognitive paradigm bound up with determinate judgement. This seems fine as far as public policy is concerned, though it may not be sufficient for policy, because the way people perceive risks and experience risk should also be a matter for policy (Harvey, 1996). But, although policy about dangers, threats and risks is important, the experience of risk victims is about more than just policy. It is indeed about forms of life; its symbolism being nowhere better explicated than in the death of Diana, Princess of Wales.

There are thus two ways of dealing with 'bads' in the risk culture: through the 'realism' of determinate judgement and through what amounts to the constructionism of reflexive judgement. We have Beck's 'risk society' as paradigmatic realism, though it is not as simple as that, and Douglas' cultures of risk as paradigmatic constructivism. Beck and Giddens would give us a reflexive modernity in which the 'bads' resulting from uncontrolled technology of an earlier and 'simple' modernity would come under the reflexive monitoring (I would call this determinate judgement) of the counter-experts of the present era. These would themselves produce some undesirable unintended consequences, but on the whole, things might be getting better. For Douglas the 'bads' would be constructed as 'bads' through a process of reflexive judgement: from the point of view of the background assumptions of the horizons, the habitus of different social groups.

Although determinate judgement is, for better or mostly for worse, quite clearly here with us to stay, reflexive judgement is integral to a much fuller sort of modernity than is determinate judgement. That is, full modernity is not exclusively or even primarily about cognitive (the monitoring or self-monitoring) judgement, but (also) about reflexive (aesthetic) judgement. Both Kant's determinate judgement and sociological cognitive reflexivity do presume the demise of heteronomous legislation or determination from the social. This said, such external legislation is displaced by another sort of internal, yet still heteronomous legislation from the logical categories, from the probabilistic and calculative reasoning of cognitive monitoring. Kant hence called the will of determinate judgement the 'empirical will' (in contradistinction to the 'pure practical will') in that it was heteronomously legislated by interests. This empirical will is very much the effective prototype for the notion of instrumental rationality as found in the work of Weber and Critical Theory. The rule finding activity of reflexive judgement is far more autonomous. Further, determinate judgement presumes a sort of subject–object dualism. Determinate judgement presumes the legislation of cognitive reason to all forms of life, all value spheres. Whereas reflexive judgement presumes a set of differentiated self-legislating value spheres: each finding their own rules to cope with events and objects coming into their purview (Weber, 1946). Finally, the notion of subjectivity itself only develops, not with determinate but with reflexive judgement. The 'I' of determinate judgement might be a 'Subject', but he/she judges objectively. That is the 'I' of determinate judgement is not yet subjectivity *per se*. Subjectivity puts the 'I', not above the world, but into the world, involved in orienting activities, sometimes confused, often bricolaging, bumping up against objects and other subjectivities, muddling through, making do. Subjectivity is embodied, can be more or less centred, while the 'I' of determinate judgement has as its condition a 'transcendental unity'. The subjectivity that Michel Foucault (1984) talks about in his later work on Enlightenment is surely that of reflexive judgement.

Now this idea of reflexive judgement is not only fully modern but constructionist. A number of scholars have contrasted the pre-modern speculative model of knowledge with the modern practical or praxis based model (Caygill, 1989; Schluchter, 1987; Todorov, 1982). In the pre-modern model, for example in Thomism, God was understood in terms of not practice but speculative knowledge. God thus had 'absolute intuition'; could know or 'see' nature as it was in itself . This is the sort of knowledge which follows the Greek model of mimesis, or passive imitation. This bears similarities with the knowledge of pure reason and logical categories. Though pure reason operates synthetically, it is objective. Modern notions of the symbol, in contrast, are based in practice, a constructionist practice of '*poesis*' (Todorov, 1982: 168–70). Anti-positivist sociologies of practice have their basis in Kant's second and practical critique, not the first and theoretical one. The objectivist and still partly pre-modern knowledge of the first critique was instantiated in physics and mathematics. The meaning at issue in the second critique was the more indeterminate meaning involved, not in the sciences, but in forms of life: and here 'man' was fully constructionist, creating meaning. Caygill (1989) has shown that meaning via reflective judgement is created not logically (as in determinate judgement) but *ana*logically. This entails the establishment of meaning, not through estimations of a logical concept subsuming an appearance, but through the approximation of 'configurations' to one another. We operate via a set of background figures or configurations, through which we analogically judge configurations that we come across in our activities. Here determinate judgement or logical knowledge is just one variation of the more general analogical knowledge, i.e. determinate judgement is just one form of reflexive judgement. Here subjectivity proceeds via analogy with the configurations in his/her horizon, encountering objects or events in his/her environment, and through judgement, synthesizing or producing or constructing yet further configurations, yet further meanings.

Aesthetic reflexivity and the sublime

Mary Douglas has an (at least implicit) philosophical anthropology. Her 'bias' is, as she says, 'towards the centre'. Towards a sort of 'centre that holds'. Her bias is surely not towards the sectarian borders, nor towards the market individualists, but towards the 'hierarchical institutionalists'. In this context, like Peter Berger (1967) she presumes an instinctual underdetermination, an *Instinktarmut*, as our species' specific lack. Other animals do not have this lack. Human beings compensate for this poverty of instinct by building institutions. We 'suture' the lack, we close the lack up with institutions. This explains why similar to Berger, Douglas emphasizes the 'sacred canopy' of the church as an institution since sects cannot compensate for that lack.

For Mary Douglas, institutions need some kind of hierarchy; however, more crucially, they incorporate memory. They inscribe it and pass it down from generation to generation. They are also vessels for trust. For individuals to trust in institutions is to trust in memory. This is paradigmatically different from Giddens' trust in expert systems. Expert systems are built on the model of cognitive or determinate judgement. They incorporate a non-narrative knowledge. Expert systems are based on a certain kind of forgetting. When Beck talks about institutional reflexivity he too means modern expert systems, incorporating structural feedback not memory or narratives. Again we are talking about forums for determinate judgement, not culturally constructed memory. Douglas' institutions incorporate tradition. They pass on memory; they (like art and architecture) give us stability and permanence. Trust in the 'goodness' of institutions say Douglas and Wildavsky (1983: 123), is also trust in future generations who then place trust in those same institutions. Stable memory-grounding institutions incorporating such trust, she observes, need not be heavily rule bound, need not follow an economy of determinate judgement. They can be flexible and rule-finding in terms of future risks and the risks of future generations. Here – in the face of the permanence of institutions, against the background of the permanence, the collective memory incorporated in art, in cultural artefacts, in architecture – human beings can recognize their finitude.

But this is also the problem. The institutions are 'the house' of collective memory, of narratives of cultural artefacts and rituals. Institutions are nothing without the permanence of the latter. These cultural artefacts are the configurations, the forms through which we judge aesthetically, judge reflexively the risk events, the objects that we encounter and from which we produce other cultural artefacts, other configurations, other forms, other meanings. Gadamer (1986) says that this is the basis of the continuing relevance of the beautiful. By this he means reflexive judgements of the beautiful as opposed to reflexive judgements of the sublime. The above discussion of reflexive judgement has mostly been in the context of reflexive judgements of the beautiful. In judgements of the beautiful we come across objects or events, including the possible future 'bads' which are risks. We do not subsume these under the logical concepts of the understanding but, instead, these judgements are a sort of 'feeling' as we intuit them through the *imagination*. The imagination for Kant (1929: 81) is the faculty of intuition. Intuition is itself a synthesis. In the imagination, objects and events are intuited through, not logical categories, but 'the forms of time and space'. It is the imagination which produces or synthesizes 'distinctions'. On some accounts it does so through 'schemata'. Here the form of time and space are gridded, as it were, by schemata. But most importantly, what the imagination synthesizes or produces through the schemata are 'representations' or 'presentations'.

In all aesthetic judgements, the faculty of judgement bridges on the one hand perception and, on the other, reason. Judgement bridges on the one hand the trivial meaning of particulars and on the other hand (skipping over the logical meaning of the understanding) indeterminate or existential meaning (Kant, 1952: 119). In 'sublime' judgements, the event or object is so powerful that the imagination cannot make a presentation. We experience such events and objects not through the imagination, but through *sensation*, through pure perception. Sensation is raw. The body takes in the world through sensation. As such, it is unable to make a presentation. It is unable to effect a productive (or constructive) synthesis. The body is open and receptive. The body experiences its constitutive *Instinktarmut*; it lives with its lack. Thus judgements of the sublime bridge, on the one hand, sensation and, on the other, indeterminate or exlstential meaning. They connect sensation of subjectivity as singular and as exposed beings. Aesthetic judgements of the sublime expose bodies with lack, expose open bodies to the ravages of contingency, to darkness to 'fear and trembling'. Hence we also experience this as confirming our finitude. Risks and threats, thus experienced and subsumed under neither determinate judgement of the understanding nor the judgements and syntheses of the imagination therefore bring us in touch with our finitude. Kant called this the 'terrible sublime' in which dangers were actually physical. This is a very important means by which we ascribe meaning not only to risks but also to the sensibilities of risk culture.

At issue here is a third sort of logic of the judgement of risk, of danger, of 'bads', a logic that is counterposed to the productionism, the syntheses, the closed body and the nature domination of both determinate judgement and reflexive judgements of beauty. If determinate judgements follow a logic of the 'I', then judgements of beauty operating though the imaginary (or imagination), follow a logic of the 'eye'. Judgements of the sublime in contrast follow not a visual logic but a logic much more tactile, sensuous, materialist and immediate; they follow what might be called a 'logic of sensation' (Deleuze, 1981). That is, objects and events, including those 'future possible bads' known as risk events, escape the concept and the 'I' of realism and determinate judgement only to come under the subsumption, the productive syntheses of the 'eye' of the (constructivist) imagination. Or to change register, the reality principle of the ego, the 'I' of the conscious mind is displaced by the constructivist syntheses of the imaginary. In realist notions of risk we paper over our lack, we close off our bodies through the 'I' of determinate judgement. In constructivist notions of risk we paper over our lack, our wounded body through the 'eye' of judgements of beauty.

This is the stuff of Kant's aesthetics of beauty. It is 'figural': dependent on configurations in perceptual fields, governed by the more loosely bound energies of figural signification, again through productive syntheses. The figural entails at the same time the hegemony of form and the 'Greek' and ancient principles of 'vision' and 'architecture'. In the place of the visual fixity of 'Greek' architecture is the sensual sublime, the contingent temporality of urbanism, of the metropolis – destroying the figural space of architecture. As against form, against figure, against the aesthetics of beauty, the sublime involves destroying the domination of the eye.[1] It is the logic of a body with lack that lives with the threat of contingency, of the threat of overwhelming forces; it recognizes its finitude in the face of them, and does not try fully to control, to subsume risks.

Futures

So what future for the 'risk culture' in today's technological culture? What future for risk positioning in the global information culture? How will risk be positioned in what Manuel Castells (1996) calls the 'network society' in which the logic of structures is displaced by the logic of flows? In which the predominance of material and industrial goods is displaced by a new prevalence of information and communications. On the one hand, the flows of information and communications, replacing the heteronomy of social structures, introduces an overwhelming flow of determinate judgements as images, sounds and narratives are brought twice under the logic of determinate judgement: as they are digitized first as information and yet again for transmission as communications. Worse, contemporary techno-capitalism attempts to colonize the future against risks with the extended memories of its cyborganizations: of a great chain of being as systems with memories, performing determinate judgements on incoming data. Each organism in the chain is hierarchized according to how distanced its memory is, ranging from the one-celled organism to God him/herself with a more distanced memory. God as absolute monad has the perfect memory, the most distanced memory. S/he is able to see into the future as well as the past, neutralizing contingency, nullifying risks, neutralizing the event. But techno-capitalism with its expanded and prosthetic computer memory is sensitized to information unavailable to the natural body (Lury, 1998). It can, according to principles of probabilism, peer into the future to guarantee long-range future narratives of self-identity. It can develop an insurance principle of anti-risk security such as never seen before. Techno-capitalism can guarantee the future: it can nullify risks, neutralize the event (Lyotard, 1991).

On the other hand are the unintended consequences of such risk control which implicate further risks, further disorganization. Moreover, determinate judgement is carried out by expert systems. And these expert systems themselves must be extraordinarily complex in order to perform such difficult judgements. The very complexity (and not just their unintended consequences) of the determinate judg*ers*, i.e. the expert systems, builds in more risk, more uncertainty into the system. Further, the system, the global information economy, can only expand in the face of uncertain markets through invention, through a design-intensivity that works not from determinate judgement but forces innovation, forces rule–finding behaviour. Finally, this itself is only possible through risk cultures, through flexible organizations that are effective disorganizations.

Risk culture is like Kantian judgement caught in the grips of an *aporia*. Systemically, it forecloses risk and 'guarantees the future' through the digital cyborganization of its economies of signs and space as well as its meta-regulation by cultural policy. Yet, at the same time, these digitized information and communication flows themselves are dependent on and create 'wild' and danger-filled zones of social, cultural and economic disorganizaton. As for subjectivity, its necessity is its determinate judgement, through which it establishes its niche and then thrives to dominate nature, to control risks and uncertainties. In its openness, its incompleteness, its reaching out for infinity, in its self-difference, subjectivity is profoundly engaged in reflexive judgement. As reflexively judging animals, we embrace lack; we live with risks; we entertain *fortuna*.

Positioning risk in technological futures must take account of the growth of hierarchies, from Murdoch's media empire to supra-national bodies. This may be an expansion of the reaction of the centre against the borders and can be expressed in enhanced nationalism, racism or 'occidentalism' (Venn, 1997). Alternatively, there is the challenge from what Douglas and Wildavsky call the 'sectarians' from the borders, from the margins. Unlike institutions which are characterized by closure, sects are open, vulnerable, lacking collective bodies. Sects are in the first instance non-institutions; indeed they are anti-institutions. Typically they are without hierarchy; they bond through intense affective charge; they are based in friendships, in affinity groups. They are rooted in common practices, with ideas of the good life, with notions of internal goods. Sects are not means to ends like institutions, like the church. In the sect means and ends are not separated. Democratic and participatory forms of life in future society are already lived in the sect. Communists form institutions. Anarchists form sects. Sects tend not to distinguish the private from the public – in contrast to institutions like churches. Sects by definition practice 'life politics' or 'sub-politics'. They are 'disorganizations'. They form reflexive and flexible communities, enduring only a short while and then forming once again. *Pace* Douglas, sects can have collective memories. But these are not embedded in institutions; they are instead extra-institutional. The church has a richness, a plenitude of being, while the sect exists in contingency, in darkness, in insecurity, on the borders. Churches and other institutions are grounded in the self-identity of individual members. As members of churches and other institutions, we are self-identical, self-enclosed and self-interested subjects. As sect members, in contrast, we form communities, not in our self-identity, but only in our self-difference: that is, with that part of ourselves that is not subsumed under narratives of self-identity; with that part of ourselves in which we are incomplete and unfinished subjectivities, unfinished, lacking bodies. If in churches trust is in institutions or in expert systems, in sects trust lies in the face-to-face or the mediated face-to-face of the affinity group. The institution (church) operates in the idiom, the certainty, the security of Weberian tradition or legal rationality; the sect along with the prophets is adrift in the sea of insecurity of charisma.

At stake in this are not sects *per se*, but new forms of non-institutional sub-politics in the risk culture. For Beck (1993) and Giddens sub-politics is the displacement of non-institutional practices from the private sphere and their politicization into institutional practices in the public sphere. Thus Giddens (1992) reconceives such sociations as intimate relations along the lines of the contractualism and rights language of the public sphere. It seems to me on the contrary that sub-politics involves an opposite movement: the displacement of institutional sociation from the public sphere into non-institutional practices more closely resembling the private sphere.

This is where the issue of norms versus values comes in. In modernity public institutions tend to be structured by not values but norms. There are vast differences between norms and values. Most important for our purposes is that norms are procedural whereas values are substantive. Thus modern constitutions and modern law are based on procedural norms within which individuals can pursue their own values. Ancient constitutions for their part are based on the set of substantive values of a given social formation. Hannah Arendt in this context noted that modern institutions in this sense presuppose utilitarian politics, in which each individual pursues his or her own interests, maximizes his or her own utility subject to a set of procedural rules. Ancient politics and the true public sphere, on the model of the Greek *polis*, in contrast, presuppose not a utilitarian politics but a politics of the good life, a politics of the pursuit of substantive values (Denhubib, 1996).

I am not arguing here for an orthodox communitarian return to Thomism or the Classical *polis*. Instead, I am arguing for new reflexive sociations which are neither *Gemeinschaft* nor *Gesellschaft*, based not in a normatively structured and utilitarian politics of interests, but in a politics of value and the good life. In antiquity this was the *Öffentlichkeit*, the public space of the *polis*. In modernity, especially in reflexive modernity this can no longer be. Classical sociology thus stressed the contradistinction of norms and values. In classic accounts of 'simple modernity' (for example, Parsons, 1951), norms are quite clearly a question of public life, of especially the social functions of the state, whereas values are involved in 'pattern maintenance'. Values are cultural rather than social (as norms are) and they are the mechanism by which a culture is passed from one generation to the next. The locus of values is primarily in the private realm, especially in the family. Values mean the core values of private morality, of language, of religion, of the forms of life surrounding death, birth, marriage, war, child rearing. Norms are located in rules, values primarily in symbols. It is notable that Parsons locates values in the private sphere much like the assumption of modern western constitutions that norms are public and for all to see, while values are private, personal and subjective. The sort of sociations that make up the critical risk cultures of reflexive modernity are not normative but value groupings that operate in the margins, in the third space, the boundary that separates private and public life. They are cultures and not institutions in the sense that they operate in the media of values not norms. But they are characteristically risk cultures (unlike communitarian traditional bodies, which are not risk, but 'security cultures') in that there is a chronic uncertainty, a continual questioning, an openness to innovation built into them. They deal with risk, with identity-risks and ecological risks, not so much through rational calculation or normative subsumption, but through symbolic practices and especially through symbol innovation.

It is these risk cultures which seem to be the emergent present and hopefully the future of reflexive modernity. These risk cultures no longer deal primarily with technology as the unintended consequences of technological development. In Beck's view, primary among risk sociations would be environmental movements dealing with risks stemming from industrial technology, e.g. oil slicks, air pollution from factories and cars. But the risk society that emerges from an industrial society is in a relatively fast decline, as the market capitalization of Intel and Microsoft rival those of General Motors and Ford. On the agenda and rapidly emerging is clearly a post-industrial context in which risk must be positioned. In this pre-eminently technological future, risk sub-politics will be dealing with a whole new set of unintended consequences, no longer from material goods-producing industry but from the information sectors, from bio-technology, from the communications and software sectors, generating new, for example, financial and existential risks. In the post-industrial risk context and its overwhelmingly technological culture, the primary form of risk sociation will probably no longer involve the sub-politics of 'consequence takers', i.e. the receiving end of risks. More central will be the risk makers, the techno-scientists and techno-artists in the emergent sectors. These sociations, these disorganizations will be operating, not in response to somebody else's unintended consequences, but largely taking their own innovation risks. So we need perhaps to begin to say farewell to the risk society. Its day has been and it may now be starting to wane. We need instead to embrace, perhaps with lots of trepidation and with no small measure of fear and trembling, the risk culture.

Note

1 Now the eye – a figure repeated endlessly in surrealism – becomes no longer an organ for seeing, but of tactility and pain as it is sliced with a razor blade; it is an organ for eating as the *oeil* is transformed into an *oeuf* (egg), and approaches the basest of sensibilities when transformed (in *the Story of the Eye*) into a bull's testicles. Thus Georges Bataille (1985: 118–20) rages against figure, against form, argues for the 'informe' that unlike the concept, unlike the imaginary is incapable of productionist syntheses. Against such productionism, Bataille argues for *dépense*; against form for a logic of sensation. This is a logic of sensation of the wounded body, the gashed eye.

References

Alexander, J. (1996) 'Critical Reflections on "Reflexive Modernization"', *Theory, Culture & Society*, 13 (4): 133–8.

Barker, E. (1984) *The Making of a Moonie, Choice or Brainwashing*. Oxford: Blackwell.

Bataille, G. (1985) 'The Notion of Expenditure', in Bataille, G. *Visions of Excess, Selected Writings, 1927–1939*. Minneapolis: University of Minnesota Press. pp. 116–29.

Bataille, G. (1987) *Story of the Eye*, San Francisco, CA: City Lights Books.

Beck, U. (1988) *Gegengifte: die organisierte Unverantwortlichkeit*. Frankfurt am Main: Suhrkamp. Trans. as *Counter gifts: the organized irresponsibility.*

Beck, U. (1993) *Die Erfindung des Politischen*. Frankfurt am Main: Suhrkamp.

Beck, U., Giddens, A. and Lash, S. (1994) *Reflexive Modernization*. Cambridge: Polity.

Benhabib, S. (1996) *The Reluctant Modernism of Hannah Arendt*. Thousand Oaks, CA: Sage.

Berger, P. (1967) *The Sacred Canopy, Elements of a Sociological Theory of Religion*. New York: Doubleday.

Castells, M. (1996) *The Rise of the Network Society*. Oxford: Blackwell.

Caygill, H. (1989) *The Art of Judgement*. Oxford: Blackwell.

Deleuze, G. (1981) *Francis Bacon, Logique de la Sensation*. Paris: Editions de la différence.

Douglas, M. (1966) *Purity and Danger*. London: Routledge Kegan and Paul.

Douglas, M. (1970) *Natural Symbols*. London: Barrie.

Douglas, M. and Wildavsky, A. (1983) *Risk and Culture*. Berkeley: University of California Press.

Foucault, M. (1984) 'What Is Enlightenment?', in P. Rabinow (ed.), *The Foucault Reader*. New York: Pantheon.

Gadamer, H.G. (1986) *The Relevance of the Beautiful and Other Essays*. Cambridge: Cambridge University Press.

Giddens, A. (1992) *The Transformation of Intimacy*. Cambridge: Polity.

Harvey, D. (1996) *Justice, Nature and the Geography of Difference*. Oxford: Blackwell.

Heelas, P. (1996a) 'Detraditionalization and its Rivals', in P. Heelas, S. Lash and P. Morris (eds), *Detraditionalization*. Oxford: Basil Blackwell. pp. 1–20.

Heelas, P. (1996b) *The New Age Movement: The Celebration of the Self and the Sacralization of Modernity*. Oxford: Blackwell.

Hetherington, K. (1993) The Geography of the Other, Lifestyle, Performance and Identity. PhD dissertation, Lancaster University, Department of Sociology.

Kant, I. (1929) *Critique of Pure Reason*. London: Macmillan.

Kant, I. (1952) *The Critique of Judgement*. Oxford: Oxford University Press.

Lash, S. (1994) 'Reflexivity and its Doubles–Structure Aesthetics Community', in U. Beck, A. Giddens and S. Lash, *Reflexive Modernization*. Cambridge: Polity. pp. 110–73.

Lury, C. (1998) *Prosthetic Culture: Photography, Memory and Identity*. London: Routledge.

Lyotard, J.F. (1991) *The Inhuman: Reflections on Time*. Cambridge: Polity.

McNaughten, P. and Urry, J. (1998) *Contested Natures*. London: Sage.

Parsons, T. (1951) *The Social System*. London: Routledge and Kegan Paul.

Schluchter, W. (1987) 'Weber's Sociology of Rationalism and the Typology of Religious Rejections of the World', in S. Whimster and S. Lash (eds), *Max Weber, Rationality and Modernity*. London: Allen & Unwin. pp. 92–117.

Todorov, T. (1982) *Theories of the Symbol*. Ithaca, NY: Cornell University Press.

Venn, C. (1997) 'Beyond Enlightenment? After the Subject of Foucault, Who Comes?', *Theory, Culture & Society*, 14 (3): 1–28.

Weber, M. (1946) 'The Social Psychology of the World Religions', in H. Gerth and C.W. Mills (eds), *From Max Weber: Essays in Sociology*. Oxford: Oxford University Press.

Wynne, B. (1996) 'May the Sheep Safely Graze? A Reflexive View of the Expert-Lay Knowledge Divide', in S. Lash, B. Szerszynski and B. Wynne (eds), *Risk, Environment and Modernity*. London: Sage. pp. 44–83.

3

Risk, Trust and Scepticism in the Age of the New Genetics

Hilary Rose

Living with risk but not in a risk society

Like many sociologists I found the *Risk Society* (Beck, 1992) a compelling and optimistic analysis, and yet as someone preoccupied for a number of years with 'science' and 'society',[1] I remain enough of a Gramscian to go on arguing for both optimism of the will and also pessimism of the intellect. Thus I want to support Beck's core and optimistic argument that the only way to manage the risks integral to rapid technological change is through a radically new openness – which requires new institutions that will both reflect and create more trust between the manifest social stakeholders and also the citizen who presently exists only as a 'virtual stakeholder' (Cronberg, 1996). However, I read this global task of building trust between 'science' and 'society' as having to be worked through locally not least because of very different histories of the civil society–state relationship. What can be done, for example, within the democratic traditions of Denmark and a relatively small biotechnology research base in managing new technologies, as against what can be done in Britain with its pathological love of secrecy, and as the second largest producer of molecular biological research, has to be confronted with an appropriate level of intellectual pessimism. But a spate of home-grown catastrophes has in this one medium-sized European country generated intense public debate. Dunblane, Milford Haven and BSE (commonly known as mad cow disease) have aroused very different feelings: the shared grief of an entire nation at the killing of the children and their teacher, the tired disgust at yet another oil spill, together with the knowledge that even the experts do not know whether or when nature can heal herself, to disbelief that any government and industry could so mismanage the food chain that the risk of Creutzfeldt-Jakob Disease in humans is now hideously real but of an incalculable incidence. But what is new in the public discussion is the question of how can society better manage the risks posed by incessant technological change.

For a country like Britain, which by and large does not see social theorists as part of its public intellectuals, it has been fascinating to see that they are at last seen as having something useful to say about risk, so we find Beck and Giddens discussed in the media. The cultural contrast with the Torrey Canyon oil disaster of the 1960s could not be more complete, for then the government of the day turned to the Royal Society. The assumption then was that the elite of British science was the ultimate repository of Truth about Nature, and as such the culturally authorized group to speak to Power. Whether the Fellows of the Royal Society actually knew anything about marine ecology, oil or risk was all rather secondary.

A number of disasters later, from Bhopal to Chernobyl, we all know it is a bit more complicated. It is not necessary to buy into the wholesale deconstruction of truth at the hands of postmodernism to acknowledge that generally within society the claims of the elite natural scientists are seen as rather more limited. Instead of elite knowers of Truth we look for competent experts. Today there is another difference, for it is not only sociologists who think that people, as the human part of a local ecological system, have potentially something intelligent to say about both the prevention of risk and the management of disaster. Increasingly, the media represents the voices of local people as providing trustworthy accounts to be set alongside the accounts from scientific experts. What is newer is to find the media discussing the arguments of social theory that risk has to be understood as integral to late modernity. The question becomes, not only how do we understand and respond to a particular disaster, but how do we understand and manage risk as a necessary task of a technologically innovatory society.

Yet there is a danger that, because we are faced with continuous risk, the idea of a risk society is seen as detachable from historical context, to apply anywhere. Social theory too has to be situated. Thus currently Britain does not meet Beck's definition of a risk society even though we are facing technological risks in abundance. It is this, together with profound changes occurring in the knowledge system itself, and a cultural turbulence in the social standing of science, which makes the development of scepticism and trust as crucial partners in the project of successfully managing risk, peculiarly difficult. Nowhere is this more evident than in the debate around the new genetics. So while I want to give support to the optimistic argument about the general direction, for social theory to be useful it has also to be grounded in the specifics of particular shifting and contradictory societies and cultures.

Beck's concept of the risk society, not least as superseding the old industrial society, is contingent on a strong economy and collective security. This, while present in Germany at the time of publication of Beck's book, surely did not exist in Britain, which for 18 years as part of hard Anglo-Saxon capitalism had been in long-term industrial decline, with rotting cities, an undereducated people and a cruelly unravelling welfare system. *The State We Are In* (Hutton, 1996) with its portrayal of the 30:40:30 society, with the bottom 30 simply struggling along to survive, has to be brought into the discourse of risk management. For that matter today it is not only Britain which cannot meet the definition of a risk society, all of Europe[2] is in economic trouble, with deep and stubborn unemployment. Scandinavia cuts its vaunted welfare state, Austria slashes its university system, in France 30% of young people are unemployed, and even the corporate consensus of Germany begins to crack as those problems, which Beck assured us were part of the old industrial society, demonstrate that they have the capacity to reappear with new intensity. Getting the whole of Europe back to work, reducing the high levels of male violence and xenophobia, responding more effectively to the re-emergence of genocide are arguably as big problems as managing risk to the environment, and, so far as the new genetics are concerned, to 'us'.

Also integral to Beck's concept of this new risk society is the disaggregation of the family and the search for new subjectivities with love as crucial for personal survival. In this preoccupation with both subjectivity and the environment, the theory of the risk society is part of that interesting development in mainstream social theory which at last includes both nature, not least the body, and love as an integral part of its agenda.[3] Concerns which were previously almost exclusively the objects of feminist theorizing[4] are now common to both, and that has to be a welcome development. Even so, despite the diversity of the feminisms, I think it would be fair to say that most are rather more cautious about the contemporary project of heterosexual love; more aware, to put it no more strongly, of its riskiness.

Thus Beck-Gernsheim and Beck (1995) provide an account of the emotionally perilous search for new subjectivities and a new longing for the support of love. But they leave something out, namely the really nasty events that go on between rather too many of those relationships of 'me' and 'you'. The book is silent about the failures of love, from the horrific levels of male violence to the widespread sexual and violent abuse of children in family life. Yet rape and violence against women and the sexual and violent abuse of children are as much part of late modernity as Chernobyl or the new genetics.[5] UNICEF's 1997 report reminds us that to be a girl or a woman in large parts of the world, is to be at risk.

So it seems to me that the possibilities of a risk society with its nice face of love, are being analysed in a rather over-optimistic way. As if the management of technological risk and the pursuit of new middle-class subjectivities dissolved away both ugly old problems and also some interesting new ones such as the new subjectivities of young black and white working-class women. Most negatively, it is evident that the old goals of social justice and social inclusion are today rather weakly supported, with the result that issues of wealth distribution, let alone re-distribution, are simply politically and academically uninteresting. By contrast problems of technological risk are politically and academically hot. Many of the old industrial societies have not been able to hold onto (and in the case of the USA never did achieve) modernity's promise of collective security; naming this the risk society serves to erase the still unfinished tasks of modernity.

An old problem but new to social theory?

Ironically I would suggest that there is quite a good case to be made that Britain, because it was one of the victorious allies, was able to enter and pass through, what was an unnamed and unacknowledged risk society rather earlier in the mid-twentieth century. It was of course the risk society of Mutually Assured Destruction with MAD its appropriate acronym. Hiroshima and Nagasaki as the first fruits of Big Science were the violent expressions of the profoundly gendered product of science, the military and the state. Thinking the unthinkable put what was claimed to be the quantifiable risk of nuclear holocaust onto the cultural and political agenda. That older risk society was different from the new; today it is techno-economism, not Cold War militarism, which is the primary, though not exclusive, generator of risk. However while 1989 ended the Cold War it opened a door to some new instabilities, and the new genetics have significant military potential and are rather cheaper to develop (Wright, 1990).

Despite this huge and evident danger from accelerating technological innovation since the mid-century, social theory, until its recent conversion, has been peculiarly resistant to thinking about science and technology and their relationship to nature. In the 1960s, Rachel Carson was reaching many audiences but not the social theorists. Even the dominant version of Marxism refused to consider science and technology as part of culture and society. Indeed, in an otherwise brilliant essay on the 'Components of the National Culture', Perry Anderson (1968) rubbished the intellectual endeavours of those Marxist scientists, above all Desmond Bernal who had pioneered the analysis of *The Social Function of Science* (1939). Nor was the cultural high ground of 1970s Marxism any more willing to make space for the attempts by the radical science movement to include nature in the material world (Rose and Rose, 1976). It was a long time before Red was conscious of Green.

This is not to say there were no social or cultural reflections. Artist and cultural analyst Jeff Nuttall published an extraordinarily interesting book which discussed what he called *Bomb Culture* (1968).[6] A cartoon published at the time of Nuttall's book, showed a Christmas party with paper-chains festooning the ceiling and from them hanging a large thermonuclear bomb. In this sceptical unofficial sociology, Britain was understood as a risky place to be, an aircraft carrier for the American warheads, and as such a perfect nuclear bomb target. Indeed calculating the chances of getting to the millennium was integral to thinking about the unthinkable. My point is simply how very slowly mainstream or critical social theory began to recognize either the risk to nature and to ourselves as part of nature or the discourse of science and technology.

The birth of techno-economism and its risks

This neglect was all the more conspicuous in that national and international science policy has since 1945 been substantially techno-economist in direction.[7] This hegemonic discourse has for almost half century been able to take public support for science for granted, with only two major cultural interruptions. The first was when the radical science movement called into question the neutrality of science in the Vietnam War. Then the 1971 Brooke Report for the influential OECD marked the first official acknowledgement of the weakening of social support for science. The second time is today, in the face of accelerating risk to the ecosystem produced by crude techno-economism, and is exacerbated and expressed culturally in the current debates over the social standing of science, better known as the 'Science Wars'.[8]

Today the questioning comes from very disparate social currents, new ageism, environmentalism, feminism, postmodernism and the sociology of scientific knowledge. In very different ways these challenge the epistemological claims of natural science and its asocial concept of rationality.[9] This epistemological debate has not significantly entered social theory, thus Beck and Giddens take a realist view of science and do not see it either as socially constructed or, rather more subtly, as constructed by a network of human and non-human actors. There is little trace, therefore, in risk theorizing of the relatively optimistic message coming particularly clearly from the sociology of technology, that not only is technology socially constructed but it can also be socially deconstructed.[10] For the risk theorists the issue is the management of risk which inevitably arrives; for the motley array setting siege to the epistemological gates of science and technology, the issue is precisely that inevitability.

In the domain of politics, not social theory, public anxiety to protect the environment is rather obviously connected to economic well being. In Europe, for example, pressures for ecologically sensitive technology policies increase with job security and social confidence, and go on the back burner in hard times. Currently, Europe is rather more concerned that technological innovation, historically both a job destroyer and a job maker, does rather more of the latter. 'Sustainable development' is in this context more of a political mantra than an effective and visible policy concern. Today the media is more concerned with vast hikes in the share value of biotechnology companies and a possible cancer drug than exploring the risks also on offer.

The new genetics

The new genetics is central to today's techno-economic project. Thus while the leading scientific ideologues of the Human Genome Project (HGP), as its international institutional expression, claim its potential contribution to medicine and to knowledge, most have shares in biotechnology companies. Not only does the HGP mark the moment when the life sciences entered Big, that is industrialized, Science (De Solla Price, 1963), it is also the moment when they made a new relationship to capital. As only the joint support of capital and the state could underwrite this long-term investment, this required selling the new genetics to diverse audiences.

One sales pitch was to re-enchant fundamental science; thus we saw metaphors of the Genome as the 'Holy Grail' and the 'Code of Codes' routinely evoked in the discourse of the molecular biological elite as they sought to capture cultural support. The second, made by the geneticists in alliance with the molecular biologists, was the power-charged claim of genetic therapy. In what has to be one of the most quoted editorials in *Science*, one of the two most influential scientific journals in the world, gene therapy was promised, not only for well-recognized genetic disorders, but also for cancer and heart disease. And as if this was not enough, the editorial went on to promise to solve alcoholism and homelessness.[11]

The new genetics is potent for they shape society both as culture and as artefact. As the science of difference, human genetics has had a long and frequently negative association with eugenics (Kevles, 1985), for the science of difference has never taken place in the context of an egalitarian society but always in the historical context of strong social hierarchies. A massively funded new genetics thus intensifies the risk of exacerbating and naturalizing social hierarchies. The initial gung-ho promise of gene therapy fundamentally modelled itself on single gene defects, argued that with the powerful and reductive tools of molecular biology, the new genetics would be able to find and fix faulty genes. The media swiftly picked up the claim and aired the possibilities and the ethical desirability of the 'perfect baby' and 'designer genes'. Science critics were rather more concerned with the political problem of who was going to decide what was a 'faulty' gene and who was to decide what was 'normal' let alone 'perfect' (Keller, 1992). There was also a widespread public questioning about both the safety and also the morality of 'tampering with nature'.

The promise of the HGP was unable to deliver therapeutic performance. Human Genome research ran into a number of technical problems, notably that closing the gap between the first approximation of the 'faulty' gene – the marker – and the gene itself, turned out to be slow and difficult. Then even single genes turned out to be complex and unstable. What had been understood as one condition with one gene sometimes became a set of similar conditions associated with slightly different genes. Despite a cascade of short-lived claims reported with uncritical enthusiasm by the media, there are currently no effective genetic therapies. Instead we have proliferating numbers of genetic diagnostics. Culturally these bring science into medicine in a new and dangerous way (Nelkin and Tancredi, 1989). While science and medicine are close they are not identical. Thus science holds that knowledge, in itself, is a social good; medicine, by contrast, is interested in knowledge which helps prevent, treat or manage conditions. Indeed clinicians have long held an ethic of not adding to the burdens of patients by sharing knowledge of conditions which they cannot treat. Today this paternalistic ethic is giving way as patients demand to share doctors' knowledge, but this new torrent of diagnostic information without therapy is qualitatively different from such negotiations.

The new diagnostics claim to be able to tell us, if we have the gene for the neuro-degenerative disease Huntingdon's, when it will express itself and how severely. However science's enthusiasm for knowledge is not evenly shared by people from families at risk of Huntingdon's. Many refuse this offer of certainty and prefer to live with uncertainty. Similarly a study I was engaged in, of people with genetically-produced high cholesterol, revealed almost certainly affected kin who refused to enter the risk discourse of disembodied knowledge, even though in this case there was the possibility of therapy. These fragments of resistance underline the material power of this new technoscience to reach into our most intimate lives disturbing our created narrative of the self as going forward, uncertainly in time, but always hoping to reach a good old age.

What energizes these new material powers is the determinant cultural shift which informs the new genetics. While geneticists formally say that genes are not determinant, the unambiguous cultural message that comes through is that they are. Thus when Foucault (1978: 84) wrote in his history of sexuality, of that general biomedical project which searches 'in the depths of the organism', today's molecular biology insists on searching ever deeper and weakening the possibility of our narrative of self. In this discourse of the molecular biologists the organism itself, never mind about culture, is reduced to the sequenced four letters of the genetic code. Strings of sequenced DNA 'R' us.

Geneticists rarely publicly resist this bio-cultural determinism. When the Human Genome Project was being proposed to Europe under the name 'Predictive Medicine', it was not the geneticists or molecular biologists who mobilized against this title as inappropriately determinant, but the German Greens and eventually the European Parliament. The cartoonists are well aware of this new determinism; one shows Madam Rosa, crystal ball gazer, being driven out of business by the new rival, a genetic diagnostician, setting up shop next door.

In turn the bio-cultural determinism is then reinforced by the claimed performativity of the technologies. In the increasingly marketized and individualized society which loses each day a little more collectivity, the new genetics as diagnostics can produce a new form of cultural terror. I speak of terror because genetic diagnostics in the context of hard Anglo-Saxon capitalism works to mobilize fear and to deny space for scepticism and social trust.[12] The best way that I can convey the problems of risk, trust and scepticism is through an iconic tale of two sisters. They are American. One is diagnosed as having cancer and subsequent testing indicates that she has the BRCA-1 gene. She 'chooses' to have a double radical mastectomy. Her sister who shares the gene but who has no diagnosis of cancer 'chooses' to follow her example. These women are not isolates, some 20,000 US women have accepted this genetic risk assessment and surgical intervention.

But what underlies these 'choices'? Do these risk assessments and surgical choices which produce extreme bodily mutilation indicate trust in science and surgery? Or do they conversely speak of the lack of trust felt by these women in the capacity and willingness of American society to take care of women with either cancer or the threat of cancer? Is their 'choice' biologically cruel but 'socially smart' – based on an unglamourized reading of the US medical care scene?

I read these 'chosen' double mastectomies, not as the choices of cultural dopes, but as acts of grim social rationality faced with a medical care system based on private insurance, where 30 million Americans are without health care and where long term, or chronic illness can destroy the security of even the well-insured individual or family. Resisting genetic pre-destinationism in a marketized context is particularly difficult. Theoretical opposition has come from feminist biologists such as Ruth Hubbard who argues that such determinism is both bad biology and also harmful to women. Empirical opposition has been launched by the recent publication of detailed epidemiological studies tracking family histories of breast cancer which provide the evidential basis for rejecting determinism. Given that alternative accounts have more cultural efficacy in displacing 'bad science' than mere criticism, such studies may help to weaken the currently iron genetic determinism.

Genetic diagnostics also raise new questions of risk within health insurance. First to impact as a policy question in the marketized US health care system, the new diagnostics have led some ten states to legislate against genetic status being used to determine health insurance eligibility. In Europe the social policy response has been slower and there is little willingness to grapple with the emergent risk even as we witness the weakening of collective solidarity. Without stringent regulation of the insurance industry it takes little foresight to predict the emergence of a genetic underclass of the uninsurable and probably unemployable.

When a pregnant woman is told that her foetus has an 'abnormal' gene, what 'abnormal' means in terms of biological and social risk is less than transparent. If she then chooses to have an abortion, 'choice' itself demands contextualizing. If she lives in a society hostile to, and unwilling to care for, disabled people, which way will she choose? If she elects to keep the pregnancy and the infant is seriously disabled, could she, at least in the US, find herself sued for 'wrongful life'? Which way will she choose? This new consumer eugenics based on choice is not to be confused with the old state eugenics of the Nazis, nor indeed the less-well publicized parallel variants of numbers of northern and western European countries and of course today's India with its widespread, if now illegal, amniocentesis clinics and female foeticide.

Consumer eugenics and a genetic underclass defined and made possible by the ultimate in technoscience appear at the same moment that a recrudescent neo-Nazism angrily searches for some hate-able *Untermenschen* and new forms of genocide manifest themselves in the world. There is no state link as between Aryan genetics and the death camps, but there is some mutually reinforcing cultural echo between the new horrors of ethnic cleansing and the exclusionary differences determined by these new dangerous diagnostics.

For that matter although social scientists have, since the UNESCO statement of 1946, fundamentally assumed that the concept of race has no support from the life sciences, increasingly 'race' is being transfused with new energy. A biologized concept of race is seeking to make a comeback, an early augury is the apparently beneficent search for the gene for breast cancer in Jews. At the same time and less benignly, it would be absurd not to be conscious of evident actor-networks within the new genetics whose members are actively mobilizing both market and state seeking to re-ground both violence and race once more in nature. Politically putting huge resources into the science of difference in such a hard context is to court, not manage, risk. At the same time, social theory which thinks that the UNESCO statement holds as a permanent Truth, does not grasp how 'race' and 'biology' can be socially if very dangerously reconstructed within a reductionist discourse.[13]

For that matter, choices are made and generation, gender and historical context enable people to understand and respond to risk rather differently. The pleas from Eastern Europe to keep open dangerous nuclear plants are not because people living near them do not know the risk, but because they also know that severe winters without heating are even more quickly lethal. A recent set of ethnographic studies of particular publics facing risk that explores which knowledge source is trusted by which public faced with risk, echoes this (Irwin and Wynne, 1996). Far from being cultural dopes, these diverse publics held coherently developed analyses which recognized which experts they could trust, and displayed an evident social rationality in critically bringing scientific knowledge together with their own pre-existing knowledges about themselves and their social and natural worlds. Context counts.

Fostering trust and scepticism

Denmark and Holland have made some of the most energetic attempts to improve the 'science' and 'society' relationship, by increasing the democratic shaping of new technology by developing new institutions, such as consensus forums and constructive technology assessment. While it would be unwise to suggest that there were no problems with these initiatives they have fostered a high level of scepticism on the part of the public about new technologies, but this scepticism comes together with a strong level of trust in the government. By contrast German and British governments command much weaker levels of public trust. Thus the Conservative government's reiterated claim that it was guided by science in the management of the 'mad cow crisis' produced only derision.

Yet, the research system and its cultural elite is conscious of the trust gap and the problems that this poses for the social – and potentially financial – support of science. Thus there have been attempts to introduce consensus fora in Britain, first those of the Kings Fund on biomedical issues and then more recently one on plant biotechnology sponsored by the Biotechnology and Biological Sciences Research Council (BBSRC), but these have to work against a strong belief among the scientific elite that like Daddy, it knows best. For instance, the Royal Society's Committee for the Public Understanding of Science (COPUS) is committed to telling the public how to understand science, and shows little intention of asking the public what it thinks of science and what directions it should and should not take.[14] They are committed to a monologic not dialogic communication which cannot work in a society where risk is endemic. Instead COPUS' conception of the public understanding of science is conflated with the belief that 'understanding' is something to do with how many science 'facts' the public knows. Paulo Freire's deficit model of those to be educated lives on in the discourse of PUS. Yet even the 'facts' the public is quizzed on in such surveys (Durant et al., 1989) reflect what the surveyors think the public should know and often fails to grapple with the historically changing constructions of nature.[15] The scientists' (sociologically informed) adage that 'yesterday's science is today's common sense and tomorrow's nonsense' points to the futility of the quest. Many, except this nostalgic elite, are beginning to see that to manage risk there are many forms of expertise, not least the local, that are needed. The problem is how to develop new institutions through which this democratic impulse can be supported.

Trust at the cross roads?

The elite's attempt to restore the past position of Science as Truth which can speak to power is part of a complex picture. There is also an international move to restructure the research system, moving from the state being the chief patron to industry taking over. This has un-discussed implications for public trust in science. We can see this process very clearly in Britain as it is in painful transition from a system which guaranteed some measure of academic autonomy in the definition of research problems to one where, through the Foresight Exercise, academic research goals are increasingly industrially driven. New hybrid forms of private public research are located in universities, above all in the science parks. The development of information technology is profoundly linked to the new genetics culturally and economically. Charles Simonyi of Microsoft finances the personal chair at Oxford in the Public Understanding of Science occupied by Richard Dawkins, the influential popularizer of genetic determinism. Microsoft also funds genomic research at Cambridge, UK as his European base, and has supported Washington University's bid for the leading molecular biologist Leroy Hood to speed up work on the Genome near to Gate's Seattle base. It is only fitting that Dolly the cloned sheep was a product of such a hybrid alliance between industry and the state, and unsurprising that the industrial partner was more ready and willing to talk about the human and environmental implications than was their Ministry of Agriculture co-financer. While the relativistic social scientists talk about the purely social construction of scientific knowledge, the biotechnologists working from within their new hybrid organization forms, claim to be doing nothing less than constructing new life forms.

In this fast changing research system, basic research resources from the state are in increasingly short supply, yet in the scramble for funds, where groupings of elite institutions attempt to situate themselves so that at least they will survive, few in Europe are willing to discuss publicly the dangers – very evident from the US system – that extreme competition damages the reliability of knowledge. Fraud and theft can become part of science at the highest levels. Scandals proliferate; the story of the American Robert Gallo's probable theft of the AIDS virus from his French collaborators, as the prize of being first was too tempting, and even the presence of a Nobel prize winner as the laboratory chief, as in the case of David Baltimore, was not able to inhibit the manipulation of data to get results.[16]

But if research is more dependent on industrial funding, how far the public will put trust in knowledge produced by profit-making institutions is yet to be seen. There are some pointers that politicians have a feeling for this in the response of the government to the salmonella crisis of the 1980s, when with one speech Edwina Currie alerted the public to both the chicken and the egg problem and enraged a risk producing industry. The rush to privatize key public agricultural research institutions was quietly halted. But there is little public trust in government science as both the BSE and the Chernobyl risks demonstrated. In the BSE case the public believes that the most critical scientists are not consulted and is well aware that the committee has been constrained in giving advice by what it is thought ministers are willing to hear. In the case of caesium pollution the advice of the Ministry scientists and thence compensation, was rapidly seen by local farmers as simply failing to meet the real world of sheep rearing. The disastrous history of the British government's management of risk from nuclear power pollution has long retreated to re-labelling its most dangerous institutions, first Windscale became Sellafield and now British Nuclear Fuels are widely seen as ripe for the process. The contrast with Denmark is marked; there scepticism, not cynicism, flourishes and so does trust.

While the risk discussion is about incessant technological innovation and its management, the dominant policy discussion (except at the moment when a disaster is taking, or about to take, place) is about intensifying technological innovation and international competitiveness. We have to recognize that distrustful Britain does much more genetic research than trustful Denmark, and it is easier to mobilize around 'caveat emptor' than around 'caveat factor'. Facilitating and intensifying innovation increases the risk rate. The arrival of what Gibbons and his colleagues (1995) call the new production system of knowledge – or 'mode two' – is part of this speeding up. In 'mode two', fungible research teams are taken on, used and fired. In these conditions, which Ziman (1995) speaks of as 'post academic science', rather few scientists are in a position to point to risk. In numbers of British research universities there are for example more staff on soft money than on 'permanent' appointments. Keeping one's mouth shut and one's eyes down is wise advice for the fungible. Today scepticism, at least in other than extremely moderate versions, receives rather little social support and the fate of research whistle blowers, whether in the US or in Britain, is not encouraging. The old forms of trust in the reliability of knowledge are under pressure, yet we are only beginning to think about new forms to develop social responsibility/democratic accountability in research.

Goodbye truth: hello trust!

The theorists of the social management of risk have to respond to the challenge that if the main arguments of 'mode two' science and 'post academic science' hold, or even partly hold, then the truth-claiming character of science is undergoing a sea change. Yet theorists' account of a risk society which better manages risk, still shares the older conception of science as speaking truth. For the social studies of science community the changing research system and the cultural debate over the social standing of science feed on each other, so as to weaken science's old universalistic truth claims. In 'mode two' science universalism and objectivity are no longer central: Elzinga's 'epistemic drift' has become a flood tide (Elzinga, 1985). Science takes its (real but more modest) place: and the scientist becomes an expert.

Culturally we stand at a crossroads. One road points towards trust and its allies scepticism and democratic debate with experts as one of several voices. The other points towards distrust, cynicism with the experts that can be marshalled behind a more or less unbridled techno-economic project. Of course, the real world is much messier than the metaphor, nowhere more so than in the case of the new genetics, where recognition of public concern has forced an unprecedented 3% of the US and 7% of the EU budgets for Genome research, to be allocated to the consideration of the ethical, legal and social ethical aspects. Thus the new genetics is politically and culturally understood to be more socially and ethically disturbing than say information technology. As a result of this concern, we now have detailed empirical studies of genetic counselling and testing in a number of countries. While the message from these empirical studies is summed up by the titles: *Eugenics by the Backdoor*, Duster (1990) which focuses on the African-American experience or Green's (1990) survey of UK work *Harming not Calming* which focuses on the experiences of British pregnant women. But as Duster observes what matters is the location of the person within the social order as much as any problems with the genes, and indeed the nature of the social order itself.

The crucial difference between the US and Europe is that despite evident signs of strain, not least in the UK, most European countries provide universal health care. To return to Beck, although we do not have the preconditions for the risk society, in Europe we still have the preconditions for managing the risks from the new genetics. But this structural precondition still leaves everything to play for culturally, and the new genetics is not standing still. What began with the DNA analysis of the transmission of physical traits is extending towards the transmission of 'behaviour'. Claims that sexuality, sexual difference, alcoholism, spinach eating are in our genes, offers the power-charged discourse of molecular biology the chance to reaffirm biology as destiny.

So while we have to defend what is left of the old welfare state not least as a precondition for managing technological risk, we have to think about new institutions, consensus fora, citizens' juries and the like to bring more of society into the social shaping of the new genetics. There are encouraging auguries such as in the close caring interactions between geneticists who work directly with patients and their families who carry the burden of very serious genetic disorders. These relationships at the micro level need acknowledging and seeing how we can build larger structures from them. A social theory which can foster scepticism and thence social trust with its ability to be comfortable with inconsistency, in the age of the new genetics has to be complex enough so as to resist a double determinism: both the cultural determinism which emanates from the new genetics (which in turn so easily slips into the new consumer eugenics) and also the determinism which emanates from an unqualifiedly realist concept of science. If science is understood as free of culture then the possibility of different ways of knowing nature are precluded, and technological risk can only be managed. If we take the alternative reading that science and technology are socially shaped, and however subtly are an integral part of culture, then the chances of reshaping science and technology and changing the construction of risk itself comes onto the agenda. That project, while still hugely difficult and requiring the mainstream risk theorists' optimism and more, is, I would argue, better sociologically founded.

Notes

1 Beginning with Rose and Rose (1969).

2 If we think of the southern hemisphere rather than just Europe then the situation is only more brutal, and of course the countries of the northern hemisphere have been exporting their chemical and nuclear risks to the southern hemisphere.

3 Benton (1991), Giddens (1992), Turner (1984), Featherstone et al. (1991).

4 Examples from a huge literature would include: Birke (1986), Haraway (1989), Harding (1991), Keller (1985), Martin (1989), Merchant (1980), Rose (1994), Shiva (1989), Traweek (1988).

5 Giddens (1992) is better able to acknowledge violence as integral to domination.

6 The novelist A.S. Byatt (1996) also picks up on Nuttall's analysis of 1960s' culture.

7 Basically Bernal's thesis but with his class politics removed.

8 This debate has taken the form of the 'Science Wars' in the USA and the debate between sociologist of science Harry Collins, and the chair of COPUS (see p. 71) Lewis Wolpert at the British Association for the Advancement of Science (BAAS) in 1995. See special issue *Social Text* 46–7, 1996 and Ross (ed.) (1996).

9 Feminists have sought to construct a 'caring rationality' (Rose, 1994: 28–51) and environmentalists a 'social rationality' (Wynne, 1996).

10 Numbers of sociologists of technology are moving again towards the democracy project e.g., Beijker (1995) and Van den Daele (1994). Others such as Mackenzie and Wajcman (1995) are very clear that technology can be deconstructed.

11 Editorial, *Science*, 246: (1989): 189.

12 One study reported that those without insurance were four times less likely to request BRCA-1 testing. Kristin White (1997).

13 Maybe British social theory will see the challenge. During 1996 the highly media visible snail geneticist Steve Jones has affirmed this reconstruction in a number of places: his book *In the Blood* (1996), his television series with the same name, his article 'Don't Blame the Genes' *Guardian*, 7 June 1996, and on local radio in a phone-in on genetics and race, *Pennine Radio*, 9 June 1996. The genie if it ever really was in the bottle, is now surely out.

14 COPUS' 1996 mission statement begins to recognize also 'the scientists' need to understand the public'.

15 Thus the 'does the earth go round the sun or the sun go round the earth' question represented by the quiz researchers and the media as showing scientific literacy is treated as a slightly embarrassing joke by scientists when they talk with one another. At a recent PUS meeting at the Royal Society the Chief Science Adviser gently, but not unpointedly, observed that 'it all depends where you are standing'. The concept of scientific literacy is overdue for deconstruction.

16 Both of these cases have been extensively covered in *Science, Nature* and *Science and Government*.

References

Anderson, P. (1968) 'Components of the National Culture', *New Left Review*, 50: 3–58.

Beck, U. (1992) *Risk Society: Towards a New Modernity*. London: Sage.

Beck-Gernsheim, E. and Beck, U. (1995) *The Normal Chaos of Love*. Cambridge: Polity.

Beijker, W. (1995) *Democratization of Technology – Who are the Experts?* Aachen: Mimeo.

Benton, T. (1991) 'Biology and Social Science: Why the Return of the Repressed should be given a (Cautious) Welcome', *Sociology*, 25 (1): 1–29.

Bernal, J.D. (1939) *The Social Function of Science*. London: Routledge and Kegan Paul.

Birke, L. (1986) *Women, Feminism and Biology: The Feminist Challenge*. Brighton: Harvester Wheatsheaf.

Byatt, A.S. (1996) *Babel Tower*. London: Chatto and Windus.

Cronberg, T. (1996) 'Do Marginal Voices Shape Technology?', in S. Joss and J. Durant (eds), *Public Participation in Science: The Role of Consensus Conferences in Europe*. London: Science Museum.

De Solla Price, D. (1963) *Big Science: Little Science*. London: Macmillan.

Durant, J., Evans, G. and Thomas, G. (1989) 'The Public Understanding of Science', *Nature*, 340: 14–15.

Duster, T. (1990) *Eugenics by the Backdoor*. New York: Routledge.

Elzinga, A. (1985) 'Research Bureaucracy and the Drift of Epistemic Criteria' in B. Wittrock and A. Elzinga (eds), *The University Research System*. Stockholm: Amquist and Wiksell.

Featherstone, M., Hepworth, M. and Turner, B.S. (1991) *The Body: Social Process and Cultural Theory*. London: Sage.

Foucault, M. (1978) *The History of Sexuality*. Vol. I. Harmondsworth: Penguin.

Gibbons, M., Limoges, C., Nowotny, H., Schwarzman, S., Trow, M. and Scott, P. (1995) *The New Production System of Knowledge: The Dynamics of Science and Research in Contemporary Societies*. London: Sage.

Giddens, A. (1991) *Modernity and Self-Identity: Self and Society in the Late-Modern Age*. Cambridge: Polity.

Giddens, A. (1992) *The Transformation of Intimacy: Sexuality, Love and Eroticism in Modern Societies*. Cambridge: Polity.

Green, J. (1990) *Harming not Calming: A Critcal Overview of Psychological Effects of Foetal Diagnosis on Pregnant Women*, Vol. 2. London: Galton Institute Occasional Papers.

Gross, P. and Leavitt, N. (1994) *Higher Superstition: The Academic Left and its Quarrels with Science*. Baltimore: Johns Hopkins University Press.

Harding, S. (1991) *Whose Science? Whose knowledge? Thinking from Women's Lives*. Ithaca, NY: Cornell University Press.

Hutton, W. (1996) *The State We Are In*. London: Cape.

Haraway, D. (1989) *Primate Visions: Gender, Race and Nature in the World of Modern Science*. New York: Routledge.

Irwin, A. and Wynne, B. (eds) (1996) *Misunderstanding Science: The Public Reconstruction of Science and Technology*. Cambridge: Cambridge University Press.

Jones, S. (1996) *In the Blood: God, Genes and Destiny*. London: Harper Collins.

Keller, E.F. (1985) *Reflections on Science and Gender*. New Haven, CT: Yale University Press.

Keller, E.F. (1992) 'Nature, Nurture and the Human Genome Project', in D. Kevles and L. Hood (eds), *The Code of Codes: Scientific and Social Issues in the Human Genome Project*. Cambridge, MA; Harvard University Press.

Kevles, D. (1985) *In the Name of Eugenics: Genetics and the Use of Human Heredity*. New York: Knopf.

Mackenzie, D. and Wajcman, J. (eds) (1995) *The Social Shaping of Technology*. Milton Keynes: Open University Press.

Martin, E. (1989) *The Woman in the Body*. Milton Keynes: Open University Press.

Merchant, C. (1980) *The Death of Nature: Women, Ecology and the Scientific Revolution*. London: Wildwood.

Nelkin, D. and Tancredi, L. (1989) *Dangerous Diagnostics*. New York: Basic Books.

Nuttall, J. (1968) *Bomb Culture*. London: MacGibbon Kee.

Rose, H. (1994) *Love, Power and Knowledge: Towards a Feminist Transformation of the Sciences*. Cambridge: Polity.

Rose, H. and Rose, S. (1969) *Science and Society*. Harmondsworth: Allen Lane.

Rose, H. and Rose, S. (1976) *The Political Economy of Science*. London: Macmillan.

Ross, A. (ed.) (1996) *Science Wars*. Durham, NC: Duke University Press.

Shiva, V. (1989) *Staying Alive: Women, Ecology and Development*. London: Zed.

Turner, B.S. (1984) *The Body and Society: Explorations in Social Theory*. Oxford: Blackwell.

Traweek, S. (1988) *Beamtimes and Lifetimes: The World of High Energy Physicists*. Cambridge, MA: Harvard University Press.

Van den Daele, W. (1994) *Technology Assessment as a Political Experiment*. Berlin: Wissenschaftzentrum für Soziale Forschung.

White, K. (1997) 'Notebook', *Women's Journal of Health*, 5 (5): 415.
Wright, S. (ed.) (1990) *Preventing a Biological Arms Race.* Cambridge, MA: MIT Press.
Wynne, B. (1996) 'Misunderstood Misunderstandings: Social Identities and Public Uptake of Science', in A. Irwin and B. Wynne (eds), *Misunderstanding Science: The Public Reconstruction of Science and Technology.* Cambridge: Cambridge University Press. pp. 65–83.
Ziman, J. (1995) 'Post Academic Science'. Lecture at the Royal Society, London.

PART II

CHALLENGING BIG SCIENCE

4

Nuclear Risks: Three Problematics

Alan Irwin, Stuart Allan and Ian Welsh

INTRODUCTION
(Stuart Allan and Ian Welsh)

The nuclear age dawned in the early days of August 1945, as the world learned of the atomic destruction of the Japanese cities of Hiroshima and Nagasaki by the US military. This transition, characterized by some as 'the end of innocence', came as a profound shock for a public who had previously known of 'atomic bombs' only in the realm of science fiction. 'Just as people recall the circumstances under which they first heard the news of the attack on Pearl Harbor,' proclaimed *Scientific Monthly* at the time, 'so they will remember how the atomic bomb first burst upon their consciousness' (cited in Boyer, 1985: 3).

The intense secrecy surrounding the Manhattan Project (the international team of nuclear physicists and engineers co-ordinated by the US military to build atomic weapons as part of the war effort) had ensured that the risks related to the development of this technology, let alone its threatened use, had not been subject to public scrutiny. Early in 1944, Leo Szilard, who together with other scientists such as J. Robert Oppenheimer was instrumental in designing the weapons, wrote: 'It will hardly be possible to get political action ... unless high efficiency atomic bombs *have actually been used in this war* and the fact of their destructive power has deeply penetrated the mind of the public' (cited in Lifton and Markusen, 1990: 96; emphasis in original). It was this issue of public opinion or, more specifically, the potential for an enraged popular outcry and subsequent political dissent, which US President Truman reportedly struggled to come to terms with prior to his fateful decision to proceed with the bombings.

If, for Truman, the atomic bomb was to be understood as 'a harnessing of the basic powers of the universe', he nevertheless sought to justify its use as merely the next logical stage in 'the science of city-burning'. For some of his critics, however, the rationale for this action was untenable in 'strategic' terms, while others denounced any such appeal to rationality as being morally reprehensible. Following the atomic obliteration of Hiroshima, and with it the eventual deaths of over 200,000 people, public opinion was anything but settled over the purported rationality of Truman's decision. 'Hiroshima inspired more debate than the rest of the war's destruction put together,' contends Weart (1988: 107); 'It was as if all the other recent massacres could be set aside and the entire moral problem of modern war could be concentrated in this one question'.

It is this question of rationality as it pertains to public debates about nuclear risks today, both in the spheres of nuclear weapons and nuclear energy, which informs each of the three contributors to this chapter. Turning first to consider the public saliency of ongoing disputes about nuclear weaponry, it would seem that the risks engendered by such technologies have been all but relegated to the dustbin of history. The discourses of 'nuclear deterrence', 'strategic nuclear forces' and even 'arms control' are recurrently projected by political elites as being almost anachronistic in nature – at best indicative of a Cold War which has long since thawed out. Indeed, following the 1994 agreement between the US and Russian governments to stop aiming nuclear weapons at one another, the risk of global nuclear war has virtually fallen off the public agenda. This when both nations still retain their nuclear arsenals with thousands of warheads on 'hair-trigger alert'.[1]

> Even more ominous is the acute deterioration of the 'command and control systems' in those countries which made up the former Soviet Union. In Russia, for example, the threats posed to 'nuclear stability', itself a deadly illusion, range from a fractious, demoralized military elite which has seen its lines of command unravel, to an increasingly precarious reliance on 'computer management strategies' to detect 'hostile incursions'. Meanwhile, the number of potentially catastrophic 'false alarms' is reportedly growing due to the absence of adequate funding for the regular maintenance and replacement of key surveillance structures. Compounding the perils of possible 'non-authorized nuclear launches' are the worsening conditions underpinning the 'physical security' of the nuclear warheads themselves. The prospect of 'nuke-napping', that is, the seizure of these weapons by 'rogue states' or terrorists either for financial ransom or for political 'blackmail' purposes, is becoming more conceivable as control procedures break down. 'The missile forces must be fed,' declares Robert Bykov, a retired colonel of the 'Strategic Rocket Forces': 'If those who guard Russia's nuclear weaponry go hungry, we might face some terrifying consequences'. (*Time*, 19 May 1997)

The pressing need to enhance public scrutiny of this ongoing crisis is all too obvious, and yet these developments are being, at best, systematically under-reported by the news media. Disturbingly, such is also the case with respect to public awareness of the risks associated with nuclear power technologies. This is not to suggest that British or North American journalists, for example, are failing to report on various problems with these technologies. Typical of this coverage, however, is an emphasis on specific events, such as accidental 'leaks' or 'spills', to the detriment of a thorough accounting of the embodied risks for the public over a period of time longer than yesterday's headline. A careful consideration of the competing discourses of nuclear risk being articulated across the public sphere can reveal how definitions of 'environmental friendliness', particularly when coupled with those of 'cost effectiveness', recurrently displace arguments for alternative, non-nuclear technologies as being both 'impractical' and 'uneconomical'.

The main consequence of this displacement is that the scientific, political and economic rationales being mobilized to legitimize the continued production of nuclear technologies appear to be evermore firmly entrenched in public opinion. Members of the public are being encouraged to believe that the risks of nuclear power are minimal, that they are well within 'reasonable safety limits'. To the extent that the attendant dangers are acknowledged, they tend to be framed by politicians and journalists alike as simply an unfortunate part of everyday life, an inevitable price to be paid for enjoying the benefits of modernity. The parameters of public debate over nuclear power are now largely defined by disputes among 'experts' regarding how best to 'administer' and 'regulate' these technologies. We are regularly asked to accept that nuclear power is 'clean', 'efficient' and 'harmless'. Usually left implicit is the postulate that, in any case, this form of energy is here to stay – in other words, because these technologies cannot be 'un-invented', it will be up to future generations to decide how to deal with the implications of 'our' decision to pursue 'the nuclear option' today. The question of responsibility is thus ostensibly deferred by this projection of a risk-free future.

This chapter suggests some initial bearings for a historically informed appraisal of nuclear risks, one which seeks to dismantle many of the seemingly 'commonsensical' presuppositions embedded in current public (including academic) discourses. Alan Irwin opens the discussion by exploring the relationships between nuclear technologies, rationality and modernity. He argues against making too ready a linkage between the nuclear case and modernity *per se*, pointing out that the kinds of certainty associated with nuclear power never existed but were constructed through rationalized forms of commentary and discourse. Stuart Allan develops the notion of 'nuclearism' in order to elucidate the ideological mechanisms by which nuclear risks are rationalized as being simply a 'normal part of everyday life'. Drawing upon a range of textual examples, he shows how the language of nuclear discourse may be analysed so as to disclose how hierarchical relations of definitional power shape what counts as 'the nuclear status quo' at the level of truth-claims. Finally, Ian Welsh argues that approaching nuclear risks through categories of rationality neglects the importance of other affective dimensions, such as desire, in framing and defining 'acceptable' risk trajectories. In addressing the situated desires of scientists, politicians and constituent publics, he argues that the 'promise' of nuclear technologies produced a mutually reinforcing resonance which substantially displaced more 'rational' registers shaping the introduction of these technologies.

Collectively, then, these three interventions suggest that before nuclear risk can be adequately positioned as an analytical category within critical modes of enquiry, greater care must be taken to attend to the historical specificity of the concomitant appeals to rationality. This shared concern speaks to the dangers of reproducing in our theorizing the very 'invisibility' of the contested rationalities underlying nuclear risk that we should otherwise be at pains to render visible.

RISK, TECHNOLOGY AND MODERNITY: RE-POSITIONING THE SOCIOLOGICAL ANALYSIS OF NUCLEAR POWER
(Alan Irwin)

This section reviews and reconsiders the relationship between nuclear power and modernity in the light of contemporary sociological discussions over technology and risk. Arguments about the 'risk society' have certainly assisted our analytical appreciation of current social and environmental concerns. However, it is also necessary to examine the specifically technological dimension to risk debates from a sociological perspective and to consider the consequences of this examination for our understanding of modernity. This is all the more relevant given the strong relationship generally assumed within the current sociological literature between technology, risk and modernity – and also the theoretical and practical significance of recent developments in the sociology of scientific knowledge. As will be argued below, in focusing on questions of technology and modernity, we are simultaneously dealing with key sociological and theoretical issues concerning the flexibility and responsiveness of current systems of knowledge and social practice.

A series of publications from sociologists such as Beck (1992, 1995), Giddens (1991) and Bauman (1991) have accorded substantial importance to the social conditions of late-modernity in explaining the contemporary public awareness of risk and environmental degradation. Technology, however, tends to play a rather weakly developed and one-dimensional role within these theoretical accounts. For many sociologists, science and technology continue to represent a 'special' and 'technical' field rather than a major focus for theoretical and empirical research of central concern to the discipline. Nevertheless, science and technology are routinely presented as being highly-significant for the current condition of modernity.

Put in slightly exaggerated form, technology is portrayed either as reflecting the 'logic of modernity' or representing an inevitable and exogenous force. Notions of 'technological rationality' and 'technocracy' (Beck) and of 'scientific culture' (Bauman) can be found throughout the sociological literature on risk. Meanwhile recent work within the sociology of scientific knowledge and the sociology of technology, which is at best poorly integrated into the work of social theorists, strongly suggests that more grounded and insightful accounts of 'risk, technology and modernity' are required. Such work has typically adopted a contextually-specific and empirical focus – dealing with the social, institutional and technical processes through which technologies become constructed, enacted and maintained (Jasanoff et al., 1995). This research has generally not made use of the discourse of 'modernity' except in the most general and descriptive terms.

In this section, I especially want to explore just what it might mean to describe nuclear power as 'modern'. What social and technological relationships does this imply? What connection might there be between the structural accounts of the 'risk society' genre and the more empirical and case-specific analyses of the sociologists of science and technology? To do this we need to discuss the relationship between sociological accounts which generally 'black box' the social processes of technology production, highlighting structural social relations, and those which deal explicitly with the social production of technology in a way distanced from 'mainstream' social theory. This account will necessarily be brief, and so suggestive and programmatic rather than detailed and empirical. Nevertheless, it will be argued that there is considerable scope for future sociological work at the interface between risk, technology and modernity.

In addressing the technological dimension within risk debates, this analysis also challenges the explanatory status of modernity as a unitary and over-arching edifice. Rather than advocating a monolithic presentation of modernity, the argument is that this concept needs to be understood in a more diverse and less 'essentialist' manner. From the sociological perspective adopted here, both 'technology' and 'modernity' are open to numerous interpretations and are the products of varied practices and constructions. A sociological refusal to deal with the social constructedness of technological processes, therefore, also limits our capacity to explore more differentiated and divergent experiences of 'being modern'.

At first approximation, the relationship between nuclear power and modernity seems unarguably close. High-tech, high energy and high consequence, nuclear power stands as one of the most visible products of the post-1945 faith in science, truth and progress. The history of civil nuclear power also conveniently marks the subsequent decline in this public faith as the social response to Three Mile Island and Chernobyl epitomized the more troubled and critical conditions of the late-twentieth century. Of course, the accidents themselves did not actually create these new conditions – a more complex relationship between risk construction and social response is at work. However, the tenth anniversary of the Chernobyl accident strongly reinforced the image of the stricken plant as an enduring symbol of modernity's negative consequences.

In order to disentangle the relationship between modernity and nuclear power, it is necessary to consider briefly the general features of civil nuclear energy and the relationship they suggest between risk, knowledge and authority. Is there any evidence to suggest that modernity can indeed stand as a unitary concept? Nuclear power has been characterized from the start by an explicit confidence in science and technology as a basis for social progress. Generated out of the wartime Manhattan Project,[2] and thereby marking one of the first manifestations of Big Science, the case for nuclear power has always been made in the form of technical argumentation which in turn depended upon an underlying belief that, while problems will inevitably be found, they can surely be ironed out as our technical understanding advances. This scientific resilience has also meant that accidents are dismissed as part of the technological learning-curve or else viewed as a consequence of non-scientific design choices (frequently seen as occurring in 'other countries'). Such a faith in 'science and progress' has also meant that critical voices are generally dismissed as either (at best) uninformed or (at worst) irrational (Irwin, 1995; Irwin and Wynne, 1996; McKechnie, 1996).

This sense of 'nuclear rationality' is also apparent in the view of risk and the environment held within nuclear institutions (broadly defined to include both sponsoring and regulatory bodies). The environment is presented as resilient and robust in the face of radioactive contaminants provided that emissions are kept at a 'reasonable level'. Risks are judged to be 'acceptable', usually on quantitative scales, implying that 'acceptability' can be determined independently of institutional processes and particular contexts. Risk is also measured according to rational calculation – a calculation which includes both potential environmental damage and the material benefits of power generation. The quantified calculation of risk and benefit offers a material and 'rational' basis for safety assessment. Opposing notions of nature as possessing intrinsic value or of life as being of incalculable benefit have been readily dismissed by nuclear institutions as misguided and anti-scientific.

These perspectives on science/technology and risk/environment are embedded in the institutional forms and practices within which nuclear power has been conceived and developed. Internationally, the nuclear industry developed in a closed climate of secrecy concealing the links between civil nuclear power and its military origins. A major consequence of this is that nuclear power has been protected by an institutional web of social and technological practices. Such institutional structures and belief systems engender a restricted view of the scope for public discussion and democratic involvement within nuclear decision-making. The process of public alienation is particularly clear within numerous British public inquiries with opposition groups regularly finding themselves disenfranchised by the largely technocratic and legalistic operating assumptions behind the inquiry process. The emphasis on factual issues addressed in an adversarial manner, as revealed in the 1976 Windscale Inquiry, serves to overrule conventional notions of due democratic process and accountability (Wynne, 1982). As one contemporaneous editorial described the role of the High Court Judge who chaired the Windscale Inquiry:

> Parker was there to decide, not to illuminate controversy ... Once (he) had decided that the decision should go in BNFL's favour he went out of his way to find for them on almost every issue – rather as a judge confronted by a bunch of witnesses prepared to testify to a man's innocence, might dismiss their evidence *in toto* once satisfied that the man is guilty. (*Nature*, 23 March 1978: 297)

These characteristics suggest that 'nuclear rationality' and 'modernity' are indeed extremely close to one another. Moreover, other characteristics of nuclear technology reinforce this perspective. Thus, the globalization of nuclear power has taken a number of obvious and less obvious forms, including the spread of the technology across otherwise disparate national settings (including the developed and developing worlds), the consequent adoption of 'rational' institutional practices (so that it is not just technology that is being transferred but also a whole 'risk culture'), and the 'global' nature of the environmental problems raised. Equally, nuclear energy is not easily separable from a *materialist and capitalist commitment*. The very notion of progress upon which it depends contains a logic of material growth and expanding capitalistic horizons – any other scenario (based on zero-growth or energy conservation) becomes naive and (again) irrational. The response to doubters has been to extrapolate previous growth trends forward – as if future energy scenarios are socially predetermined. At that point social and technological futures fuse into one vision of nuclear progress.

Of course, there are those who dissent from this triumphalist note. It is impossible to discuss 'nuclear modernity' without also recording the various social challenges to such a vision. For reasons which may be economic rather than simply environmental or risk-oriented, nuclear programmes world-wide find themselves under threat – at least in terms of the international expansion of nuclear facilities. Such a reaction to one of modernity's 'dream technologies' can only raise further doubts about the promise of the so-called 'emerging technologies', e.g. biotechnology, and their social consequences.

Put in these rather sweeping terms, nuclear power fits well with the overall vision of 'troubled modernity' presented within current discussions of late-modernity and the 'risk society'. Science, technology and authority are mutually-reinforcing. Institutional practices embody this modernistic nexus. Fundamental uncertainties are denied, even when events like Chernobyl bring these to the fore. Meanwhile, extra-institutional forces are challenging 'nuclear rationality' and its vision of the future. The consequence is a critical climate both for institutions and the notions of technological-social progress upon which they depend for their legitimation.

While this overview certainly possesses descriptive merits, it is also necessary to consider a number of analytical deficiencies with the simple juxtaposition of 'nuclear power' and 'modernity'. In particular, approaching technology as either a product or cause of modernity implies an unfortunate element of both technological and social determinism. On the one hand, this suggests the need to conduct more careful empirical analysis into 'what it means to be modern'. Equally, however, it causes us to reconsider the very concept of modernity in this and other contexts. In the points that follow, I particularly want to challenge the notion of modernity as a homogeneous or monolithic phenomenon. Instead – and here the sociological study of technology can be especially useful – I want to consider its dynamic and varyingly constructed character.

As the account stands thus far, nuclear technology and nuclear risk somehow 'resonate' with the rationality of modernity but the nature of this causal connection remains unexplored both in theoretical and empirical terms. Technology is viewed either as an independent force or as a social consequence – but with little sense of the cognitive and institutional interactions involved. Meanwhile, modernity is left at the level of *Zeitgeist* rather than grounded in the specific social and technical practices of varied groups of actors. Thus, the plural character of both 'technology' and 'modernity' becomes reduced to a single-dimensional framework. However, it is precisely this relationship which emerges as a focal point for sociological investigation and fresh theoretical interpretation.

A number of observations based on a constructivist approach to science and technology may serve to suggest the kinds of sociological work which are required. Once again, these can only remain observations within such a brief analysis but may serve to stimulate further discussion. In the first place, sociological commentators need to be careful not to equate challenges to a specific technology with either generic challenges to technology or indeed challenges to the wider social structures framing operational principles. On the one hand, writings in the risk society genre need to avoid uncritically harnessing specific forms of environmental protest to the idea of broader challenges to the structure of modernity, while on the other they need to avoid presenting 'modernity' as an oddly a-social force which is somehow pulling the historical strings.

This is not to deny that certain forms of modernist discourse are a characteristic of the development of nuclear energy. Environmental groups are as likely to draw upon technical argumentation as the 'nuclear establishment' – and for reasons which go beyond the merely tactical and rhetorical (Yearley, 1996). Very often, the same (much criticized) model of a scientifically ignorant and uninformed public is employed by anti-nuclear groups, the nuclear industry and supporter governments. In this manner, nuclear protest can be less about the rejection of some putative modernity than the application of a very similar form of discourse to areas where it has been seen to fail. Far from negating public faith in science and technology, this offers the promise of better technical fixes to the social and environmental problems of our age. The problem for many environmentalists is thus how to communicate the 'right' set of facts. Equally, the critique of nuclear power has emphasized issues of technological inefficiency and economic cost rather than opposition to 'nuclear rationality'. Recent research among critics of nuclear power suggests that rather than an anti-technology backlash or wholesale rejection of science there is an attempt to develop more 'appropriate' technological forms which reflect new patterns of living and working (Irwin et al., 1994). This situation of working with, as well as against, technology is also reflected in the often close, if at times strained, relationships between environmentalist and governmental organizations. These shared concerns suggest that modernistic discourses can be flexible in their technological and social expression and far less dogmatic than is often argued by critics.

Secondly, it is important that we move beyond the monolithic or essentialist presentation of nuclear technology – the notion that it is an alien force on the landscape or that it has simply been imposed by dominant institutions. Instead, an established sociological tradition argues that we should consider the processes which socially construct and maintain such technologies (Bijker et al., 1987). At one level, it must be recognized that this 'technology' actually takes a number of distinctive forms according to different designs and operating systems. Technologies also have precursors and 'pedigree' – in this case involving various particular parts of the chemical industry and general engineering. The technological and social 'uniqueness' of nuclear power can be over-emphasized. Instead, a more cautious and critical study is needed of both the unique and overlapping nature of nuclear power and nuclear institutions.

At the same time, it is necessary to consider nuclear technology not as simply 'given' but as varyingly constructed, experienced, opposed and, indeed, enjoyed. For example, anthropological research suggests that the technology may be differentially constructed even within a nuclear installation. Thus, Zonabend's study of a French nuclear waste processing plant conveys strongly this sense of diversity rather than simply the dead hand of modernity. Zonabend focuses not on 'nuclear power' as a separate category but on 'the turns of speech (and silence), the procedures and stratagems, the tactics and practices – in short – the whole spectrum of methods by which the people of la Hague deal with *le nucléaire*' (1993: 121). Certain workers may see the plant as exciting, dangerous and risky while others see it as controlled, measured and reassuring. The local experience of a nuclear site can also vary, from a positive valuation of the impact on local jobs and services to anxiety at the hidden consequences. Macgill has noted a set of widely different interpretations held by those who live close to the British Sellafield nuclear site. To quote two residents from her study:

'My family work there – therefore I feel the risk is nil.'

'I would stand up for the area – it's still a far healthier area
than a smokey city – I'd prefer to bring children up here than there.'
(Macgill, 1987: 181–2)

Related studies around chemical sites reinforce this notion of a complex and often contradictory experience of technology (Irwin, 1995: 81–103). Such studies typically suggest that, for example, a feeling of alienation is less an inherent characteristic of the technology itself than of the social and contextual processes within which it is located (although this is not to deny that such factors as the scale, pollution record and visibility of technologies will be of significance within this contextual treatment). Technologies are not experienced in some immediate and unmediated fashion. Instead, they are differentially constructed and consumed within a variety of social and institutional contexts.

A third element within this discussion of 'nuclear modernity' is found within the voices of science itself – a science which is considerably more plural and heterogeneous in form than most externalist accounts suggest (and especially those which portray science as the 'logic of modernity'). Rather than simply pursuing one 'technical rationale' or slavishly following institutional dictates, the generation of nuclear energy builds upon a number of cognitive frameworks and disciplinary perspectives – from high energy physics to plant biology, from epidemiology to electrical engineering. Of course, it must also be recognized that scientists have spoken both for and against nuclear energy. While one portrayal of the role of science within modernity has emphasized its denial of risk and uncertainty, our very awareness of nuclear risk and uncertainty is largely dependent upon the public statements of scientists and engineers. Once again, we witness the plurality of this category – a plurality which undermines ungrounded and over-abstract talk of 'science and modernity'.

Fourthly, we must consider the varying construction of nuclear power's threat to the human and natural environment. Again, it is not possible to summon up some unmediated notion of 'nuclear danger' – as if sociologists could claim in this context to know better than the key participants in the nuclear debate, or as if there indeed existed an unproblematic epistemological basis for such claims. Various accounts of nuclear risk are available – one important sociological task, therefore, is to explore their foundations and operating assumptions rather than dismissing certain accounts on the grounds of their apparent institutional origins.

The need is for a 'symmetrical' form of analysis rather than the unreflexive identification with one assessment. It must be acknowledged that such a constructivist perspective also raises analytical dilemmas – but that these need to be explicitly addressed rather than concealed within sociological claims-making.

Competing risk constructions thus become an important topic (and resource) for empirically-based sociological research: how do certain accounts gain and maintain credibility, under what circumstances, and within what changing parameters? The social construction of 'global risk' becomes an especially important topic for investigation, particularly since it links nuclear threats to other matters of contemporary social concern. Rather than weakening the radical import of sociological analysis, such a perspective opens up the social, technical and environmental uncertainties within policy-making to wider discussion and strategy-making. In that way it also becomes possible to draw upon the varied experiences of both technologies and of 'being modern' (and, importantly, the inter-connections between these). In so doing, sociological research can reveal the ethical, value-related and institutional questions which are otherwise obfuscated by variations on social/technological determinism and by retreat to the 'logic of modernity'.

The study of modernity and technology should therefore represent a central element in the sociological analysis of risk. This contribution has argued that rather than imputing a causal relationship from afar – which tends to grant independent status to either modernity (i.e. social determinism) or technology (technological determinism) – we need to examine the cross-cutting and mutually-dependent interactions in play. This strategy will involve a more fine-grained and contextually-sensitive approach than has been apparent in a number of recent theoretical contributions to the discipline. Especially important sites for such research will include environmentalist groups, the generators of nuclear energy, government bodies and those who live and work with the technology. This analysis has specifically advocated a symmetrical, empirical and constructivist approach to such sociological investigations. One consequence of this approach may be a more inhibited, differentiated and cautious usage of sociological 'key-words' such as modernity and post-modernity. This would indeed be a most gratifying development – especially if it opened up a creative discussion of the possibilities for social and institutional flexibility within the processes of technology development.

RISK AND THE COMMON SENSE OF 'NUCLEARISM'
(Stuart Allan)

This section discussion focuses on the problem of risk as it is implicated in the cultural imperatives of nuclear discourse. More specifically, it is my intention to engage with the discursive strategies being used by various institutional voices to articulate the risks associated with nuclear weapon technologies, in general, and the threatened use of these weapons in the name of 'deterrence', in particular. By rendering problematic the seemingly *rational, reasonable* or *logical* presuppositions underpinning these articulations, I hope to highlight some of the ways in which the construction of 'nuclear normality' (Lifton and Markusen, 1990) is being achieved in cultural terms. Accordingly, I shall argue that our mundane, day-to-day 'acceptance' of the 'need' for these nuclear technologies is actually contingent upon the ideological displacement of alternative ways of speaking their attendant risks as being transgressive of 'common sense'.

In order to discern the (always provisional) cultural codes or rules by which these risks are being routinely defined as simply a *normal* part of everyday life, we need to establish a conceptual space for examining contending discourses about nuclear weapons not only in terms of what is said, but also in terms of what remains unspoken (ostensibly too obvious for words). Here it is evident that the 'specialist' language of nuclear weaponry is replete with a formalized lexicon organized, in part, to lend legitimacy to the dictates of the pertinent 'strategic considerations'. If risks, as Ulrich Beck (1994: 30) writes, presuppose decisions, and thereby 'deepen the dependency on experts', then the statements made by various 'accredited' and 'authoritative' institutional voices, such as those of government and military officials, 'arms experts', 'security advisers', 'weapons analysts', and other members of the 'strategic community', may be read as attempts to regulate and rationalize the preconditions of nuclear risk.[3] Significantly, while it may be fair to suggest that there is a growing public awareness of the role of military language in mystifying certain uncomfortable truths about warfare, I would argue that the same cannot be said about the official language employed to define the threat of nuclear war. By way of an example, a consistent theme in the news media coverage of the 'Persian Gulf War' was the scrutiny of military jargon ('surgical strikes', 'smart bombs', 'collateral damage', 'friendly fire', 'soft targets', 'acceptable losses' and so forth) and its 'effects' *vis-à-vis* the 'sanitization of reality'. Regarding nuclear issues, however, there remains in operation an officially sanctioned vocabulary which is only rarely made the subject of news media attention. Certainly the notion of 'nuclear deterrence', among others, would appear to be a prefigured feature of most news treatments of 'nuclear weapons issues' (see also Allan, 1996, 1997).

A brief illustration of this latter point may be found in a news account published in *The Independent*, a British 'quality' broadsheet newspaper, on 14 May 1996 (page 2). Entitled 'Last voyage as Polaris ends 30 years of secret patrols,' it reads as follows:

> The haunting strains of 'Auld Lang Syne' drifted across the Clyde as the Polaris nuclear era came to a distinguished end yesterday. A watery sun filtered through the early-morning mist to cast an eerie glow on the black shape of HMS *Repulse* as the submarine completed the last Polaris patrol after almost 30 years. ...

> Controversy has dogged the fleet of four Polaris boats since they took over the role of carrying Britain's nuclear deterrent from the RAF amid great secrecy in 1968. For 28 years they guaranteed Britain's national security with continuous patrols in the North Atlantic with their arsenal of 16 strategic nuclear weapons.

> Despite the end of the Cold War, Russian submarines are still trying to track the Navy's ballistic-missile submarines. Now responsibility for Britain's nuclear deterrent will fall on two new Trident submarines.

> The 16,000 ton *Vanguard*, which entered service in 1994 and *Victorious*, which entered service last September, are more advanced than Polaris and carry the more potent D-5 missile with a 5,000-mile range. ...

'It's like losing an old friend', said Admiral Whetstone. '*Repulse* has served everyone who has commanded her very well'.

By reading this example of newspaper discourse 'against the grain', so to speak, it is possible to pinpoint several discursive strategies which have been utilized, knowingly or not, to help normalize the perilous uncertainties of nuclear risk. Examples of these interrelated discursive strategies include:

- The restriction of perspectives to official sources accredited with expert status. The news account's actors are: 'Sea Lord, Admiral Sir Jock Slater'; 'Commander David Philips, 40, *Repulse*'s Commanding Officer'; 'Philip Ullathorne, 47, from Selby, West Yorkshire, a veteran of 25 patrols'; and 'Admiral Whetstone' (the latter three of whom are quoted);
- the use of metaphors, such as 'Polaris nuclear era' or 'the Cold War', to help render abstract strategic rationales into ostensibly concrete entities;
- the use of euphemistic descriptions of nuclear deterrence: 'For 28 years they guaranteed Britain's national security with continuous patrols in the North Atlantic with their arsenal of 16 strategic nuclear weapons';
- the use of formal acronyms and abbreviations, such as 'HMS', 'RAF', or 'D-5', to reinforce the authority of bureaucratic discourse;
- the displacement of human agency, and with it public accountability: 'the Polaris nuclear era came to a distinguished end yesterday'; 'Controversy has dogged the fleet of four Polaris boats since they took over the role of carrying Britain's nuclear deterrent'; and: 'Now responsibility for Britain's nuclear deterrent will fall on two new Trident submarines';
- processes of naming: just as in the 'Persian Gulf War' where we saw 'Patriots battle against Scuds', here we have '*Repulse*' and '*Vanguard*' (with their defensive and proactive connotations, respectively), as well as '*Victorious*';
- and un-naming: the word 'nuclear' is dropped from 'D-5 missile' and is replaced in favour of 'ballistic' in 'the Navy's ballistic-missile submarines'; also, nuclear-powered submarines become 'boats';
- the humanization of nuclear technology: nuclear-powered submarines enter service, complete patrols, take over roles, have responsibilities; '*Repulse*' becomes 'an old friend';
- the use of gendered terms: the pronoun 'her' is used for '*Repulse*'; the 'D-5 missile' is described as 'potent';
- and, finally, Britain's technological capacity is conflated with defence (an 'arsenal of 16 strategic nuclear weapons' is seen to have 'guaranteed Britain's national security') while, in marked contrast, that of the Russian Other constitutes a threat to be deterred: 'Despite the end of the Cold War, Russian submarines are still trying to track the Navy's ballistic-missile submarines'.[4]

In looking to deconstruct the public projection of nuclear risk, then, it is this language of nuclear discourse or 'nukespeak' (the latter term is a play on Orwell's 'Newspeak') which needs to be carefully explicated. Underpinning much of the available research on nuclear discourse is the contention that its use by politicians and military officials, among other interested actors, represents a consciously systemic effort to naturalize a need for the continued design, development, production and 'deployment' of new forms of nuclear weapon technology (see Chilton, 1985; Hook, 1985; Ruthven, 1993; Schiappa, 1989). Investigations have shown how nuclear discourse, as a distinct linguistic genre, is working to reproduce certain preferred ways of talking about nuclear risk across the contested terrain of the 'public' sphere, as well as in the 'private' realm of everyday life. This research suggests that what is at stake is the naturalization of the strategic postulates which inform the rhetorical features of these ideological appeals to support the 'pro-nuclear consensus', despite its inherent contradictions. To the extent that the news media re inflect this terminology and its nuclearist presuppositions, then, they are facilitating the larger 'strategic' appropriation and codification of the threat of nuclear war. The actual language used to construct the reality of this danger will necessarily shape the parameters within which the popular exchange of viewpoints about the risks engendered by 'nuclear strategy' take place. All too often it is the case, according to this research, that the veracity of nuclearist truth-claims, such as 'nuclear weapons have kept the peace' or 'our national security depends on nuclear deterrence', is made to appear to be little more than a matter of common sense in newspaper and televisual accounts (see also Allan, 1995).

For those researchers seeking to address the materiality of this common sense, the term 'nuclearism' is often employed to advantage. To clarify, 'nuclearism' may be invoked to designate the popular negotiation of the ideological relations embedded in discourses about nuclear weapons as they work to authorize a continued need for their threatened use.[5] To the extent that fears of nuclear annihilation have been displaced (if not erased) from the popular imaginary, then, Beck's (1992: 24) observation that the risk society is a 'catastrophic society' in which 'the exceptional condition threatens to become the norm' assumes a new resonance. Nuclearism is constitutive, in part, of a discursive re-appropriation of everyday language into nuclearist categories, thereby making the unspeakable horrors of a potential nuclear war safely speakable within the administrative logics of risk calculation. The normality of nuclear weapons and their role in 'national security' has become, to varying degrees, part of our day-to-day experience of life in the 'post-Cold War era'. And yet this normality requires a continuous series of interventions to be sustained: its ideological presuppositions, always threatening to come unravelled, need to undergo active renewal as they are promulgated across an extensive array of institutional sites.

Accordingly, in my view, the oft-repeated assertion that the risks posed by nuclear weapons are as constant as they are 'unimaginable' while, in contrast, public perceptions of them are shifting dramatically over time, requires substantive qualification.

- First, is it not the case that nuclear discourse allows, indeed routinely encourages, the imagining of the potential destructive force of nuclear weapons? This imagining is to take place, however, within certain normative 'rules of inclusion and exclusion', that is, in such a way that the preparation for nuclear war may be seen as normal, even desirable, because the event itself will never be 'allowed' to happen to 'us' only to 'them'. This endless deferral of the decision to 'push the button' in the name of 'nuclear deterrence' accords to the processes of 'nuclear escalation' a rationality consistent with the strategic management of risk.

- Second, I would suggest that the reality of the nuclear threat is far from static or unchanging. Rather, the threat of nuclear war (and here I follow, if in only very general terms, a line of argument advanced by Derrida, 1984) is made comprehensible to us through the language we have to articulate it. There is no 'pure experience' of nuclear risk outside of words; rather, the reality of the nuclear threat is contingent upon the (culturally specific) meaning practices we draw on to interpret it, to make it signify. Perceptions of the nuclear threat may be seen as being constitutive of its reality; by privileging for critique this complex activity of discursive construction, then, the social relations of signification may be located *vis-à-vis* the social hierarchies of time, space and place.

- And third, following the dissolution of a rigid dichotomy between the nuclear threat, on the one hand, and perceptions of it, on the other, we may proceed to ask how 'dramatic' are these 'shifts' in public perception? Is it reasonable to assume that there is an arbitrariness to these perceptions being played out at the level of the individual (and thereby be in danger of reifying a further dichotomy between cognitive and social processes), or is it not more advantageous to look for regularities in the dispersal of (necessarily partial and selective) discourses about the nuclear threat as they are produced, contested and transformed? By adopting the latter approach, I would argue, analyses may disrupt the common sense of the truth-claims embedded in our language about nuclear war precisely as they work to police the ideological limits of 'what can and should be said' about the reality of nuclear risk.

In recognizing that the shifting modalities of this naturalization process need to be explicated in relation to calculable risks, attention may shift to address the issue of common sense as it is implicated in nuclear normality. Historical research into the popular dispersal of nuclearism is rich with insights into the origins of the nuclear threat, and how the tenets of 'strategic doctrine' were publicly presented as being commonsensical. In one such study, Paul Boyer (1985) argues that the principal elements of 'our contemporary engagement with the nuclear reality' began to assume a recognizable form almost immediately after the atomic obliteration of Hiroshima on 6 August 1945.[6] He proceeds to cite a transcript of a US radio broadcast, one of the first to announce that the bombing had taken place:

> This is Don Goddard with your news at noon. A little less than an hour ago, newsmen were called to the White House down in Washington, and there they were read a special announcement written by President Truman ... This was the story of a new bomb, so powerful that only the imagination of a trained scientist could dream of its existence. Without qualification, the President said that Allied scientists have now harnessed the basic power of the universe. They have harnessed the atom. (cited in Boyer, 1985: 4)

As Boyer's research indicates, this 'harnessing of the atom' is a recurrent feature of news accounts attempting to describe processes which seemed to belong more to the realm of science fiction (H.G. Wells coined the phrase 'atomic bomb' in 1913) than everyday reality. The first five post-war years were particularly crucial with respect to the naturalization of both 'the friendly atom' and, simultaneously, the need to maintain 'atomic superiority' over the Russians. The degree to which official nuclearist discourse succeeded in realizing the naturalization of its imperatives is difficult to assess; claims that popular opinion was acquiescent to the dictates of the new 'atomic era' are contradicted by widespread evidence that public anxieties over nuclear weapons in this period were profound (see also Spinardi, 1997; Weart, 1988).

Indeed in this regard, and further to the issues raised in the newspaper account concerning the end of 'the Polaris nuclear era' discussed above, we may briefly examine an anti-nuclearist article written at the time when the Polaris nuclear submarine programme was under development (the first test flight of its missile, minus the 'nuclear warhead', occurred in 1958, while the first Polaris submarine, the USS *Daniel Webster*, went on 'patrol' six years later). The article in question, written by Robert Bolt, appeared in the *New Statesman* on 24 December 1960, and is entitled 'Do You Speak Nuclear?' There Bolt (1960: 1000) writes:

> Nothing is so dangerous as the Bomb. No danger is so inescapable, if the Bomb goes off. Nothing seems more likely than that the Bomb is going to go off. In a word, nothing is so important as the Bomb. Yet nothing is so boring as the Bomb. Printed matter on the subject has the property of turning paper grey, and as a topic of conversation it is to the mind what the Atlantic is to a castaway, nauseous, of hideous extent, hideously boring. And it's not that any of us imagines that the matter has anywhere by anyone been even partially dealt with; it is known to be a live issue and open question. It must be panic that makes it so boring, makes us believe as though it were a dead issue and the question closed.

Bolt's article clearly succeeds in mapping several of the more salient contours of nuclearism in relation to risk. Of particular interest, in my view, is his identification of the paradoxical juxtaposition of panic and boredom. Implicit to this passage is the recognition that the danger of 'the Bomb' transcends geography, national boundaries, lines of class and privilege, and so forth – the danger is 'inescapable'. The calculation of risk associated with this danger is marked by the phrase: 'Nothing seems more likely than that the Bomb is going to go off', thereby subverting in dramatic fashion the presuppositions underpinning nuclearist re-articulations of safety (for 'us') and risk (for 'them'). Related to this is the sceptical reading of the expertise of official truth-claims, the partial (and, therefore, dangerous) nature of which is highlighted. The delusional quality of the public negotiation of the significance of 'the Bomb' is then recognized as being characteristic of a response to an unimaginable reality, a response that is at once understandable ('panic') and yet inadequate ('boredom') under these new circumstances.

As Bolt's anti-nuclearist thesis unfolds, he proceeds to address the problem of naturalization directly, arguing that: 'we seem always to speak as though ... the Bomb were a natural phenomenon which threatens from without, and against which we must prepare ourselves, as against a high tide on a low coast, with a calculated system of checks and dispersals' (1960: 1000). 'The Bomb' as a 'natural phenomenon' is thus set in relation to the pernicious dynamics of risk, such that the rationality otherwise implied by 'a calculated system of checks and dispersals' is directly challenged. Moreover, when he writes that: 'We speak of 'avoiding' it, exactly as though the Bomb had some volition of its own', Bolt is observing how nuclear discourse works to attribute agency to 'the Bomb' (science, technology, nature, etc.) at the expense of the human agents (scientists, militarists, politicians, etc.) actually responsible for its development and threatened use. This dichotomy obfuscates more than lines of responsibility, or what Beck (1996) identifies as 'conflicts of accountability', for it also calls into question the very tenets of modernity. In Bolt's words: 'In fact, while every new contrivance (like Polaris) increases our "readiness" there is no counter-balancing increase in our reluctance, for whereas scientific progress seems to proceed quite helplessly, we have no such built-in disposition for increasing our awareness' (1960: 1000). By advancing his critique in opposition to the interpellations of modernist discourses of scientific rationality and progress, Bolt is able to show how the 'margin of safety has gone, and the old motions are not appropriate' (1960: 1000).

New research into this common sense of nuclearism as it relates to the problem of risk may be able to radically elaborate upon the points of ideological tension discernible in the above illustrations. Beck (1996: 32) rightly points out that 'there are no bystanders anymore', yet his attendant claim that 'under this [nuclear] threat everyone is affected and involved and accordingly can speak in their own right' needs to be contextualized in relation to the hierarchical politics of nuclearist truth-claims. One way to proceed is by asking questions such as: whose articulation of nuclear risk is being advanced as commonsensical, and what are the criteria by which this common sense is being re-validated? In what ways, and to what extent, are its presuppositions being aligned with the natural, the obvious and the inevitable? As I have sought to argue above, in my view it is by addressing the ideological struggles transpiring over the common sense of nuclearism that its contested nature may be best rendered visible. This is to say that the language of nuclear discourse needs to be analysed so as to disclose how an unequal dispersion of power to communicate the attendant risks of nuclear war conditions the very normality of official, popular and resistant nuclear discourses as they are lived out in everyday experience. Once again, Bolt's (1960: 1001) article of almost 40 years ago pinpoints the issue with elegant clarity:

And as normal day succeeds to normal day we allow ourselves the illusion that normality accumulates and is brought forward. We are leaving the war behind, we feel, allowing ourselves to forget that in the past this has always meant: we are moving towards the war. Comforting illusion, necessary comfort, but we ought not to call it realistic. To contain our own violence, to love life, to know that our own particular truths are limited, these are not traditionally political problems, and will not yield to traditional political methods. (1960: 1001)

DESIRING RISK: NUCLEAR MYTHS AND THE SOCIAL SELECTION OF RISK

(Ian Welsh)

In this short contribution I argue that desire plays an important, though neglected, role in the social selection and prioritization of the risks which societies are prepared to engage with. It is part of my argument that the situated desires of various actors, from groups of scientists, to politicians, regulators and constituent publics, mediate collective approaches towards certain risks.[7] At certain critical moments the desires of particular constellations of actors enable society to embrace projects which are openly acknowledged as risky. Among other things, desire mobilizes symbolic resources as it compensates for gaps in knowledge which inevitably accompany periods of intense technical advance and preclude early scientific closure.[8] If one accepts this argument then approaching risk exclusively in terms of rationality diverts attention away from these less comfortable affective dimensions.

Nuclear issues are particularly evocative of a number of registers of desire producing actions which fly in the face of apparently rational behaviour. One particularly clear example of situated desire at work is embodied in the iconic images of US citizens seated in specially constructed stands watching atomic bomb tests during the 1950s. Photographs of these stands, packed with sunglasses-wearing Americans, now evoke incredulous responses in many. A classic case of 'if only they had known' things would have been different. But, this retrospective rationalization misses the prevailing *zeitgeist*; better to ask what did it mean to be a patriotic American at that time? A short answer would include allegiance to the American dream of world dominance and leadership through possession of nuclear weapons. Being invited to witness the use of such weapons was to become a member of the magic circle, to share in the wonder of the towering mushroom cloud, the crack of doom at the point of detonation, to experience the potential to become like the Grim Reaper, destroyer of worlds. It was not an invitation to be turned down lightly, especially as anti-communist hysteria grew. Despite the massive difference in public knowledge about radiation by the time of the reactor accident at Three Mile Island in 1979 an analogous media image appeared. An open top car full of youths driving down deserted streets under the banner 'Just Out Absorbin' Some Rays'. Nor has compulsory underground testing expunged the desire to witness bomb tests either. In the words of one American weapons worker: 'I've seen the films. I want to feel the heat. This is the most there is; this is the closest you get to playing God' (Rosenthal, 1990: 55). The public health implications of atomic tests were concealed, despite being recognized inside and outside government circles from the early days, until high profile public declarations by the Clinton administration in the early 1990s – long after the most intensely affected areas had been dubbed 'national sacrifice zones' by activists and critical academics (Davis, 1993). There is, then, clearly much more to the social prioritization of risks and risk behaviour than knowledge-based recognition and rational responses.

Nuclear power has long been recognized as a 'Faustian bargain' even among scientific circles. Part of this bargain has always involved the potential for dual use of nuclear facilities, their capacity for mass destruction or massive power generation. What I want to argue here is that detonation of the first atomic weapons was a kind of founding moment, an event of such intensity that it threatened the integrity of self within those associated with the project. Confronted with an event which exceeded their vocabulary of rational expression the temporary vacuum was filled through other expressions evoking registers widely regarded as irrational. In order to understand the subsequent efforts to reapply rational categories to the nuclear domain within both scientific and political circles it is useful to paraphrase a question posed by Lacan, 'what is it that the physicist desires?' (Lacan, 1979: 10).[9]

Among the answers to this question lay desire for power, control, dominance and omnipotence associated with nuclear weapons and the compensating desire for recompense and reparation associated with the 'peaceful atom'. Perversely the scientific desire for, and pursuit of (rational) power-knowledge over the fundamental forces of nature evoked other registers widely defined as irrational, primitive and instinctual. Far from being secret, from the beginnings of nuclear power, the risk of mass death and the possibility of mass prosperity were actively invoked via pre-existing mythic structures as 'depoliticized speech' (Barthes, 1993: 142) in high profile public discourses. Given these initial expressions of public candour, the analytical challenge becomes one of explaining why these articulations of destruction and prosperity have been steadily withdrawn from the public domain and obscured by secrecy.

My argument here is that public recruitment to a nuclear future via mythic registers proved too unstable and led to the political and scientific need to re-impose rational categories of control and dominance over the nuclear genie. In short there was a driving new desire, a desire to re-impose rational categories on the nuclear domain to re-establish secure functional identities for political and scientific leadership in the nuclear age.[10] In part the re-establishment of rational categories became more and more pressing as public scepticism and ambivalence about the mythic promise of the new technologies began to appear in Britain from the mid-1950s (Welsh, 1993). In this context public desires also play an important part in the selection and prioritization of risk agendas.

To understand this point one has to recognize the depth of transformations in state/citizen relations implicit in the nuclear bargain. Nuclear weapons, for example, transformed political exchange theory by rendering entire populations tradable within ladders of nuclear escalation. After the Second World War it became, in Lacan's words 'a well-known fact that politics is a matter of trading – wholesale in lots, in this context – the same subjects, who are now called citizens, in hundreds of thousands' (Lacan, 1979: 5). In Britain civil nuclear power was the foil to this, holding out the promise of unlimited prosperity congruent with other welfare state promises of provision which emerged almost simultaneously. The separation in the popular mind between nuclear weapons and nuclear power thus mirrored the separation between the warfare and welfare state.

Understanding the role of desire in the social selection of nuclear risks requires an articulation between the desires of military leaders, politicians, constituent publics and Lacan's physicists. As these intersect and influence each other, these desires are not separate categories though they may be separated for analytical purposes. The separation imposed here will flow from physicists, to politicians and military leaders to constituent publics.

Physicists' desires

The quest for atomic weapons encapsulated a wide range of desires within the scientific community. Harnessing usable energy from the atom had been declared impossible by no less a figure than Rutherford in the 1930s. By 1943 the impossible had become the centre of one of the most ambitious scientific projects of the century – the Manhattan Project. This high prestige enterprise to build an atomic bomb was driven by political will fuelled by wartime expediency. Scientists demonstrated their willingness to pursue a goal determined by political representatives and seen as vital to the survival of western civilization itself. At the same time, they operated on a desire to conquer intensely challenging theoretical and engineering problems at the behest of society's elected representatives. This was the physicist war. The risks of success as well as failure were perceived as enormous. There was, for example, widespread scientific speculation about the possibility of nuclear weapons setting the atmosphere on fire. The risk of being beaten to the bomb by Hitler's Germany was patently obvious and overrode all other considerations. Against this background the successful testing of the first atomic bomb evoked the recourse to mythic language noted earlier.

Oppenheimer, head of the American atomic bomb team, wrote that 'we knew the world could never be the same ... I remembered the line from the Hindu scripture the Bhagavad Gita: "Now I am become death, destroyer of worlds"' (cited in Prins, 1983: 65). Oppenheimer's well-documented response resonates with the statements of other eminent scientific figures. The British observer, Sir Edwin Chadwick, declared that it was 'as if God himself appeared among us', it was 'a vision from the book of Revelation' (cited in Prins, 1983: 65). Sir William Penny, head of the British bomb project at Aldermaston, described nuclear power as 'a talisman of his times' (Penny, 1968: 59–63). Lord Cherwell, the British Government's chief scientific advisor during this early nuclear era, echoed the theme when he stated that 'Without atomic weapons we shall be like savages armed with boomerangs and bows and arrows confronting armies with machine guns. Not only will our days as a great power be numbered but we shall be faced with slavery or even extinction' (House of Lords Debates 172: 671).

These specific examples illustrate the general point made, by Margaret Gowing (1978), that in certain respects the official response to this pre-eminent scientific break-through resembled the:

> practice of magic among the most primitive tribes. Having in their possession a fearful image of the god of war, which makes them stronger than all their enemies, the tribe is obsessed with the fear that the image may be stolen or duplicated and their extensive claim to the deity's favour lost. (Gowing, 1978)

The collective horror at the potential for destruction embodied in atomic weapons was balanced by the hope that nuclear energy would be an equally formidable force for good. The late Sir Kelvin Spencer, Chief Government Scientific Advisor at the Ministry of Fuel and Power in the mid-1950s, considered that nuclear energy resembled 'to some small extent ... some sort of redemption for having created this ghastly power for making war' (interview with author 16 June 1981). This hope for nuclear power was completely congruent with the post-war ethos of science as a progressive force vital to the future of democracy which led many scientists with socialist leanings to seek employment in the nuclear power industry in the UK. The vision of substantive transformation inherent in the technology offered by both scientists and popularizers of science extended from projects of global significance like greening deserts to the most mundane level of day-to-day life.

Political and military desires

In the UK the complex of risks confronting the nation in the post-Second World War era became woven into a political fabric which portrayed nuclear prowess as both a practical and symbolic currency of national renewal. The risk of losing 'great nation' status was real, the problems of domestic reconstruction enormous, and the risk of bankruptcy haunted the country throughout the 1950s. The response to the atomic bomb among leading political figures closely resembled those of the scientists involved. Churchill described the event as 'the second coming' (Moran, 1966: 280). I have already quoted the views of his close friend and political ally Cherwell. The US Government issued public assurances that 'substantial patent control had been established to make certain the weapons would not fall into the hands of the enemy (*The Times*, 7 August 1945), substantially underlining Gowing's point about primitivism. In the UK possession of atomic weapons became an imperative, vital to continuing status as a top nation, with the production of plutonium for bombs taking primacy among British nuclear ambitions. Military aspirations were, however, closely tied to civil nuclear developments in terms of both institutional structures and legitimation strategies.

It is here that the political desire for continued international prominence and restored national fortunes can be seen to combine in a positive disposition towards nuclear risk-taking, albeit with the technical and population risks being heavily translated into economic terms. Even allowing for the fact that the early policy documents were extensively written by senior figures within the United Kingdom Atomic Energy Authority (UKAEA) the extent of political recruitment to the science-driven agenda remains hard to account for in purely rational terms. Indeed, it seems reasonable to identify the 1950s as the decade of, what I would term, peak modernity – that period when the desire to believe in the technical advances being promised by wartime developments in physics, cybernetics and general systems theory was readily translated into political will despite the acknowledged risks (See Welsh, 2000).

In the UK these processes are particularly transparent in relation to the launch of the first nuclear power programme in 1955, an event timed to divert domestic public attention from the explosion of Britain's first H-bomb. There was a wider attempt to symbolically recreate a 'Second Elizabethan Age' which provided an opportunity for Britain's fledgling civil nuclear ambitions to be launched by HRH Queen Elizabeth in person. Her valedictory speech placed nuclear power in the context of Britain's glorious past as a continuation of the 'visionary ideals and practical methods which have gone from our shores', and speculated that it may be 'among the greatest of our contributions to human welfare' (*The Times*, 18 October 1956. 1).

Symbolic spectacles such as this apart, the economic and technical risks were openly acknowledged in high profile public discourses including the government's own white paper (HMSO, 1955). J.A. Jukes (1956), economic advisor to the UKAEA, noted that the projected costs of nuclear energy were based on a 'large number of assumptions', stressing that we 'must assume that various problems which are known to exist will be solved successfully'. It would, he warned, 'not be possible to take full advantage of future similar advances unless the risk is also taken that they may not in fact take place'.

> In Britain today we have a rapidly developing atomic energy industry. This new industry is not for the cautious or timid it is one where innovation and experimentation pays and where economic risks must be taken if adequate rewards are to be achieved ... if we are to play our proper part in world affairs we in Britain must remain in the vanguard of technical progress. (Jukes, 1956)

In short the combined effect of these discourses was to assert that it would be profoundly unpatriotic not to take the necessary economic and technical risks even if this meant sacrifices in the short term. In Parliament it was asserted that while 'Britannia no longer rules the seas, it is a certain fact that she rules the isotopes and reactors' (House of Commons Debates 569: 146–9).

At the level of the state then, scientific, military and political desires drove policy in the direction of nuclear expansionism based on positive risk acceptance in both scientific and economic domains. Once injected into the public domain, where it was avidly received in commercial circles, this elite consensus created a tide of euphoria which, in the words of the late Sir Christopher Hinton, 'was impossible to swim against'. Desire had displaced rationality, with criticism over technical or economic risk being immediately read as signifying unpatriotic behaviour, leading to the active marginalization of internal critics and dismissal of public sceptics.

Public desires and nuclear dreams

The attempt to recruit publics to the nuclear future in the USA and the UK involved bombarding them with positive images of nuclear technology which portrayed a transformation of life from the global to the most mundane levels. In Bruno Latour's terms there was massive recruitment to an actor-network. As one popularizer intoned 'perhaps the slogan "Gamma Washes Whiter" will become quite familiar to us when our ultrasonic washing machines are equipped with some gamma source to sterilise shirts and socks and napkins' (Larsen, 1958: 136–7). The apparent exaggeration of this claim pales into insignificance against those of senior scientists whose vision extended to nuclear powered space flight, among other things.

In Britain the public desire for peace and restored prosperity was widespread; in America the public had to become accustomed to the end of isolationism and America's new role as world leader. In terms of the UK the central analytical point here is that the establishment's vision of taking risks for a brighter collective future occurred within the prevailing class relations embodied in the political, military and scientific realms. In short, the public desire to be recruited to the atomic actor-network was mediated by the embedded relations of trust between publics and the various bodies of class-bound expertise. Despite the exhortations towards positive risk acceptance and trust from Britain's eminent cadre of scientific experts, belief and recruitment were never wholehearted.

My basic argument here is that the promise of control and mastery initially extended by physicists had a symbolic resonance with significant desires within political circles, military elites and the wider public milieux which not only insulated nuclearism from critical scrutiny but also created an ambiguous public quiescence in the nuclear adventure. It was the discursive creation of nuclear power as a technology capable of fulfilling political and public desires for a new era of prosperity and peace which ultimately created problems of legitimation for the mythic language through which the breakthrough had initially been legitimated.

By ambiguous quiescence I am invoking the tension between the public desire to believe in the better future on offer and residual scepticism arising from the embedded class and expert relations within governmental and nuclear institutions respectively. In approaching this area it is important not to reify the processes involved in the management of quiescence, since public quiescence requires constant attention and is not a given. In the context of the immediate post-war period the political and public mood of the UK reflected a commitment to collective renewal through collective planning and increasingly rational i.e. technocratic and 'scientific' leadership. In the USA the post-war mood was one of accommodation to the new found position of world leader. In each country military and civil nuclear technology became means by which citizens could share in the realization of these various collective triumphs by association. As I argued earlier, through the example of atom bomb spectators, recruitment even ambiguous recruitment, produces attitudes towards risk and risk behaviours which cannot be interpreted entirely in terms of knowledge and rationality.

UK atmospheric tests were conducted in Aboriginal tribal lands, making a direct comparison with the American example impossible (see Blakeway and Lloyd-Roberts, 1985). Having been invited to share in the establishment's positive disposition towards nuclear risks it might, however, be expected that the strongest enrolment would take place in areas selected for nuclear power stations, structures referred to as 'the cathedrals of our times'. In 1955 and 1956 the first two proposed stations met sufficient local hostility to force heavily contested public inquiries (Welsh, 1993). In 1957 the political and scientific capacity to manage the transition to the nuclear age received a potentially fatal blow when one of the plutonium-producing piles at Windscale caught fire irradiating large tracts of Cumbria and beyond.

Many citizens of West Cumbria had lived with and worked in the nuclear industry since construction began in 1947, developing a set of relevant knowledges while benefiting from a materially high standard of living. Initial press attempts to portray a prosperous local community under headlines like 'All the Advantages of the Atom' (*Daily Express*, 12 October 1957: 1) quickly gave way to reveal the underlying fracture lines inimical to both trust and full recruitment. The Windscale site had a dependency culture with workers relying on managers and experts for information; it was possible said one, 'to work there for ten years and still not know what was going on' (*Manchester Guardian*, 12 October 1957).

The public desire (bolstered initially by sweeping symbolic appeals couched in mythic language) to believe that the risks were worthwhile became increasingly permeated with scepticism. Such scepticism can be seen arising from within a number of discourse coalitions. In a narrow sense the unambiguous desire for success and achievement expressed within scientific, technical and political arenas was discernibly challenged in 1957. Beyond this, the state as 'author' of a number of interlocking discourses, reprised here under the warfare/welfare tensions, clearly failed in a number of respects. Possession of nuclear weapons did not forestall Britain's declining ability to act independently as a geo-political player as the failed Suez expedition in 1956 revealed. Far from nuclear power leading to a new era of economic prominence it led to a paralysing and acrimonious debate between advocates of different types of reactor (Welsh, 1994).

Conclusions

Ionizing radiation formed the paradigm case of Beck's *Risk Society*; as such the nuclear case provides one of the most extensively documented areas containing many generic issues of continued relevance to the academic analysis of risk. The need to recognize the role of collective desires in prioritizing the acceptance of such risks advanced here is not intended to replace approaches emphasizing rationality but to supplement them. I have shown, in collapsed form, how the pursuit of (scientific) power-knowledge raised important symbolic and mythic expressions among scientists, politicians, military leaders and situated publics. The ensuing efforts to rationalize deterrence, nuclear warfighting, and the peaceful atom during the 1960s and 1970s should be seen as a reassertion of the desire for rational control. The successive veneers of rationality used to overlay the mythic primitive responses were vital, as it was only this intensely constructed nuclear rationality which subsequently enabled the establishment to dismiss anti-nuclear views as primitive and irrational.

I would also lay claim to the continued relevance of the insights argued for here. There is an urgent need to become sociologically 'literate in desire' (Copjec, 1995). In an era when the collective aspirations shaping socially articulated desires has been replaced by individualist ones perhaps the clearest example lies in bio-technology and its implicit promise of the perfectly engineered, even immortal body. This apparently free market development has in effect grown from the same institutional networks central to nuclear technology being identified by the European Union, USA and the then USSR as a key technological development node early in the 1980s. Krimsky (1991) shows how US State funding, including a significant military component, combined with venture capital to create a contemporary big risk business.

In terms of academic and political interventions within these new risk horizons it is important not to lose sight of the continued relevance of the situated desire for absolute control. Perhaps more importantly it is vital to recognize the boundary conditions of the new climate of positive risk acceptance which are now set to appeal to both collective and individual desires for a better future. Biotechnology promises to solve world famine and holds out the prospect of 'better' individuals through private means.

In place of pathological desires orchestrated through flirtations with mass destruction lie others conducted through the lure of plenty and immortality. To ignore the power of these discourses of desire would be to misunderstand risk at the start of the twenty-first century.

Notes

1   The precise number of nuclear warheads held by the US and Russian governments is, needless to say, a matter of considerable dispute. Recent press accounts tend to place the figure at 7,900 apiece (under the 1993 Strategic Arms Reduction Treaty or START II, which has yet to be ratified, this number was to drop to 3,500 each), the majority of which are reportedly on 'alert status'; that is, they can be launched on less than 15 minutes notice.

2   The Manhattan Project was a major collaborative project among the Allied Powers which led to the construction in 1945 of the atomic weapons dropped at Hiroshima and Nagasaki.

3   Here Beck's (1996: 32–3) observation that: '[e]xperts are relativized or dethroned by counterexperts' underscores the point that each of the institutional sites within this 'strategic community' is itself continuously criss-crossed by contradictory discourses of expertise. For an account of the patriarchal dimensions of 'nuclear strategic thinking' amongst 'defence intellectuals', see Cohn (1987). For a discussion of the importance of Beck's formulation of 'risk society' for news media studies, see Anderson (1997) and Cottle (1997).

4   Readers of a news account published on the same day in *The Guardian*, a rival British newspaper, are informed of the technological crises associated with the Polaris nuclear submarines, including reports about cracked pipework in the primary cooling system which has caused 'propulsion problems' for the nuclear reactors. Official cost estimates of £12 billion for the fleet of four Trident nuclear submarines are also cited.

5   Arguably, the initial conceptual formulation of this phenomenon is to be credited to Lifton and Falk (1982). Their deployment of 'nuclearism' provides a name for what they consider to be the *deformation* of cultural beliefs and attitudes manifest in the current (globalized) psychological, political and military dependence on nuclear weapons. More precisely, for Lifton and Falk (1982: ix), nuclearism is made to represent 'the embrace of the weapon as a solution to a wide variety of human dilemmas, most ironically that of security'. At the centre of nuclearism as an 'illusory structure', they argue, is a struggle for a sense of power over death: nuclear weapons have become a source of 'vitality' or 'salvation', even of 'symbolic immortality' (1982: 87, 95; see also Allan (1995) for an evaluative assessment of this research literature).

6   In addition to this example, Boyer (1985) offers further evidence to support this theme, including material from the 26 August 1945 issue of the *Washington Post*. He points out that voices in this newspaper were: 'already vigorously discussing whether some type of Star Wars-like defense could be developed to destroy incoming nuclear missiles. A science writer felt sure such a defense was possible – he spoke of 'rays' that would disrupt the missile's control system. The *Post*'s editorial writers, however, were sceptical: 'The possibility of discovering any defense against atom bomb rockets shot from thousands of miles away seems ... out of the question ... As far as we can discover, there is no loophole or joker in this new contract with the devil' (cited in Boyer, 1985: xix).

7   I use the term 'situated desire' here in an analogous manner to that used by Donna Haraway to argue for the significance of 'situated knowledges' see Haraway (1995). The argument that desires are situated and thus mediated within specific social groupings is vital to differentiate the social component of desires from overarching psychoanalytical arguments.

8   Desire is used here as a means of denoting the willingness or necessity of invoking symbolically potent appeals in order to discount risks and uncertainties highlighted by rational scientific discourse. I deal with two main categories of such symbolic supplements to rational discourses here, namely appeals expressed through mythic categories and those mobilized by more instrumental registers such as renewed economic, political and military prominence.

9   My use of Lacan's formulations, here and later, should not be read as the adoption of a Lacanian approach to desire which denotes a 'lack' which can never be fulfilled. On this see Copjec (1995).

10   I am grateful to Stuart Allan for clarifying comments on an earlier formulation of these points.

References

Allan, S. (1995) '"No Truth, No Apocalypse" Investigating the Language of Nuclear War,' in T. McCormack and R. Avery (eds), *Studies in Communications*. Greenwich, CN: JAI Press. pp. 171–214.

Allan, S. (1996) 'Words at War: Canadian Press Coverage of the End of the Cold War', *British Journal of Canadian Studies*, 11 (2): 233–53.

Allan, S. (1997) 'News from NowHere: Televisual News Discourse and the Construction of Hegemony', in A. Bell and P. Garrett (eds), *Approaches to Media Discourse*. Oxford: Blackwell. pp. 105–41.

Anderson, A. (1997) *Media, Culture and the Environment*. London: UCL Press.

Barthes, R. (1993) *Mythologies*. London: Vintage.

Bauman, Z. (1991) *Modernity and Ambivalence*. Cambridge: Polity.

Beck, U. (1992) *Risk Society: Towards a New Modernity*. London: Sage.

Beck, U. (1994) 'The Reinvention of Politics: Towards a Theory of Reflexive Modern-ization', in U. Beck, A. Giddens and S. Lash, *Reflexive Modernization*. Cambridge: Polity. pp. 1–55.

Beck, U. (1995) *Ecological Politics in an Age of Risk*. Cambridge: Polity.

Beck, U. (1996) 'Risk Society and the Provident State,' in S. Lash, B. Szerszynski and B. Wynne (eds), *Risk, Environment and Modernity*. London: Sage. pp. 27–43.

Bijker, W., Pinch, T. and Hughes, T.P. (eds) (1987) *The Social Construction of Technol-ogical Systems: New Directions in the Sociology and History of Technology*. Cambridge, MA: MIT Press.

Blakeway, D. and Lloyd-Roberts, S. (1985) *Fields of Thunder: Testing Britain's Bomb*. London: Unwin.

Bolt, R. (1960) 'Do You Speak Nuclear?', *New Statesman*, LX (1554): 1000–1.

Boyer, P. (1985) *By the Bomb's Early Light: American Thought and Culture at the Dawn of the Atomic Age*. New York: Pantheon Books.

Chilton, P. (ed.) (1985) *Language and the Nuclear Arms Debate.* London: Frances Pinter.

Cohn, C. (1987) 'Sex and Death in the Rational World of Defence Intellectuals', *Signs*, 12 (4): 687–718.

Copjec, J. (1995) *Read My Desire: Lacan Against the Historicists.* London: MIT.

Cottle, S. (1997) 'Ulrich Beck, "Risk Society" and the Media: A Catastrophic View?', *European Journal of Communication*, 12 (4): 429–56.

Davis, M. (1993) 'Deadwest: Eco-cide in Marlboro Country', *New Left Review*, 200: 49–73.

Derrida, J. (1984) 'No Apocalypse, Not Now (Full Speed Ahead, Seven Missiles, Seven Missives)', *Diacritics*, 14 (2): 20–31.

Giddens, A. (1991) *Modernity and Self Identity: Self and Society in the Late Modern Age.* Cambridge: Polity.

Gowing, M. (1978) *Reflections on Atomic Energy History.* Cambridge: Cambridge University Press.

HMSO (1955) A programme of nuclear power, Cmnd 9389. London: HMSO.

Haraway, D. (1995) 'Situated Knowledges: The Science Question in Feminism and the Privilege of Partial Perspective', in A. Feenberg and A. Hannay (eds), *Technology and The Politics of Knowledge.* Indianapolis: Indiana University Press. pp. 175–94.

Hook, G.D. (1985) 'Making Nuclear Weapons Easier to Live With: The Political Role of Language in Nuclearization', *Bulletin of Peace Proposals*, 16 (1): 67–77.

Irwin, A. (1995) *Citizen Science: A Study of People, Expertise and Sustainable Development.* London: Routledge.

Irwin, A. Georg, S. and Vergragt, P. (1994) 'The Social Management of Environmental Change', *Futures*, 26 (3): 323–24.

Irwin, A. and Wynne, B. (eds) (1996) *Misunderstanding Science? The Public Reconstruction of Science and Technology.* Cambridge: Cambridge University Press.

Jasanoff, S., Markle, G.E., Peterson, J.C. and Pinch, T. (1995) *Handbook of Science and Technology Studies.* London: Sage.

Jukes, J.A. (1956) 'Britain in the Atomic Age', *Atomic Energy A Financial Times Survey*, 9 April: 7–10.

Krimsky, S. (1991) *Biotechnics and Society: the Rise of Industrial Genetics.* New York: Praeger.

Lacan, J. (1979) *The Four Fundamental Concepts of Psycho-Analysis.* Harmondsworth: Penguin.

Larsen, E. (1958) *Atomic Energy: A Layman's Guide to the Nuclear Age.* London: Hennel Locke.

Lifton, R.J. and Falk, R. (1982) *Indefensible Weapons.* Toronto: Canadian Broadcasting Corporation.

Lifton, R.J. and Markusen, E. (1990) *The Genocidal Mentality.* New York: Basic Books.

McKechnie, R. (1996) 'Insiders and Outsiders: Identifying Experts on Home Ground', in A. Irwin and B. Wynne (eds), *Misunderstanding Science? The Public Reconstruction of Science and Technology.* Cambridge: Cambridge University Press.

Macgill, S. (1987) *The Politics of Anxiety.* London: *Sellafield's Cancer-Link Controversy*: Pion.

Moran, Lord (1966) *The Prof in Two Worlds.* London: Collins.

Penny, W. (1968) Untitled. *Atom*, (137): 59–63.

Prins, G. (1983) *Defended to Death: A Study of the Nuclear Arms Race.* Harmondsworth: Penguin.

Rosenthal, D. (1990) *At the Heart of the Bomb.* Wokingham: Addison-Wesley.

Ruthven, K. (1993) *Nuclear Criticism.* Victoria: Melbourne University Press.

Schiappa, E. (1989) 'The Rhetoric of Nukespeak', *Communication Monographs*, 56 (3): 253–72.

Spinardi, G. (1997) 'Aldermaston and British Nuclear Weapons Development: Testing the "Zuckerman Thesis"', *Social Studies of Science*, 27: 547–82.

Weart, S.R. (1988) *Nuclear Fear: A History of Images.* Cambridge, MA: Harvard University Press.

Welsh, I. (1993) 'The NIMBY Syndrome: Its Significance in the History of the Nuclear Debate in Britain', *British Journal for the History of Science*, 26: 15–32.

Welsh, I. (1994) 'Letting The Research Tail Wag the End-user's Dog: The Powell Committee and UK Reactor Choice', *Science and Public Policy*, 21 (1): 43–53.

Welsh, I. (2000) *Mobilizing Modernity: The Nuclear Moment*. London: Routledge.

Wynne, B. (1982) *Rationality and Ritual: The Windscale Inquiry and Nuclear Decisions in Britain*. Chalfont St. Giles: British Society for the History of Science.

Yearley, S. (1996) 'Nature's Advocates: Putting Science to Work in Environmental Organizations', in A. Irwin and B. Wynne (eds), *Misunderstanding Science? The Public Reconstruction of Science and Technology*. Cambridge: Cambridge University Press. pp. 172–90.

Zonabend, F. (1993) *The Nuclear Peninsula*. Cambridge: Cambridge University Press.

5

Genotechnology: Three Challenges to Risk Legitimation

Lindsay Prior, Peter Glasner and Ruth McNally

INTRODUCTION
(*Lindsay Prior*)

According to Jacob (1974), somewhere near the end of the nineteenth century and the beginning of the twentieth century the science of biology fractured into several sub-disciplines – each focusing on distinct objects of study and adopting clearly differentiated strategies of investigation. Of the emergent objects, two in particular came to dominate twentieth century scientific discourse; the gene and the molecule. Clearly, it was in relation to these objects that the modern sciences of genetics and biochemistry developed.

Genetics, of course, focused mainly on the study of populations or species. The attendant technology was pivoted on the practices of selective breeding and its theory was underpinned by statistics. So much was this the case that at the turn of the century Pearson confidently argued that genetics was, 'in the first place statistical, in the second place statistical and only in the third place biological' (1930: 3, 128). Biochemistry on the other hand took as its focus of study the cell and attempted to elaborate upon the order within rather than the relations between individuals in a population. Only during the second half of the twentieth century, and after the emergence of knowledge concerning the structure of DNA, did the two strands of inquiry intertwine, and recombine as it were, to form what is sometimes called the new genetics. And only after that recombination did the possibilities for new technologies of genetic engineering arise.

This contrast between a focus on order within the organism as against a study of order in the relations between organisms (that is, order at the level of populations), offers us a ready frame through which problems of risk may be viewed. In human terms, of course, few of us worry much about the fate of the species as a whole, or of the slow and languid process of adaptation by means of which our collective destiny will be revealed. Instead we are more usually concerned with our personal and individual fates in the here and now – whether we might fall subject to this or that pathology, whether or not there is a risk in our eating genetically engineered foods, or what the personal consequences of releasing designer viruses into the environment might be for ourselves or our near relatives. Naturally, in the vast panorama of eternity what is a risk for the individual can signal a risk for the species as a whole, especially if too many critical incidents occur over too short a period of time. Yet, the ways in which genetic risks are identified, framed, packaged and translated for public consumption frequently serve so as to block out the problems relating to collectivities and to highlight merely the particular, the singular and the personal. Indeed, one might argue that the ways in which genetic risks are understood and perceived have relatively little to do with genetics or bio-chemistry *per se*. For the processes of identification and translation are ultimately social, cultural and political ones. Not surprisingly, perhaps, it is essentially these latter processes which are discussed and surveyed in the sections below.

In the opening section, Lindsay Prior argues that in the modern world questions of risk have been effectively transposed into questions of probability, and that probability assessments can only be derived from studies of collectives and collectivities. At the twentieth century's end, however, it would seem that there is a distinct process under way whereby assessments of risk have been privatized in such a manner as to make it seem as if it was individuals rather than populations that carry genetic risks. Yet by definition, if nothing else, the human genome and its aberrations belong to all.

This is followed with a contribution from Peter Glasner. It is structured in terms of C.W. Mills' distinction between public issues and personal troubles. The 'public issues' in this instance are those which flow in the train of the Human Genome Project (HGP), and the private troubles are those concerning everyday anxieties about possible genetic predispositions to identifiable medical pathologies (such as breast cancer). The question is, how can a lay public potentially subject to such pathology interface with, and participate in, the scientific project? For it cannot be the case, as some might argue, that a cadre of technocrats should simply hand down expert knowledge about attendant risks to a relatively ignorant public. Not least because, as Glasner argues, '[a]ny discussion of risk is as much about culture, institutions, perceptions, control, and activity as it is about how risks are framed by experts' (p. 111).

The final section by Ruth McNally adopts the question of risk in the context of Actor-Network Theory. In particular she outlines the ways in which vaccine producers, national state agencies (such as MAFF), the European Commission and a genetically engineered virus have been enrolled into a struggle against the risk from rabies in the European Union. In so doing she provides a concrete empirical instance of the ways in which a specific risk has been identified, edited and translated into a form suitable for public consumption.

MATHEMATICS, RISK AND GENETICS
(Lindsay Prior)

In this section I intend to focus my attention on mathematical concepts of probability in order to indicate how risk is essentially a property of collectives rather than of individuals. Risk and probability are not, of course, synonymous, but since all quantitative (and many qualitative) assessments of risk are framed in terms of the language of chance and/or probability (Adams, 1995), the transposition seems justified.

According to contemporary historians of probability theory (Crombie, 1994; Daston, 1988; Gigerenzer et al., 1989; Hacking, 1975,1990; Hald, 1990; Krüger et al., 1987), the modern world opens without a place for chance for, as Ian Hacking has argued, the only space in which chance could operate was 'a space repugnant to reason' (1990: 13). Toward the end of the seventeenth century, however, a new vista on chance began to open. The entry to the new panorama was discovered by the mathematicians and their first point of contact was with what are commonly called the games of chance. So whereas in the pre-modern world the fall of the dice or the receipt of a playing card appeared to be entirely haphazard, in the world of the late-seventeenth century such things came to be recognized as precisely calculable. Thus the chance of throwing two sixes with two throws of a six sided dice was calculable as 1/36; the chance of selecting a three from a full pack of cards as 1/13, and the chance of obtaining three heads with three tosses of an unbiased coin as 1/8.

The selection of a card, the toss of a coin and the fall of the face of a dice invoke what we now call a priori independent equiprobable outcomes, and it was around consideration of such outcomes that probability theory seems to have languished during the long eighteenth century. Yet, even during that century it had become clear that there were some events in the universe that did not take an equiprobable form. One set of events of this kind related to the chances of life and death, and according to Daston (1988) it was consideration of such events that served as the catalyst for a new nineteenth-century theory of probability.

The early probabilists had argued that the probability of an event occurring in any given population – whether that population be of cards, people or asteroids – lay not so much in the event itself as in our subjective expectation of it. Thus, given a priori equiprobable assessments we might, for example, expect to obtain a 'six' in six throws of fair dice, and we might expect to obtain heads in about half of every batch of coin tossing experiments – but we may be, and frequently are, disappointed in a particular empirical outcome. The same would be true of our 'expectation of life'. A given man or woman might be expected to live for many years, but empirical events may conspire to cut his or her expectation short.

During the nineteenth century, however, and for various reasons, this subjective notion of probability came to be regarded as mathematically and philosophically unsatisfactory. In its place was developed a new concept of chance. It was a concept that was to have a major impact on mathematics, physics, biology and the social sciences. In retrospect it was a simple yet stunning strategy. Its beauty lay in the fact that it forsook a concern with the singular and unique, the particular and the individual, and focused instead on the properties of the collective.

A clue to the new theory was provided by J.S. Mill in the very first edition of his *Logic* (1843), when he stated that, 'To be able to pronounce two events equally probable ... experience must have shown that the two events are equally frequent' (2: 71). And this interpretation of probability as reflecting a long-term relative frequency of events served to mark off the nineteenth and twentieth century interpretations of the concept from their eighteenth century counterparts.

(Strangely, Mill himself reverted to a subjectivist theory of probability in later editions of his work.)

The second, frequentist interpretation of the concept of probability was of course more attuned to the demands of a newly emergent social science which, following the precepts of Quetelet, Poisson and the like, tended to pivot around the study of large numbers. For when we study large populations, the perturbations evident from a study of individual heights, weights, wishes, demands and behaviour, are smoothed out and patterns can be seen to emerge. Somewhat inevitably then, it was the frequentist interpretation that came to dominate the social sciences during the nineteenth and twentieth centuries. More interestingly, perhaps it was this interpretation which dominated the science of statistical mechanics, and the study of genetics. Indeed, one might go as far as to argue that without this interpretation the entire edifice of mathematical statistics itself may well have collapsed.

During the 1920s, Von Mises (1957/[1928]: 83) was to plead that it was the emphasis on the collective, evident in modern physics, that stimulated the development of his own concept of probability, and which led him to produce what is undoubtedly the most robust defence of the frequency theory ever written. Moreover, the accent on the collective was, in various contexts, to reappear in twentieth century work on topics as diverse as the general epidemic model, the (Hardy-Weinberg) law of genetic equilibrium and the study of Brownian motion. In the framework of the philosophy of mathematics it was also a focus much favoured by the likes of Popper (1959/[1935]), Reichenbach (1949), and the aforementioned Von Mises – each of whom argued that the concept of probability only has meaning in as far as it refers to the limiting value of a relative frequency in long series of observations. (During the twentieth century new and novel modifications to the frequentist and the subjectivist theories of probability were made and useful overviews of such theories are provided by Black, 1967 and Sklar, 1993.)

Given its significance, perhaps I could illustrate the nature of the frequency theory of probability with an example. Imagine a series of events that either occur or fail to occur. Say, the birth of girl babies as against boy babies in a single country during a single year, or the presence/absence of accidents among individuals in a three month period, or the presence/absence of genetic markers in a sample population, or red/green traffic lights along a 1000 kilometre journey or whatever. All such events can be symbolized as a series of ones and noughts thus:

$$0\ 0\ 1\ 0\ 1\ 0\ 1\ 0\ 0\ 0\ 0\ 1\ 0\ 0\ 1$$

We therefore have 15 'events' in all, and the probability of an event occurring can be easily determined by simply adding up all of the 'ones' in the series. Thus:

$$p = 0, 0, (1/3), (1/4), (2/5), (1/3), (3/7), (3/8), (1/3), (3/10), (3/11), (1/3), (4/13), (2/7), (1/3)$$

So, in my example, the long run relative frequency is 1/3 and it is this kind of a fraction to which we refer when we use the term probability. I will simply emphasize, without labouring the point, that it is quite clear that the probability belongs to the series and not to the individual events. In short, probability is the property of a collective.

Clearly, probability assessments in the realm of genetics must have the same mathematical basis as the above, and consequently genetic risk must also be considered as a property of populations rather than of singular individuals. (In the strict sense of course a single, unique event cannot, by definition, be assessed in probabilistic terms.) Indeed it was this insight which enabled the English geneticist G.H. Hardy and (independently) the German mathematician-geneticist, Weinberg, to propose the use of simple probability models in population genetics. For example, according to the Hardy-Weinberg law of genetic equilibrium, in any large population where discrete generations reproduce by random mating, the distribution of a gene with two alleles can be modelled by the function $(p + q)^2$. That is AA, Aa, and aa would be distributed in the proportions p^2, $2pq$, q^2.

This result is surely one of the most magnificent in all of population genetics. Not least because it highlights the absolute stupidity of any eugenic programme, and the poverty of thought which was and is associated with those who advocate a focus on the individual as a source of genetic 'risk'. Indeed, it was results of this kind which enabled Penrose to finally understand why haemophiliacs are always with us and why those with 'amentia' (later called mental handicap), are present in all populations despite the fact that such individuals rarely reproduce in any numbers. To follow their insight simply assume that a recessive and 'damaging' allele has a low probability (say 0.01), and carry out the calculations. The results will tell you that the unwanted condition will be evident in only 0.0001 of the population. The recessive allele, however, will be carried by 0.0198 of the population (that is the Aa's). In other the words, the risk belongs to all and not simply to the singular and isolated individual.

RISKS, THE PUBLIC AND THE HUMAN GENOME PROJECT
(Peter Glasner)[1]

If, as C.W. Mills (1970) suggested, the essential project of sociology is to use the imagination to 'grasp history and biography and the relations between the two in society', we must accept his stricture to uncover the relationships between 'the personal troubles of milieu', and 'the public issues of social structure'. This means we must 'range from the most personal and remote transformations to the most intimate features of the human self'. Mapping and sequencing the human genome, while constituting an example of De Solla Price's (1963) Big Science project, is unlike many of the new technologies in that it directly affects all of us at a very personal level. It poses a threat to the boundary between ourself and others in a way quite different from, for example, the virtual realities of the new electronic technologies (Bloomfield and Verdubakis, 1995; Jones, 1995; Glasner, 1996), which liberate individuals from their particular social and biological characteristics (gender, class, ethnicity, age, etc.). In genotechnologies, the connections are obscured, and the boundaries defined by (predominantly) medical experts (Carter, 1995; Gieryn, 1994).

The Human Genome Project (HGP)

HGP, an international programme costing billions of dollars, has been likened to the biological sciences' equivalent of landing on the moon (see, for example, Cook-Degan, 1994). In 1988, an organization called HUGO, the Human Genome Organization, described as 'United Nations' for the Human Genome, was established to *inter alia* encourage public debate on the ethical, social, legal, and commercial implications of the project (Bishop and Waldholz, 1990). These include fairness in the use of genetic information in, for example, employment; the impact of knowledge on the individual through stigmatization and labelling, issues of privacy and confidentiality; impact on genetic counselling and reproductive decisions; issues of education, standards and quality in medical practice; the past uses and misuses of genetics; and commercialization and other intellectual property rights. HUGO has signally failed to address these in a concerted fashion at this time (Glasner, 1993).

Others have been less reticent, writing about for example the reductionist nature of the project (Lewontin, 1993), with its attendant danger of a resurgence of eugenicism; its impact on reproductive technologies (Stacey, 1992); its use in employment and insurance areas (Nelkin and Tancredi, 1994); its application to policing and the law (Lander, 1992); and the possibilities which arise from commercial exploitation – patenting 'life' itself (Cook-Degan, 1994).

British scientists initially involved in the project generally argued that the HGP posed no new ethical problems for society to address. This was most evident during the complicated processes of 'enrolment' and 'translation' (to use the actor-network terminology of Latour) needed to ensure the funding of the project in the late 1980s (Balmer, 1993). At the Royal Society meeting on 'Genes, Ethics, and Embryos' in 1991, the view expressed was that this research did, however, place emphasis on *existing* dilemmas (Brenner, 1991) even if no new ones were apparent. In a recent survey a substantial proportion of scientists involved in the UK HGP were of the opinion that their work did indeed pose *new* ethical problems (Glasner et al., 1995). The views of these respondents, working away from the political epicentre with its policy-oriented concerns for the shaping and funding of research in molecular biology, are probably more representative of laboratory scientists. One suggested that opinion about the novelty of ethical issues in this area depended on whether the focus was on the present use of discoveries already made, or the uses to which they may be put in the future. It is the latter which should exercise the public more.

Public participation in technological and scientific decision-making

In the spirit of Mills' sociological imagination, we might, therefore, usefully address the issue of public participation in decision-making in this key area. We already know that within Europe, public knowledge and concern about the impact of the new genetic technologies is differentially located. Thus, for example, the northern European countries tend to be more active and informed than those in the south. We also know that within the former, the issues are given greatest prominence in Denmark and Germany. The best informed groups in Europe are men, the young, and the financially better off (Marlier, 1992; Terragni, 1992). In comparison with the United States, however, the Europeans are much less critical about scientific and technological advances in general, and medical advances in particular (Evans and Durant, 1989). HGP straddles all three areas: science, technology and medicine.

This recognition of the contextual nature of expert knowledge is reflected at the micro as well as the macro level. Recent studies in the sociology of science and technology have done much to dispel the simplistic view of an 'ignorant' public faced with a superior array of technical experts whose mission is to fill their deficiencies of knowledge (Irwin and Wynne, 1996). Scientists, wedded as they like to think to approaching all problems coolly, calmly and rationally, work with a stereotype of the public as emotional and irrational as well as sadly ignorant. We have learnt that what counts as a fact is actually problematic. Risk as a concept should be seen as situated, contextualized and negotiated. Any discussion of risk is as much about culture, institutions, perceptions, control, and activity as it is about how risks are framed by experts (Douglas, 1985). Studies have shown that disputes between experts are not only normal but often conducted in rhetorical rather than empirical terms (see, for example, Nelkin, 1985).

Significantly, for both Giddens (1990) and Beck (1992), expertise is also a temporary phenomenon, since the development of new knowledge coupled with the new reflexivity, results in a continuing process of expert replacement. Knowledge, for Giddens, becomes valid only until further notice. In this way, in a culture faced by society-wide hazards, the concept of 'expert' becomes problematic. Experts in the fields of medicine, as well as science, may be held to be no more expert than knowledgeable and informed lay people in certain circumstances. But, as Giddens notes, while the key to late modern risk society is knowledge, such knowledge may not be distributed equally. In addition, it is likely to be rooted in differential experience, and may, as a result, be opaque in practice.

The perceived risks associated with mapping the Human Genome are not part of a futuristic, Jurassic Park-inspired, doomsday scenario (Nelkin and Lindee, 1995). To think that the public perceives them as such is to fall, as Sydney Brenner (who gave HUGO its name) often seems to, into stereotyping the public in a most unscientific way. Of course there are no new ethical problems associated with HGP if you think that those who pose them are off the wall.

The issue, then, is how best to constitute fora in which less stereotypical exchanges can take place. The list is extensive, ranging as it does from science shops, citizens' courts and scenario workshops to public representation on advisory groups and consensus conferences (Irwin, 1995). On the only recent occasion when scientists voluntarily called a halt to their research, following the publication of the 'Berg letter' calling for a moratorium on experiments using genetic engineering techniques in 1974, public involvement in the USA took the form of local, lay citizens' courts (Krimsky, 1982), while Britain involved representatives of 'the public interest' in its national, Genetic Manipulation Advisory Group (Bennett et al., 1986). Consensus Conferences originated in the United

States in the late 1970s with the first dealing with breast cancer screening. The UK held its first national Consensus Conference on Biotechnology in 1994 in London, but this focused on plants rather than humans or animals (Joss and Durant, 1995). All of these different methods exhibit both strengths and weaknesses, with the most participatory (by lay people) suffering from lack of representativeness, and only reaching a small proportion of the public (Fiorino, 1990).

Conclusion

These examples do not prevent experts defining the boundaries of risk (Purdue, 1995). However, they help the public identify the existence of such boundaries in an environment which attempts to reverse the coercive (Douglas, 1985: 59) privileging of 'boundary' over the 'connections' between adjacent spaces such as 'us' and 'them' (Carter, 1995). These connections, as I suggested earlier, are more obscure as well as more personal in the genotechnologies. As illustrated in a recent television programme on the hereditary characteristics of breast cancer in women, the problems are as much about whether to find out if you are genetically predisposed, and with what associated risk, as they are about whether to have a double radical mastectomy. C. Wright Mills' injunction to link personal troubles with the public issues is thrown into stark relief when scientific and technological advance poses questions of such complexity, ignores the fact that those who receive them are poorly equipped to come to their own conclusions, and sidelines further discussion as the responsibility of the professional ethicist. As Beck (1995) notes, there appears to be an obligation by society to cross the boundary between safety and risk before being in a position to make even a qualified decision. I am reminded of the words of the rocket scientist, who joined the US space race after the Second World War, and who is purported to have justified his work with the observation: 'I aimed at the stars, but I hit London'.

STRATEGIC USE OF 'RISK' IN GENE TECHNOLOGY: THE EUROPEAN RABIES ERADICATION PROGRAMME[2]
(Ruth McNally)

Rabies has been in the news, following pressure from Chris Patten, former Governor of Hong Kong, and the interest groups 'Passport for Pets' and 'Vets in Support of Change'. From January 2000 a pet passport scheme will be piloted under which, quarantine restrictions will be dropped for rabies-free cats and dogs travelling from Western Europe (Meikle, 1999). In coverage of the debate in British and European newspapers, magazines, on the radio and on television, you may have noticed a reference to the European rabies eradication programme. By the year 2000, it was claimed, the European Union (EU) would be rabies-free, thanks to a European Community (EC) initiative to immunize foxes against rabies with a vaccine called Raboral V-RG. Portrayed in this way one would consider this to be an entirely laudable goal. However, there is no such thing as a free lunch. In this case, the price of a rabies-free Europe could be a new viral epidemic caused by the vaccine itself, which is a living genetically engineered virus. This section tells the story of the programme to eradicate rabies from the EU using Raboral V-RG. I have previously applied Actor-Network Theory for this case study to illustrate innovation through translation[3]. In this section, I focus on two theoretical aspects of risk: the strategic use of a 'natural' risk to justify the taking of a 'technological one'; and risk assessment as a 'rite of passage' for achieving closure on debate about 'technological risk'.

Raboral V RG

Since 1987 millions of genetically engineered viruses have been released in the European Union (EU). The virus – Raboral V-RG – is a genetically engineered hybrid resulting from the insertion of part of the rabies virus (glycoprotein GcDNA from strain ERA) into the genome of vaccinia virus (Copenhagen strain). It is a living hybrid organism – a vaccinia virus which expresses a rabies virus protein. It is also a vaccine, whose purpose is to immunize foxes against infection with the rabies virus. Risk assessment of genetically engineered organisms which are released into the environment falls into three categories: safety, containment, and genetic stability. Below I briefly summarize the risks of Raboral V-RG under these three categories.

Safety

Data on the human health risks of vaccinia virus have been collected following its use by the World Health Organization (WHO) as a vaccine to eradicate smallpox. Vaccinia is a minor human pathogen causing impaired vision, eczema, neurological symptoms and even death in some susceptible people. While human health experts considered the risks of vaccinia to be acceptable when smallpox was widespread, they now argue that the disease's eradication is a strong contraindication to any further immunization with vaccinia. In addition to which, the US Department of Agriculture concluded that the safety of Raboral V-RG (genetically engineered vaccinia) in humans is unknown, and that it would be unwise to draw conclusions concerning human safety from observations of experimental animals.

Containment

The method of vaccinating wild foxes is oral vaccination. Raboral V-RG is loaded into edible bait which is then dropped onto field sites from the air. Each bait contains 10^8 TCID$_{50}$ (tissue culture infectious doses), the equivalent of 100 million viruses, and the baits are dropped twice a year, at a density of 15 baits per km^2 per drop. Millions of copies of this novel virus are being dropped onto the countryside in France, Belgium and Luxembourg as part of the European rabies eradication programme. This makes these releases among the largest authorized open field releases of genetically engineered organisms anywhere in the world.

The idea is that when foxes eat the bait, the virus inside will immunize them against rabies. In due course, it is argued, if enough of these baits are dropped, a sufficient proportion of the fox population will become immunized to eradicate rabies from the EU. However, although intended for foxes, the bait containing the vaccine can be eaten by other animals. Animals that might come into contact with and/or eat the bait include cats, dogs, badgers, hedgehogs, hares, rats, mice, voles, squirrels, and birds. The researchers claim that the genetic engineering of vaccinia has not changed its host range. However, this is not very reassuring since its host range includes humans, cows, rabbits, pigs, sheep and rodents.

There is historical evidence that vaccinia has been transmitted from one organism to another. During the smallpox vaccination campaign, it was transmitted from vaccinated humans to non-vaccinated humans. It has also spread from vaccinated humans to dairy cows, and from cows to farm workers in El Salvador. It is also suspected of having become established outside of the laboratory in India, where a virus believed to be a variant of vaccinia used in the smallpox eradication programme has become established in buffaloes, causing a kind of buffalopox. Raboral V-RG is also alleged to have been transmitted from vaccinated cows to workers when used at an experimental farm in Argentina.

Genetic Stability

Genetic recombination is a process in which one piece of DNA or RNA exchanges parts with another. The more similar the two genetic molecules are, the more likely they are to recombine (hybridize) with each other. Vaccinia is a member of the family of pox viruses, which includes cowpox, monkeypox, camelpox, variola and ectromelia, and pox virus family members readily hybridize with each other in the laboratory.

The host range of vaccinia overlaps with the host ranges of other pox viruses, which gives rise to the risk that the bait containing genetically engineered vaccinia could be eaten by, or transmitted to, animals already harbouring another pox virus. If genetic recombination between Raboral V-RG and another pox virus were to occur, the properties of the resulting virus would be unknown.

A particular risk is posed by the cowpox virus. Contrary to its name, the most commonly reported host of cowpox virus is the domestic cat. Virologists believe it may also be maintained in small wild mammals where, because it is not pathogenic, it is undetected. One route of human infection by Raboral V-RG (or a mutant version of it) would be via pet cats which prey on small mammals which have eaten the bait.

Six years after the first release of genetically engineered vaccinia in Europe, Raboral V-RG researchers stated that 'the eventual risk of recombination with orthodox viruses which might exist in wildlife still needs to be investigated' (Boulanger et al., 1992, 1993). Yet in October 1993 the European Commission gave written consent under the deliberate release Directive 90/220/EEC to place Raboral V-RG on the market for use in aerially distributed bait as a vaccine against rabies in rural populations, and in November 1994 the vaccine was given a favourable evaluation as a veterinary medicine under Directive 87/22/EEC. Moreover, the European Commission has not only given consent to the release of Raboral V-RG, but has also funded its development, and it is used in the EC rabies eradication programme.

In the following sections I use actor network theory in an attempt to explain how such a risky, genetically engineered virus could gain regulatory approval in the EC.[3]

Actor-Network Theory

Actor-Network Theory is a form of story-telling in which the story teller describes events in terms of the attempts of an 'enrolling actor' to build an Actor-Network – a constellation of human and non-human actors. In the course of 'enrolment' in the Actor-Network, the identities of the actors are 'translated': among the competing identities which they might have, a particular identity, which is compatible with the strategy of the enrolling actor, is adopted. The Actor-Network I am going to describe comprises the vaccine producers (to whom I have allocated the role of the enrolling actors), fox rabies, the institutions of the EC (especially the Commission), and Raboral V-RG. The story is as follows.

In the beginning ...

When the Raboral V-RG vaccine was developed in the early 1980s, the enrolling actors had produced a living genetically engineered virus designed to immunize a range of animals against rabies infection. What they required were target populations of animals at risk of rabies in which there was sufficient economic interest to create a market for the vaccine. Furthermore, in order to bring in a financial return, Raboral V-RG required the appropriate product licences.

One such target population they identified was cattle in Argentina. This field trial was terminated when it was alleged it was being conducted without the consent of the Argentinean authorities, that it violated ethical and legal principles, and that farm workers had become infected with the virus. Another target population they identified was wild racoons in the USA. A third target population was foxes in the EU, where rabies was endemic in fox populations in France, Belgium, and Germany and also present in Luxembourg and Italy.

In order to build the actor-network in the EU, the vaccine producers required regulatory approval for the vaccine from the EC institutions. The question for the vaccine producers was how to enrol these institutions in the Raboral V-RG network? The methods by which the enrolling actor enrols others in the actor-network is called 'translation'. One method of translation is 'problematization' whereby the enrolling actor defines a general problem which can only be resolved by the solution of a much more specific problem posed by the enrolling actor (see Callon et al., 1986). In this case, the general problem was rabies, the specific problem was fox rabies and the solution – the 'obligatory passage point' – was Raboral V-RG.

The problematization of fox rabies

The strategy for the problematization of fox rabies is most clearly illustrated by the Ministry of Agriculture, Fisheries and Food's (MAFF) attempts to persuade travellers of the need for pet quarantine. Although the vaccine producer's methods were not as graphic, they used the same principles (see, for example, Brochier et al., 1991).

On entering the port of Dover, having crossed the Channel from Calais on a ferry, you cannot fail to notice multiple copies of a huge poster displayed at immigration control. The poster, published by the MAFF, pictures a young girl cuddling a cat underneath the heading: 'It's this easy to pick up rabies'. The picture and the heading above it suggest that the young girl is at risk of 'picking up' rabies from the cat she has brought back with her from the Continent. However, if the cat has merely come from another EU Member State, the probability that it will give her rabies is virtually zero. This is because the type of rabies which is endemic on the Continent differs in significant ways from canine rabies which is endemic in Asia and Africa.

The type of rabies on the Continent is fox-adapted and is not very threatening to other species. The victims of a bite from a rabid fox can only pass the disease back to another fox. Since 1977, when the WHO began collecting data, there have been no reported human deaths from indigenously-contracted rabies in EU countries. The last such case in France was in 1928. The little girl in the poster is not at risk of 'picking up' fox rabies from her pet cat. I suggest that what the poster illustrates is the translation of fox rabies into an organism with the characteristics of canine rabies. Indeed, the representation of fox rabies as canine rabies in this poster and in the media generally is so successful that most people are unaware that the translation has taken place. Both the MAFF in this poster, and the vaccine producers in their documents on Raboral V-RG, have problematized fox rabies as if it posed the same risks as canine rabies.

Enrolling the EC institutions

In order to become enrolled in the actor-network, the EC institutions must consider it to be in their interests to perceive fox rabies as a serious problem and adopt Raboral V-RG as the solution. Here I suggest what these interests might be.

Firstly, like any sovereign power, the European Commission is liable to crises of legitimation. By enrolling in the actor-network, the European Commission can assume a heroic role: the protector of EU citizens from the terrible scourge of rabies.

Secondly, the vaccine itself provides a much needed flagship for the genetic engineering industry, an industry identified by the European Commission as crucial to European economic growth, competitiveness and employment, but which often seems to be a technology in search of a marketable product.

Thirdly, the eradication of rabies from the EU would transform it into one pure free zone in which livestock, people and their pets could circulate freely, thereby removing one of the obstacles against the realization of the ideals of the Single European Act 1986.

Whether for these strategic reasons or for others, the EC institutions did indeed enrol in the actor-network as sponsors, regulators and users of Raboral V-RG. Once enrolled, the EC institutions had an interest in combining forces with the vaccine producers in translating Raboral V-RG into its ideal identity so that it too could join the network.[4]

Enrolling Raboral V-RG

The ideal identity of the genetically engineered virus in the network is as a safe, veterinary pharmaceutical product – a vaccine which is effective in eradicating fox rabies. However, the virus has other identities in competition with this ideal identity, for example, a new genetic construct with unpredictable properties, and a living virus with the potential to cause harm, spread and mutate. These competing identities were obstacles to its enrolment as a safe vaccine to be aerially distributed in the open countryside. A method of translation was needed whereby the virus could be stripped of these competing identities. Fortunately for the enrolling actors, a method for such a translation already existed. As a 'rite of passage', the regulatory process itself performed the necessary translation under Directives 90/220/EEC and 87/22/EEC.

In order to enter the regulatory process, the vaccine producers had to compile a technical dossier evaluating foreseeable risks of the genetically engineered virus. Compiling such a dossier was both costly and time-consuming. However, the European Commission proved a useful ally in this task by supplying financial support for gathering information for the dossier under the various biotechnology programmes.

Even with such support, convincing data for the translation could not be gathered fast enough. At the same time as the dossier was being submitted to European Commission regulators, European Commission-funded researchers were reporting to the European Commission that they had not yet completed their risk-assessment research, and that further work was necessary (see Crouch et al., 1993; Skinner et al., 1993).

But this lack of risk-assessment data was not an obstacle because both of these Directives are themselves hybrids. On the one hand, they are measures to protect human health and the environment, and to ensure that veterinary pharmaceuticals are safe, efficacious and pure. On the other hand, they are measures for the completion of the internal market. Thus, the protection of the environment and human health under Directive 90/220/EEC is not paramount; in the event of a difference of opinion between the Member States the matter is decided by a qualified majority vote among the Member States. Provided the number of dissenting votes is below the specified majority, consent is given (the EC's version of quantified risk assessment!). With risk assessment thus reduced to the ballot box, and with only Germany (incidentally, the Member State with the highest level of fox rabies) dissenting, Raboral V-RG successfully completed its passage through the regulatory process.

The virus entered the risk-assessment process as a bundle of competing identities and emerged as just one: a safe and efficacious licensed product for the eradication of fox rabies. Thus translated by the rite of passage through the regulatory process, the virus could take its place in the actor-network as a safe, efficacious veterinary vaccine for use in the campaign to eradicate rabies from the EU.

The enrolment of fox rabies?

The story might be considered to be complete at this stage. The EC institutions have been enrolled and so has Raboral V-RG. But what about fox rabies? Has it assumed its ideal identity in the network, yielded to Raboral V-RG, and been banished from the EU? No and nor is it likely to be.

According to the Commission's Scientific Veterinary Committee on Rabies (1997), the rabies eradication campaign has dramatically reduced the number of fox rabies cases in Belgium, France, Luxembourg and Germany. However, the EU itself is undergoing a constant translation by its enlargement to the east. Fox rabies is believed to have originated in Poland and it is even more prevalent in Eastern Europe than in existing EU Member States. With every eastward enlargement, the realization of the goal of a rabies-freee EU retreats[5].

Translation of Raboral V-RG?

And what about Raboral V-RG? What is there to prevent Raboral V-RG from resisting its enrolment as a safe, predictable product, and expressing itself as a pathogenic, infectious, mutating organism? Nothing except the Network. As long as the Network is stable, Raboral V-RG will retain its identity as an effective vaccine. However, destablize the network, alter the risk-assessment procedure, change the representation of risks of fox rabies – and the saliences could be reversed: Raboral V-RG could be perceived as the problem and not the solution.

Notes

1   An extended version of Peter Glasner's section appeared in Adam, B., Allan, S. and Carter, C. (eds) (1999) *Environmental Risks and the Media.* London: Routledge.

2   Ruth McNally's section is based on the following published papers: McNally, R. (1995) 'Mad Dogs or Jackasses: The European Rabies Eradication Programme', in P. Wheale and R. McNally (eds), *Animal Genetic Engineering: of Pigs, Oncomice and Men.* London: Pluto Press. pp. 109–23; McNally, R. (1995) 'Genetic Madness: The European Rabies Eradication Programme', *The Ecologist,* 24 (6): 207–12; McNally, R. (1996) 'Political Problems: Genetically Engineered Solutions: The Socio-technical Translations of Fox Rabies', in A. van Dommelen (ed.), *Coping with Deliberate Release: The Limits of Risk-Assessment.* Tilburg and Buenos Aires: International Centre for Human and Public Affairs. pp. 103–19.

3   For a more detailed account, see McNally, 1996, *op. cit.*

4   *Idem.*

5   However, the more foxes that are immunized, the fewer that die through rabies infection. German animal biologists are already warning that immunization of the fox population has led to an increase in their numbers of between three- and five-fold in the Black Forest. So many of these foxes are straying into urban areas that the vaccine has had to be placed in some city parks. See R. Boyes (1997) 'Victory over rabies brings hidden peril', *The Times,* 26 November, p. 16. See also McNally, 1995, *op. cit.*

The actor-network has only one response to the growing problem of fox rabies: more Raboral V-RG: extend the vaccination campaigns to the east, use even more Raboral V-RG, immunize even more foxes.

References

Adams, J. (1995) *Risk*. London: UCL Press.

Balmer, B. (1993) *Mutations in the Research System? The Human Genome Project and Science Policy*. Unpublished D Phil Thesis, University of Sussex.

Black, M. (1967) 'Probability' *Encyclopedia of Philosophy*. New York: Macmillan and The Free Press. pp. 464–79.

Beck, U. (1992) *Risk Society: Towards a New Modernity*. Trans. M. Ritter. London: Sage.

Beck, U. (1995) *Ecological Politics in an Age of Risk*. Cambridge: Polity.

Bennett, D., Glasner, P. and Travis, D. (1986) *The Politics of Uncertainty: Regulating Recombinant DNA Research in Britain*. London: Routledge and Kegan Paul.

Bishop, J. and Waldholz, M. (1990) *Genome*. New York: Simon and Schuster.

Bloomfield, B.P. and Verdubakis, T. (1995) 'Disrupted Boundaries: New Reproductive Technologies and the Language of Anxiety and Expectation', *Social Studies of Science*, 25 (3): 533–51.

Boulanger, D., Brochier, B. and Pastoret, P.P. (1992) 'Infection of the Red Fox (*Vulpes Vulpes*) with Cowpox Virus', *BRIDGE First Sectoral Meeting on Biosafety*. Wageningen and Brussels: CEC. pp. 74.

Boulanger, D., Brochier, B. and Pastoret, P.P. (1993) 'Infection of the Red Fox *(Vulpes Vulpes*) with Cowpox Virus', *BRIDGE Final Sectoral Meeting on Biosafety and First Meeting on Microbial Ecology*. Granada and Brussels: CEC. pp. 99.

Brenner, S. (1991) 'Old Ethics for New Issues', *Science and Public Affairs*, (August): 35–8.

Brochier, B., Kieny, M.P., Costy, F., Coppen, P., Bauduin, B., Lecocq, J.P., Languet, B., Chappuis, G., Desmettres, P., Afiademanyo, K., Liboid, R., and Pastoret, P. (1991) 'Large-Scale Eradication of Rabies Using Recombinant Vaccinia-Rabies Virus', *Nature*, 354 (19–26 December): 520–22.

Callon, M., Law, J. and Rip, A. (eds) (1986) *Mapping the Dynamics of Science and Technology*. London: Macmillan.

Carter, S. (1995) 'Boundaries of Danger and Uncertainty: An Analysis of the Technological Culture of Risk Assessment', in J. Gabe (ed.), *Medicine, Health and Risk: Sociological Approaches*. Oxford: Blackwell.

Cook-Degan, R. (1994) *The Gene Wars: Science, Politics and the Human Genome*. New York: Norton.

Crombie, A.C. (1994) *Styles of Scientific Thinking in the European Tradition*. Vol. II. London: Duckworth.

Crouch, A., Bennett, M., Gaskell, R.M., Gaskell, C.J. and Baxby, D. (1993) 'Epidemiology and Pathogenesis of Cowpox Virus in its Reservoir Hosts', *BRIDGE Final Sectoral Meeting on Biosafety and First Meeting on Microbial Ecology*. Granada and Brussels: CEC. pp. 96.

Daston, L. (1988) *Classical Probability in the Enlightenment*. Princeton, NJ: Princeton University Press.

De Solla Price, D. (1963) *Little Science, Big Science*. New York: Columbia University Press.

Douglas, M. (1985) *Risk Acceptability According to the Social Sciences*. London: Routledge and Kegan Paul.

European Commission DG XXIV (1997) 'Rabies and the movements of animals in the European Union. Report of the Scientific Veterinary Committee on Rabies, adopted 16 September.

Evans, G. and Durant, J. (1989) 'Understanding Science in Britain and America', in R. Jowell et al. (eds), *British Social Attitudes: Special International Report*. Aldershot: Gower.

Fiorino, D.J. (1990) 'Citizen Participation and Environmental Risk: A Survey of Institutional Mechanisms', *Science, Technology and Human Values*, 15 (2): 226–43.

Giddens, A. (1990) *The Consequences of Modernity*. Cambridge: Polity.

Gieryn, T.F. (1994) 'Boundaries of Science', in S. Jasanoff et al. (eds), *Handbook of Science and Technology Studies*. London: Sage.

Gigerenzer, G., Swijtink, Z., Porter, T., Daston, L., Beatty, J., Krüger, L. (1989) *The Empire of Chance: How Probability Changed Science and Everyday Life*. Cambridge: Cambridge University Press.

Glasner, P. (1993) 'Programming Nature and Public Participation in Decision-Making: A European Perspective', in J. Durant and J. Gregory (eds), *Science and Culture in Europe*. London: The Science Museum.

Glasner, P. (1996) 'From Community to Collaboratory? The Human Genome Mapping Project and the Changing Culture of Science', *Science and Public Policy*, 23 (2): 109–16.

Glasner, P., Rothman, H. and Scott, P. (1995) *Mobilising Resources in Genomic Research: a Study of Users of the Human Genome Mapping Project Resource*. Bristol: Centre for Social and Economic Research, University of the West of England.

Hacking, I. (1975) *The Emergence of Probability*. Cambridge: Cambridge University Press.

Hacking, I. (1990) *The Taming of Chance*. Cambridge: Cambridge University Press.

Hald, A. (1990) *A History of Probability and Statistics and their Applications before 1750*. New York: Wiley and Sons.

Irwin, A. (1995) *Citizen Science*. London: Routledge.

Irwin, A. and Wynne, B. (1996) *Misunderstanding Science? The Public Reconstruction of Science and Technology*. Cambridge: Cambridge University Press.

Jacob, F. (1974) *The Logic of Living Systems: A History of Heredity*. Trans. B.E. Spillman. London: Allen Lane.

Jones, S.G. (1995) *CyberSociety: Computer-Mediated Communication and Community*. London: Sage.

Joss, S. and Durant, J. (1995) *Public Participation in Science: The Role of Consensus Conferences in Europe*. London: The Science Museum.

Krimsky, S. (1982) *Genetic Alchemy: The Social History of the Recombinant DNA Controversy*. Cambridge, MA: MIT Press.

Krüger, L., Daston, L.J., Heidelberger, M. (eds) (1987) *The Probabilistic Revolution*. Vol. 1. Cambridge, MA: MIT Press.

Lander, E. (1992) 'DNA fingerprinting. Science, Law and the Ultimate Identifier', in D.J. Kevles and L. Hood (eds), *The Code of Codes: Scientific and Social issues in the Human Genome Project*. Cambridge, MA: Harvard University Press.

Lewontin, R.C. (1993) *The Doctrine of DNA: Biology as Ideology*. Harmondsworth: Penguin.

Marlier, E. (1992) 'Eurobarometer 35.1: Opinions of Europeans on Biotechnology', in J. Durant (ed.), *Biotechnology in Public: A Review of Recent Research*. London: The Science Museum.

Meikle, J. (1999) 'New year holidays for tourist pets'. *The Guardian*, (4 August): p. 4.

Mill, J.S. (1843) *A System of Logic Ratiocinative and Inductive*. 2 Vols. London: John Parker.

Mills, C.W. (1970) *The Sociological Imagination*. Harmondsworth: Penguin.

Nelkin, D. (1985) *Controversy: The Politics of Technical Decisions*. 2nd edn. London: Sage.

Nelkin, D. and Tancredi, L. (1994) *Dangerous Diagnostics: The Social Power of Biological Information*. 2nd edn. Chicago: University of Chicago Press.

Nelkin, D. and Lindee, S. (1995) *The DNA Mystique. The Gene as a Cultural Icon*. New York: W.H. Freeman.

Pearson, K. (1930) *The Life, Letters, and Labour of Francis Galton*. 3 Vols. Cambridge: Cambridge University Press.

Popper, K. (1959/[1935]) *The Logic of Scientific Discovery*. London: Hutchinson.

Purdue, D. (1995) 'Whose Knowledge Counts? "Experts", "Counter-Experts" and the "Lay Public"' *The Ecologist*, 25 (5): 170–72.

Reichenbach, H. (1949) *The Theory of Probability*. Berkeley, CA: University of California Press.

Skinner, M.A., Cowley, R., Patel, R. and Green, P. (1993) 'Systems for the Assessment of Recombination between Homologous and Heterologous Poxviruses'. *BRIDGE Final Sectoral Meeting on Biosafety and First Meeting on Microbial Ecology*. Granada and Brussels: CEC. p. 95.

Sklar, L. (1993) *Physics and Chance. Philosophical Issues in the Foundation of Statistical Mechanics*. Cambridge: Cambridge University Press.

Stacey, M. (1992) *Changing Human Reproduction: Social Science Perspectives*. London: Sage.

Terragni, F. (1992) *Bioethics in Europe: The Final Report*. Luxembourg: European Parliament, Directorate General for Research.

Von Mises, R. (1957/[1928]) *Probability, Statistics and Truth*. London: George Allen and Unwin.

6

Health and Responsibility: From Social Change to Technological Change and Vice Versa

Elisabeth Beck-Gernsheim

Introduction

Technological research in the social sciences frequently focuses on the relationship between technological change and social change. Roughly summarized, two positions have initiated the debate (see for example Joerges, 1988; Weingart, 1989a). On the one hand there is technological determinism which sees technology as destiny: technology dictates whether and in what way it will be applied. On the other hand there is the position of social reductionism. Here it is the users who decide whether and in what way technology will be applied. Cultural influences, social norms and interests play a crucial role in the shaping and use of technology.

Meanwhile, of course, the deficiencies and lacunae of both positions have become evident. Both perceive only segments, not the whole, as sociologist Peter Weingart puts it: they are the 'two great traditions of one-eyedness' (Weingart, 1988: 145). Consequently recent research focuses on the relationship between the cultural prerequisites of technology and what it offers. Here technology may be seen as a spiral-shaped process (Mettler-Meibom, 1990: 61). It appears as both the product and the instrument of social needs, interests and conflicts. Technology is effect and cause at the same time.

In the following, I want to explore this spiral-shaped process for the sphere of genome analysis. I shall argue as follows: first, I shall look at the concept of health – and later, responsibility – which represent two major values of modern society. I shall give a brief sketch of their origin and social rise, the point being that they act as the cultural prerequisites of gene technology. Second, I shall look at their interaction with genome analysis. Therefore the focus is on the *special relationship of health, responsibility and genome analysis* and with the central question being: what happens when new technologies link up with socially established values? Here, the spiral-shaped process moves forward, and I shall suggest the following spiral: at first, the values of health and responsibility create cultural acceptance of genome analysis; they pave the road. Then, through the spread of genome analysis, the values themselves are changed. Seen like this, genome analysis is not just a neutral means for reaching a predefined end, but rather the rapid expansion of this technology will affect the end itself. In other words, genome analysis will bring about a radical redefinition of the concepts of health and responsibility.

Health as a major value of modern society: the life course as an individual task

In the first step of my analysis, I want to point out how health functions as a cultural prerequisite of gene technology. Here we need a brief look into history. Over and over again, studies from social history have shown that in pre-industrial society the life course was to a very large extent pre-shaped. On many levels, the radius of action was limited from birth. Above all social status, religion and gender regulated everyday life.

Then, with the transition to modern industrialized society, the changes set in. The life course became more open and malleable. On the one hand, this implies that the radius of action is expanding, offering more options and choices. But, on the other hand, it also means that the individual is facing new demands and expectations. Above all, the labour market, the state and institutions of all kinds, set up their regulations, rules and requirements (Mayer and Müller, 1989: 41–60). If a person will not adhere to these norms, he or she will suffer the consequences. S/he will not be explicitly punished or sent to prison, but may lose his or her job, income and social status. 'In the individualized society, the individual must ... learn, on pain of permanent disadvantage, to conceive of himself or herself as the centre of action, as the planning office with respect to his/her own biography, abilities, orientations, relationships and so on' (Beck, 1992: 135). Increasingly, an active and self-directed way of life is expected from the individual, and this implies a skilful handling of and reacting to institutional prerequisites. As Martin Kohli puts it: 'Life is no longer ... a "Wonderful Gift of God", but rather an individual property, to be defended continuously. Even more so it becomes a productive task, an individual project' (Kohli, 1986: 185).

Health as an individual task

One area in which this kind of task shows itself very clearly is the modern idea of health. Of course, people in earlier centuries also hoped to be healthy and to live without pain. But then the outlook on life was also defined by religion, promising a life after death and delivery from pain. Life on earth was seen against a background of the Eternal, and when measured against that, it was less important. If one lived for two years or 20 or 70, what did it really matter, if what followed was Eternity?

Against this background, sickness and suffering were seen in a different manner (Illich, 1981). Very often, they were a heavy burden indeed. But, at the same time, a reason was ascribed to them. They were seen as part of the eternal cosmos, a task allotted by God in order to lead man toward purification, consciousness, and salvation. Throughout the great philosophies and religions of mankind, this idea of a higher reason can be found. Time and again philosophers and spiritual leaders have attributed a sanctifying power to suffering. Even more so, it has been said that only s/he who has emptied the cup of suffering may expect salvation. As Novalis put it 200 years ago, illness and disease 'are years of apprenticeship to the art of life and to emotional development'. The romantic poet, who died of tuberculosis at the age of 29, knew well enough that 'suffering can petrify', but he also knew that 'the one who flees from suffering has given up love'. And Schopenhauer concludes his famous chapter 'On the Theory of Abnegating the Will to Live' with a frequently quoted sentence by the Cologne Dominican Master Eckhardt 'The obedient beast carrying you to perfection is suffering'.

In modern society, for more and more people this faith in God, eternity and salvation has become brittle. What remains is the individual in the here and now and his or her physical condition. When faith in a world beyond has been dissolved, health gains in significance and value, it turns into the expectation of earthly salvation. Studies from social history, social psychology and sociology draw similar conclusions. 'What can no longer be expected from the world beyond is now ... projected to this world: immunity from troubles and impairment, from sickness and suffering – all in all, happiness and immortality' (Mergner et al., 1990: 18). Increasingly, the body is shifting into the focus of attention. For good health and a well-functioning body now constitute 'the one and only guarantee of our life, that is of our *entire* life. Once the body begins to wilt, our life will automatically wilt along with it' (Imhof, 1984: 223). Health even gains a 'transcendental significance: without health, everything else is nothing' (Van den Daele, 1989a: 208). In other words, salvation has been dethroned; healing has taken its place (see Rohde, 1974: 130).

This development gains added impetus, because health consciousness and health care neatly fit into the life course expected in modern individualized society. For in order to stand up to competition and to succeed in the labour market, people have to display health and fitness. Take, for instance, a slogan the Siemens Company issued in 1938. It declares openly: 'Health is not your private affair. Health is your obligation' (Sachse, 1990: 189). Or take a slogan advertising a cold remedy today. Though somewhat less harsh in tone, its message is similar: 'Who can afford having a cold? Today everybody has to be a hundred percent fit'.[1] Given these conditions, health is no longer so much a gift of God but rather the task and duty of the responsible citizen. S/he has to safeguard, control and care for it, or else s/he must accept the consequences. For if one's health is being impaired, one has fewer chances in the labour market, or even none at all. This is the danger potentially threatening everyone. It creates a climate of latent but widespread insecurity which, in turn, gives health a high priority in public opinion and media. Or to paraphrase Oscar Wilde: 'the importance of being healthy' is a characteristic of modern society.

Seen like this, the modern striving for health is not just a product of personal wishes or fears. Rather it is part and parcel of modern life, and it points to the new pattern of the life course, to its options as well as its demands. In the next step of my analysis, I want to explore how this modern idea of health paves the road for biotechnology and genome analysis.

Health and genome analysis

With the rise and spread of the new biotechnologies, the radius of action with regard to health has increased enormously, and at an unprecedented speed. Taken together, medicine, biology and genetics are opening up new dimensions of interference with the very substance of life. For precisely this reason, these technologies have become the subject of numerous discussions in science, politics, and public life. By breaking through the hitherto valid barriers, taboo thresholds are being touched. What man is, should be or can be, now stands open to discussion.

Barriers of acceptance

At the same time, a new stage has begun in the social awareness of technology and its consequences. Technological optimism carried the natural sciences and technology over many years; recently this optimism has become controversial with many groups, not only within political and public groups, but even within, and among, the different scientific groups themselves.

These controversies become particularly sharp when it comes to genetic technology as applied to humans. However, in an international comparison we can find some interesting differences. While in the USA the model of the liberal market is prevalent, with 'freedom of choice' being the catchphrase, the basic tone in some of the European countries, and especially in Germany and Switzerland, is distinctly more restrictive. Here a number of groups state doubts and apprehension, and for many different reasons. Representatives of the churches see manipulations of God's creation; followers of the Greens see a rape of nature; feminists see yet another case of patriarchy oppressing women. But throughout the different groups, there is a common apprehension relating to Germany's recent past. When gene technology is being discussed, the memory of eugenics comes up together with the fatal consequences of a policy that differentiated between genetically 'superior' versus genetically 'inferior' people and races, and made selections accordingly. The memory of this past leads to public sensitivity, in politics, in political parties, and also in the profession of human genetics.

The promise of health

Nevertheless, research concerning the human genome goes forward, not only in the USA but also in Europe, including Germany. Similarly, genetic counselling finds acceptance. In growing numbers, men and women are privately making use of what in public discussion often becomes the subject of criticism and even attack.

At least on the surface this seems to be a contradiction, and there is probably no single or simple answer. However, in the framework I have sketched here, one answer comes to mind. It suggests that along with other factors, health as a major value plays a decisive role. As I see it, 'health' is the magic word for gaining agreement. Health, or more precisely the promise of health, opens doors, elbows aside resistance, brings public support and money.

There is, of course, an ongoing debate over the actual linkage between health and gene technology. While some scientists expect enormous progress, others express doubts or even regard such expectations as grossly overrated. So far, we only know for certain that there is an enormous gap between the possibilities of diagnosis and those of therapy. Whether this gap will ever disappear, when this will happen or whether the promise of health will come true one day, is much disputed even within the natural sciences. In public discussion, however, the advocates of gene technology, especially the pharmaceutical industry, time and again use the promise of health in order to paint the picture of a better, healthier and happier future. For instance Renato Dulbecco, Nobel prize winner in medicine, in co-operation with the journalist Riccardo Chiaberge, writes:

> Meanwhile, the complete deciphering of the genome has moved within reach. We are on the eve of a Copernican revolution in the realm of medicine. Once many of the traditional methods of treatment have been put *ad acta*, we are going to transform our procedures with illnesses, our diagnostic and therapy procedures entirely. Every pathological change of the organism, be it hereditary, chronic or due to infection, will be analysed and assailed on the basis of the genes determining or at least favouring it. Health will find new, invincible allies, life on the average will be of longer duration, and a future of greater well-being will open up before us. (Dulbecco and Chiaberge, 1991: 117)

Bridgehead strategy

Some scientists and physicians are sure to read such statements with feelings of scepticism. Nevertheless we can expect that such promises will prove effective with the public. This is not to say that all social groups will change their minds, but some may. And once some begin, others might follow. This may also hold true of men and women who look upon gene technology with apprehension, or tend to reject it on principled grounds. But they too will be touched by what is sometimes called the 'business of hope' (Klein, 1989). I suggest the following pattern:

What might be emerging here is a separation between principle morals and private morals and, within the same person at that, following the compass of his or her needs. This sounds hardly surprising to psychologists, after all that is known of the mechanisms of need-oriented perception and cognitive dissonance. If this is true, the resulting mixture of apprehension and hope leads to internal ambivalence. And ambivalence, in turn, plays an essential role in abolishing taboos and expanding the radius of what is socially accepted. For this interpretation we can refer to Peter Weingart and a pattern he calls 'bridgehead strategy'. According to Weingart, the introduction of a new technology always needs a kind of bridgehead in the social system, serving as a starting point for expansion. From this point of view, 'a situation of at least partial acceptance' proves extremely useful. 'Take the image of colonization: the victorious campaign of the colonizers, even in face of an overwhelming superiority of the "old cultures", can be explained only by the fact that they are split and ambivalent *vis-à-vis* the intruders' (Weingart, 1989b).

Thinking of gene technology, we can expect such a partial acceptance for the very reason that health is a major value of modern society. Seen like this, the priority of health is the bridgehead, the starting point for expansion. By referring to health, obstacles are pushed aside, doubts are allayed, critics are silenced (or fall silent of their own accord). One cannot argue against health, particularly not so in a society where many no longer know a god, or have universally binding morals or firmly established traditions. Some doubts may remain here or there; some apprehension may linger; some groups may not join up right away. But nevertheless, gene technology begins to move in. Wolfgang van den Daele who was a member of the 'Gene Technology' Commission of the German parliament has analysed this bridgehead function of health closely:

> In so far as technologies expand the options for the realization of values established in culture, they redefine the range of these values.... The technical possibilities [become] integrated into the protection area of the values.... Thus, for example, from the protection of health guaranteed by the Constitution ... individual claims are derived for the right of making use of existing technical possibilities. Such claims are legitimate and can only be passed over by a regulative policy under increased burdens of argumentation and proof. The hardest to justify would be without doubt a blanket prohibition of technologies that can be deployed in medicine. It is simply not possible to be against the healing or prevention of diseases. 'Health' ranges in our society at the top of individual hierarchies of value. It is at the same time – with an investment of 10% of the gross national product and about one million employees – a central public good. In general one may rightfully criticize that it is precisely the impending medical applications of modern biology which are going to strengthen the tendency, in a hazardous manner, toward a technicalization of human life. In a concrete case the right of those affected to protection of their physical soundness (Constitution, Art. 2, Par. 1) also fundamentally includes the access to precisely these technologies. (Van den Daele, 1989b: 212)

From this Van den Daele draws the following conclusion: 'Morality is changeable.... Seen against the background of new technology, existing morality becomes obsolete' (Van den Daele, 1985: 15, 205). This means that with the arrival of a new technology that promises health, hitherto valid taboos are overruled. In secularized and individualized society health is a major value ranging before other values and displacing other values.

Expansion of the concept of health

Let us look now at the next stage of that spiral-shaped process, the interaction between social change and technological change. So far I have argued that health functions as a cultural prerequisite and door opener for gene technology. Now I shall try to show that with the growing acceptance and use of gene technology, our very concept of health begins to change and to expand.

Let us start with two examples from the media. In 1992 *The Economist* published an article on gene technology,[2] entitled 'Changing Your Genes'. The first sentence referred to that famous dictum by Freud: 'biology is destiny', then the vision of a future followed in which Freud's statement no longer would hold true, because people will choose, select and rearrange their genes. Today, so it said, therapies are aiming at malignant genes. Tomorrow, however, it might be genes that will not only turn a malfunctioning body into a well-functioning one but might also make a well-functioning body even better, faster, stronger and more beautiful. Then followed a wholehearted praise of such a future, the main idea being: genetic choice brings a new era of freedom. And the last sentence was: 'With apologies to Freud, biology will be best when it is a matter of choice'.

In 1990 the physician and novelist Michael Crichton published an article in *Newsweek* on the future of medicine. Its tone is similar, its optimism even more marked, the future is described in shining colours. With a hint of Dickens, 'Greater Expectations' was chosen as the title, and it is meant literally:

> The physician as life-style expert, as wellness adviser, has already begun to appear. And as genetic profiles and other predictive tools improve, the art of prevention will grow far more sophisticated. Physicians will administer tests and, armed with the results, prescribe measures just as precisely as they now dispense medications.... Fundamental will be gene-replacement therapy, in which missing or defective genes are supplied by the physician. Such procedures are being developed to treat serious illness, but they will eventually be used to boost enzyme levels and hormone production to retard aging [*sic*] and to increase vigor.... What all this means is that our present concept of medicine will disappear.... Medicine will change its focus from treatment to enhancement, from repair to improvement, from diminished sickness to increased performance. (Crichton, 1990)

Rising expectations

To some, such forecasts may seem exaggerated, even absurd. But here is not the place to discuss whether this kind of genetic interference will or will not be possible in the foreseeable future. (This is a question to be answered by the natural sciences.) Whatever the future possibilities will be, for the study of social change it is highly interesting to note the visions emerging today. Clearly, the media examples quoted above signal a turning point. With the promise of health linked to gene technology, an expansion of the concept of health is being introduced, gradually, silently, but nonetheless radical in its results. The old concept of health appears far too narrow, far too modest now. Expectations are rising: change and improvement are in demand. Nature is not altogether passé, it is still the necessary base supplying the raw materials, so to speak. With the help of technology a new body should come from the old one, much healthier and better. Consequently, the role of the physician is newly defined. S/he is no longer expected just to preserve and protect life, s/he is also appointed as lifestyle expert. The physician guides us, because s/he knows us, that is: s/he knows our genes. S/he knows what we should do or not do, from food to jobs, sports and leisure time.

One might raise the objection that the two articles mentioned above are atypical. But in the works of many prominent scientists we can find similar statements (see, for example, the statement by Dulbecco and Chiaberge quoted on p. 126). And when looking into the history of technology, time and again we find a similar pattern. With the arrival of a new technology, the quality standards in this field of action will rise and new ideals of perfection will come up. Household research is a case in point. Take the history of washing as studied by historian Karin Hausen (1987: 204–19). She argues that with the introduction of the washing machine the physical effort of doing laundry work has been reduced, but at the same time there was also a shift in the socially accepted norms of 'cleanliness' versus 'dirtiness'. A norm of frequent washing was introduced and (with strong support coming from the detergent industry) 'whiter laundry' became the housewife's obligation.

In other words, it is naive realism to believe that human needs are static, pre-set by 'Eternal Nature'. Rather these needs are expandable and open to a wide range of interpretations. And it is precisely technology which often sets into motion a spiral of rising expectations. What holds true for washing laundry may hold true with regard to health. Ideas of the perfectibility of 'man', reaching back to the classic philosophies, today take on the shape of biotechnology and its promises (Rothschild, 1988). Take for instance prenatal testing:

> In the case of prenatal diagnosis, the technology, building on a perfectability [*sic*] ideology already in place, specifically reshapes those beliefs through the health ideology it creates. In the language of prenatal screening, what is imperfect becomes anything that can be diagnosed as a pathological condition, from a fatal affliction to a genetic predisposition for a non-life-threatening, treatable malady.... Although tests for most of these conditions are not routinely performed ... this growing list of diagnosable defects helps to create and reinforce a mode of thought that demands a 'perfect child'. (Rothschild, 1988)

Voluntary compulsion

At first, gene technology offers to rationalize our life and then, continuing along this line, it leads into new dimensions. The next offer is to find our individual risk factors (like a proneness to heart attacks or diabetes) and to take this information as a guideline for shaping our lifestyle. Preventive care is:

> an element of self-management expected from modern individualized man. If a methodical way of life becomes established practice, from the planning of education ... to provision for 'successful aging', then preventive health care must become a priority. (Van den Daele, 1989a: 207f)

On closer reading, one word catches the eye, four letters only: 'must'. What does it mean? Compulsion and punishment? Penalties if a person should not comply? Certainly not. A more subtle pressure is meant here which nonetheless – or perhaps precisely for that reason – is all the more effective. To put it paradoxically, it is a pressure most people will submit to voluntarily, again for the sake of that magic word: 'health'. 'Health oils voluntariness, makes it submissive to "necessity"' (Beck, 1988: 57).

So this 'must' does not mean direct compulsion, but even less so does it mean a plain voluntary act. It is something in between. We might call it 'voluntary compulsion' or 'preventive compulsion', as Van den Daele (1989a: 207) puts it. According to him, preventive measures easily obtain a status of legitimacy and rationality today, barely allowing for objection. For on the one hand, the option of avoiding health risks is seen as enlarging our freedom of choice, and on the other hand, such measures are turned against the state in the form of benefit claims. Today people seek protection against the oddities of life (for instance, against sickness and accidents) via all kinds of insurance, and there is also a broad range of social policies, many paid for by the general public. Given these conditions, it becomes a public problem if people do not make full use of preventive measures and the possibilities of a health-oriented lifestyle.

In general, the social role of the sick person includes a corresponding expectation from his environment that he will be making every reasonable effort to get well soon. This expectation is the compensation for the privileges extended, like, for example, being excused from the obligation to work, and increased care. Claims in case of illness for benefits coming from the joint community are equal to obligations toward health. The transferability of this idea to the healthy person who, "in an irresponsible manner", does not make use of the opportunities offered for prevention, is obvious'. (Van den Daele, 1989a: 208)

In the late nineteenth and early twentieth centuries health campaigns were initiated in order to introduce working-class women to hygienic rules of household management. The historian Ute Frevert (1985: 420–46) called these campaigns 'social sieges', and perhaps we will soon experience further forms of sieges. At the 1992 Meeting of German Physicians, the President, Karsten Vilmar, spoke out for a fundamental change in health policy. In order to ease the financial burden of the health system, among other things he demanded risk premiums, that is, people engaging in behaviour dangerous to their health should pay higher contributions.[3] And in a book by two pioneers of medical technology, we find the following sentence: 'Knowing our genes should induce us to a responsible lifestyle' (Bräutigaum and Mettler, 1985).

Now responsibility, like health, ranges among the major values of the modern age. Hardly anyone would plead against it. But of course the essential question is, what does this concept include, what is gathered under this headline? And then, just as it is in regard to health, the next question is, what happens when gene technology comes in? Will the arrival and spread of gene technology bring about, and change around, yet another basic value?

The expansion of responsibility

Again, let us start with examples. The statement of a pregnant woman: 'I felt in a terrible quandary. All the time I was asked, "Have you been to the check-up? You really have to, now that it exists.... And what if the child is disabled? You've got two children now, you've got to think of them, and of your husband!"'. Or a gynaecologist's advice to a 35-year-old woman: 'For a woman of your age there is no question about it. Over 35, it *must* be done'.[4] Or a book of popular science, informing about prenatal diagnosis: 'You should definitely read this book if you ... take responsibility for your pregnancy and want to make well-founded decisions.... [With this information] responsibility is put where it belongs: with you' (Blatt, 1991: 16, 25).

A new sound

There is ample evidence that these examples are not just haphazard. What we see here is how the concept of responsibility is undergoing a subtle but significant change. In earlier decades, when safe methods of contraception became available, the idea of 'responsible parenthood' began to spread. At that time, the idea was meant in a quantitative way: people should have only as many children as they could feed and bring up adequately (Häussler, 1983: 58–73). Meanwhile the concept of responsibility has been adapted to the new options of reproductive medicine and prenatal diagnosis. Now it is interpreted in the way of a qualitative selection taking place before birth, perhaps even before conception. However, the terms used here often do not spell out the goal directly, rather they use the 'plastic words' (Pörksen, 1988) of administrative language. For instance, there is much talk about 'prevention' (Schmid, 1988) or 'prophylactic measures'.[5] Such words have a positive meaning in modern society. They sound up-to-date, rational, hygienic, as if they were a part of the publicly promoted health care, like, for instance, brushing your teeth. They point to goals which are widely accepted because they serve the interests of the individual (maintaining health, avoiding pain) as well as the interests of society (cost saving).

However, more is at stake here than dental hygiene. What is actually meant is avoiding the birth of a handicapped child, either by way of renouncing biological parenthood altogether or (more likely in practice) by way of a 'tentative pregnancy' (Katz-Rothmann, 1988) and induced abortion in case of a genetic deficiency. In the public debate we can already find prominent scientists praising such behaviour as a new example of responsible choice. In a lecture on 'Genetics and Ethics' Hubert Markl (1989), former president of the German Research Community, said: 'I want to express very clearly, because it is sometimes described differently, that the renouncing of children due to such [genetic] reasons ought to be praised as much, or perhaps even more, as the decision of a mercilessly fatalistic piety to let a possibly cruel fate simply run its course'.[6]

Do ethics in the age of genetics mean that avoiding the birth of a handicapped child becomes the obligation of today's responsible citizen? Hardly any German official would say this publicly. But ideas somewhat more subtle are gaining ground, like those put forward by the philosopher Hans-Martin Sass. He calls reproductive risks 'irresponsible in regard to the society that accepts severely handicapped people into the community'.[7] And in everyday life, we can also see a change of attitudes creeping in. Increasingly, women who do not undergo prenatal testing are seen as ignorant, stupid or even egoistic: 'Obviously they prefer to stick their heads in the sand rather than learn the truth' (interviewee cited in Schindele, 1990: 66).

Responsibility brings blame

This attitude does not arise from nowhere. Rather, there is a certain logic behind it. Like health, responsibility is a major value of the modern age, and in a way it is based on the philosophy of the Enlightenment. Responsibility means more autonomy, taking fate into one's own hands, as Kant said of the Enlightenment: it is 'a way out of self-inflicted ignorance'. But even in this phrase there is a double meaning pointing toward the other side of the coin. Indeed, the person who does not take part in this kind of responsibility is now being labelled 'irresponsible'. His or her behaviour is seen as a failure: blame comes in. This is exactly what happens today with prenatal and genetic testing. On the one hand, freedom of choice is proclaimed as a basic right, with a great deal of goodwill and good intentions. The basic tone of all official statements is that there must be no compulsion to undergo the test, it is up to the individual to decide. But on the other hand, there is the momentum of technology, and in gradual steps – albeit at first hardly noticeable – the concept of responsibility changes its content; it is being expanded and adapted along with the increasing options of technology. Seen against this frame of reference, the person who does not play along must appear irresponsible, suspect, if not outright guilty.

Furthermore, the responsibility at issue here has many addressees and reference points. For one there is responsibility *vis-à-vis* society. Then there is responsibility *vis-à-vis* the family, *vis-à-vis* the husband/partner and the children who are already here (maybe also *vis-à-vis* the grandparents hoping for a healthy, cuddly and presentable grandchild). Not to forget the responsibility for the unborn child: is it right to burden it with disease, a life of pain and dependency? (see Rapp, 1984: 319). Last but not least, in individualized society there is also responsibility towards the self, an obligation to safeguard one's life course with all its needs, rights, and demands. Today, many young women have been brought up with this lesson, and they have learned to act accordingly. Take this interview statement for instance:

> The main reason for me having the test was that I have a profession which I want to continue practising.... With a handicapped child I would be tied down for years.... The idea of having a child with Downs Syndrome means to care for 20 years or more for a child who has the developmental stage of a toddler. And then you are caught again in a 'woman's role'. (cited in Leuzinger and Rambert, 1987: 87)

The more levels of responsibility, the more sources for reproach, for social and moral pressure, the more potential for blame. This prepares the way for taking the tests. For instance, take those women who are labelled as 'risk group' because of their age. Figures from Germany suggest that in 1988, more than half of those women underwent prenatal testing (Schroeder-Kurth, 1990: 39). And later data indicate that meanwhile, the trend has accelerated considerably.[8]

Can technology be checked?

In the light of the trends analysed so far, the future seems obvious. Gene technology is booming and blooming. Success follows success. With each scientific development new options are opened up, and the area of 'responsible behaviour' is widened accordingly. Opposition and doubts are overruled by the sheer force of this trend. Due to its enormous speed, the process cannot be checked: Medicine becomes 'sub-politics' (Beck, 1992: 204ff, 1997: 94–109).

So, is technology destiny after all? Even if this assumption were wrong on the general level, it could prove true as a metaphorical description and phrase when applied to a specific situation, place and time, for instance to what happens today. But even here, the picture is not yet complete. For even today we are witnessing some countertrends. In recent years, a slow but distinct shift of attitudes with regard to technology has set in, with a growing awareness of the potentially dangerous side effects of technology, at least among some groups. In effect, another value is on the rise, namely: 'Nature'. In the public debate, nature is a symbol that can be used and is being used by the critics of technology. And gene technology is clearly a case in point. When the label 'unnatural' is brought into the debate, gene technology seems suspect, and apprehension is growing. So along with all the factors promoting acceptance, there are still some deep-rooted cultural and social barriers, and they may even gain in momentum (Heins, 1992).

If this diagnosis holds true, we are facing a paradox. The values of 'Nature' and of 'Health' though closely connected at first glance, move apart here. They compete with one another and are being mobilized for opposing standpoints. While the advocates of gene technology cry 'Pro Health', the critics counter 'Pro Nature'. This polarization runs right through the established parties and groups, right through the sciences, not least through the natural sciences. It may be measured by the number of panels, commissions and meetings discussing the pros and cons of genome analysis, and it can easily be felt in the emotionally laden atmosphere of such debates.

Maybe all this has just an alibi function, and we are witnessing the last moments and motions of a bygone culture. But maybe not. Maybe there is a growing awareness that the achievements of the modern age very often have two sides, options and risks, in gene technology as well as in other fields. If taken seriously, this would imply the claim that technology will move from sub-policy to the political level, that is, become open to scrutiny and public decision-making. Then careful scrutiny of technology could begin, with a conscientious effort to look at both sides, the promises as well as the potential side-effects. For instance in regard to the global promise of health linked with genome analysis, the question could be, for each and every step:

What concept of health and *what* concept of responsibility are we talking about when it comes to this step? Which step implied in the general promise of health is helpful and humane, which step will bring growing control and coercion, of whom and by whom? With the implementation of this step, who will carry what kind of responsibility; which burdens will be eased; which conflicts might arise here; and whose interests are at stake? Seen like this, the question is not whether or not we want health and responsibility. Rather, the question is, or could be: *What kind of health, what kind of responsibility do we want?*

Acknowledgement

This chapter is reprinted from Haker, H., Hearn, R. and Siegleder, K. (eds) (1996) *Ethics of Human Genome Analysis*. Tübingen: Attempto Verlag, pp. 199–216, with kind permission from the publishers.

Notes

1 Published for instance in the *Süddeutsche Zeitung*, 29 November 1990.
2 'Changing your Genes', *The Economist*, 25 April 1992, pp. 11f. (editorial).
3 See *Süddeutsche Zeitung*, 13 May 1992, p. 2.
4 Both statements are from interviews cited in Schindele (1990: 64).

5 'In Familien mit genetischem Risiko ist präkonzeptionell eine humangenetische Beratung anzustreben. Gegebenenfalls sind ... prophylaktische Maßnahmen anzuraten' (Bach et al., 1990: 41). 'For families where there are genetic risk factors it is highly advisable that they opt for genetic counselling. Advice may be needed on prophylactic measures.'

6 Hubert Markl 'Genetik und Ethik'. Speech delivered at the reception of the Arthur-Burkhardt-Prize. Stuttgart, 16 April 1989; photocopied manuscript.

7 Cited in Bundesministerium für Forschung und Technologie (1989).

8 Institut für System- und Technologieanalysen (1992) *Perspektiven der Anwendung und Regelungsmöglichkeiten der Genomanalyse in den Bereichen Humangenetik, Versicherungen, Straf- und Zivilprozeß*. A study for the office for the assessment of technological consequences (an office of the German parliament) (Bad Oeyenhausen, photocopied manuscript, 1992, p. 26).

References

Bach, H. et al. (1990) 'Orientierung humangenetischer Betreuung – genetische Beratung in der DDR', *Medizinische Genetik*, (4): 40–2.

Beck, U. (1988) *Gegengifte: Die organisierte Unverantwortlichkeit*. Frankfurt am Main: Suhrkamp.

Beck, U. (1992) *Risk Society: Towards a New Modernity*. Trans. M. Ritter. London: Sage.

Beck, U. (1997) *The Reinvention of Politics: Rethinking Modernity in the Global Social Order*. Cambridge: Polity.

Blatt, B. (1991) *Bekomme ich ein gesundes Kind? Chancen und Risiken der vorgebürtlichen Diagnostik*. Reinbek: Rowohlt.

Bräutigaum, H.H. and Mettler, L. (1985) *Die programmierte Vererbung: Möglichkeiten und Gefahren der Gentechnologie*. Hamburg: Hoffman and Campe.

Bundesministerium für Forschung und Technologie (ed.) (1989) *Ethische und rechtliche Probleme der Anwendung zellbiologischer und genetischer Methoden am Menschen. Dokumentation eines Fachgespräches im Bundesministerium für Forschung und Technologie*. Munich: Schweitzer.

Crichton, M. (1990) 'Greater expectations: The Future of Medicine Lies not in Treating Illness but in Preventing it', *Newsweek*, 24 September.

Dulbecco, R. and Chiaberge, R. (1991) *Konstrukteure des Lebens: Medizin und Ethik im Zeitalter der Gentechnologie*. Munich: Piper.

Frevert, U. (1985) '"Fürsorgliche Belagerung" Hygiebebewegung und Arbeiterfrauen im 19. und frühen 20. Jahrhundert'. *Geschichte und Gesellschaft*, 11 (4): 420–46.

Hausen, K. (1987) 'Große Wäsche, soziale Standards, technischer Fortschritt. Sozialhistorische Beobachtungen und Überlegungen', in B. Lutz (ed.), *Technik und sozialer Wandel: Verhandlungen des 23. Deutschen Soziologentages in Hamburg 1986*. Frankfurt: Campus.

Häussler, M. (1983) 'Von der Enthaltsamkeit zur verantwortungsbewußten Fortpflanzung. Über den unaufhaltsamen Aufstieg der Empfängnisverhütung und seine Folgen, in M. Häussler, C. Helfferich, G. Walterspiegel and A. Wetterer (eds), *Bauchlandungen: Abtreibung – Sexualität – Kinderwunsch*. Munich: Frauenbuchverlag.

Heins, V. (1992) Gentechnik aus der Verbraucherperspektive – Symbolische Kämpfe um neue Konsummodelle, *Soziale Welt*, (4): 383–99.

Illich, I. (1981) *Die Nemesis der Medizin: Von den Grenzen des Gesundheitswesens*. Reinbeck: Rowohlt.

Imhof, A.E. (1984) *Die verlorene Welten*. Munich: Beck.

Institut für System-und Technologieanalysen (1992) *Perspektiven der Anwendung und Regelungsmöglichkeiten der Genomanalyse in den Bereichen Humangenetik, Versicherungen, Straf- und Zivilprozeß*. Bad Oeyenhausen. Unpublished document.

Joerges, B. (ed.) (1988) *Technik im Alltag*. Frankfurt am Main: Suhrkamp Verlag.

Katz-Rothmann, B. (1988) *The Tentative Pregnancy: Prenatal Diagnosis and the Future of Motherhood.* London: Pandora Books.

Klein, R.D. (ed.) (1989) *Das Geschäft mit der Hoffnung, Erfahrungen mit der Fartpflanzungsmedizin: Frauen berichten.* Berlin: Orlanda Frauenverlag.

Kohli, M. (1986) 'Gesellschaftszeit und Lebenszeit. Der Lebenslauf im Strukturwandel der Moderne' in J. Berger (ed.), Die Moderne. Kontinuitäten und Zäsuren. *Sociale Welt,* special volume 4. Göttingen: Schwartz.

Leuzinger, M. and Rambert, B. (1987) 'Ich spür es – mein Kind ist Gesund' in C. Roth (ed.), *Genzeit. Die Industrialisierung von Pflanze, Tier und Mensch.* Zurich: Limmat Verlag Genossenschaft.

Markl, H. (1989) 'Genetik und Ethik' Speech delivered at the reception of the Arthur-Burkhardt-Prize. Stuttgart, 16 April.

Mayer, K.U. and Müller, W. (1989) 'Lebensverläufe im Wohlfahrtsstaat, in A. Weymann (ed.), *Handlungsspielräume. Untersuchungen zur Individualisierung und Institutionalisierung von Lebensläufen in der Moderne.* Stuttgart: Enke.

Mergner, U., Mönkberg-Tun, E. and Ziegler, G. (1990) 'Gesundheit und Interesse. Zur Fremdbestimmung von Selbstbestimmung im Umgang mit Gesundheit', *Psychosozial,* 2.

Mettler-Meibom, B. (1990) *Mit High-Tech zurück in eine Autoritäre Politische Kultur?* Essen: Essener Hochschulblätter.

Pörksen, U. (1988) *Plastikwörter.* Stuttgart: Klett-Cotta.

Rapp, R. (1984) 'XYLO: A True Story', in R. Arditti, R. Duelli Klein and S. Minden (eds), *Test-Tube Women: What Future for Motherhood?* London: Routledge and Kegan Paul.

Rohde, J.J. (1974) *Soziologie der Krankenhauses.* Stuttgart: Enke.

Rothschild, J. (1988) 'Engineering Birth: Toward the Perfectability of Man?', in S.L. Goldman (ed.), *Science, Technology and Social Progress.* Bethlehem, PA: Lehigh University Press.

Sachse, C. (1990) *Siemens, der Nationalsozialismus und die moderne Familie: Eine Untersuchung zur sozialen Rationalisierung in Deutschland im 20. Jahrhundert.* Hamburg: Rasch and Röhring.

Schindele, E. (1990) *Gläserne Gebär-Mütter: Vorgeburtliche Diagnostik: Fluch oder Segen.* Frankfurt: Fischer.

Schmid, W. (1988) 'Die Prävention des Down-Syndroms (Mongolismus). *Neue Zürcher Zeitung,* 20 January: 77.

Schroeder-Kurth, T. (1990) 'Medizinische Genetik in der Bundesrepublik', *Medizinische Genetik,* 2 (4): 38f.

Van den Daele, W. (1985) *Mensch nach Maß? Ethische Probleme der Genmanipulation und Gentherapie.* Munich: Beck.

Van den Daele, W. (1989a) 'Das zähe Leben des Präventiven Zwanges', in A. Schuller and N. Heim (eds), *Der Codierte Leib: Zur Zukunft der Genetischen Vergangenheit.* Zürich: Artemis.

Van den Daele, W. (1989b) 'Kulturelle Bedingungen der Technikkontrolle durch Regulative Politik', in P. Weingart (ed.), *Technik als Sozialer Prozeß.* Frankfurt am Main: Suhrkamp Verlag.

Weingart, P. (1988) 'Differenzierung der Technik oder Entdifferenzierung der Kultur', in B. Joerges (ed.), *Technik im Alltag.* Frankfurt am Main: Suhrkamp Verlag.

Weingart, P. (ed.) (1989a) *Technik als Sozialer Prozeß.* Frankfurt am Main: Suhrkamp Verlag.

Weingart, P. (1989b) '"Großtechnische Systeme" – Ein Paradigma der Verknüpfung von Technikentwicklung und Sozialem Wandel?, in P. Weingart (ed.), *Technik als Sozialer Prozeß.* Frankfurt am Main: Suhrkamp Verlag.

PART III

MEDIATING TECHNOLOGIES OF RISK

7

Child Organ Stealing Stories: Risk, Rumour and Reproductive Technologies

Claudia Castañeda

The United States Information Agency's (USIA) Program Officer for Countering Misinformation and Disinformation is charged with responding to false stories considered to pose a risk of some kind to the United States and its citizens. The Program Officer, Todd Leventhal, estimates that he has spent 80% of his nine post-Cold War years in office countering a single rumour: the 'child organ stealing' or 'baby parts' rumour (Leventhal, 1995a). The child organ stealing rumour is a story about Latin American, Korean, and other children being kidnapped for organ harvesting. In its many different versions, the kidneys, corneas, liver, or heart are removed from the stolen child and sold in a global human organs market for eventual surgical transplant. The child is eventually found with organs missing, sometimes dead and sometimes still alive, its body visibly wounded or otherwise marked by the ordeal. Among the more graphic versions is one in which a child is found dead as a result of organ theft, with US one-dollar bills and a thank-you note stuffed in its wounded body (see Kadetsky, 1994; Leventhal, 1994; Orlebar, 1994).

According to Leventhal, the child organ stealing rumour began to pose a risk significant enough to come under his jurisdiction when it moved from word of mouth to the world 'prestige' press (1995a). The importance of countering this rumour, from Leventhal's point of view, lies in the risk posed by the rumour as a false story. Not only has the rumour's own prolific word of mouth reproduction been exponentially increased by the world media's technology, but also because the world media initially authorized the rumour as true (see Cordier, 1988; Mauro, 1988; Pinero 1987). As part of his countering strategy, Leventhal has published reports on the rumour and its risks for the USIA (1994; 1995b), and tried to promote news reports that present the rumour as a patently false, if compelling, story. The rumour itself locates risk in the workings of medical technology combined with a global market in organs, and identifies poor children in poor countries as the principal targets of that risk. In Leventhal's version of the rumour, it is the rumour itself that poses a risk. For him, the rumour is a false story wrongly authorized and disseminated as true by the global media which, as will soon become apparent, poses an entirely different set of risks. His strategy for countering the child organ stealing story aims to use the global media's power to re-represent the child organ stealing as a false rumour.

Taken together, the child organ stealing rumour and its coverage by the world press as variously true or false suggest a much more indeterminate relationship between risk and rumour. Indeed, many issues are woven into this complex relation. Among these, transnational adoption suggests the kinds of indeterminacies that might be at issue. Both Leventhal's report and news media versions of the child organ stealing rumour document child stealing for the purposes of transnational adoption as an uncontested fact. Most recently, a report published in the *New York Times* (Schemo, 1996) confirmed the existence of child kidnapping for this purpose in Paraguay. The *New York Times* reported that an extensive network of agents in Paraguay have been processing kidnapped children through official foreign adoption channels. The illicit activity included personnel at every level of the adoption process, from women posing as biological mothers, to nursery operators, psychologists, notaries, lawyers, and judges.

The relatively uncontested existence of child stealing for transnational adoption makes child stealing for organ theft and transplant seem quite a bit less impossible. Is it possible that a similarly elaborate network of accomplices could be carrying out child kidnapping for organ harvesting for a lucrative world market? As it turns out, the relation between rumour and risk in the case of child organ stealing is even more elaborate than even this brief example can suggest. A rumour is a story without an author, information without a definite origin, whose truth is always in question. Consequently, many risks, and many different effects, can be associated with a given rumour. Indeed, the power of rumour lies not in its simple repetition, but in its continual embellishment and alteration, its self-generation.

It is in this sense that rumour, as well as the technologies named and associated with the rumour, are reproductive technologies. In using the term 'reproduction' to describe the rumour's appearance and transmission, I mean to emphasize generativity rather than mere replication. In the case of the child organ stealing rumour and its association with risk, four key reproductive technologies emerge in a complex relation to one another, and bear an equally complex relation to risk. In the media reports, rumour can be, first, a reproductive technology of its own narrative and indeterminate truth. Second, the rumour's narrative itself also identifies organ transplantation, a reproductive technology of life and death or dismemberment, as the source of risk. Third, the rumour is generated through the reproductive technology of the media, its risks located specifically in its media-assisted reproductions. Finally, the rumour of child organ stealing is associated with transnational adoption, and shares the same risk group of poor and destitute children in non-western countries. Transnational adoption is considered here as an analogue to some new reproductive technologies in that it, too, generates parent–child relationships from non-biologically related individuals. At the same time, Leventhal and others also identify the child organ stealing rumour as a risk *to* transnational adoption, because foreign programmes have been encumbered, limited, or closed in response to allegations of child organ theft in some countries (see Leventhal, 1994).

While the multiple risks identified across the spectrum of reports considered in this chapter are different in fundamental ways, it is also the case that they intersect in the figure of the child. Along with the global media, it is the spectre of the child torn apart by unseen hands and instruments, its body emptied out into a collection of organs by the powers of medical technology and the lure of the global market-place that propels the rumour. It is this image that contributes powerfully to the rumour's capacity to captivate, and so also to its continued reproduction and recirculation. Posed so as to emphasize this aspect of the rumour's power, the question of risk becomes: does the child-figure that appears in accounts of the child organ stealing story represent an actual risk of theft, mutilation, and possible death to children? Or does it, perhaps, only signify a more diffuse set of fears?

Redefining risk

A significant link between risk and technology has been articulated by Beck (1992) in his theory of the 'risk society'. Beck's theory describes contemporary societies as so profoundly affected by technologically-induced risk that risk is their defining feature. Paradoxically, the importance of risk in Beck's sociological description of contemporary societies corresponds to the inability of experts to adequately determine or assess dangers posed by technological change as a defining feature of modernity. The 'risk society' is modernity in a state of excess. It is modernity at risk, ultimately, to itself. And it is not just risk, but rather *indeterminate* risk that Beck identifies as its central problem.

There is little doubt within the theory of the 'risk society', however, as to the actual existence of risk. Risk is indeterminate only to the extent that it has surpassed predictive control, spreading beyond definable geopolitical boundaries and the limits of expert knowledge. Indeed, the certainty with which risk is invoked is linked to its predictable uncertainty; the less definable, predictable, and controllable the risk, the more risk it potentially entails. But this notion of risk has also been amplified and questioned by other social analysts. For example, Beck-Gernsheim (1996) emphasizes social and political dimensions of risk. For her, debate among relevant professional groups, or 'contestation between concepts of risk', is an important sociological factor in the determination of risk (emphasis deleted, 1996: 150). That is, the assignment of risk to a given technology may be the result of socio-political debate over risks differently identified by each of these groups.

Ruth McNally's (Chapter 5, this volume) analysis of risk further complicates available conceptions of risk as a descriptive and analytical category. For McNally, risks are constituted as such through 'problematization', a social process of authorization and legitimation in which relevant actors are enrolled in the very making of risk as a given. As McNally's example of The European Rabies Eradication Programme shows, risks are constituted through social processes, sometimes in the absence of empirical evidence as to the nature and extent of the dangers involved. Social actors can be mobilized in relation to a risk that does not, according to such empirical evidence, actually pose much of a risk. Risk, then, does not simply exist in relation to a given technology, nor can it simply be discovered by experts. Its 'existence' is contingent upon social processes by which risks are constituted as such in the first place.

Together, these elaborations of the sociological analysis of risk suggest that risk is not simply given, either for the actors involved in defining or assessing risk, or for sociological analysis (see also Adam, 1996; Wynne, 1996). The contingency of risk as elaborated by both McNally (with regard to the constitution of risk itself) and Beck-Gernsheim (with regard to contestation between groups over the definition of risk) suggests that there is no simple link between a given technology and risk. Most importantly for my purposes here, this contingency also implies that some potential risks never gain the status of risk as such. Similarly, some dangers may be identified as risks by some groups, while at the same time being *de*authorized as risks by others. The analysis of risk, then, should consider within its purview dangers that are identified in some way or by some groups as risks but never achieve the status of risk on a broad scale. This, too, is part of its indeterminacy.

Rumour is a site in which the play of authorization and deauthorization of risk makes itself especially evident. Rather than consider the relation between rumour and risk in the abstract, I consider the child organ stealing rumour in terms of the multiple risks associated with this rumour and the different worlds of evidence, truth, and authority to which these evaluations of risk belong. The following discussion takes a closer look at the complex of technology, reproduction, and indeterminate risk through the most recent spate of global media reproductions of the child organ stealing story, in which the rumour is said to have caused terrible violence in a rural Guatemalan town. Here, it becomes important to watch how the relation between rumour and risk shifts with each reproduction of the rumour, and how risks are variously authorized and deauthorized in the process. I argue that media reports of the rumour associate it with proliferating and contradictory risks, leaving the reader without any clear way of determining their validity or legitimacy, and exposing the indeterminacy of risk. The indeterminacy of risk exemplified by this rumour and its technological reproduction poses the following questions: does the indeterminacy of risk undermine the concept of modernity as an explanatory framework for contemporary risks? Is risk a function of modernity in the process of its own undoing, or does risk, redefined by rumour, suggest a social ordering that is more likely *a*modern?

The global media: localized rumours and multiplied risks

The child organ stealing story was reported widely in the mainstream world press in the spring of 1994 when news stories and images about a 'wave of panic' in

Guatemala hit the newspaper stands and flashed across television screens. The international page of the *New York Times* carried the story on 5 April under the headline 'Foreigners Attacked in Guatemala'. Its lead sentence read: 'Fed by rumours that Americans were coming to kidnap children, cut out their vital organs and ship them to the United States for transplantation, an extraordinary wave of panic has swept Guatemala over the last month'. Reports on this 'wave of panic' focused on an attack that occurred in San Cristóbal Verapaz, a small town in southwestern Guatemala, where a 52-year-old woman from Alaska named June Weinstock was beaten into a comatose state by a group of men after a local resident claimed that her 8-year-old son was missing. The story was covered not only by the major Guatemalan media, but also by newspapers, magazines, and major television networks in Europe and the US. In addition, the British Broadcasting Corporation (BBC-TV) produced and aired a documentary on the question of organ harvesting, and Reuters distributed internationally three-minute excerpts from videotapes of the attack on Weinstock which had been made available to Guatemalan cable television viewers in their full 5-hour length (Kadetsky, 1994). The small portion of global media reports considered here are indicative, but certainly not representative, of the spectrum of available reproductions of the child organ stealing rumour.

According to these reports, the crowd believed that Weinstock had stolen the child in order to harvest his organs for a lucrative transnational market, and a group of approximately 75 men stormed the courthouse where Weinstock had been taken in order to further investigate the allegations. Aided by a truckload of machetes and metal poles brought by a crew of striking road-workers, the crowd torched the courthouse and attacked Weinstock who was left in a comatose condition as a result of the attack. This attack was also linked in media reports to three other incidents in which local residents took violent action against a New Mexico tourist, a Swiss volcanologist, and a Salvadoran couple, all of whom were also suspected of stealing children, possibly for organ harvesting (Frankel and Orlebar, 1994; Johnson, 1994; Kadetsky 1994; López, 1994; Maclean's, 1994).

News media reports of the Weinstock incident have attempted to analyse how something as evanescent as a rumour could create a 'wave of panic' powerful enough to result in the absolutely material fact of June Weinstock's comatose condition. Some have attributed the attack to Guatemalans', especially rural and largely indigenous groups', susceptibility to the rumour due to Guatemala's history and contemporary politics. Among these accounts, some focus on the workings of right-wing military power as a catalyst for the attack. The *New York Times*, for example, published a piece by Victor Perera[1] about the Weinstock incident that associates child organ stealing with a right-wing attempt to destabilize the work of human rights monitors:

> The recent mob attacks in Guatemala on two American women suspected of kidnapping children for organ transplants may be part of a right-wing strategy to create a climate of instability hostile to human-rights monitors. In the more serious of the two incidents, June D. Weinstock, an environmental writer from Fairbanks, Alaska, was engulfed by an enraged mob in San Cristóbal Verapaz, in the Mayan Highlands, after she was seen caressing a child whose mother reported him missing immediately afterwards. (Perera, 1994)

This account locates risk in the rumour identified as a means of instigating violence. It also authorizes the rumour as a catalyst of violence while simultaneously deauthorizing the rumour as a legitimate account of the risk of child organ theft.

In addition to suspecting military instigation, some accounts of the Weinstock incident name the local press as a second catalyst. A front page *Los Angeles Times* article that appeared on 1 April 1994, makes the link as follows:

> Hard line factions of the Guatemalan military are believed to be exploiting visceral fears – perhaps even encouraging them – to undermine public security and to generate suspicion of foreigners.... The collective psychosis has been stoked by inflammatory reports in the local press of sightings of long-haired foreigners, driving Jeeps with tinted windows, supposedly hunting for children in remote villages. (Orlebar, E., 1994)

Note that Jeeps with tinted windows have been routinely used by the military in 'disappearing' citizens in Guatemala, such that the image of the Jeep with tinted windows signifies state terror to anyone familiar with these habits.

To understand the plausibility of accounts that emphasize the military's use of the rumour involvement requires a brief review of recent Guatemalan history, in which such involvement is not only plausible, but all too frequent. The spring of 1994 marked a watershed in Guatemala's 33-year undeclared civil war in which the military-controlled government, backed by the US, had waged a genocidal campaign against its largely poor and indigenous population. Naming anyone a guerrilla or subversive justified their killing, and by this convenient means the military massacred entire highland communities. The killings extended as well to individual middle-class Latinos suspected of sympathizing with the opposition to military rule or the economic exploitation of 80% of the Guatemalan population (Jonas, 1991; Manz, 1988). That spring, peace talks in Mexico between the civilian government and leftist guerrillas of the Guatemalan National Revolutionary Union (URNG) had reached an agreement that would permit a United Nations truth commission to investigate human rights abuses committed by both sides.

Perera's (1994) account states that 'the military's displeasure with this agreement is hardly surprising, as foreign observers accuse them of responsibility for as much as 95% of human rights violations committed by all sides during Guatemala's 33-year war of counterinsurgency'. In other words, it was the military that stood to lose by foreign investigations of human rights abuses, and it was the military that would benefit from a disruption of the plan by making Guatemala seem unsafe for foreigners. According to both the *New York Times* and *Los Angeles Times* articles, the military saw the truth commission as posing the greatest risk, because it was charged with uncovering human rights abuses committed by the military and other forces. Used by the military to generate the (unfounded) risk to unsuspecting foreigners like June Weinstock, a risk whose incontrovertible truth is palpably inscribed on June Weinstock's beaten body and in the travel warning issued by the US Embassy in Guatemala in the wake of the attack. And rumour simultaneously becomes the military's means of avoiding the risk posed by the truth commission.

From the point of view of the news reports themselves, however, the risk posed by the child organ stealing rumour is precisely that it allows such military manipulations of townspeople's fears. The rumour's capacity to generate a risk usable by the military to destabilize the country also entails a risk in itself, precisely because of its power to captivate the imagination and to incite action. Indeed, the risk of child organ stealing named by the rumour is directly opposed to the risk attributed to the rumour itself: to believe the rumour (and act on it) is to remain complicit with the right-wing attempt to impede human rights efforts.

Reports siding with this general analysis cite the following evidence to support their claim that the military was indeed involved in manipulating fears about child stealing for organ trafficking to their own ends: the presence of two known military men in the crowd of Weinstock's attackers; the appearance of a crew of workers who provided the men with sticks, which they used to beat Weinstock; and the arrival of military assistance three hours too late to prevent any damage (Frankel and Orlebar, 1994; Gleick ,1994; Johnson, 1994; Kadetsky, 1994; Orlebar, 1994; Perera, 1994). Two additional facts are cited as signs of the military's intent to destabilize the civilian government at this time. First, then Guatemalan President Ramiro de Leon Carpio replaced two high-level officials sympathetic to human rights efforts with supporters of the army's bid for immunity from all prosecution for human rights abuses. It is thought that he succumbed to military pressure in making this decision. Second, there is the assassination of Guatemala's Constitutional Court President, who had prevented the previous 'civilian' president Jorge Serrano Elias from installing yet another dictatorship, and was considered to be friendly to human rights efforts (Perera, 1994; White, 1994).

The military may well have harnessed the power of the child organ stealing rumour to explicitly political ends within Guatemala, but the question remains, once such a possibility is entertained, why this particular rumour might have been available and effective as a means of generating such powerful effects. Never questioning the rumour's power as a galvanizing force, accounts of the rumour that emphasize its manipulative use by the military insist that there is no actual threat of child organ stealing, only the (unreasonable) perception of risk. They account for the rumour's power in terms of Guatemalans' susceptibility to this kind of story on both cultural and political grounds.

In these reports, the risk of child organ stealing named in the rumour has been reproduced as an unfounded risk by relying on myth. Perera makes the explicit suggestion, for example, that the attacks on foreigners 'tap into indigenous fears that are at least 500 years old' (1994: M1). He then attributes these fears to the fact that '[w]hen the Spanish conquistadors invaded the Guatemalan Highlands in the 16th Century, Mayan mothers believed the men with pale complexions and blond beards were anaemic, and required the blood of brown-skinned infants to become well'. Orlebar's article makes the similar suggestion that the 'hysteria ... builds on local legend of Miculash, a Guatemalan bogeyman who stole children to make soap out of them' (Orlebar, 1994: A22).

Like the *New York Times* and *Los Angeles Times* accounts of the Weinstock incident, the *Village Voice* article by Elizabeth Kadetsky (1994) invokes myth as an explanation for the power of the child organ stealing story, but perhaps because it is concerned with the 'female face' of the rumour as an indicator of the 'national fixation on body parts', this account invokes the myth of La Llorona, said to be Cortés' lover. 'La Llorona', writes Kadetsky in a storyteller's mode:

> so curses the betrayal of the murderous white man and colonizer that she slips off to the nearest river and drowns her new infant, the first offspring of a white and Indian union. Forever after, La Llorona, the wailing woman, slinks along late-night riverbanks as she howls her song of mourning, searching for her lost child and snatching those children unlucky enough to cross her path. (1994: 26–7)

According to this account, the fear of kidnapping lives on in the bodies of contemporary indigenous children: 'Throughout Latin America and in Guatemala, where memories of conquest remain central to Mayan culture, children shiver on windy nights in fear of La Llorona's thieving grip' (Kadetsky, 1994: 28).

In some cases, these reports also link myth to contemporary Guatemalan events and realities. Perera suggests that 'ancient fears' have 'resurfaced' due to reports from the Guatemalan Attorney General's office of '20 kidnapping rings and at least 65 fattening houses operating in Guatemala'. Kadetsky's article explains the rumour's power in terms of the indigenous Pokonchí language's oral (rather than written) mode by way of a linguist from Guatemala City: 'People tend to hear something and they repeat it. This is an oral society. This is how knowledge is passed on, and often something is added' (Kadetsky, 1994: 25). But whether or not this additional link is made, these reports generate versions of the child organ stealing story both as naming an *unfounded* risk, and as a powerful story by creating a distance between a rational 'us' and an indigenous Guatemalan 'other'. Mired in mythological fantasies, this 'other' psychically inhabits a prior historical time, or employs an oral mode of communication, through which the rumour's power does its dangerous work. By this means, the 'real' risk of the rumour as a military agent gains authority, while the potential risk of child organ stealing identified by the same rumour is simultaneously *de*authorized as risk.

In contrast to other versions of the Weinstock incident, the *Village Voice* rendition points out that while the events cited took place mostly between foreigners and indigenous Guatemalans in rural areas, the fear of child organ stealing had spread widely. Middle class Guatemalans were also circulating the rumour in various forms, and protecting their children on sight of a foreigner. While this account also extends 'gruesome fantasizing' from the indigenous population to the middle class in Guatemala (Kadetsky, 1994: 26), it refuses the possibility that there might be any validity to the risk of child organ stealing feared by those who repeat the rumour and act on it as a possible truth.

In these reports, then, the rumour itself is reproduced as a technology of a specific risk, the risk to the Guatemalan peace process posed by the rumour. It is this second version of the rumour that is authorized as the more rational and politically valid. The risk it poses, furthermore, is located specifically in Guatemala, and in the transnational peace efforts devoted to the nation. But while the rumour's risk has been located in this specific local-global nexus in the above accounts, other news reports on the rumour are oriented to risks dispersed across a 'modern' and global terrain. As the folklorist most cited by Leventhal puts it, the 'baby-parts story shows a mixture of spontaneous creation and sophisticated manipulation that is characteristic of our global village' (Campion-Vincent, 1990: 9).[2] Newspaper reports countering the child organ stealing stories reproduce it as a 'modern urban legend' whose appeal is not associated with ancient myths or even national political conditions, but rather with more generic and universal fears associated with modernity. According to this set of reports, it is because of these compelling fears that the rumour has confused the United Nations, the European Parliament, and consumers of the global media, along with the residents of San Cristóbal Verapaz.

Globalizing rumours and countering risks: the rumour as a 'modern urban legend'

The 'modern urban legend' is a category used by folklorists to describe the child organ stealing rumour as a false but powerful story (Brunvand, 1993; Campion-Vincent, 1990; Turner, 1992). This category's usage in news reports is often accompanied by quotes from Todd Leventhal. Indeed, given that Leventhal's overall countering strategy can be read in these counter-reports as well, it seems likely that these reports represent the USIA's success in generating counter-stories, as Leventhal himself claims (see Leventhal, 1994; 1995a). I have already suggested that the Program Officer's concern with the rumour's appearance in the world press lies in its presentation as a legitimate story, a factual report. Child organ stealing was first published as a fact supported by the testimony of judges and other officials. Both the London *Daily Telegraph* and the French *L'Humanité* published reports of child organ trafficking in Brazil in the 1980s (Mauro, 1988; Pinero, 1987). *L'Humanité* also published follow-up reports documenting further cases of child organ trafficking in 1988 and 1992 (Cordier, 1988; Pinero, 1992). The rumour has also been maintained as a valid allegation by the United Nations, the European Parliament, and numerous newspapers, as well as a number of television magazine programmes, and documentary films. *Le Monde* documented cases of child organ stealing as part of a report on the European Parliament's official ban on organ trafficking in 1993 (Scotto, 1993). Various United Nations investigations on child organ trafficking have been undertaken, leaving the Special Investigator convinced of the existence of such trafficking in spite of inconclusive evidence (Muntarbhorn, 1993; 1994a; 1994b), and these conclusions, too, have been cited in news reports. The initial weight of media attention, then, was not directed at debunking the rumour as completely false. Leventhal's reports and associated news counter-stories charge that all of the evidence offered is simply passed from one report to another, even when that evidence has been contradicted by counter-testimonies given by families, judges, and other parties (Frankel, 1995; Leventhal, 1994; Pukas, 1995).

Leventhal's current strategy in countering these reports is only partially devoted to providing counter-evidence. The problem with misinformation (as opposed to disinformation), he argues, is that it progresses not because of an identifiable agent (a foreign government, etc.), but in accordance with its appeal, its compelling power.[3] Particularly in the absence of any nameable origin or culprit, this power makes the rumour prolifically reproductive. Once further enhanced by the reproductive capacity of the global media, the self-generativity of misinformation becomes intractably difficult to stop. The best way to accomplish this task, according to Leventhal, is to counter the child organ stealing rumour by promoting counter-stories that do not simply denounce the story as false (by providing counter-evidence), but work at both levels of the rumour's power.

The 'modern urban legend' is used to achieve precisely this goal. 'Modern urban legends' are false stories that are obviously false. (Among Leventhal's favourites is a story told about a pet owner trying to dry a dog in a microwave oven, thereby exploding the dog.) 'False stories ... we've all heard them, we've all believed them, and a lot of people have realized they're not true ... You can ... list dozens of different stories that people believe that are *totally* false' (Leventhal, 1995a). To place the child organ stealing rumour in this context, then, is to make its own falseness apparent; any validity that the rumour might carry is rendered invalid by its similarity with other fantastic stories. Rather than simply countering rumours already heard as true, Leventhal hopes to predispose his audience to recognizing false stories as such. As Leventhal puts it, the aim is to 'pigeonhole it in people's minds ... I prefer them to hear about it as a false rumour or as an urban legend first' (Leventhal, 1995a). His best strategy is to pre-empt versions of the rumour as true by supplying a view of the rumour as false. In his report, Leventhal posits 'rational scrutiny' against unfounded credibility in the rumour, given the absence of valid evidence combined with the technical impossibility of clandestine organ transplant. His aim is to reproduce the rumour according to these terms: the rumour as a false story, and as itself a risk rather than as a valid identification and assessment of risk.

Two recent counter-stories that Leventhal claims as his successes bear the mark of this strategy. A *Newsweek* magazine article and a London *Sunday Times* piece are considered here as examples of counter-stories that employ a series of strategies to *de*authorize the rumour as true. In both reports, this deauthorization is advanced partly on the grounds that the rumour itself poses risks, this time not related to the Guatemalan peace process, but on a different global scale. These risks are related to the rumour's effectiveness not just in Guatemala, but everywhere the rumour has been reported as true, and wherever it resonates with the fears of modern urban existence.

In June 1996, *Newsweek* ran an article headlined 'Too Good to be True'. Its subtitle read: 'Tall Tales: Everyone's Heard the Heartbreaking Stories about Third World Kids being Killed for their Internal Organs. Just One Problem: They're False' (Frankel, 1995; hereafter cited as NW). The London *Sunday Times*' slightly more sensational headline read: 'A horrifying story began as local gossip and spread to fool the world: the global lie that cannot be silenced' (Pukas, 1995; hereafter cited as LST). Both reports provide specific 'factual' counter-evidence. They offer the suggestion that organ trafficking is impossible because, along with the fact that organ trafficking is illegal, 'the entire US transplant system is highly controlled by the United Network for Organ Sharing (UNOS), which registers and tracks each donated organ' (NW; see also Leventhal, 1994, 1995b).

Additional counter-facts cited are that organs also have a short 'shelf life' (a heart lasts 4 hours before degenerating, and a kindey 48 to 72 hours) (NW, LST), and organs must be tissue-matched in order to avoid rejection (LST). Both counter-stories also quote UNOS spokesman Joel Newman's remark that: 'You can't just turn up with a kidney in a cooler and say to some hospital, "Hey, are you interested"' (NW, LST) which, by its tone, dismisses child organ stealing as an unfounded rumour.

The two reports also include 1996 versions of the rumour culled from local Brazilian and other Latin American newspaper reports. In one such version, men and women dressed in costumes lure children into a van, cut out their vital organs, and sell them to rich foreigners for transplant. As *Newsweek* put it, this initial rumour proliferated into even 'wilder' rumours as it was retold (NW). A second recent version of the rumour reproduced in these reports involves an account of child organ stealing published in São Paulo's newspapers, which tell of Eduardo Feliciano Oliveira Jr's death in a local hospital. The infant's parents charged the hospital with removing the infant's organs in order to cover up medical wrong-doing when the autopsy revealed that his eyes had been removed, his abdominal organs were missing, and his abdominal cavity had been stuffed with sawdust. While the family's lawyer made no charge of organ stealing, the story was, as the *Sunday Times'* Anna Pukas put it, 'caught up in the myth of Third World children murdered for their internal organs that keeps surfacing around the world'. That is, it became part of a global myth according to these accounts.

While some stories reproduced in these reports are simply dismissed as 'preposterous, bunk, hokum' (NW), others that have circulated through the world press are granted a more detailed response. These longer-standing and more widely-circulating versions of the child stealing rumour are printed in these reports together with retractions issued in response to publicity, or investigations undertaken by Leventhal and other authorities that are said to prove the rumour false. For example, both reports display half-page photographs of blind boys whose eyes had been claimed to have been stolen, but who, the text asserts, actu-ally lost their eyes to infection. In the London *Sunday Times'* version of this story, the visual 'evidence' (the captioned photograph) is corroborated by Leventhal himself, who is reported as having obtained the pictured boy's medical records documenting the infection. Both articles report a retraction made by the boy's half brother, in which he admits to lying about the eye theft, and grants that his eyes, too, were lost to infection.

In keeping with Leventhal's strategy, these reports' reproductions of the rumour provide counter-evidence while 'recontextualizing' the rumour as an effective but false story with considerable risks, whose effectiveness extends across a modern, global world. Moving from the apparent absurdity of the rumours to an alternative mythological logic, evidenced by the existence of child stealing rumours since antiquity and in all parts of the world, these reports note the power of the rumour as an urban legend, rather than as a potential fact. It is this mythological power, they claim, that explains why, 'in spite of the lack of evidence', this story 'has been swallowed by the United Nations, the World Health Organization, the European Parliament, and much of the international media' (LST).

The rumour's classification as 'whispers of allegation … transformed into pseudo-fact' (NW), as 'urban myth,' (LST) and 'legend' (NW) is also combined with the alternative explanations of the rumour's power that this strategy requires. For example, the *Newsweek* article cites Campion-Vincent's analysis of the rumour as follows:

> Writing in a 1990 issue of *Western Folklore*, a journal of the California Folklore Society, [Campion-Vincent] notes that though body snatching is a myth, illegal adoptions by foreigners are a real, albeit small, problem. The body-parts rumour began to spread at the same time that illegal adoption rackets were uncovered in both Honduras and Guatemala; children of unknown origin were discovered in so-called fattening houses, from which they were sold to overseas couples.

Having posed the 'fact' of child stealing and selling for transnational adoption against the 'myth' of child stealing for transnational organ-selling, *Newsweek* goes on to suggest that the child organ stealing rumour is also generated by a cultural misunderstanding between the First and Third Worlds:

> 'The humanitarian impulse of the First World is totally misunderstood in many countries where these rumours arise', says Bill Pierce, chairman of the Washington-based National Council for Adoption. 'In that culture it can be really impossible to understand why a couple of middle-class Americans would want to adopt such a child. The "logical" answer is that they must want to profit from the child in some way'. It's sometimes easier to imagine the evil within the human heart than to perceive the real mercy.

Due to an intelligible but ultimately illogical line of thought, then, Latin Americans have failed to appreciate the generosity of US adoptive parents. Like these Latin Americans, the UN investigator of the rumour, journalists all over the world, and documentary filmmakers like Judy Jackson (British director of *The Body Parts Business*, a film on the subject), 'swallowed the myth whole', all the while 'jettisoning or ignoring facts that get in the way of what is admittedly a compelling fable' (NW).

These two counter-stories, then, appeal to the readers' rationality, asking us to accept the 'true' facts. While admitting our susceptibility to the rumour, we can help to avoid the real risks posed by it. These risks include the risk to continued transnational adoption, to organ donation, and so on. The London *Sunday Times* adds a new twist to this list, however. Its quote from folklorist Paul Smith of the University of Newfoundland, reads: 'The important thing is why people believe them, the ideas and fears the myths express and the way some myths eventually come true'. With this observation, the risk of rumour comes full circle, as the *Sunday Times* concludes: 'It would be tragic indeed if the legend of the organ-snatchers were to become reality just because it was too horrible to believe' (LST). The risk of the rumour identified here, as elsewhere, lies in its generative power. But that power is not turned to an alternative task such as disturbing a peace process, or explaining a culturally inscrutable gesture of 'mercy'. It is, rather, a power so great that it might actually bring about the impossible truth that it names.

Risking rumour: the child-body as a site of global risk

In the end, unravelling the allegations and counter-allegations that run through
the stories either documenting or debunking the child organ stealing story is
nearly impossible. Both sides recycle information such that the reports themselves become as indeterminate as the rumour they attempt to pin down. The
relation between rumour and risk that emerges from these news reports is
indeterminate as well: the risks reproduced in relation to the rumour can be different according to different global locations, for different constituencies, different bodies, and, ultimately, different regimes of truth. How are 'we' as readers
or consumers of media reports on rumour to evaluate the resulting array of
contradictory yet equally volatile risks, the insistent indeterminacy of rumour?
The complex of rumour and risk variously authorized and deauthorized in the
rumour's multiple reproductions offers no easy answers, not least because the
power of rumour to capture our own imaginations, to stimulate our own sense of
horrified fascination with risk, works in excess of the available evidence.

And yet, contrary to the folklorist's claim that the truth of a rumour does not
matter as much as its compelling power, I would argue that it does matter whether
or not the child organ stealing rumour is true or not, because the consequences of
each possibility are different, and require different responses. While there can be
no certainty as to the risks involved, my own assessment of the story attempts to
make recourse precisely to rumour's indeterminacy, asserting not so much that
the story is true as that it is not possible to be certain that it is false. With the
United Nations, the European Parliament, and some news reports, I am compelled
to insist that the child organ stealing is potentially true, if only in order to retain
the possibility of further investigations of the matter, to refuse the deauthorization of the child organ stealing rumour as a reasonable, if possibly erroneous,
assessment of risk. While there are good reasons to resist the child organ stealing
rumour's pull – most notably the risks it has posed for human rights efforts in
Guatemala – there are also good reasons to attend to its insistent reproduction of
child organ stealing as a potentially legitimate risk.

No doubt there is some validity to the contention that the child organ stealing
story gives voice to diffuse fears associated with bodily integrity, the power of
medical science, and so on. But this does not necessarily exclude the possibility
that the rumour also identifies a possible truth, an actual practice undertaken
in historically and geopolitically specific conditions. That is, child organ stealing
is what Jean Comaroff has called a 'generic category with an extensive cultural
history' (Comaroff, n.d.: 9). For Comaroff, a category like 'witchcraft' – or,
in this case, 'child organ stealing' – can be simultaneously generic, widely
employed across a range of locations, and specific to a given time and place.
Comaroff distinguishes between the 'general sign' and the 'particular instance' of
such categories, and argues that 'it is the tension between the general sign and the
particular instance that generates insight' when considering such categories
(Comaroff, n.d.: 9).

Considered in these terms, the child organ stealing rumour can be a technology
of plural kinds of risks that are differently located, but in which the child remains

a central figure. Indeed, Comaroff observes that contemporary anxieties often centre on children's bodies as the vulnerable targets of global capital as it is manifested in everyday life. These anxieties are often organized around the literal and figurative consumption of children, and on capital profit extracted from the alienation of bodily substances by forces operating beyond the reach of formal authority or state control. For Comaroff, the child at risk is the product of a particular historical conjuncture, which in the late-twentieth-century has been characterized by a global economy. But as global effects take local shape, the dangers they entail and the anxieties they reproduce change. In Nigeria, Cameroon, and South Africa, witches are said to steal children and eat their souls, while in the United States (and Europe), 'child abuse' has become the quintessential crime. The child figures as a central target of risk in either case not only because its appearance in these stories names the actual vicitimization of children, but also because it condenses a multitude of anxieties, 'collaps[ing] into one carnal sign, diverse sources of angst about an endangered mode of domestic reproduction; about the breakdown of the nuclear family and the commercialization of bodies, procreation, and childcare; about sharp shifts in a gendered division of labour' (Comaroff, n.d.: 25–6). Comaroff further extends the already double work done by the category of child abuse to its expression of 'more profound crises' lying behind the 'sense of loss ... of a moral home in the world', and even further, to 'the terms of Western modernism itself, among them, the secure contrasts of male and female, gifts and commodities, public and private, white and black, West and other, local and global' (Comaroff, n.d.: 26).

It is this plural work of stories suggested by Comaroff's analysis that I wish to emphasize here. For while Comaroff tends to emphasize witch stories and child abuse as 'moral commentaries on contemporary experience' and 'ways of phrasing local interventions in global histories', and on the child as an 'icon' endangered in the 'standardized nightmares' of communities, she also suggests that stories can chronicle risks or the possibility of risks otherwise denied. Such stories are 'transcripts from particular moral worlds' where the 'worlds' are both metaphorical and material. The 'truth' in such worlds 'lies in the details' (Comaroff, n.d.: 26).

The child organ stealing rumour can also be considered as an account of risk whose 'truths' may lie in both metaphorically and materially consequential details. Considering the rumour in this way presupposes and implies a specific world, with its own standards of evidence and legitimacy. One of the main features of the world described by Comaroff in relation to witchcraft is the economization of bodies through modern technologies of extraction and commodification (18–19). This point can be made with regard to the child organ stealing rumour as well, since two of the reproductive technologies associated with the rumour – organ transplantation and transnational adoption – are also implicated in the economization of bodies. In these two technologies, the economization of the child-body is a key factor in the reproduction of risk to the child. From this point of view, the child organ stealing story highlights the shifting value of the child in a global economy of value generated in relation to reproductive technologies. Tied to global capital (a transnational trade in body parts), to the possibilities generated by modern medical science and technology (the possibility of organ transplantation), and to the documented value of children in a transnational market (child-stealing for transnational adoption), the stolen child named by the rumour as the victim of organ stealing is literally globalized as its body parts are disseminated transnationally. That is, the child-in-pieces conjured by the rumour's insistent reproduction is distributed to other bodies that receive its missing organs.

This dissemination implies at least two categories of children existing within this globalized domain. In some versions of the rumour, the missing child is returned after its organs have been extracted and then bought by wealthy foreigners for transplant into their own children. For every child missing an organ, then, there is another who receives that organ. The two categories of children that appear in this version of the child organ stealing rumour also map a global economy of value constituted through organ exchange. The missing child's value in this economy is measured in terms of body parts, while the child-recipient of the organ is valued in terms of bodily integrity and continued life. In other versions of the rumour, the missing child disappears or is found dead. In this case, it is not an organ alone that is transferred from one child to another according to this same economy, but life itself.

As we have seen, it is not difficult to maintain that the rumour reproduces a story that names metaphorical risks associated with a globalized world and its economies. In fact, Todd Leventhal's reports as well as most news reports provide descriptions of the rumour as just such a story, a story about globally relevant fears regarding bodily integrity under conditions of modern technological progress, as well as economic inequalities across a north–south divide (Leventhal, 1994; 1995b). Comaroff's analysis, however, suggests that even metaphorical stories are both more 'local' in their particular negotiation of the global, and more historically relevant, than such generalized interpretations allow. For her, 'witches animate an alternative modernism that is also an alternative mode of authorization and a critical moral commentary on the contemporary global condition as it collides with the local social world' (Comaroff, n.d.: 10–15). According to this analysis, seemingly identical stories that circulate globally may be related to quite different material conditions and metaphorical meanings depending on the particular historical, political, social, and cultural conditions through which they are reproduced.

The child organ stealing rumour, then, may be more effectively described not as a single rumour, but as a series of 'local' stories in a global frame. I can now suggest that the rumour's story of child organ stealing reproduces an account of a potentially legitimate risk, and embodies reasonable fears. I make this claim specifically about the rumour as a 'local' story, that is, in its circulation through Guatemala. In the context of the reign of terror that continues (at this writing) to operate in Guatemala with almost unimaginable impunity, and the documented fact of child stealing for transnational adoption, in conjunction with the well-known shortage of transplant organs worldwide (New et al., 1994), and the fact that neither the United Nations nor the European Parliament have changed their position on child organ stealing as a legitimate risk, child organ theft does not seem entirely impossible. As I suggest in the following section, it is the insecurity of doubt, rather than the confidence of certainty, that compels this conclusion.

Conclusion: whose risk, whose rumour?

In the course of my writing this chapter, the BBC aired a documentary about exhumations of mass graves in Guatemala (Rosin, 1996), which suggested the importance of relying on alternative regimes of evidence and truth in order to sustain that which one believes to be legitimate even though it is deauthorized as abnormal and indeed impossible according to reigning standards. Forensic anthropologists have been occupied since the 1980s with exhumations, aimed at identifying the cause of death detectable in the skeletons found in mass graves. Titled *Traces of Guilt*, the BBC documentary featured a team of Guatemalan and foreign investigators who identified the buried bodies through forensic methods with the help of local residents. The team concluded that the dead had been killed by military forces on the basis of the bullets used and the forms of torture employed.

At one point in the documentary, local residents in Plan de Sánchez were filmed helping to identify the bodies of their friends and relatives. The grave site was surrounded by armed government personnel. A familiar presence, the police stand for some as a reminder that reprisals, including disappearance, torture, and death, might ensue for anyone who collaborated with the exhumation effort. The documentary intermittently cut from the gravesite to an interview with an unnamed local resident, whose words were translated through an English voice-over. Among the comments cut into the grave-digging sequences were the following:

> The army keeps harassing us, trying to stop us talking to you. But they have to understand that there is a law for us as well, and this has to stop. We're speaking out to break the cycle of impunity so that we are an example to other nations and this can never happen again.

The cycle of impunity to which this statement refers includes the massacre of entire villages, including six others which occurred at the same time as the killings in Plan de Sánchez, according to the documentary. Given its reference to Guatemalan resistance as an example to other nations, it also signifies the much broader orchestration of disappearance, torture, and death suffered by the largely indigenous and poor citizens of Guatemala.

Among the skeletal remains exhumed from Plan de Sánchez were those of two children, both of which showed signs of torture and death by shooting. According to Amnesty International, among other observers, children have been the targets of other violent campaigns as well. Specifically, Amnesty International has documented disappearances, torture, beating, raping and harassment of street children in Guatemala City by police and other security agents, including private security firms and other civilians, all of whose actions have gone unchecked. Some children have been forced to swallow glue (children living in the streets are known to sniff glue to stave off hunger and for its hallucinatory effects), or had glue poured on their heads by police (Amnesty International, 1990, 1992). Some of these children have been further subjected to violence at the hands of police for testifying to child agencies and the courts about the violence perpetrated against them and their companions (1992: 1–2).

Given the level of impunity under which Guatemalan children as well as adults have lived, combined with the persistent denial of wrongdoing on the part of the government, often with US and media complicity, it seems imperative to support accounts of unimaginable violence, including child organ stealing. The level of clandestine organization required to carry out secret organ removal does not seem much greater than that required for state genocide or child kidnapping for transnational adoption. If the child organ stealing story is true in any way, a sustained effort will be required to prove it. If the story is false, that sustained effort could contribute to maintaining vigilance over the conditions of Guatemalan children who live the cycle of impunity. It could be used to support their efforts, along with the efforts of many others in Guatemala and abroad, to bring economic, cultural, social, and political justice to the majority of Guatemalans, in terms responsive to its local and global histories and contemporary conditions.

The case of the child organ stealing story suggests that reproducing risk is a highly political matter, which involves deciding what counts as risk while sustaining concern for both the metaphorical and profoundly material consequences of risk. Questionable by definition, 'rumour' can be understood as an unauthorized risk, whose indeterminacy highlights the uncertainty of risk itself, and even of modernity as the generator of risks beyond its own powers of assessment and control. Rumour may reasonably identify risks, but reason cannot answer rumour's captivating and reproductive mode, its power to generate and regenerate, to be taken up and be generated again, to move emotions and motivate action. Rumour is not modern, but *a*modern: if rumour is associated with multiple risks, perhaps one of them is a risk posed to the certainty that underlies the very notion of modernity as an adequate historical and sociological description of the world.

Acknowledgements

I wish to thank Joost van Loon and an anonymous referee for their valuable comments on earlier drafts of this chapter, together with Donna Haraway and James Clifford for their readings of the dissertation chapter on which this is based.

Notes

1   Perera's *Rites: A Guatemalan Boyhood* (1986) chronicles his upper middle class childhood in Guatemala City. His *Unfinished Conquest: The Guatemalan Tragedy* (1993) offers a historically informed analysis of the then current political situation in Guatemala.

2   The author, Veronique Campion-Vincent, cites Leventhal in this work, so that the two are citing one another as experts on the rumour. Leventhal charges news reports of the

rumour with recycling evidence from one report to the next, but this same circularity of citation is evident, as this example shows, in the counter-stories as well.

3   Counter-stories published in 1988 bearing Leventhal's mark identify the rumour as the product of both disinformation and misinformation. For example, in the *Washington Post*'s 1988 report titled 'Nailing Disinformation: The Slum-Child Tale', 'USIA officials' cite the Soviet Union's 'disinformation propaganda apparatus' as a key actor in the rumour's global dissemination (Goshko, 1988). However, disinformation is not mentioned as an important factor with regard to more recent continued reproductions of the rumour. Leventhal's reports and news counter-stories now identify the rumour only as disinformation.

References

Adam, B. (1996) 'Re-vision: The Centrality of Time for an Ecological Social Science Perspective', in S. Lash, B. Szerszynski and B. Wynne (eds), *Risk, Environment and Modernity: Towards a New Ecology*. London: Sage. pp. 84–103.

Amnesty International (1990) *Guatemala, Extrajudicial Executions and Human Rights Abuses Against Street Children*. New York: Amnesty International.

Amnesty International (1992) *Guatemala: Children in Fear*. New York: Amnesty International.

Beck, U. (1992) *Risk Society: Towards a New Modernity*. Trans. M. Ritter. London: Sage.

Beck-Gernsheim, E. (1996) 'Life as a Planning Project', in S. Lash, B. Szerszynski and B. Wynne (eds), *Risk, Environment and Modernity: Towards a New Ecology*. London: Sage. pp. 139–53.

Booth, W. (1994) 'Witch Hunt'. *The Washington Post*, (17 May): C1.

Brunvand, J.H. (1993) *The Baby Train and Other Lusty Urban Legends*. New York and London: W.W. Norton & Co.

Campion-Vincent, V. (1990) 'The Baby-Parts Story: A New Latin American Legend', *Western Folklore*, 49 (January): 9–25.

Comaroff, J. (n.d.) 'Consuming Passions: Child Abuse, Fetishism, and the "New World Order"'. Unpublished manuscript.

Cordier, J.M. (1988) 'La Baby Connection', *L'Humanité*, (21 October): 22.

Fabian, J. (1983) *Time and the Other: How Anthropology Makes its Object*. New York: Columbia University Press.

Frankel, M., (1995) 'Too Good to be True', *Newsweek*, (26 June): 20–2.

Frankel, M. and Orlebar, E. (1994) 'Child Stealers Go Home', *Newsweek*, (18 April): 24.

Gleick, E. (1994) 'Rumour and Rage', *People*, (25 April): 78–80.

Goshko, J.M. (1988) 'Nailing Disinformation: The Slum-Child Tale', *The Washington Post*, 25 August.

Johnson, T. (1994) 'Rumours, Rage, Xenophobia in Guatemala', *Miami Herald*, (27 March): 1A.

Jonas, S. (1991) *The Battle for Guatemala*. Boulder, CO: Westview Press.

Kadetsky, E. (1994) 'Guatemala Inflamed', *The Village Voice*, (31 May): 25–9.

Leventhal, T. (1994) '*The Child Organ Trafficking Rumor: A Modern "Urban Legend"*'. Report submitted to the United Nations Special Rapporteur on the Sale of Children, Child Prostitution, and Child Pornography. Washington, DC: United States Information Agency.

Leventhal, T. (1995a) Interview by author at USIA in Washington, DC (November).

Leventhal, T. (1995b) 'The Illegal Transportation and Sale of Human Organs: Reality or Myth?'. Paper presented at European Police Executive Conference, Ghent, Belgium.

López, L. (1994) 'Dangerous Rumours', *Time*, (8 April): 48.

Maclean's (Staff writers) (1994) 'Stolen Children? A Child Snatching Hysteria Sweeps the Country', *Maclean's*, (May): 36.

Manz, B. (1988) *Refugees of a Hidden War*. Albany: State University of New York Press.

Mauro, L. (1988) 'Babies Kidnapped for US Organ Banks', *The Daily Telegraph*, 9 August.

Muntarbhorn, V. (1993) *'Sale of Children'*. Report submitted by Mr Vitit Muntabhorn. Special Rapporteur appointed in accordance with Commission on Human Rights resolution 1992/76 (E/CN.4/1993/67). United Nations Economic and Social Council, Commission on Human Rights.

Muntarbhorn, V. (1994a) *'Sale of Children'*. Report submitted by Mr Vitit Muntabhorn. Special Rapporteur appointed in accordance with Commission on Human Rights resolution 1992/76 (E/CN.4/1994/84). United Nations Economic and Social Council, Commission on Human Rights.

Muntarbhorn, V. (1994b) *'Sale of Children, Child Prostitution and Child Pornography'*, addendum. Visit by the Special Rapporteur to Nepal (E/CN.4/1994/84/Add.1). United Nations Economic and Social Council, Commission on Human Rights.

New, B., Solomon, M., Dingwall, R. and McHale, J. (1994) 'A Question of Give and Take: Improving the Supply of Donor Organs for Transplantation'. London: King's Fund Institute, Research Report on Health Policy Issues. No 18.

Orlebar, E. (1994) 'Child Kidnapping Rumours Fuel Attacks on Americans', *Los Angeles Times*, (1 April): A1/A22.

Perera, V. (1986) *Rites: A Guatemalan Boyhood*. San Diego: Harcourt Brace, Jovanovich.

Perera, V. (1993) *Unfinished Conquest: The Guatemalan Tragedy*. Berkeley: University of California Press.

Perera, V. (1994) 'Behind the Kidnapping of Children for their Organs', *New York Times*, (1 May): M1/M6.

Pinero, M. (1987) 'A Vendre Coeurs d'Enfants', *L'Humanité*, (14 April): 18.

Pinero, M. (1992) 'Enlèvements d'enfants et trafic d'organes', *L'Humanité*, (August): 17.

Pukas, A. (1995) 'The Global Lie That Cannot Be Silenced', *The Sunday Times*, 19 July.

Rosin, I. (1996) *Traces of Guilt*. London: BBC/A&E Network.

Schemo, D.J. (1996) 'Courts Condone Illegal Baby Trade', *The Guardian* (Manchester), (22 March): 14.

Scotto, M. (1993) 'Le Parlement Européen Condamne le Commerce des Organes', *Le Monde*, 16 September.

Turner, P.A. (1992) 'Ambivalent Patrons: The Role of Rumour and Contemporary Legends in African-American Consumer Decisions', *Journal of American Western Folklore*, 105 (418): 424–41.

UNOS (1994) 'Questions and Answers about US Organ Allocation', information pamphlet. Richmond, Virginia: United Network for Organ Sharing.

White, I. (1994) 'Who Is Stealing Guatemala's Children? Behind the Attacks on US Tourists', *Report on Guatemala*, (Spring): 2–5.

Wynne, B. (1996) 'May the Sheep Graze Safely? A Reflexive View of the Expert-Lay Knowledge Divide', in S. Lash, B. Szerszynski and B. Wynne (eds), *Risk, Environment and Modernity: Towards a New Ecology*. London: Sage. pp. 44–83.

8

Liturgies of Fear: Biotechnology and Culture

Howard Caygill

During the 1980s the locus of anxiety regarding the technological threat to the future of human life shifted from nuclear technology in its civil and military guises to biotechnology. In many respects this shift marked the reprise of an earlier, pre-Cold War cultural anxiety focused upon eugenics and the biological control of populations. The earlier anxiety was sufficient in the case of Germany (and in other ostensibly more democratic societies) to mobilize support for political movements and legislative initiatives dedicated to biologically selecting the character of future human populations. The current wave of anxiety in some respects repeats the unstable fusion of fear and desire that characterized the earlier culture of eugenics, with the difference that now the object of concern is less the survival of a particular 'race' or 'nation' than that of the human species itself. Developments in biotechnology are perceived to pose a potentially irreversible threat to the future of human life, producing a culture of anxiety which is framed and debated within the limits of existing religious, political and aesthetic culture even while exceeding and challenging them.

Whatever the accuracy of the perceived risk to human life posed by biotechnology, the anxiety which surrounds it is proving a central and productive feature of contemporary culture. The positive and negative fantasies which constitute this anxiety manifest themselves in the actions and proclamations of such public institutions as the State, the Church and the medical profession as well as in art, popular science, film, music and fiction. Together these internally inconsistent and often competing versions of the biotechnical imaginary aspire to create a culture capable of reflecting upon, assessing and perhaps even managing the risks posed by biotechnology.

The range of perspectives contained within this emergent culture can be illustrated by three ideal–typical responses to the threat of biotechnology: the 1995 encyclical letter of Pope John Paul II, *Evangelium vitae: the Value and Inviolability of Human Life*; the 1992 report of a Working Party of the British Medical Association, *Our Genetic Future: The Science and Ethics of Genetic Technology* and the work since the late 1980s of the Australian performance artist Stelarc. All three works – religious, scientific and aesthetic – are devoted to framing the risk to the future of human life posed by biotechnology, but do so in ways which, while predictably diverse, display some surprisingly convergent features.

Each of these texts and works attempts to frame the threat posed by biotechnology in terms of an existing repertoire of cultural interpretation and resistance, but finds that these are themselves transformed in the process. Each presents an imagined future for the human species, and from this dream (or nightmare) attempts to frame cultural responses which will either counter, or promote, the feared/desired future. The ambivalence with respect to the future may be registered in the ambiguous cultural strategies that each of the texts contrives in order to manage the effects of anxiety, strategies which oscillate between the retreat to a religious, scientific-professional or artistic subculture and the megalomaniacal ambition to inaugurate a wide-ranging cultural revolution.

Evangelium vitae

In the encyclical letter addressed to 'Bishops, Clergy, Monks and Nuns, the Faithful Laity and all Persons of Good Will', Pope John Paul II called on behalf of the Catholic Church for a 'culture of life' opposed to the prevailing, secular 'culture of death'. The letter defines the culture of death in terms of an extension of the 'crimes and attacks against human life' detailed in a document of the Church Council of Vatican II (1965) which encompassed a depressing range of violations of the human body and human dignity. After citing the conciliar document John Paul II extends its list of violations to include recent scientific and technological developments: 'Unfortunately this disturbing panorama, far from being reduced, has been extended: with the new perspectives opened by scientific progress and technology are born new forms of attack on the dignity of human beings...' (1995: 8).

The threat posed by biotechnology is thus aligned with those actions identified by the Church as injurious to the flourishing of human life. Biotechnology is a central feature of the 'culture of death' which in the wake of liberal individualism and moral relativism has made it 'difficult to maintain a grasp on the meaning of the human, its rights and obligations' (1995: 19). The unqualified value of human life in itself is succeeded by 'the conception of an efficient society' (1995: 20) in which all other values are subordinated to those of economic and political efficiency.

For the encyclical letter, the concept of efficiency is an insidiously disguised exercise of violence on the part of the economically and politically powerful, a form of 'conspiracy against life'. The victims of the 'culture of death' are the 'inefficient', namely the poor, the ill and those with a 'handicap' and the key agents of their persecution are those who decide what constitutes an efficient life. These are above all the scientists and biotechnologists who pursue their research within the parameters of a naturalistic understanding of human life. Those engaged in genetic research and the development of techniques of artificial reproduction are in the vanguard of this culture, especially in so far as they regard their object of research – human embryos – as raw material for research or technological manipulation:

embryos are produced in numbers greater than are necessary for implantation in the wombs of women and these so-called 'surplus embryos' come to be destroyed or used for research which, under the pretext of scientific or medical progress, in reality reduce human life to a simple 'biological material' which may freely be disposed of. (1995: 23)

The encyclical letter declares such research, 'the expanding field of biomedical research legally permitted in some states' (1995: 94), as thoroughly inconsistent with human dignity. This is because the 'life and integrity of the embryo' is injured when it is treated naturalistically as raw material for the production of efficient human beings. The document aligns this treatment of the fertilized egg with pre-natal screening and selective abortion of 'abnormal embryos'.

The position adopted by the document is consistent with the Church's doctrine regarding the integrity of the human person at the moment of conception. Yet even while reiterating the position sustained by the 'Christian tradition' regarding the spiritual integrity of the embryo, the encyclical letter resorts to citing the 'precious confirmation furnished by modern genetic science' (1995: 90). It is difficult to imagine how the 'individuality' of a fertilized cell as conceived by genetics can accord with the traditional position of the Church regarding the integrity of the human personality. For the former, the fertilized cell is individual in so far as it is a product of a singular combination of the genetic heritage of the parents. Unless this moment of chance combination is made the unfathomable, perhaps divine origin of the singular being, then the positions of Church and genetics are not compatible. Indeed, such individual combinations of genetic material cannot support a definition of the singularity of a human life since such unique combinations characterize all the products of sexed reproduction, not solely those of human beings.

Before the fact of the 'culture of death' – whose scientific ideology seems to have penetrated even the documents of the Vatican – *Evangelium vitae* proclaims a culture of life. Yet this cultural politics is extremely ambiguous, and takes a number of forms in the final part of the encyclical letter. At its broadest, the promotion of a 'culture' of life entails a wide-ranging cultural politics entailing a 'general mobilization of conscience and a common ethical effort to put into action a grand strategy in favour of life. Everyone must join together to create a new culture of life' (1995: 139). This entails a mobilization of believers and non-believers as well as an institutional cultural politics directed against medical scientists and practitioners (1995: 131), educational practitioners, intellectuals and 'workers in the mass media' (1995: 145).

In this version of the revolutionary culture of life 'everyone has an important role to play' (1995: 144). Against the hegemony of the culture of death, a broad alliance of forces has to be united to pursue a counter-hegemonic culture of life. But as in the Gramscian cultural politics of the Italian Communist Party, whose experience uncannily informs this document, the dangers of a sectarian retreat of the true believers to their own churches, or party cells, is omnipresent. Consequently alongside the calls for a broad cultural politics can be found those recommending a retreat to the narrow, sacramental culture of the Church and the 'celebration of the liturgical year' (1995: 125). In many respects the pursuit of both a grand and a modest cultural strategy has been a characteristic of the

Church and ecclesiology since Augustine's description of the two cities in the *City of God*. In the case of biotechnology the implications even for believers are so considerable that the Church's universal mission is accentuated, almost to the point of reducing to insignificance its sectarian mission of providing a sacramental liturgy for the benefit of believers. This tension is evident in the appeal to the evidence of genetics, which marks an attempt to mediate between the Church's sacramental role and the terrain of secular ideology (genetic science) with which it must engage if it is to pursue a broader cultural strategy.

Evangelium vitae recognizes the role of the medical professions as central to any cultural politics of life:

> These professions serve and protect human life. In today's cultural and social context in which the science and art of medicine risk losing their native ethical dimension, they may be occasionally strongly tempted to transform themselves into tools for the manipulation of life or even into workers of death. (1995: 131)

The encyclical letter reminds medical practitioners of their ethical obligations under the Hippocratic Oath, but the force of this oath has already been considerably qualified in modern medical practice. This is recognized in the British Medical Association's (BMA) working party report (1992) *Our Genetic Future: The Science and Ethics of Genetic Technology*, which addresses many of the concerns of the papal encyclical letter.

Our Genetic Future

Our Genetic Future begins in a similar way to *Evangelium vitae*, except that the spectre of the body and soul threatened by sin is succeeded by that of the physical body beset by genetic illness. The threat to life posed by the 'culture of death' is in its turn replaced by a culture of ignorance which surrounds gene therapy. The culture of ignorance, and thus, at least for this enlightenment document, of anxiety, produces the typical effects of uncritical support and uncritical rejection of biotechnology. In the face of such widespread 'ignorance' and anxiety the report maintains that the increased knowledge of genetics and a broader diffusion of its results will create a culture or community capable of making informed assessments of the risks involved in a given genetic therapy. However, this enlightenment confidence in the liberatory potential of knowledge is qualified by a sceptical undertone which doubts whether sufficient knowledge will ever be attained to make an accurate prediction of the potential effects of a particular genetic intervention.

The BMA report provisionally resolves this potentially paralysing ambiguity by postulating that 'biotechnology and genetic modification are in themselves morally neutral. It is the uses to which they are put that create dilemmas' (1992: 4). Yet this neutrality is almost immediately qualified by the self-evident admission that the increase in biological knowledge and its biotechnical application will create 'some new ethical dilemmas' but their main effect will be 'to magnify existing ethical problems in medicine' (1992: 5). Here the BMA follows the same strategy as the Vatican, regarding the developments in biotechnology as intensifying existing problems rather than creating new ones. However, this stated view is qualified on several occasions throughout the document when it appears as if the new biological knowledge will indeed create unprecedented ethical dilemmas. The ambiguities in the text offer a clear example of what Adorno and Horkheimer (1979) described as the 'dialectic of enlightenment', that is to say, the way in which the promise of liberation offered by science creates new and novel forms of subjection.

Underlying the argument about the intensification of existing 'ethical dilemmas' is the deeper concern over the possibility of ever accumulating sufficient knowledge to minimize the risk produced by the same increase in knowledge. If the dilemmas remain the same, and are only magnified by the increase in knowledge and its application, then it may theoretically be possible in the future to gain sufficient knowledge to minimize the risks of its technological application. Yet if the very increase in knowledge and its application produces new areas of risk, then the pursuit of knowledge becomes at best asymptotic, at worst catastrophic. It may never be possible to achieve sufficient knowledge to outweigh the risks generated by the technological applications of existing stocks of knowledge; indeed scientific discoveries may exponentially increase risk, making it potentially unmanageable. As the BMA's report ingenuously admits 'no one is yet [*sic*] in a position to forecast accurately either the benefits or the risks from some of the developments of genetic modification' and 'The totality of scientific knowledge which we would like to have available when making judgements about the future is rarely [*sic*] available' (1992: 5). It may well be that the deficit of knowledge available for making assessments of risk (judgements of the future) is paradoxically enhanced by the very increase in knowledge.

In the light of the fundamental dilemma of scientific knowledge the 'challenge which faces us' of how 'to achieve an optimal future: one which maximises the benefits of genetic modification and minimises the harms' (1992: 4) is more complex than can be answered in a cost-benefit analysis. Yet any possible objection to the principle of pursuing genetic research as such, a position which is approached in *Evangelium vitae* in the name of the 'totality of *theological* knowledge', is pre-emptively neutralized by the claim that biological research and biotechnology is in itself ethically neutral, regardless of how it is conducted or its effects. Thus, for example, the 'abuse' of prenatal diagnosis – which 'can be used to prevent children being born with seriously incapacitating disease' (it is not clear from this whether they will be born without the disease or not born at all) – is cultural and not generated by the research and technology. Nevertheless, the report finds it necessary to elaborate a principle which can serve as a criterion for assessing levels of future risk, not to an individual but to the species as a whole.

For this principle the report has resort to the distinction commonplace in genetics between genotype and phenotype. The distinction was first elaborated by the Danish geneticist Wilhelm Ludwig Johannsen not simply in order to better describe the phenomena of population genetics, but also to provide a metaphysical legitimacy to the descriptive science of genetics (see Caygill, 1996). By introducing a platonic distinction between timeless essence and time-bound appearance, Johannsen was able to confer metaphysical dignity upon the 'science' of genetics, making it into the practice of neutral scientific investigation and separating it from some of the less-than-neutral ideological positions of some of its other earlier practitioners such as Galton. In addition the distinction serves many further purposes, notably that of inserting genetics within a powerful paradigm of religious and scientific experience. The axiom of a genotype or genetic substance underlying but separate from the phenotype or appearances provided a potential terminus for the pursuit of genetic knowledge as well as a moral even theological legitimation for genetic researchers and politicians.

The recommendations proposed by the report all assume the legitimacy of the axiomatic distinction between geno- and pheno-types, translated into the therapeutic correlate of germ and somatic cell therapies. In the case of gene therapy this translates into the ban upon 'interfering with DNA in egg cells or spermatozoa (germ line therapy), as in the production of transgenic animals' ('at least in the foreseeable future') but support for 'altering genes in particular tissues of the body (somatic cell gene therapy)' (1992: 116). The latter affects only the individual subject of therapy, while the former is bequeathed to subsequent generations and thus poses an incalculable risk. The report shies away from such risk on the grounds that interventions may prove irreversible and produce unanticipated effects in future generations (1992: 231).

On occasion the report seems to qualify the distinction, but only tangentially. Yet if it were to remain consistent with its broad enlightenment premises, then it should assume that any defect in current germ line therapy will be corrected in future generations by vastly improved genetic knowledge. Furthermore, biological risk does not simply involve an individual organism but the interaction between organism and environment. Somatic cell interventions are also capable of producing catastrophic effects in their interaction with the environment, but in the present and without the (questionable) insurance policy of the superior knowledge of future generations. In this light it would appear as if somatic cell therapy potentially holds greater risk than germ line. Whether it does or not, what is important is the point that the acceptance of the distinction between somatic cell and germ line therapy as a criterion for assessing risk is itself a decision fraught with risk.

Our Genetic Future is beset by ambiguity, notably in its view that genetic research and its biotechnical application is culturally neutral while at the same time posing a fundamental threat to existing culturally founded understandings of the body and human life. The existence of the document itself marks an attempt to address a cultural anxiety with the enlightenment panacea of improved knowledge. Yet the attempt to create an informed culture cannot go so far as to question its own premises, and so becomes apologetic, seeking to minimize the risk already taken in genetic research and its therapeutic applications by neutralizing their impact. The Report concludes with a dual cultural strategy similar to that adopted by the Vatican in *Evangelium vitae*: Ignorance rather than sin has 'given rise to fear and opposition to new developments' (1992: 227) which should be countered by the creation of an 'informed' popular culture of genetics:

> The scientific community, both in academia and commerce, has a duty to inform the general public of new developments in the applications of genetic modification in a

manner comprehensible to lay people. Schools, radio, television and publishers of books, journals, and newspapers also have an important role to play in achieving this end. (1992: 228)

At the same time as informing the public about the science of genetics the Report recommends that scientists and medical practitioners be informed of 'the link between the ethics and the practice of medicine' (1992: 228). The cultural strategy involves remedying both the knowledge deficit of the lay public and the ethical deficiency of the medical profession. The title *Our Genetic Future* consequently expresses the aspiration of creating a community of compromise between the future feared by the lay public but desired by the scientific and medical professions: the grounds of the compromise are established through an exchange between the professions' knowledge and the public's ethical *sensus communis*. The very terms of this exchange are unfortunately endangered by the threat that the increase in knowledge may produce unprecedented dilemmas which render the ethical culture of the community inflexible or obsolete. In this case, the perplexity of the ethical culture is supposed to be remedied by the increase in knowledge, an unconvincing appeal to what Nietzsche described as the new religion following the death of God, namely, 'faith in science'.

Fractal Flesh

One of the leading practitioners of 'faith in science' is the Australian performance artist Stelarc. Since the late 1980s his work has moved increasingly towards a quasi-liturgical staging of the possible futures opened by developments of biotechnology. Performances such as the 1986 and 1990 *Amplified Body, Laser Eyes and Third Hand*, the 1992 *Host Body/Couple Gestures: Event for Virtual Arm, Robot Manipulator and Third Hand* and the recent *Fractal Flesh* explore the possibilities of prosthetically re-organizing the body and redefining the limits and character of human life. In these works Stelarc re-organizes the body's flows of information by linking his stomach muscles with motor prostheses such as a third arm, and in the later work with remote signals from the Internet processed through STIMBOD software (see Armstrong, 1996: 24–7).

In both the work and the theoretical reflections upon it, Stelarc stages a faith in science as uncompromising in its formulation as the opposed position of the Vatican in *Evangelium vitae*. His clumsy prostheses are deliberate liturgical anticipations of a transformation of human life through the micro-prostheses made possible by developments in nano-technology. The possibility of technologically manipulating molecules and atoms – producing self-replicating machines that operate at a molecular level – promises to transform the human body, making it the host of micro-technological devices which can effect changes not only at the level of the cell, but also at the level of the proteins that make up the cell. The locus of Stelarc's work is the organism and not the genetic code informing its reproduction. Indeed, Stelarc seems to refuse the distinction between information and organism which informs genetics and the medical distinction between somatic and germ line cell therapies. By turning the external prostheses already ubiquitous in human life into the interior of the body, imagining them operating at a sub-cellular level, he envisages the possibility of a totally prosthetic body which would no longer be subject to the limits of human life: 'Thus life would no longer commence with birth and end with death! Life would become a digital experience and no longer a development, a maturation and a decline as in an analogue experience' (Stelarc, 1992: 28). This is a view of the future which embraces and takes to an extreme the tendency, feared in the encyclical letter and discreetly overlooked in the BMA report, of the human body becoming the raw material of technological manipulation.

Stelarc's work performs an uncompromising inversion of the Christian view of the value of life and the uniqueness of the individual. In a gesture of extreme naturalism he imagines the technological re-organization of the body made possible by biotechnology. He imagines, for example, the creation of a 'human' skin capable of photosynthesis:

> With such a skin we would no longer have need of a mouth to chew, of a throat to swallow, of a stomach to digest, of lungs to breathe. We would be able to leave the human and replace useless organs with technologies. Ha-ha-ha-ha-ha-ha-ha-ha-ha-ha-ha!... (1992: 29)

By driving the logic of biotechnology to its inhuman extreme Stelarc affirms both its ultimate tendency and the modern aesthetic fantasy of a *Gesamtkunstwerk* in which the human body becomes the raw material of an irreversible scientific and aesthetic re-organization. As a consequence of his extreme naturalism the future imagined by Stelarc is devoid of risk. If the human being and human life are simply particular forms of organized matter, then their transformation or even destruction are a matter of indifference. This is expressed in his view that the process of evolution ends with the development of biotechnology:

> The end of the Darwinian concept of evolution through organic change. From now on, with nano-technology, mankind can absorb technology. Thus the body must no longer be considered as the seat of the spirit or as the instrument of human relations but must be considered as a structure. Not as an object of desire, but as an object to be redesigned. (1992: 27)

Extreme naturalism combined with the ambition to produce a *Gesamtkunstwerk* thus gives rise to a secular eschatology of the end of the human body.

The staging of the ultimate direction of tendencies feared in the Vatican document and informing that of the BMA is also dedicated to the formation of a culture. Stelarc regards his work as provoking a wide-ranging cultural debate by means of the liturgical staging of a possible future *in extremis*:

> There are of course social, ethical and religious arguments to oppose to what I am proposing. But these ideas are the result of what I am doing. At first these are not clearly ideas easy to accept. When I began to have these sort of ideas I also questioned myself about their problematic nature. But they are my contribution. (1992: 29)

The view that the work of art can provoke wide-ranging debate and contribute to the formation of a culture is questioned by the location of Stelarc's practice within the institution of avant-garde art. While his work goes further than any other in using a fantasy of biotechnology to challenge the limits of art and aesthetic reflection, it still remains within the view of art as effecting an aesthetic transformation of life which has informed avant-garde theory and practice since its beginnings in Schiller's *Letters on Aesthetic Education* (1796). The solemn liturgy of Stelarc's performances anticipates a future in which the human body itself, and not just this exemplary human body of the artist, will have become an object of technological and artistic manipulation.

Conclusion

Evangelium vitae, Our Genetic Future and *Fractal Flesh* all attempt to frame the threat to human life posed by biotechnology in terms of existing cultural codes, whether those of religion, medical professional ethics, or avant-garde art, but in each case the codes are themselves challenged and transformed. Each of these responses to biological research and its biotechnical applications attempts to create a culture capable of negotiating the risk perceived to be posed by biotechnology. In each case, moreover, this culture is anticipated in liturgical terms, as a staged transformation of the meaning of everyday life by the implications of biotechnology.

At the one extreme, the Papal encyclical letter asserts the uniqueness of an individual human life in the face of its biological transformation into a naturalistic combination of genetic information and proteins. However, even this extreme formulation of the uniqueness of human life finds itself appealing to the evidence of genetics, thus undermining the purity of its own position. With this the encyclical letter approaches the position of the British Medical Association Working Party which attempts to find a compromise position between a naturalist and a religious-moral understanding of human life. Stelarc's position, finally, is located at the affirmative extreme of naturalism, where the human body is conceived technologically, and life is considered as a 'digital' rather than 'analogue' experience.

The differences in the positions adopted by the Church, the BMA and the avant-garde artist regarding the understanding of the future of human life are reflected in their cultural strategies. The encyclical letter establishes a Manichean opposition between the cultures of life and of death, regarding future developments of biotechnology as representing an absolute danger to human life. The response is ambiguous, with a militant call for a cultural politics (or cultural crusade) dedicated to creating a new civility immediately tempered by a call for a retreat of believers to the Church and the celebration of the liturgical year. The British Medical Association's document is also ambiguous, staking compromise positions on both the tension between genetic research and its therapeutic applications and that between the ethical culture of the community and the scientific culture of the profession. The key to the compromise is increased knowledge, so the report concludes by urging the creation of a cultural and institutional climate favourable to continued research and technological development. Stelarc's position, at the extreme opposite pole to that of the Church, inversely replicates its stance. The future is imagined eschatologically as the end of evolution in the realization of a new form of post-human life, although the cultural strategy adopted by the artist is strangely liturgical, performing a small anticipation of the future in the secular retreat of the art world.

Between them the three documents bear witness to the diverse ways in which contemporary culture positions the risks posed by biotechnology. They show both the extent to which this culture is inconsistent and internally divided, as well as the ways in which the various fantasies of the future at risk affect each other. Not only do all the texts show the ways in which religious, professional/moral and aesthetic discourses borrow from each other, but also the ways in which together they mark the creation of a divided but creative culture which stages and reflects upon the anxieties which drive and motivate its development.

References

Adorno, T. and Horkheimer, M. (1979) *Dialectic of Enlightenment*. Trans. J. Cumming. London: Verso.

Armstrong, R. (1996) *Totally Wired: Science, Technology and the Human Form*. London: ICA.

British Medical Association (1992) *Our Genetic Future: The Science and Ethics of Genetic Technology*. Oxford: Oxford University Press.

Caygill, H. (1996) 'Drafts for a Metaphysics of the Gene', *Tekhnema*, 3: 141–52.

John Paul II (1995) *Evangelium Vitae: Il Valore e l'Inviolabilità della Vita Umana*. Milano: Paoline Editoriale Libri.

Stelarc (1992) 'Interview Jean-Yves Katelan', *L'Autre Journal*, 27 September.

9

Virtual Risks in an Age of Cybernetic Reproduction

Joost van Loon

In this chapter, I am concerned with the future of the risk society. This future is placed in the context of a world marked by an ongoing restructuration due to the influence of electronic mediation. The increasing pervasiveness of electronic mediation in everyday life, in particular in industrialized societies, has had important yet hardly acknowledged transformative consequences for the very nature of 'risk' and the social conditions and institutions it engenders. I will argue that whereas the language of science and politics still appropriates a rudimentary distinction between real and imaginary risks, they are better understood as *virtual risks*. Moreover, only by scrutinizing the new sociations that have become possible with these relatively recent media-connectivities, can one begin to develop a grounded theoretical understanding of virtual risks in an age of cybernetic reproduction.

The title of this chapter is a play on Walter Benjamin's (1973: 219–53) famous essay 'The Work of Art in an Age of Mechanical Reproduction'. In this work, Benjamin's central argument is that the emergence of mechanical reproduction (for example, photography, film, gramophone, books and television) has eroded the uniqueness and singularity (aura) of the work of art. With the demise of aura, questions of authenticity and origin which fundamentally ground the aesthetic experience of modernist contemplation, become displaced. Under mechanical reproduction, aesthetic experience is no longer isolated from the social conditions which have made its production, dissemination and reception possible, as the social and cultural become interconnected (Lash, 1990: 153–71). The dissemination of aesthetic experience by mechanical reproduction is increasingly a matter of impersonal, collective distractions, rather than personalized, individuated contemplations. One of the consequences of this shift which will be central to this chapter, is highlighted by Scott Lash (1990: 165–7) as the politicization of culture. The aesthetic experience has increasingly become a matter of a new form of politics. This politics is not that of the institutionalized representational type, but attaches itself to ensembles of (inevitably cultural) artefacts and objects in the form of what Benjamin refers to as allegories which operate as mythical resources for making historiographical sense out of the density of everyday life.

At first sight, it might seem a little odd to relate an analysis of risk arising from electronic media to that of a transformation in the social organization of aesthetic experience. However, in this chapter I argue that risk has everything to do with aesthetics (see also Chapter 2 by Scott Lash in this volume). A central assumption that will be worked out in more detail below is that particular risks cannot be understood independently from the media by which they have been generated.

Risks are generally defined in terms of a calculation of a probability that something 'bad' happens. Beck (1992), for example, talks about risk as a distribution of 'bads' (as opposed to 'goods'). Risk is further quantified by a multiplication of probability with the intensity (the seriousness of the 'bads') and scope (for example, the number of people affected) of this distribution of 'bads'. Such a calculation always implies some form of spatio-temporal delimitation. In order for a probability to be assessed, one needs to specify the parameters of time and space within which the particular risk operates. However, apart from this problematic of calculability and delimitation, Beck argues that risks also imply some form of decision-making. It is this decision-making that distinguishes risks from hazards. For example, whereas today for most people AIDS is a risk as it implies a decision to have or not to have safe sex, before the disease was known it was a hazard as such decision-making was not causally linked to the transmission of HIV. In other words, risks imply a specific form of knowledge of causal relationships between particular conditions, specific actions (decisions) and possible consequences.

It is thus not difficult to see that risks are not real in themselves; they have to be realized in causal articulations of conditions with actions and actions with effects. In their very 'essence', risks imply a certain uncertainty, a contingency of conditions, actions and effects that are therefore spatially and temporally fragmented. If there is no uncertainty, that is, if causality is spatially and temporally unified with a condition, action and effect, there is no risk (for example, it is certain that we *will* die; death-risks only make sense in terms of how and when).

Since risks are not certain, they require knowledge about causal articulations and probabilities, and they imply the involvement of particular decisions. Indeed, the realization of risks is a work of art. It involves a complex alignment between very particular and very exclusive modes of signification (most notably those of 'applied' and 'pure' science), with financial, economic, judicial, political, and administrative institutional systems of representation, and finally with popular and allegorically organized moral and practical *sense*. Risks are realized in the experience and appreciation of a variety of particular discursive and figurative alignments. This necessitates that risks must have an appeal to an audience and thus involve an interpellation: a calling upon potential receivers to respond. In an age where television is capable of instantaneous world-wide dissemination of information to an almost limitless mass of receivers, the appeal of risk is formed in a cultural matrix which exceeds that of science and institutional politics: it has the capacity to directly intervene in the social density of everyday life. Consequently, I consider the mechanisms and operations by which risks can be cultivated to appeal to audiences and hence to be realized in allegories of everyday life.

However, Benjamin's model of mechanical reproduction cannot be applied to today's risk society uncritically. The mode of standardization of mechanical reproduction is linked to that of mass culture and a fordist-type of capitalist mode of production. It is based on the logistics of uniform mass distribution and centralized planning. Since the time of Benjamin's writing, there has been a gradual but persistent shift towards a more flexible mode of reproduction, which, in analogy with the sphere of production, might be called post-fordist. The post-fordist mode of reproduction is not bureaucratic but adhocratic (Mintzberg, 1983). It consists of temporary formations, co-ordinated and controlled via (dangerous) liaisons rather than commands, and works through control rather than discipline. Electronic communications have transgressed the distinctions between mechanical and organic (similar to, for example, biotechnologics) and no longer allow an analytical separation between origin and reproduction (which is still possible in mechanical reproduction). The model I will use to theorize this mechanical–organic conjuncture is that of cybernetics: a self-regulating, self-reproducing communicative system that is capable of not only internalizing its environment and producing particular responses, but also of adjusting these inter-nalizations according to the feedback it receives from the impact of those responses to its environment (Luhmann, 1982).

A cautionary warning must be made in advance. Although I argue that the aesthetic experience of risks in an age of cybernetic reproduction is quite differ-ent from that in mechanical reproduction and has radically different spatio–temporal implications, I do not want to suggest that the mechanical reproductive systems are no longer important. The whole point of cybernetics is not the erad-ication of the mechanical age, but a reappropriation of it according to organic principles. Indeed, the very transgression of the boundary between the mechani-cal and the organic was already initiated by mechanical reproduction. Cybernetic reproduction appropriates mechanical reproductive technologies such as tele-vision, photography and printing but follows a different principle. The central principle of cybernetics is that of *assemblage*: a specific form of linking up differ-ent media by which their (re)productive potential becomes radically amplified.[1]

A simple example would be the use of computers in transforming photo-graphic (analogue) pictures into video-graphic (digital) images which in turn allow further manipulation and crossovers into more textual modes of reproduction (to a degree that CD-ROMs can now contain textual, visual as well as audio information bits). The computer-mediated connectivities have created a virtually organic universe where everything can be transformed into everything else. This is due to the uniformity of the binary code. In this fluid universe, origins are no longer fixed. The nature of the origin in the work of art before mechanical reproduction was always the 'genius' of the artist him/herself. In contrast, with mechanical repro-duction there are only copies. Now with cybernetic reproduction, the copies too have vanished: everything is a pseudo-original (a simulacrum). However, at the same time, every origination becomes a question of fabrication. In this universe, to talk about 'real risks' versus 'perceived risks' is to get lost in hopelessly stag-nating and regressive parochial discourses. Risks are realized in their fabrications. If the virtuality of risk is all we can deal with, we must allow ourselves to connect to the technologies of its fabrication and grasp its political moment in the heat of its multiform and instantly mutating manifestations.

This argument is explored in more detail in the following way: first, I briefly consider the ways in which current developments in information and communication technologies have affected the social. This will be followed by a more detailed discussion of the possibilities of integrating a more extensive understanding of mediation into Beck's (1992) risk society thesis. I argue that whereas his approach has many strengths, a potential weakness is to be found in the rather uncritical use of a model of mediation as based on mechanical reproduction without adequately considering the effects on 'risk' itself. This weakness spills over into a dualism based on a realist ontology and a constructivist epistemology. Such a dualism is not only at odds with the very promise of risk society but is also becoming fundamentally inadequate in the face of current changes in the dominant modes of signification through which media work.[2] In order to come to terms with the possibilities that new media herald, I discuss some of the consequences for understanding our relationship with the future in terms of virtual risks.

Media and social transformation

Electronic communications have vastly transformed the world. The sets of connections (assemblages) they have made possible have amplified not only our capacity to transcend many of the physical limitations of spatio-temporality, but also fundamentally transformed the sense of being human to something rather peripheral to information and communication technologies.[3] Theorists as diverging as Baudrillard (1990, 1993), Deleuze and Guattari (1988), Haraway (1988, 1990, 1991, 1997), Lyotard (1991), McLuhan (1964), Thompson (1995) and Vattimo (1992), not to mention many others, have all been concerned with and offered a wealth of insights into the socio-political and technocultural consequences of such developments. John Thompson for example, argues that:

> [i]n a fundamental way, the use of electronic media transforms the spatial and temporal organization of social life, creating new forms of action and interaction, and new modes of exercising power, which are no longer linked to the sharing of a common locale. (1995: 4)

The proliferation of information and communication media, and the growing variety of connections between them (for example, satellite – telephone – computer – television) have reconfigured the spatio–temporal flows of sociation. Assemblage, however, not only implies that technologies are linked up (connectivity), but moreover, that their functions intersect and constitute new forms and imperatives of social interaction, which in turn engender shifts in responsibilities and accountabilities. Hence, assemblage affects the moral constitution of solidarity (sociality) as the basis of social and collective being (community).[4]

These information and communication technologies intervene in everyday interactions, for example, by removing the need for face-to-face contact in many of our routine conversations (via the telephone), or speeding up the circulation of documents both in the old paper or new electronic forms (facsimile and e-mail respectively). Electronic media have facilitated what McLuhan (1964) terms 'a world information order'; anything that happens anywhere can potentially be brought instantaneously into the here and now of 'our' presence. This facilitates globalizing information flows. However, these flows are not a simple consequence of media technologies themselves (as this would amount to an untenable techno-logical determinism), instead, they have to be situated in a highly complex set of economic, political, social and cultural relationships. The point is simply that global information and communication flows are unthinkable without this emer-gent technological infrastructure.

Media-connectivities emerge as satellites connect more and more people and media technologies. Television, telephone and computer are now linked up to 'information super highways' which sprawl far beyond media hype and have already materialized in global economies, politics, laws and cultures. This requires not only a reconsideration of what is meant by 'society' as 'global' but also with what is meant by 'local'. The local is now radically disembedded from its tradi-tional environment to a degree that 'location' is itself a displaced, temporary phenomenon.

With the expansion of this 'global media mix' (see Chapter 10 by Deirdre Boden in this volume) our social networks have also extended globally; we are all implicated as if in an extended global presence in which we are at once spatially and temporally distanciated and compressed (Adam, 1995; Nowotny, 1994). In such an imagined presence, we find it increasingly difficult to locate ourselves in space and time. We face constant flows of displacement, disorienta-tion, desynchronization. This is not only true for people living in the industrial-ized world, everyone has been affected, albeit in different ways. For example, the panics associated with viral epidemics such as Ebola and AIDS also travel throughout the African continent, often via short-wave radio transmissions. The rationality of development, which originated in the West, finds an acute resonance on the Kinshasa highway, which, alongside goods, people and services, also allowed for diseases such as AIDS, to spread very rapidly across the continent (McKechnie and Welsh, 1994; Myers et al., 1993: 122–3).

There is a correlation between population density and the risk of epidemics. Not only can we find illustrations of these connections in the urbanization of nineteenth-century Europe, but also in for example computer networks. With more and more people connected to ever-extending networks, the risk of infec-tion from a growing amount of viruses disproportionately accelerates. Computer viruses have been capable of laming computer networks across the globe; and likewise, as will be shown below, BSE (mad cow disease) is – although perhaps not a virus but a prion – apart from the cause of a terminal disease, also a highly infectious and lethal electronic phenomenon.

The age of cybernetic reproduction

We now live in a world of hypermediation. Virtual reality has displaced the boundaries between real and representation. In writing about the Rodney King incident, Fiske (1994), for example, provides a strong argument for a con-ception of the 'media event' that defies the binary opposition between real and representation (see also Van Loon, 1999). What 'the real' is, cannot be conceived of outside of the mediations with which it is brought into 'presence' and 'the present'. The relation between ontology and epistemology requires some serious rethinking. In order to understand what sort of risks we face in an age of hyper-mediation, I need to discuss in a bit more detail the modes of reproduction with which these risks come into existence.

A good starting point is perhaps Roland Barthes' (1977) distinction between textual (code) and photographic (analogon) modes of representation.[5] These two modes institute different notions of time and space. Textual representation evolves around a notion of reading-path – a sequence that extends over time – a becoming towards being here. In contrast, the photograph is instantaneous, it presents a frozen moment by re-presenting the having-been-there. As Benjamin (1973) noted, the photograph turns the image into a political field (for example, he referred to the key roles of film and photography in the Nazi-propaganda machinery).

In the modern age, both modes of signification have been radically transformed by first mechanical and then cybernetic reproduction. Texts and images can now be reproduced on a scale and with a speed which is virtually instantaneous. Such reproductive force institutes a systemic simultaneity of the multiplying and forgetting of origins (Baudrillard, 1993). For example, whereas the photograph implies an origin outside itself, it is in itself a new origin. It fixates a fraction of time into an image as it turns the event into a phenomenon. It thus allows for a forgetting of Being, as the image acquires a sense of timeless permanence. However, simultaneously, photography invites the re-telling of narratives, for example in holiday pictures. It thus becomes an origin in-itself for-itself. Conversely, the institutionalized systemic forgetting and multiplication of originality has produced a culture (and this is certainly not limited to the 'West') in which 'the simulacrum' plays a formative role (as a copy of which no original exists).

With the advent of television, video and more recently computer graphics, the distinctions between discursive and figurative modes of signification have become rather blurred. The videographic mode of signification ('moving images' with a more or less analogous relationship to what they represent) installs reading paths into figurative significations. That is, more than books or films, it has the capacity to integrate figurative modes of signification into narrative forms. Unlike film, which operates on a photographic principle and institutes flow through rapid succession, videographic signification is electronic and digitalized. One step further, cybernetic modes of representation have allowed these representations to constitute digital forms that can be manipulated and worked on like texts and can be generated purely internally. Three-dimensional computer simulations make it possible for us to interact with and intervene directly into the 're-presentational' forms it displays. They have acquired the capacity to internalize their environment, to make a world of their own in which 'presence' is extended and controlled to a far greater extent than any other mode of representation. This presence is at once spatial (in the sense of being located in a 'coming before', i.e. 'here') and temporal (in the instantaneous moment of 'now'). The here and now of cybernetic videography is completely de-contextualized from the time-spaces of origination as well as reception. They can be stored and transmitted electronically and hence instantaneously brought into a sense of global presence. As a result this presence extends well beyond the here and now of the coming-before in instantaneous time (Adam, 1995; Nowotny, 1994).

Cybernetic and videographic reproduction come together in multi-media computer systems which have enabled hypertext, photo-videographic manipulation and a writing in images that injects new reproductive force into an older configuration of time–space politics. At first sight this politics seems split into a struggle between humanism and technocratic determinism. Humanism projects a time–space beyond that of cybernetic reproduction where the pure human resides, and a true natural equilibrium can be found. In contrast, technocracy presents time–space as a world created by intelligent machines which have already displaced humans from the course of history (Land, 1995). Whereas for humanists, the origin of both risk and risk management lies with the human will, for technological determinists they are the result of the unfolding of the programs enabled and operated by machines.

It is quite clear why both variants are unappealing. Both claim to master a sense of orientation while being adrift in an ocean of distractions. By cultivating a notion of nature beyond/before technology, the humanist variant falls prey to the paranoid neurosis of the Oedipus complex. In contrast, the technocratic variant succumbs to a fascistic, cynical and predatorial power fetishism. Both types of politics strive for a hegemonic homogenization of life itself: humanism by overwriting ethics with human nature, technocracy by overwriting ethics with historicist determinism. If we are to come to terms with virtual risks in an age of cybernetic reproduction, we must challenge the very ethical basis (or lack of it) which underscores this dualism.

Originary illusionism and technocracy presuppose each other. They are oppositional poles in a singular elliptical field. Both are part of an oedipalized capitalist machinery that links risk to the fear of loss and the desire for purified unification. What humanists fear technocrats desire and vice versa. By linking risks to desire and fear, or Eros and Thanatos, we can relate Beck's risk society as 'an *other* modernity' to Deleuze and Guattari's (1977) demythification of the Oedipus complex. In their famously acclaimed *Anti-Oedipus* (1977), they argue that pyschoanalysis presents us with a particular story, the Oedipus complex, which it tries to pass for absolute and universal, that is, myth. Rather than explaining desire, the Oedipus complex fixes it in a narrative that has to be told and re-told indefinitely. By accepting it as a universal myth, psychoanalysis normalizes and naturalizes its undercurrent of neurosis and paranoia that is wrapped up in phantasies of reunification with the Mother (the origin). The Oedipus Complex is thus nothing but a historically situated psychopathology of modernity-capitalism. Hence, if there is nothing essential about a desire for origins or a fear of death, why should we still be forced to cling to them?

Risk society is a transitional, and as Lash (Chapter 2 this volume) argues, paradoxical moment. In this moment, the old hegemony is dying, but the new cannot (yet) be born. Humanism and technocracy are merely discourses that express a desire to rescue the waning institutionalized structures of certainty and stability, in fear of their imminent collapse. What thus unites both sides is a desire for mastery and control on the one hand and fear on the other. We 'humans' (men at least) are granted (masculine) fantasies of mastery and domination, playing with our joysticks, voyeuristically zooming into the scopophilic realism of the visual. However, this comes at a price. Cybernetic reproduction holds no guarantees for truth, everything is vulnerable to deception; we can no longer trust origins (we never could, but whereas it used to be a matter of choice/ethics it is now a matter of fact). The price we pay for entering the simulacrum is that our subjectivities too have lost all grounds for authenticity (Haraway, 1990).

In other words, there is no ethics to be found in either the desire (or fear) for (of) lost origins or the desire/fear for/of technocratic domination. Ethics come from a completely different possibility, a different form of desire. This possibility is connected to the very deception, or better de-con-ception, of the cybernetic process itself. The de(con)ception that no longer implies an originary truth, differs from conception, that essentialist metaphor of reproduction, in that it always deviates from what it seemed before. The aura of a unique singularity does not completely vanish but has a residue in de(con)ception. In a world of total visibility, we have become blinded by the sheer force of illumination. We cannot plan strategies, because we don't know where we are. We have to move around tactically, via sensing, touching, smelling and hearing. Indeed, as McLuhan (1964) already suggested more than 30 years ago, the world of electronic media marks a return to acoustic and tactile space.

Deception implies vulnerability. However, this is not the same vulnerability of originary illusionism which invokes the fear of loss and the desire for unification. It is a vulnerability that never closes in the desperate certainties of nature and power. Hence, it is not the same vulnerability as that posed by tech-nocratic determinists for whom there is always a final solution for everything. Vulnerability in an age of cybernetic reproduction is not a matter of survival. Instead it is a matter of opening up oneself to lose oneself, to allow oneself to slide off a seemingly infinite chain of signifiers, to allow oneself to become part of something larger, something that can neither be understood as a unique integrity (as a work of art before mechanical reproduction), nor from a singular perspective (the cultivated gaze). It is the dissemination of spatio–temporal con-tingencies that are re-assembled in particular connectivities. We are always 'only' partially implied in particular tactical chains.

Virtual risks

Vulnerability, it could be argued, is integral to the virtual risk society itself. Both videographic and cybernetic modes of signification mediate between the having been there and being here (e.g. media events). Both reality and representa-tion have been displaced by simulacra (Baudrillard, 1993; Deleuze, 1994). Although it emerged in an age of mechanical reproduction, cybernetic reproduc-tion has begun to transform the world and engenders new sensibilities. Machines, or better machine–humans (cyborgs), rather than humans, are the most likely agents of social transformation, as human mastery of technology is increasingly incapacitated by the velocity and speed that is required to control risk.

The reality of virtual risks cannot be 'fixed' through some form of transcendental logic (for example counterfactual thinking) or crude empirical observations. It is in the practices of everyday life that such virtualities matter. Virtual risk is always a media event. Virtual risks are reflexive in their mediation, that is, the very act of mediating a virtual risk feeds back to the very 'essence' of this risk, with the potential to transform it. If risks do not 'exist' outside of their mediation (for it is impossible to render an account of existence without recourse to some form of making sense) then the only way we can come to terms with them is through reflexivity (Beck, 1992; Beck et al., 1994; see also Lash, Chapter 2 in this volume).

It is here where the proliferation of information and communication technologies have radically disturbing effects. An increasing dependence on (that is, the vulnerability of) information and communication systems results in a decreasing capacity to understand, represent and control risk. This is a serious paradox. The more we know about the world, the more we know about risk, but the more we know about risk, the less we know about the world.[6] This paradox can be represented in a slightly different way: with increased mediated global connectivities and integration into a global media mix, comes an increased differentiation and fragmentation of our sense of 'present' which on the one hand extends to 24-hour around the clock ongoing flows of exchanges and communications, but on the other hand has a speed and velocity which reduces time to a mere sequence of 'instantaneities'. In this continuously growing complexity, we become saturated with information but simultaneously, we become more and more disconnected from the future as everything revolves around an instantaneous but continuing presence. With the information overload and the growing speed of events, we have already been displaced by an ensemble of apparatuses which select and control the risks we should attend to. Reflexivity in a virtual reality is thus not a matter of comprehension (reflectivity), but of selectively connecting to 'matters', to make and keep them 'present', even if only for an instant.

Central to understanding virtual risks are, therefore, notions of chaos and complexity. In the language of risk, chaos and complexity function as problems which in turn can be used to mobilize resources to reduce their (unknown) predicaments. However, the relationship between the unknown predications and the identified 'need' to control or limit them, is paradoxical if not contradictory. For how can something be controlled if it is not known? Consequently, information and communication technologies mobilized to render the unknown more visible have been instrumental in the very proliferation of risks. The uncertainty of futures marked by chaos and complexity thus results in a techno–social configuration in which the human is increasingly displaced by his/her own instrumentalism and desire for mastery.

I propose to conceive virtual risks in an age of cybernetic reproduction in terms of what Deleuze and Guattari (1988) have called *flow*. Flow is not a unidirectional, linear (phallic) exchange relationship, but dispersed, disseminated across a smooth space. It can be traced in trajectories and strange attractors of an order constituted on the way (nomadic). It does not relay between scapes but spatializes them. That is, flows are not linear but involve multiple disseminations, whose course can only be traced in fractions (Shields, 1997).

Analysing flows therefore involves a differential rather than an integral approach. To think of flow is to postpone a reliance on indexicality, that is, signification as dependent upon a particular context. Instead, thinking flow requires the centrality of *vortexicality*, in which contexts are induced through significations as strange attractors (Weissert, 1995). Flows induce temporary autonomous zones (TAZ) (Bey, 1991) which are interruptions in autopoietic systemic formations (when things go wrong system unity breaks down, and the system-environment boundaries are transgressed). To theorize cybernetic media in terms of flow is to think of zoning and flowing technologies. In the case of Bovine Spongiform Encephalopathy (BSE, see below), the strategy of the British government to control virtual risks hopelessly failed because they did not understand the flows and zones of its contamination. They falsely assumed that Royal Science (Deleuze and Guattari, 1988; see also Chapter 3 by Hilary Rose this volume) could fence off the incubation with a politics of thresholds. Their realist ontology was hopelessly inadequate because they still believed in an origin outside mechanical reproduction.

Media and risk society: the case of BSE

On 21 March 1996, the day after the British Government announced that there was a possibility that ten cases of Creutzfeldt-Jakob Disease (CJD) could have been related to BSE or so-called 'mad cow disease', the sale of beef plunged not only in Britain but across Europe, and a ban on the import of British beef, and products based on it, was almost instantaneously imposed on a world-wide scale. The announcement followed years of speculation about such a link, with the British government stubbornly denying any possibility, citing the lack of scientific evidence for such a link as proof that it did not exist (Ford, 1996). Connectivity must be placed at the heart of explaining why suddenly this change of tone from certainty to uncertainty had such devastating consequences on people's consumption practices (if only temporarily). Indeed, the intensive media coverage of the event has transformed BSE/CJD from a relatively local 'British' event to a global phenomenon.

Although not often mentioned by the critics, Beck's (1992: 46) *Risk Society* reserves a significant space for theorizing the role of media in the contemporary world. Risk society, he argues, is also a 'science, media and information society'. Like Thompson, he sees the central operation of these media as intervening in the public sphere, separating off the sphere of production from that of consumption. This separation also applies to risks as it furthers the spatio–temporal fragmentation of articulations between information, knowledge, decisions and consequences and (thus) responsibilities.

The BSE case highlights one of Beck's strongest claims: that in the risk society the calculating of probabilities collapses under the weight of our collective inability to conceptualize the consequences. Scientists who were called upon by the

British government could not estimate the exact probability that eating possibly BSE-infected beef results in CJD. However, while admitting the incalculability of this possibility, the science–politics conjuncture simultaneously resulted in the slogan that British beef was completely safe for consumption because the risk was very small. In a matter of days, the risk of a BSE-CJD link was replaced by another related risk: that of the collapse of the British (and European) beef industry (Ford, 1996).

The replacement of one risk by another, it could be argued, is the effect of a transition in the leading discursive articulation of BSE from humanism to technocracy. For humanists, the BSE–CJD link is a product of un-natural reproductive practices which have unbalanced the food chain. In contrast, for technocrats BSE is purely internalized as a vector within the political–economic machinery. The most grotesque manifestation of this technocratic will to power is the way in which the British Government and the Conservative Party have transformed it into an issue of consumer nationalism. In other words, far from a matter of *prima facie* scientific hegemonization, risk is a domain of political struggle. This struggle not only concerns the definition of the risk in terms of its probability and implications, but affects the very core of the problematic of what the 'actual risk' is and what 'being at risk' is supposed to mean.

The shift from a concern over public health to that of the collapse of the beef industry indicates that there were different risk positions involved.[7] On the one hand, the beef industry faced an immediate crisis with beef-sales going down. On the other hand, consumers were also facing previously unacknowledged health risks, created by the confessed uncertainty over possible links between BSE and CJD. The involvement of the European Commission in imposing a ban on the export of British beef further allowed a politicization of the so-called BSE crisis in terms of 'national interests' which were intricately tied to the fate of the British Government in the light of the Conservative Party's deep internal divisions over the desired role of Britain in the process of European integration.[8]

It is on the side of risk-consumption that the individualizing tendencies of the risk society can be traced. The risk of being infected by BSE is individualized – and since all individualization implies institutionalization (Beck, 1992: 132) – the BSE risk becomes politicized. In this very direct way, the mediation of the BSE–CJD risk transgressed the sacred distinction between public and private and between openness and secrecy. Suddenly, a connection was imposed between the newly announced 'potential risk' and our individual biographies and we were invited to retrace the eating of beef in our personal histories: When was the last time 'we' ate fast food? What was really in that steak and kidney pie 'we' had last Sunday? In what foods and brands can 'we' find beef products? We are all implied in these multiple bovine protein flows and their implications are of global importance. British beef could come from any part of the globe and could be consumed anywhere.

In *Reflexive Modernization* (Beck et al., 1994), Beck extends his analysis of the risk society in terms of his concern with reflexivity. Reflexivity, according to Beck (1994: 6–10), is a 'self-confrontation', which in the context of risk society means an encountering with the reality-effects of risk production and risk consumption in which 'uncertainty' features as the constitutive force. This reflexivity is a 'breach' with the instrumental rationality of modernity itself, as it is constantly haunted to clarify the foundations upon which it relies and the conditions under which it performs.

With this notion of reflexivity there is an interesting tension which stems from Beck's rather ambiguous notion of 'reality'. On the one hand, he understands risk to be a social construction, generated by scientific knowledge, as an institution, a particular rationality and a technological practice. In this sense, risk becomes itself an arena of contesting definitions, with adjacent socio-economic, political and professional interests at stake. On the other hand, however, he continues to discuss risk and the risk society in terms of a reality that is beyond all representation. Even if ultimately grounded in making the invisible visible, risk, for Beck, is there.

However, rather than perceiving this as the ultimate flaw, and 'therefore' refutation of his argument, I would advocate that this ambiguity needs to be cherished. Only by thinking of risk in terms of reality, or better, a *becoming-real* (a virtuality), can social materialization be understood?. Only by thinking risk in terms of a construction can we understand its indefinitely deferred 'essence'.[9] Risks cannot be understood outside their materialization in particular mediations, be it scientific, political, economic or popular.

Electronic media involved in the BSE crisis connect science, politics and popular consumer culture. In so doing, they render the invisibility of risk, for example, the mutating prions of BSE, visible. They bring them into being through digitalized imagery. We, the consumers of such images, have no means to test the adequacy of such representations, nor do we have to. Their origin is fabricated, manufactured, in laboratories, under microscopes, and further enhanced by computer simulations. Their sources are truly cybertechnological, connecting chemistry, molecular biology and medicine with computer graphics and television broadcasting. Rendering the prion visible as a computer simulation allowed news broadcasts to begin to interpret the uninterpretable (to tell us what BSE and CJD actually 'are') and to explain the unexplainable (how a normal piece of protein – whatever that might be – could become a pathological prion). The mere possibility that the pathogenesis might be linked to the banal practice of consuming beef, which is part of a banal aesthetics of everyday life (e.g. the 'taste' of food), further illustrates the force of Benjamin's claim that in an age of mechanical reproduction, all aesthetic experiences may become politicized.

The becoming-real of the risk of BSE is directly related to its mediation. Now that 'we' know that there 'are' possible risks, 'we' face a responsibility. This responsibility takes the form of a *decision* whether to eat beef and other bovine products or not. Therefore, CJD is no longer exclusively a hazard, as a strain has been identified that can be linked to BSE. Although the calculability of this risk has remained problematic, as a virtuality, it operates in exactly the same way. The sudden accessibility of the 'knowledge' of the possible relationship between BSE and CJD has thus transformed a hazard into a risk: we now have a decision to make with consequences for ourselves, our loved ones and possibly everybody else as well.

It is interesting to note that not much of the debates around BSE actually took the form of an established Royal Science versus a counterscience (or what Deleuze and Guattari (1988) referred to as 'nomadic science'). The news media were a site of a different form of struggle, one which never took place on a shared set of terms. On the one hand, there was the government quoting Royal Science that there is no, or no longer, a risk, or better, the risk is now below an unnamed but assumed threshold. On the other hand there was an entity that rarely took the form of a subject, but was merely a phantom of indirect discourse.[10] This phantom subject, or virtual subject, was often referred to as 'the consumer', 'the public' or 'the audience'. Significant in this discursive arena is the displacement of one risk, that of BSE spreading to humans, to another: that of a collapse of the beef industry due to the evaporation of consumer confidence. Like the first risk, this risk cannot be understood outside of the media which have brought it into existence. No one really questioned the virtual status of this second risk; that is, the collapse of consumer confidence is a purely internally produced simulacrum, engendered by the information and communication technologies that sparked it off. However, what is important is that the first risk, which was annulled by Royal Science (by defining it as 'negligible'), is as much a virtuality as the second. Without the mediation of a possible link between CJD and BSE, the hazard of CJD would never be articulated in relation to BSE. In fact, we would not be at risk from contaminated beef and thus never take responsibility for consuming it. However, this is no longer an option. The process of risk formation is irreversible. It is ironic, albeit not surprising, that the very agent that initiated the first connectivity of its fabrication, Royal Science, is also its first casualty, as the authority of science has itself mutated into a spongiform prion. This should function as a warning to everyone who tries to deny the force of virtual risks and continue to consume the virtual reassurances of royalty.

This also signifies a major problem in the way in which Beck's account of the risk society has been generally understood. Although his mediated world may be grounded in an age of mechanical reproduction, he does account for a mutually implicated reality/representation; they are not analytically separated into a realist ontology and a constructivist epistemology. In contrast, risk in an age of mechanical reproduction would be a paradox. On the one hand it forces one to accept that there *is* something *out there*, which might not be properly called risk, but which still exists independently of the machinery that represents it. On the other hand, the representing apparatuses (media) transform this external reality into a symbolic form which we can analyse, explain and understand as risk.

To think of risks in terms of a distinction between reality and representation requires a world view based on the domination of linear time in which the real thing outside is transformed into a representational construction. This assumption perceives the real to *precede* the construction, that is, the construction originates in the real. As the construct's origin, the real is effectively displaced from risk production. The problem with this is that in actuality risk production does not require a preceding real because risk production is, as Beck explains, always a becoming-real. The real that is displaced in cybernetic reproduction, however, is not outside of that reproduction, but always already internalized by it. It is the reproduction that is its own origin.

The scientific aura of risk is thus at once intensified and eroded by the dissemination of virtual risks via information and communication technologies. The speed of information has made both realist ontologies and constructionist epistemologies hopelessly inert. It is not only impossible but also unnecessary to trace reality as origin; this tracing itself is a fabrication of reality. In risk society, all we have are reality-effects and they are real enough! Indeed, Beck's theory can be usefully complemented with an understanding of the role of media as engendering risks without relying on a dualistic model of mechanical reproduction. Not only is this desirable because it allows us to avoid the originary fallacy of a real preceding its representation, but also because it is more attuned to the world of cybernetic reproduction.

In short, both the risks associated with BSE being transformed into CJD via beef and the risks associated with bringing this into publicity, that is, the risks of the collapse of the beef industry, the British economy and the prospects of the government cutting taxes to seduce a critical proportion of the electorate to vote for them again, are virtual risks. It is therefore futile to state, in the name of some appeal to truth, that these virtual risks are not real. There is no way to tell whether they are more or less real. But more importantly perhaps, it does not matter.

In the debates around BSE, it became once again clear that the distinctions between what is deemed 'reality' (sanctified by 'official science') and 'representation' (hyped up in a media frenzy) are completely artificial constructions. 'Consumer confidence' is not a politically or scientifically manipulable entity, but a construction that, like risk, is largely internal to the mediating apparatus which generates it. However, it is certain that as virtual risks, both the possibility of a link between BSE and CJD and its effects on the consumption of beef, have had considerable effects. Around the world, British beef was banned (until 1999), large fast food corporations recalled their products made from British beef, a law suit had been issued against the British government over its repression of information about the risks of eating beef, and every case of CJD is now carefully scrutinized for possible prion-mutations that are similar to BSE-infected cattle.

Conclusions

In this chapter I have discussed the impact of electronic media on the way we can analyse and understand risks. I have argued that in an age of cybernetic reproduction (which destroys the boundaries between the mechanical and the organic), it is no longer helpful or adequate to discuss risks in terms of reality versus representation. The notion of 'virtual risk' might have a more appealing ethos as it allows us to discuss the relationships between science, politics, economics, law, the media and popular culture as part of one and the same complexity of connectivities.

Furthermore, I argued that by following mechanical reproduction and extending it into the organic realm itself, cybernetic reproduction implies a new political moment. In this political moment, the unity beneath the old dualism between humanism and technocracy needs to be exposed as unethical. The connections between risk, desire and fear do not necessarily force us to accept either homeo-static or evolutionary dogmatism. De(con)ception and vulnerability are two possible ethical implications that can be associated with virtual risks in an age of cybernetic reproduction. This relates perhaps to the most critical of virtual risks we currently face: the death of the human. In science fiction this has already been imagined, for example in the two *Terminator* films, and films such as *The Lawnmower Man* and *War Games*. These are all born out of masculine fantasies of power and mastery, which evolve around strategies of programming based on phallogocentric masculinist desires. However, there is no way to turn here. The masculinist ethos is self-destructive. It will be either too inert or too weak to face risks sensibly. Masculinity is a form of command-control risk-taking without communication and intelligence (see Haraway, 1990). It is blind to its own inauthentic being.

The paradox of mastery and control is false, however. As Haraway (1990) has argued, we are cyborgs and the sooner we accept the challenge this sets to facing the uncertainty of our destiny, the more we might be capable of affecting its outcome in a more desirable direction. Cybernetics provides opportunities that are compatible with what could be called a new feminist ethos based on net-working (Plant, 1995), cultures of (or islands on) the internet (Shields, 1996) and cybertechnological sensibilities and affectivities (Chambers, 1994; Van Loon, 1996). The centrality of flows further allows us to think of virtual risks not as 'things' to be mastered by concepts, but as 'energy-matter', that can only be de-conceived if we acknowledge vulnerability, rather than survival, as an ethical modality of cultural politicization.

I therefore conclude that our world is marked by virtual risks, whose flows induce sociations that are instantaneous and fleeting. 'The' human is displaced and rendered visible itself as an object of information and communication tech-nologies. Cybernetically reproduced, virtual risks are effective and affective and call for an ethics that is not strategic and not grounded in a politics of urgency. In an age of intelligent machines, only cyborgs (prion-free of course) might deliver the emancipatory promise that we humans have always been used to dream up for ourselves.

This leaves us, finally, with the question of what the role of socio-cultural theory could be as regards the implications of virtual risks in an age of cybernetic reproduction. Traditionally, the role of theory has been a service in the quest for truth. Such a service has generally been embroiled in an ethos of either indif-ference (pure science) or interest-based political power. However, in an age of cybernetic reproduction, theory's role has to be more modest as it cannot assume responsibility for all that is thinkable. For me this is first and foremost a question of ethics. Socio-cultural theory becomes ethical if it enables us to liberate our-selves from the self-imposed justifications of humanism and technological deter-minism by facilitating an opening up of the human condition to technoculture, by cultivating its vulnerability, by bearing witness to the events as they unfold, but not indifferently. One cannot *bear* witness indifferently, for, as Lyotard (1988) has argued, it is an *obligation* for the thinker, the theorist. Theorizing is linking, flowing-connecting, creating assemblages. Bearing witness is not to ask 'has it happened', but 'is it happening'?[11] It is thus 'taking place' within, and thus not outside of, the events as they unfold. Theorizing cannot step outside of time, but it can temporize some of the implications of technocracy by being responsive to technology. Being responsive is not the same as 'taking (away) responsibility', but cultivating an ability to respond. This is the ethical moment of theory in a post-humanist episteme: cultivating a responsive sensibility to effect a disclosure of the transgressive implications of the mediation of technologies (in the face of the risks they engender) on subjective and biographic experiences.

Acknowledgements

I am heavily indebted to Celia Lury for her extensive comments and suggestions on earlier drafts of this chapter. I am also grateful to Barbara Adam for her comments, suggestions and editorial advice. Furthermore, I would like to thank Ian Welsh for the useful discussions we had on this and other subjects. Finally I would like to thank all participants in the round table session on electronic communications at the Risks, Technologies, Futures Conference (Cardiff, 2–3 March 1996) for their input.

Notes

1   The term 'assemblage' is derived from the work of Deleuze and Guattari (1988: 4) who used it to refer to a multiplicity that is unattributable to anything outside itself. This resembles what McLuhan (1964: 23–35) referred to as 'the medium is the message'.

2   The usage of the term 'signification' rather than 'representation' is deliberate since representation still implies a dualism of a realist ontology and a constructivist epistemology.

3   This implies a particular vulnerability at the heart of the human condition. Later in this chapter, I argue that such a vulnerability discloses a possibility for ethics.

4   For similar arguments, see McLuhan (1964) and Maffesoli (1995).

5   Following Lyotard (1971), Scott Lash (1990) has called these 'discursive' and 'figurative' modes of signification.

6   'Knowing', 'the world', 'risk' must all be understood here as virtualities.

7   Perhaps 'interests' would be a better term as it highlights the differential power-relations involved. However, the term implies a rather unproblematic set of relationships between means and goals on the one hand, and cognitive processes on the other hand. The language of goals and means versus cognition is inadequate to account for the immense complexification of (re)productive networks based on connectivity.

8   There are quite substantial differences between various national and regional media. Whereas in Europe, most media attention was given to the issues surrounding a possible link between BSE and CJD, the national English media only focused on the issue of health risks for a very short period. The issue was soon replaced by that of political risk, in particular of the Conservative Party's split over Europe. In contrast, the Welsh media were more concerned with the plight of Welsh farmers whose livelihoods were threatened by the drop in sales of British beef on domestic and foreign markets.

9   Following Teresa de Lauretis' (1989) remarks on essentialism, essence is used here to refer to a differential residue. It is not some fixed permanent matter, but constructed. An example is the essence of a circle as based on a continuity of points with an equal distance to a centre (see also Van Loon, 1996).

10 Occasionally representatives of consumer organizations did speak as subjects and sometimes members of the opposition attempted to speak in a similar role, but in the case of the latter, the battleground was significantly shifted to that of party politics, and no longer involved issues surrounding the risks of BSE.

11 I would like to thank Neal Curtis for elaborating on this point.

References

Adam, B. (1995) *Timewatch: The Social Analysis of Time*. Cambridge: Polity and Philadelphia: Temple University Press.

Barthes, R. (1977) *Image Music Text*. Trans. Stephen Heath. London: Fontana Press.

Baudrillard, J. (1990) *Fatal Strategies, Crystal Revenge*. Trans. Ph. Beitschman and W.G.J. Niesluchowski. New York: Semiotext(e).

Baudrillard, J. (1993) *Symbolic Exchange and Death*. London: Sage.

Beck, U. (1992) *Risk Society: Towards a New Modernity*. Trans. M. Ritter. London: Sage.

Beck, U., (1994) 'The Reinvention of Politics: Towards a Theory of Reflexive Modernization', in U. Beck, A. Giddens and S. Lash, *Reflexive Modernization: Politics, Tradition and Aesthetics in the Modern Social Order*. Cambridge: Polity. pp. 1–55.

Beck, U., Giddens, A. and Lash, S. (1994) *Reflexive Modernization: Politics, Tradition and Aesthetics in the Modern Social Order*. Cambridge: Polity.

Benjamin, W. (1973) *Illuminations*. Trans. H. Zohn. London: Fontana.

Bey, H. (1991) *TAZ: The Temporary Autonomous Zone*. New York: Autonomedia.

Chambers, I. (1994) *Migrancy, Culture, Identity*. London: Routledge.

de Lauretis, T. (1989) 'The Essence of the Triangle or, Taking the Risk of Essentialism Seriously: Feminist Theory in Italy, the US and Britain', *Differences*, 1 (3): 3–37.

Deleuze, G. (1992) 'Postscript on the Societies of Control', *October*, 59: 3–7.

Deleuze, G. (1994) *Difference and Repetition*. Trans. P. Patton. London: Athlone.

Deleuze, G. and Guattari, F. (1977) *Anti-Oedipus, Capitalism and Schizophrenia*. Trans. R. Hurley. New York: Viking Press.

Deleuze, G. and Guattari, F. (1988) *A Thousand Plateaus: Capitalism and Schizophrenia*. Trans. B. Massumi. London: Athlone.

Fiske, J. (1994) *Media Matters, Everyday Culture and Political Change*. Minneapolis: University of Minnesota Press.

Ford, B.J. (1996) *BSE The Facts: Mad Cow Disease and the Risk to Mankind*. London: Corgi.

Haraway, D. (1988) 'Situated Knowledges: The Sciences Question in Feminism and the Privilege of Partial Perspective', *Feminist Studies*, 14 (3): 575–99.

Haraway, D. (1990) 'A Manifesto for Cyborgs: Science, Technology and Socialist Feminism in the 1980s', in L.J. Nicholson (ed.), *Feminism/Postmodernism*. New York: Routledge. pp. 199–233.

Haraway, D. (1991) *Simians, Cyborgs and Women*. London: Free Association Books.

Haraway, D. (1997) *Modest_@Second_Millennium FemaleMan_Meets_Oncomouse*. London: Routledge.

Land, N. (1995) 'Machines and Technocultural Complexity: The Challenge of the Deleuze-Guattari Conjunction', *Theory, Culture & Society*, 12 (2): 131–40.

Lash, S. (1990) *Sociology of Postmodernism*. London: Routledge.

Luhmann, N. (1982) *The Differentiation of Society*. Trans. S. Holmes and Chr. Larmore. New York: Columbia University Press.

Lyotard, J.F. (1971) *Discours, Figure*. Paris: Klincksieck.

Lyotard, J.F. (1988) *The Differend: Phrases in Dispute*. Manchester: Manchester University Press.

Lyotard, J.F. (1991) *The Inhuman: Reflections on Time*. Trans. G. Bennington and R. Bowlby. Cambridge: Polity.

Maffesoli, M. (1995) *The Time of the Tribes: The Decline of Individualism in Mass Society*. London: Sage.

McKechnie, R. and Welsh, I. (1994) 'Between the Devil and the Deep Green Sea: Defining Risk Societies and Global Threats', in J. Weeks (ed.), *The Lesser Evil: The Greater Good*. London: Rivers Ohram. pp. 57–78.

McLuhan, M. (1964) *Understanding Media: The Extensions of Man*. Harmondsworth: Penguin.

Mintzberg, H. (1983) *Structures in Fives: Designing Effective Organizations*. Englewood Cliffs, NJ: Prentice Hall.

Myers, G., McInnes, K. and Myers, L. (1993) 'Phylogenetic Moments in the AIDS Epidemic', in S.S. Morse (ed.), *Emerging Viruses*. Oxford: Oxford University Press. pp. 120–37.

Nowotny, H. (1994) *Time: The Modern and Postmodern Experience*. Trans. N. Plaice. Cambridge: Polity.

Plant, S. (1995) 'The Future Looms: Weaving, Women and Cybernetics', *Body & Society*, 1 (3–4): 45–64.

Shields, R. (1996) 'Introduction: Virtual Spaces, Real Histories and Living Bodies', in R. Shields (ed.), *Cultures of Internet: Virtual Spaces, Real Histories, Living Bodies*. London: Sage. pp. 1–10.

Shields, R. (1997) 'Flow', *Space & Culture*, (1): 1–7.

Thompson, J.B. (1995) *The Media and Modernity: A Social Theory of the Media*. Cambridge: Polity.

Van Loon, J. (1996) 'Technological Sensibilities and the Cyberpolitics of Gender: Donna Haraway's Postmodern Feminism', *Innovation: The European Journal of Social Sciences*, 9 (2): 231–43.

Van Loon, J. (1999) 'Whiter Shades of Pale: Media-Hybridities of Rodney King', in A. Brah, M. Hickman and M. Mac an Ghaill (eds), *Thinking Identities: Ethnicity, Racism and Culture*. London: Macmillan.

Vattimo, G. (1992) *The Transparent Society*. Trans. D. Webb. Cambridge: Polity.

Weissert, Th.P. (1995) 'Dynamical Discourse Theory', *Time and Society*, 4 (1): 111–33.

PART IV

P(L)AYING FOR FUTURES

10

Worlds in Action: Information, Instantaneity and Global Futures Trading

Deirdre Boden

In his rather brilliant novel on the culture of Wall Street in the 1980s, *The Bonfire of the Vanities*, Tom Wolfe (1987) portrays the international bond traders of that era as 'Masters of the Universe', a title based on children's popular action dolls of the same name – a very muscled and masculine set of plastic supermen who were, in turn, promoted through a TV series of the same name. Early in the novel, Wolfe has his central character describing his fellow traders on the 50th floor trading room of a fictional investment banking house as Masters of the Universe who, through their telephone dealing, were 'moving the lever that moves the world' (1987: 62). In this discussion, I shall be concerned with that *interconnectivity*, which is to say with the ways in which local actors working under conditions of often global uncertainty make markets move.

In late modernity, world financial markets are taken to be the organizing force behind globalization. The sheer volume, invisibility and speed of capital markets operating on a global scale defy our imagination both to conceive their scope and to theorize their consequences, whether intended or consequentially unintended. Twenty-four hour capitalism, operating electronically and instantaneously, would seem the ultimate example of Marx's notion of time annihilating space. But time itself also collapses into a dense present moment, one in which it is possible to move huge amounts of capital continuously around the world.[1] There is a global logic often argued to shape and pace the late-modern age.

Yet, there also remains, in all economic activities, an endemically social character which is all too easily taken for granted.[2] Even sociologists who tackle the topic with special insight often miss the fine-grained structure of social relations out of which 'the market' is conjured (cf. Adler and Adler, 1984; Baker, 1984;

Granovetter, 1985). Economists may note, but only in passing, that a great deal of trust and personal contact is involved in high-speed, high-volume trading (e.g. Williams, 1986). But, in fact, a kind of calculative rationality pervades market activities, a grounded, *in situ* local set of logics that defy any clear means-ends relationship. When markets 'go global' as they have in the past 15 years, and with an accelerating pace since the spread of satellites starting in the mid-1980s, it is tempting to think that the global logic is pre-eminent. But, I believe, there exists instead a more dynamic and local logic as well, one that involves an extraordinarily delicate balance between trust and risk, between today and tomorrow.

Today's financial markets, for all their invisibility, liquidity and speed are anchored in time-space by real people, and it is their local activities which I want to consider as a means of understanding this delicate balance. Standing on the floors of stock markets and financial exchanges everywhere are everyday brokers and traders. In backrooms and boardrooms from London to Tokyo, there are their managers, investors and institutional market players. It is their individual and complexly achieved collective understandings, interpretations, insights, innovations and not infrequent misreadings that drive the market. Their understandings and actions (or inactions) are, in turn, irreducibly *interactional* in character and in realization. As we shall see shortly, even under conditions of a potentially huge number of contacts and contracts, the many human agents who move the levers that move markets operate within remarkably small and routinely face-to-face conditions of proximity (Baker, 1984; Boden and Molotch, 1994). Bounded by a rationality that is as inevitably local as its consequences are global, a broker in Chicago, for example, watches prices in London in realtime yet handles local trades through a close network of interpersonal contacts.[3]

For present purposes, I shall be examining global futures trading as a way of analysing both markets and the actions that move them. Global markets provide the social analyst with a new way of examining both the complexities and consequences of modernity, with its ability to stretch institutional and interpersonal relations across time and space (Giddens, 1990). In addition to their global reach and often arcane practices and abstract hierarchies, all markets also run on an odd and oddly compelling mix of trust and risk. They depend, pervasively, on fragile yet robust networks of interpersonal relations that are simultaneously intensive in their links yet remarkably extended in time and space. Some of the networks are very local, but others are significantly extended. Local/global qualities interact constantly. On satellite and cellular phones, Goffman's 'interaction order' and Garfinkel's 'irremediably local practices' go global.[4]

Markets are, in other words, oddly local affairs, for all the global flows of capital and complex technology that links them, indeed often just because of that same techno-mix. High quality telecommunications and information flows have accelerated modernity at a rate that has yet to be effectively theorized. The synchronous markets of today depend on them, utterly. As a result, instantaneity of communication and information has become the taken-for-granted feature both of doing business and of everyday sense-making. 'Information' as a basis for decision-making is itself highly fluid and often at full flood. And, the abstract flows of information that dominate late modernity have to be interpreted in rapid realtime market conditions by brokers, traders, market makers and punters. The ways in which people make sense and collaboratively arrive at practical working decisions under the contingent and often shifting conditions of realtime activities require what I call 'local logic' (Boden,1994).

The market for futures

Perhaps the most abstract of all markets today are those that variously trade in the future, essentially in opportunities to trade in some future price of some commodity, currency or financial product at some future point in time and even space. Futures trading is the ultimate extension of Simmel's (1990 [1907]) early observations on the power of money as a symbolic token to transform modern society. In trading a *future* price on today's electronic exchanges, social actors use immediate market conditions to instantaneously shape both present and future relations of market and economy. In so doing, they broker the future itself. To develop this topic as a vehicle for understanding how elements of time, trust, risk and local action enter into world markets, a brief overview will be useful. What follows is however a necessarily simplified and schematized description of a volatile and complex phenomenon.

What *are* 'futures'? In formal terms, futures are standardized forward contracts to buy or sell a variety of commodities. Historically, these were mainly agricultural and metallurgical products and, more recently, have also involved contracts for financial instruments and foreign currencies. These contracts are made between brokers and traders working in specific exchanges, licensed and regulated to do so.[5] Futures trading is typically done on organized exchanges, such as those in Chicago and London, and a variety of other exchanges have also opened in other major financial centres around the world. There are now approximately 75 such exchanges with trading in some 400 different contracts.[6] Standard contracts provide the normative and thus regulatory context of futures trading and it is their standardization that facilitates the 'actions at a distance' that characterize this busy world. Until recently, the dominant exchanges have been those in the US, especially the three based in Chicago, which accounted for approximately two-thirds of the contracts traded world-wide 10 years ago.[7] In recent years, however, the US exchanges have been losing market share to newer exchanges in Europe and the Far East, especially Singapore and Japan. Rather obviously, the recent Barings Bank débâcle in Singapore may have left established exchanges such as Chicago and London looking stable, but there have also been scandals in the so-called windy city[8], while London and Tokyo are currently in the grips of a growing scandal in copper futures.

Futures exchanges themselves are voluntary non-profit associations, and their members are individuals who may trade on their own account or as brokers for their firms or outside clients. In addition to the right to trade, exchange membership carries the right to participate in the running of the exchange. Associated with each exchange is a clearinghouse which acts as a guarantor for all the contracts on the exchange. Risk is thus technically contained, at least in some sense. Regulation and standardization are central to the functioning of the exchanges since the markets' liquidity depends on uniformity established by the standardization of the contract terms and the strict rules governing trading (e.g. as to the amounts prices can move, methods of making delivery, times during which trading is permitted and so on). So, it is argued, the security of the markets does not rely on personal trust, but on the role of the well-capitalized clearing-house and, most importantly, the margin deposit requirements and rules imposed on traders in their rapid, daily activities. As we shall see, below, this may be an overly optimistic view of the exchanges.

Trading in the future prices of commodities started with rice in seventeenth-century Japan, and in interesting ways modern exchanges retain much of the intense interpersonal qualities of the pre-technological era. For example, even today, much trading takes place in an 'open pit' with traders watching each other's actions. The market is full of metaphoric animals and primal practices – bulls, bears, pits, turf, open cries and so forth. The pit is a specific part of the floor of a given exchange designated for each type of contract. Brokers cluster together in close proximity, using runners to carry tickets and information further afield. Their attention appears focused on a single trading activity, watching large electronic boards and smaller VDUs, but they also constantly scan the room. They are thus acutely aware of, responsive to and occasionally dependent upon more subtle interpersonal cues such as volume of voice, posture, gesture, pace, direction of gaze and general choreographed demeanour of other brokers in their vicinity and beyond (see also Baker, 1984; Heath et al., 1993).

This territorial aspect has interesting consequences for the local organization of time and space which, in turn, has had a distinct impact on the introduction of remote, so-called screen-based trading, discussed below. There has long been an 'open outcry' system, under which any offer to buy or sell must be made simultaneously to all traders present. This results in raised voices, waving arms and cascades of paper tickets which create those frenetic scenes that film and TV-coverage captures so well. All the while, private customers and institutional brokers keep in touch with the activity on the floor and place their orders by telephone, usually through floor or telephone clerks who relay orders to dealers by hand signals or runners.

As indicated, during the past decade automated electronic systems have also been introduced into futures trading, especially in the newer exchanges in the Far East. Here, traders receive price data on world prices for contracts and other relevant information and news through screen-based systems. These systems have reduced the dependence on face-to-face contact and have therefore been greatly resisted. Electronic screen-based trading also has the potential for much greater regulation and increased opportunities to trade around the clock but traders have continued to resist such surveillance. Their insistence on the need for interpersonal cues and visual contact has resulted in the tendency only to use screen-based facilities for 'after hours' activities, which is to say for extended trading hours and the execution of trades at a distance from other time-zones.[9]

Co-presence and proximity remain however central to the realtime interactional environment of futures markets even as they go increasingly global (Boden and Molotch, 1994). Moreover, the spatial organization of the trading floor, type of information systems available, and the territorial relations embodied in the 'turf', 'booth' and various locations of traders are also critical. They are part of the politics of the exchange as well as being quite practical factors that enter into moment-to-moment enactment of this busy environment of action. Such territorial issues are shaped by the relative influence of individual dealers and firms, based on their trading volume and other factors.

Trading around the clock

Globally, futures markets now operate around the clock (see Fig 10.1), trading not only basic commodities and metals but also currencies and, most significantly, financial instruments and composites, the most complex being the recent and fraught development of the derivative market.[10] All trading in one market, for example, Tokyo, has multiple and often simultaneous effects on other markets.

Until quite recently, global trading simply meant following a certain commodity through various markets serially and spatially around the world. Now, brokers routinely trade similar contracts at the same time in several markets, going 'long' in one, 'short' in another, and speculating on the direction of one market or product against another, taking their profits in tiny margins in between. This means that a broker in Tokyo may take positions in Tokyo and Singapore, for instance, crude oil or Mexican pesos, while creating the conditions of trading for later the same day in Europe or the US. Indeed, the global financial cities of London, New York and Tokyo rarely sleep (Sassen, 1991). Both markets and individuals are rooted in close, yet extensive communities, reflexively tied by cultural practices and normative expectations involving complex regulatory arrangements.

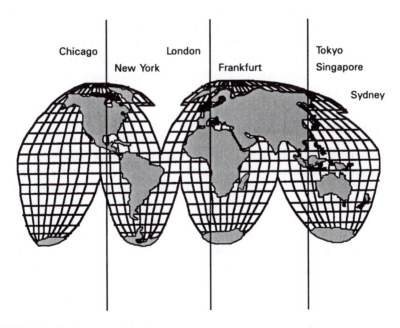

FIGURE 10.1   *Trading around the clock*

Markets open in Tokyo, Hong Kong and Singapore in rapid succession and, with variable opening hours, lunch breaks and extended trading into the evening, now operate almost continuously, moving to Frankfurt, London, New York, Chicago, and later Sydney and, again, to Tokyo. The intensive yet extensive quality of trading depends on high levels of expertise, realtime response rates, and a constant flow of electronic and interactional signs and symbols. Yet there has also been considerable debate in a number of exchanges over the past 4–6 years about whether improved electronic trading systems will replace open outcry and proximate dealing. In one New York exchange some years ago, traders were so exercised about threats to their working environment that they insisted on having monitors suspended over the pit. They claimed it was essential that they watch and have line-of-sight contact with all other relevant brokers. As these markets increasingly 'go global' and trade 24 hours, the speed-up and synchronicity have also created a global environment of action – action at a distance taken to a considerable extreme. An increasing number of contracts are now being traded in more than one exchange. The location of exchanges in different time zones means that some contracts are now traded for more than 20 hours in a given day or, more accurately, on a given date. Brokerage firms and banks have opened branches in the main urban centres around the world and can recruit and service clients and trade around the clock. London and Tokyo, for example, now have teams of brokers working ghost shifts so as to be able to trade in realtime in New York and Chicago, with Tokyo trading, interestingly enough, back to the future across the international dateline. Even brokers working regular hours, in Chicago, London and Frankfurt, arrive to find a market in action and potentially substantial changes since they went to bed the night before. They are thus obliged to respond constantly to an essentially moving set of targets, taking positions that may have to be monitored by others in other time zones. Satellite technology, fully available only from the mid-1980s, virtually guarantees a constant and dense flow of data, information and voices encircling a global market of great complexity, with phone, fax, and buzzing screens also displaying graphic summaries of incoming communications.

The time value of the future

The skill of brokers lies in their on-the-spot abilities to track and calculate a very narrow yet complex range of contracts and relevant flows of information. Futures trading brings the central workings of capitalism into sharp relief and, in the process, highlights the fragile rather than fragmented nature of work and technology in the late-modern age. Brokers watch screens and a continuous flow of incoming information while simultaneously intervening in those same flows to create new conditions of next actions by both themselves and others. As briefly outlined above, they frequently take positions on both sides of a trend and, just as often, hold multiple positions in the same kind of contract, whether oil, Yen, Eurodollars or a composite calculation of the Nikkei or Dow Jones indices. Timing is critical for brokers as are their links to other markets open at the same time or due to open shortly. In essence, these young traders are trading in time itself, which is to say in the momentary forward fluctuations of price and value. The latter are, by extension, expressions of the most abstract sort: of money itself and, even more abstractly, of the price of money at some future point in time, in other words, in future interest rates.

Exploring these issues will be best taken in three linked stages. First, we will need to reconsider the role of money in modern society and, in particular, its relation to value, on the one hand, and time, on the other hand. For this, the foundational writings of Simmel on money will illuminate the brief analysis that follows. Second, a brief example of the operation of a common futures trade will explicate some of these quite abstract considerations. In this, I shall draw on the recent work of economists and financial writers. Finally, it will be possible to begin to put some simple pieces of the puzzle together in a discussion of futures trading as an exercise in trust and risk.

Georg Simmel on money

Simmel's definition of money provides a theoretical filter which may highlight the largely invisible and instant quality of today's economic transactions. Money, for Simmel, is both a medium and measure of modernity. It is abstract and thus objective, symbolic and thus totemic. It operates independently of individuals, collectivities, objects and markets, providing a way for the value of either goods or services to appear objective and inherent (Simmel, 1990: 80). It is the 'incarnation and purest expression of the concept of economic value' yet simultaneously provides for the *relativity* of valuation necessary for any exchange (Simmel, 1990: 101). Moreover, as a free-floating and symbolic token of concrete relationships, money has the capacity to 'bracket' time and space by coupling present to future and thus instantaneity to deferral (Giddens, 1990).

Money, for Simmel, can also be located within the sequential properties of social life, as the ultimate 'extension' of humans in time/space, as a tool and an aid to their ability to act purposively yet abstractly (1990: 210–11). As such, it mediates between people and their goals. It is the 'purest reification of means ... a pure instrument' (Simmel, 1990: 211). It is 'neutral and colourless', at the same time 'more objective in relation to particular interests and more remote from any specific purpose' (Simmel, 1990: 212), and thereby a major medium of spatio-temporal distantiation while providing a quite detailed system of value. Transformed into the electronic and global impulses of today's financial exchanges, this purposive yet abstract extension of value has reached new heights (and, perhaps, depths).

Futures trading breaks with older notions of use-value however, whether those of Marx or Simmel, by providing an instant abstract set of values extended from the present moment into an increasingly calculable yet uncertain future. The future value of a commodity contract is not simply a matter of linear time – increasing or decreasing in some predictable way – but is linked instead to complex multivariate calculations, inflated, discounted, hedged and even expressly devalued. Where money, for Simmel, is a pure instrument that represents the best way to establish concrete value in the most abstract terms, the new markets of modernity are also capable of simultaneously discounting some future value to create multiple present valuations. The mediating capacity of old-fashioned money is thereby pushed into far more intensive yet extensive areas of risk. At the same time, there are almost unimaginable moments of profit making and profit taking. At each step the future itself becomes one of the bargaining chips of modernity.

The general connections between money and value, as well as between time and money become attenuated, rather obviously, in any market transaction.[11] It is not only that labour and time become commodified, as Marx and later writers have noted, but also that the abstract and abstracting quality of money means that value and time become intertwined through the deferral process that money facilitates. Money is a measure of value and medium of circulation for Marx too, while time extends value through rates of interest. In simple terms, what intervenes is the cost of money over time or, more explicitly, the *rental cost* of money. Although interest rates enter into all market calculations as a basis for the circulation of capital, the *time-buying* character of futures markets makes interest rates still more central. As we have seen, trading futures directly involves buying contracts at various prices strung out along a future timeline. The kinds of margins and liquidity required further involve variable interest rates which must also be extended along a time trajectory. The interplay of four basic elements are activated in all futures trading (Figure 10.2).

Figure 10.2 illustrates the current or 'spot' price of a given commodity or financial instrument, its various future prices at various dates of delivery, the rental price of money at interim periods, and the 'spread' between potential prices and delivery (or contract) dates. The spread is defined by one economist as the 'difference between the price of a good for two dates of delivery or at two different locations' (Williams, 1986). For instance, a trader may be interested in the spread of corn prices between June and September (through the growing and harvest period) or in the price of American wheat delivered to St. Petersburg, or the price of North Sea crude oil stored now in Aberdeen or delivered three months hence to a refinery in Wales or Japan. The spread may also be understood as the set of trades necessary to create a certain position in the market, contracts in Yen, for example, at multiple prices in different markets and at different points in time. Taking different positions in volatile contracts allows a broker to 'straddle' the

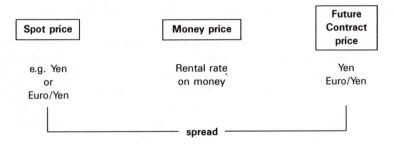

FIGURE 10.2 *The time value of money*

spread, thereby containing risk. Often, very slim profit margins and very high levels of expertise are involved and these may, in turn, require brokers and traders to shift positions, buying and selling rapidly, to maintain position and clear profit.

Figure 10.2 represents, quite simplistically, two such potential operations; one is a basic investment in Yen and, in particular, in its potential to strengthen (or noticeably weaken) within a given period. More complexly, a broker might trade in the *relative position* between Sterling and Yen, explicitly playing two areas of the global economy against each other and calculating variable spreads across time (and, we may also say, space). Cross-currency trading requires brokers to take positions in both currencies simultaneously but one may be hedged against the other and a third may even come into play at key points in the trading exercise. Most large brokers take simultaneous positions in various delivery months, typically buying contracts for one period and selling for another. In the futures pits, these are the frequently highly local deals that are enacted in close small networks. The brokers on the Chicago exchanges, where local traders are particularly common, may use key contacts to offset large positions, an operation which clearly involves a high degree of local trust. What matters to these simultaneous positions are the spreads between prices rather than the prices themselves (Williams, 1986: 18), hence a quite acute sense of the *time value* of money is apparent in these rapid transactions. Additionally, especially for institutional brokers representing large clients, variations in global conditions – of economy, politics, environment and so on – may well affect the intervening interest rates at which the financing of these huge transactions is accomplished. As a result, the temporal volatility of interest rates enters into the many individual contracts traded. As futures trading has become ever more global and instantaneous, the manipulation of positions in relation to variable spread and minor shifts in interest rates has become part of the largely invisible operation of these markets. It is in just this way that not only capital is in flight, but modernity itself floats free of its earlier moorings.

Perhaps the most abstract of all such transactions are those which move the price of contracts most abstractly around the world: the so-called 'derivatives' contracts. Table 10.1 presents a summary of the closing prices of this type of financial instrument: Eurodollar Time Deposit Futures. The items extracted for this working example need not concern us in any detail, but include opening prices, daily high/low trading levels, final settlement prices and the actual or estimated volume over 10 years.[12] The 'derivative' element here is the Eurodollar Time Deposit Futures treated as an index. Instead of (or in addition to) investing directly in Eurodollars, a broker or trader may want to trade in the combined performance of interest rates on holding Eurodollars for 90-days. Eurodollars (ED) are US dollars on deposit in Europe, usually in London. Their existence, often for tax reasons held outside the US by large transnational firms, acts as a magnet for speculators. Again the spread is central here. At first glance, the task might seem simple as the further into the future the greater the Eurodollar time deposit will cost and thus the more it is discounted. But what is indexed is not the cost of Eurodollars (ED) *per se*, but a sliding index price, calculated as 100 minus the estimated ED interest rate based on a 90-day contract. In fact, however, a broker

TABLE 10.1   *Chicago Mercantile Exchange*

Month/Strike	Session					
	Open	High	Low	Last	Settlement	Estimated Volume
JLY 96	94.35	94.36	94.34	94.36	94.35	1841
AUG 96	94.26	94.27	94.24	94.26	94.26	1211
SEP 96	94.17	94.18	94.15	94.17	94.17	34K
DEC 96	93.82	93.85	93.78	93.83	93.83	89K
MAR 97	93.63	93.65	93.58	93.63	93.63	51K
JUN 97	93.43	93.45	93.38	93.43	93.42	34K
SEP 97	93.28	93.30	93.23	93.27	93.27	13K
DEC 97	93.12	93.14	93.09	93.13	93.12	7561
MAR 98	93.09	93.10	93.05A	93.08	93.08	5922
JUN 98	93.02	93.04	92.99	93.02	93.02	4298
SEP 98	92.98	93.00	92.97	92.98	92.98	4546
DEC 98	92.90	92.92	92.88	92.90	92.90	3474
MAR 99	92.89	92.91	92.91	92.87	92.89	2221
JUN 99	92.82	92.86	92.82	92.84	92.84	1423
JUN 00	92.66	92.70	92.65	92.68	92.68	1060
JUN 01	92.52	92.54	92.51	92.52	92.52	740
JUN 02	92.36	92.37	92.36	92.36	92.37	137
JUN 03	92.22	92.23B	92.22	92.23B	92.24	142
JUN 04	—	—	92.10A	92.11B	92.13	10
JUN 05	—	—	—	—	92.00	10
JUN 06	—	—	—	—	91.88	10

These figures were taken from publicly quoted items of the Chicago Mercantile Exchange for 12 June 1996. Any other period would display the same pattern, although at different calculations of future interest rates.

may move in and out of this position within days, hours, even minutes, trading on the fine momentary fluctuations of ED interest rates and their relation to other often volatile factors in the currency markets worldwide. Brokers, on behalf of clients, or traders on their own account can, for instance, buy contracts in Eurodollars themselves while, at the same time, 'hedging' those promises to buy with derivative contracts based directly on indexes of interest rates in Eurodollar deposits. These activities, as is well known, have recently featured in various global financial scandals but, for our more theoretical purposes, offer a particularly intense picture of the globalizing properties of these markets. It is only through having continuous and often parallel streams of information, instant communication links and constant opportunities to trade that global futures markets are fully realized.

In the light of this, it is tempting yet again to assume the operation of a global logic 'driving' decisions and prices, one which dictates the discrete activities of individual and institutional brokers and traders. This is particularly tempting given academic preoccupations with markets, hierarchies, rationality and the many formulations of capitalist overaccumulation and even disorganization (for example, Harvey, 1982; Lash and Urry, 1987). Yet, as I have suggested earlier, the few studies of actual trading that have been conducted reveal a far more local, interpersonal and horizontal (or 'flat' to use Latour's term) organization of market transactions. These are now tense with technology and flooded in information yet remain highly localized and robustly interactional in their constitution and ultimate success (or failure).

Trust, risk and technology

Let me return therefore to the issues of proximity, face-to-face interaction and close interpersonal networks with which this brief examination of global futures trading began. The study of various processes of globalization demands careful consideration, I argued, of the links between local action and global consequences (and vice versa). Indeed, it may be said that globalization itself, as both process and outcome, now depends on what McLuhan (1962: 248) once called the 'instant all-at-onceness' through which we are all interconnected electronically. We live and work in an era when time and space are collapsed into a global present and where information and communication create a total field of interacting events and person-to-person relations (Adam, 1995; McLuhan, 1962: 248–55). Surrounded by high technology, traders experience a multiplicity of temporal and spatial frames simultaneously. The busy world of futures traders embodies just such instantaneous and intense practices and conditions. The results are global in both consequences and creating the continuing conditions of *next* actions. Both sequence and simultaneity are central to futures trading. The actions of brokers and traders are, in an ethnomethodological sense, reflexively tied and sequentially relevant, operating through a local logic with global results, yet simultaneously organized in terms of relentless instant conditions. Many conditions may be created through technology but they must be managed and made to work by local actors whose own sequentially unfolding activities are also fraught with tense temporal pacing.

Moreover, although many market practices are designed to conform to regulatory constraints and thereby contain risks, they also centrally depend, for their moment-to-moment enactment as well as for their long-term effect, on trust. Futures contracts are, as we have seen, ways of encapsulating time and risk by creating collective valuations of the future itself. To do so, however, entails a very local sort of trust, as well as the creation and sustained accomplishment of institutional trust at a more diffuse level.

A common assumption about futures markets is that they are mechanisms for increasing investment potential while reducing risk. Yet this is, according to some current economic theory, at best an incomplete view (Williams, 1986). Certainly traders may use, for instance, cautious positions in gold futures to offset riskier positions in currencies. But a remarkable degree of trust in the future is also involved since, as I have sketched, trading out into the future means playing with the variable price of money and thereby with the value of value. In this way, colonizing the future takes on a complex new meaning.

Trust, in this context, is a thoroughly modern matter. Luhmann (1979) defines trust in rational terms, as the mechanism through which social actors reduce complexity and as a necessary prerequisite for deriving proper rules of conduct. Trust, in this formulation, is treated as external to action and complexity is seen as part of the environment of action rather than intrinsic to it. In certain ways, markets do seem to operate on just that sort of trust, driven in just such an external way. Yet, if we observe social worlds in action, *as they happen*, a rather more sophisticated picture emerges (Boden, 1990). As people move iteratively and sequentially through social life, they are, to be sure, inclined to 'satisfice', which is to say to reduce uncertainty and complexity by selecting the nearest reasonable solution or next action. But they also move through their activities in a significantly collaborative and cumulative fashion and this involves a very high level of mutual trust.

Especially under the rapid realtime conditions of late modernity, people need a delicate balance of trust, temporal framing, interactional co-ordination and constant monitoring just to get through the day.[13] In places like the futures exchanges of Chicago, London or Singapore, there is no time not to trust your local network. It is thus not the 'function of trust' which makes it possible for actors to 'live and act in greater complexity in relation to events' (Luhmann, 1979: 151, emphasis deleted) but the fine-grained and ever-present capacity of people to sustain the conditions of trust as an ongoing accomplishment. Underpinning that ability is Garfinkel's (1967) notion of trust as the irreducible condition of social action and as internal to it. Surrounded by complex technology and variable degrees of uncertainty, social actors seek each other out, to make the deals that, writ large across the global electronic boards of the exchanges, make the market. They come together in tight social worlds to use each other and their shared understandings of 'what's happening' to reach out and move those levers that move the world.

Reordering the future

Information and instantaneity characterize this era of late modernity. The speed and intensity with which information can be transferred is facilitated by an invisible and largely unanalysed network of global satellites. Through them, which is to say, literally, buzzing across their linked positions in space, instant information has collapsed time into a single global present. Computers, telephones and television are also merging into a singular communicative environment which will radically alter the nature of both interpersonal and telecommunication. As telephonic and televisual technologies become one, the very idea of 'interaction' is taking on new meaning. This chapter offers a preliminary discussion of global futures trading as a means of analysing and theorizing the consequences of such interactive instantaneity for the global village. I am proposing that we take McLuhan seriously, and with him Goffman and Garfinkel. The global world of traders is local, everywhere, at every point and at every moment (see also Latour, 1993).

What is fascinating about futures markets, especially in the context of this volume, are the ways in which the future is reordered through everyday action: through talking, trading and tracking across the horizon of the global landscape. In addition to being a remarkable form of colonizing the future, trading futures contracts involves bartering the future itself. The currencies and commodities are 'real' in that there are plenty of hogs bellies, cotton bales, gallons of crude oil, bars of gold and lucrative Eurodollars 'out there' in the marketplaces and holding pens of modernity. There are also both producers and consumers of these commodities and whole industries whose markets are tied both back and forward in time through their raw materials. But the whole operation of futures markets is also exquisitely abstract in that, as I have tried to indicate, relatively few traders or brokers deal in actual physical commodities but in a complex array of contracts.

The action – of these *worlds in action* – is elsewhere. Futures dealers are, as we have seen, speculating in contracts to buy, sell or exchange some commodity at some point in the future. They are, as they say themselves, dealing in 'paper' and effectively gambling on or hedging against the *future* value of money extending and reorganizing the future of the markets themselves. Futures traders and brokers dance along a fine line that stretches out into a decidedly unforeseeable future. They are, in the final analysis, buying and selling at the ephemeral leading edge of the world capitalist system. Moreover, they are doing so often by juggling with just those raw commodities, exchange values and price systems that so fascinated Marx. Yet the matter is, perhaps, more complicated than Marx could imagine. Not only does the use value of money facilitate the circulation of commodities, but the future of each enters into the present instantaneously and relentlessly. How the future and present interpenetrate is what futures trading is all about.

Acknowledgements

This chapter is based on shared work with Sol Picciotto (see for example, Picciotto and Haines, 1999). I would like to thank the conference participants and organizers of the Risks, Technologies, Futures Conference in Cardiff. I also thank Kevin Boden, Anthony Giddens, Nigel Thrift, John Urry and the editors for their comments, and Joost van Loon for his excellent work on the overall manuscript.

Notes

1 See Friedland and Boden (1994: 30). David Harvey (1989) argues that through flexible over-accumulation world markets have reached the limits of spatio-temporal displacement and have been transformed into cultural flows (see also Lash and Urry, 1993).

2 See Anderson et al. (1989: 6). For an interesting discussion of an ethnomethodological approach to 'economy and society', see Molotch (1990).

3 Here I am rather consciously playing with Herbert Simon's notion of bounded rationality. The latter depends on essentially cognitive and individualistic assumptions about how humans 'satisfice' rather than 'optimize' in their decision-making (Simon, 1990). My own research suggests that the matter is far more interactional than psychological (Boden, 1994: 193–9).

4 See Erving Goffman (1983) for an extended discussion of the interaction order.

5 Brokers, as the name suggests, represent absent others and act on their behalf. In today's markets, most brokers are directly tied to specific institutions – banks, insurance companies, corporations – who in turn represent clients and stockholders. Traders (or local traders), on the other hand, may be individual investors, also licensed. The term 'trading' is however often used generically in both academic and business literature.

6   See for example, the *Report of the Presidential Taskforce on Market Mechanisms* (1986); and the US Congress, Office of Technology Assessment (1990), *Trading Around the Clock: Global Securities Markets and Information Technology – Background Paper*.

7   These are, in descending order of volume traded: the Chicago Board of Trade, Chicago Mercantile Exchange and the Chicago Board of Options Trading.

8   See for example, Greising and Morse (1991) for a very useful journalistic account of FBI 'sting' operations in Chicago in 1987.

9   For instance, one such service was developed jointly by Reuters and the Chicago Mercantile Exchange, initially in 1987. It marked an attempt to set-up a global 24-hour electronic trading system called Globex. It took five years before it was finally fully launched in June 1992 and despite its apparent promise and predictions that it would rapidly supplant local exchanges and open outcry, was reported in June 1993 to be making little headway and managing to represent only the 'tail' of the market. By late 1999, however, almost every world exchange was experimenting with various after-hours trading arrangements and contracts to authorize traders licensed on one exchange to trade on another.

10   All futures trading, in a general sense, is 'derivative' of basic prices and commodities but recent composite indices and contracts for complex financial instruments are still more abstracted from concrete market relations.

11   See Giddens' (1990: 24–6) discussion of Keynes and Simmel on the relation of time and money.

12   For simplicity, I have extracted key elements on a quarterly basis for the period of July 1996–June 1999, and then only June figures for each year to 2006.

13   The fragile business of 'getting through the day' is one that is all too often missed by sociologists and even anthropologists. It is, of course, the central focus of ethnomethodology and the phrase itself is one of Harvey Molotch's, himself quite an accomplished proponent of everyday life.

References

Adam, B. (1995) *Timewatch: The Social Analysis of Time*. Cambridge: Polity.

Adler, P. and Adler, P. (eds) (1984) *The Social Dynamics of Financial Markets*. Greenwich, CT: JAI Press.

Anderson, R.J., Hughes, J.A. and Sharrock, W.W. (1989) *Working for Profit: The Social Organization of Calculation in an Entrepreneurial Firm*. Aldershot: Avebury.

Baker, W. (1984) 'The Social Structure of a National Securities Market', *American Journal of Sociology*, 89: 775–811.

Beck, U. (1992) *Risk Society: Towards a New Modernity*. Trans. M. Ritter. London: Sage.

Boden, D. (1990) 'The World As It Happens: Ethnomethodology and Conversation Analysis', in G. Ritzer (ed.), *Frontiers of Social Theory: The New Synthesis*. New York: Columbia University Press. pp. 185–213.

Boden, D. (1994) *The Business of Talk: Organizations in Action*. Cambridge: Polity.

Boden, D. and Molotch, H. (1994) 'The Compulsion of Proximity', in R. Friedland and D. Boden (eds), *Now/Here: Space, Time and Modernity*. Berkeley: University of California Press. pp. 253–85.

Friedland, R. and Boden, D. (1994) 'Introduction', in R. Friedland and D. Boden (eds), *Now/Here: Space, Time and Modernity*. Berkeley: University of California Press. pp. 1–53.

Garfinkel, H. (1967) *Studies in Ethnomethodology*. Englewood Cliffs, NJ: Prentice-Hall.

Giddens, A. (1990) *The Consequences of Modernity*. Stanford, CA: Stanford University Press and Cambridge: Polity.

Goffman, E. (1983) 'The Interaction Order', *American Sociological Review*, 48: 1–17.

Granovetter, M. (1985) 'Economic Action and Social Structure: the Problem of Embeddedness', *American Journal of Sociology*, 91: 481–510.

Greising, D. and Morse, L. (1991) *Brokers, Bagmen and Moles*. New York: John Wiley.

Harvey, D. (1982) *The Limits to Capital*. Oxford: Basil Blackwell.

Harvey, D. (1989) *The Condition of Postmodernity*. Oxford: Basil Blackwell.

Heath, C., Jirotka, M., Luff, P. and Hindmarsh, J. (1993) 'Unpacking Collaboration: The Interactional Organisation of Trading in a City Dealing Room', in G. Di Michelis, C. Simone and K. Schmidt (eds), *Proceedings of the Third European Conference Computer Supported Co-operative Work (ECSCW)*. Amsterdam: Kluwer.

Lash, S. and Urry, J. (1987) *The End of Organised Capitalism*. Cambridge: Polity.

Lash, S. and Urry, J. (1993) *Economies of Signs and Space*. London: Sage.

Latour, B. (1993) *We Have Never Been Modern*. Trans. C. Porter. Hemel Hempstead: Harvester Wheatsheaf.

Luhmann, N. (1979) *Trust and Power*. New York: Free Press.

McLuhan, M. (1962) *Understanding Media: The Extensions of Man*. London: Routledge.

Molotch, H. (1990) 'Sociology, Economics and the Economy', in H. Gans (ed.), *Sociology in America*, ASA Presidential Series. Newbury Park, CA: Sage. pp. 293–309.

Picciotto, S. and Haines, J.D. (1999) 'Regulating Global Financial Markets', *Journal of Law & Society*, 26 (3): 351–68.

Report of the Presidential Taskforce on Market Mechanisms (1986) Washington, DC: US Government Printing Office.

Sassen, S. (1991) *The Global City*. Princeton, NJ: Princeton University Press.

Simmel, G. (1990[1907]) *The Philosophy of Money*. (2nd edn.) Trans. T. Bottomore and D. Frisby. London: Routledge.

Simon, H. (1990) 'Alternative Visions of Rationality', in P. Moser (ed.), *Rationality in Action*. Cambridge: Cambridge University Press.

US Congress, Office of Technology Assessment (1990) *Trading Around the Clock: Global Securities Markets and Information Technology-Background Paper*, OTA-BP-CIT-66, Washington, DC: US Government Printing Office.

Williams, J. (1986) *The Economic Function of Futures Markets*. Cambridge: Cambridge University Press.

Wolfe, T. (1987) *The Bonfire of the Vanities*. New York: Bantam Books.

11

Discourses of Risk and Utopia

Ruth Levitas

Recent discussions have placed not only risk but utopia at the centre of contemporary social theory. They contain both the dystopian warning 'if this goes on ...' and the associated utopian 'if only ...'. They raise the questions which brought me to sociology: What is to be done? How shall we live? – although sociology and sociologists resolutely refused to try to answer these questions, first in pursuit of a chimerical value-neutrality and then in insistence on relativism. In reinstating these questions, works by Ulrich Beck and Anthony Giddens have moved away from a discourse in which utopianism was rejected out of hand, as something associated with modernity and rationality, and with totalitarianism, fascism, Stalinism, communism and socialism, all of which could be elided into a negative monolith against which the freedom of capitalist democracy could be contrasted. Such a position was always a travesty of utopianism, which is very diverse in content, form and function. I want to endorse the necessity of utopian thinking. But I also want to argue that these analyses current in social theory do not move nearly far enough from a pro-capitalist ideological position. They are too cautious, insufficiently utopian. This is partly because of inherent weaknesses in the concept of risk, partly because of the discourses in which it is embedded, and partly because current conditions create particular difficulties for transformative utopian thinking.

There is a huge literature on utopianism, spanning fiction, literary criticism, political theory, philosophy, sociology, theology, and architecture. Definitions are contested, or more frequently simply presumed or neglected. At its broadest, utopia may be defined as the expression of a desire for a better way of living, which may take many forms (Bloch, 1986; Levitas, 1990). These forms are socially constructed: imagining an alternative society in the future is one manifestation; so too is an idealized representation of the present. Utopia may also refer to a more personal locus, in the quest for the ideal relationship, or for the perfect self/body, as if that is all over which control can be exercised. Utopia is always a form of counter-factual thinking, although not always self-consciously so. What is abandoned in this definition is the pejorative connotation of utopia, as impossible and unrealistic. It also counters the accusation of totalitarianism, routinely levelled at literary utopias as well as at social systems – an accusation which is in any case historically inaccurate even as a description of social utopias: it may be salutary to remember that William Morris' (1890) utopia, *News from Nowhere*, is libertarian, socialist and green, if not particularly feminist.

There are problems with such a definition. On the one hand, it enables us to map the different contents, forms and functions of utopianism, and the social conditions which produce shifts between these. On the other hand, it fails to distinguish between utopian images. For those who have a commitment to social change, it has always been necessary to make a distinction between utopia as compensation, as escapism, as fantasy – as Raymond Williams put it, 'a mode of living with alienation' (1980: 203) – or utopia as a vehicle of criticism, and utopia as a catalyst of change – that which Ernst Bloch called anticipatory thinking. Bloch (1986) distinguishes between abstract and concrete utopia, Edward Thompson (1977), in his discussion of Morris, between disciplined and undisciplined dreaming. Even Lenin, asking *What is to be Done?*, argued in favour of dreaming connected to an analysis of the present and a commitment to change, and regretted that 'of this kind of dreaming there is too little in our movement' (Lenin, 1975: 211). The attempt to make this distinction between transformative and other utopian visions is fraught with difficulty, and at the root of that made by Karl Marx and Friedrich Engels between utopian and scientific socialism, as well as Karl Mannheim's distinction between ideology and utopia, Thompson's assertion of the dialectic between reason and desire, Bloch's assertion of the dialectic between utopia and material analysis, as the 'warm' and 'cold' streams of Marxism, and, I suspect, at the root of Giddens' term 'utopian realism' which 'has utopian features, yet is not unrealistic because it corresponds to observable trends' (Giddens, 1995: 101).

Transformative utopianism requires not just the projection of desire, although it does require us to think seriously and creatively about the conditions for a sustainable and equitable future. This is the 'what' of utopia. It also requires an analysis of the present. How, and by whom, is the transformation to be made? What are the points of intervention into the present system which permit radical transformation? Who are the agents of change? While the imagining of the future must be tempered by this analysis, there is always the danger that where change seems difficult, utopia is either impossible to imagine, or becomes collapsed into the analysis of the present itself (and this can of course also happen in defence of the interests of those benefiting from the status quo, and, even where unintentional, tends to serve those interests). By comparison with ourselves, utopianism was relatively easy for the Victorians. A belief in progress placed utopia in the future, as the outcome of an evolutionary process. This was true even for Marx, whose view of technological development was highly optimistic; the achievement of utopia did require a radical break, but only in the relations, not the forces of production. In our own situation, technology seems less benign: fears of nuclear or ecological catastrophe are linked to a more general sense of powerlessness and insecurity. When society is seen as in a state of decline, utopia can only be envisaged in the future if there is a radical break (Levitas, 1981); and this break, for us, must include both the forces and the relations of production, but it is almost impossible to identify how, or by whom? Fatalism is not just dystopian, tending to gloomy prognoses for the future, but anti-utopian, tending to cancel out as absurd transformative utopian thinking.

If transformative utopian thinking is necessary, how is it served by current discussions of risk? How do the available discourses of risk affect how we think about the future? Risk is a broad concept, and an appealing one. It appeals for a good reason, and for a bad one. The good reason is that it makes ecological (not just environmental) questions central, and reminds us, to paraphrase Dorothy Parker, that considering how dangerous everything is, we are not nearly frightened enough, while simultaneously addressing the fact that it is very difficult for us to know just how frightened we should be. The bad reason is that it is a very elastic concept. The translator's note in *Ecological Politics in an Age of Risk* (Beck, 1995b) observes that *Sicherheit* may mean security, safety, or certainty, and 'risk' in English carries a similar penumbra of (inverted) meanings. Scanning a day's news offers risk capital, children at risk, risk of flooding; while sociologists can take up the fashionable concept in discussions of young people's sexual activity or the behaviour of motor cyclists. I fear that the title of *Risk Society* (Beck, 1992) is as evocative as that of Herbert Marcuse's *One Dimensional Man* (1968), whose title was always more quoted than its argument because it articulated the experience of a particular class fraction and generation. In this sense, the idea of risk appeals quite separately from the substance of Beck's argument. It does so less because of ecological threats than because many people are exposed to economic uncertainty, insecurity and anxiety. This is of course true for large parts of the population. It is newly true for the professional middle classes, among whom, as we know, academics have suffered the greatest relative fall in economic rewards and social status as well as among the greatest rises in 'productivity' or intensification of labour. There may be good sociological reasons for sociologists' attraction to the idea of risk. And while the breadth of the concept is largely irrelevant to the merits of the actual arguments advanced about risk society, it is not wholly so. For elastic concepts – and if risk is one, utopia is another – are more easily co-opted to alternative discourses and bent to operate in opposing interests.

For the purposes of this chapter, I want to distinguish between a discourse of risk, which undoubtedly exists beyond the confines of academia and which is part of the object of Beck's attention, and a discourse of risk society which is a theoretical discourse of sociologists, and to focus on their consequences for transformative utopian thinking. Beck defines risk as 'a systematic way of dealing with hazards and insecurities induced and introduced by modernization itself' (1992: 21). It is a mode of thinking about potential negative events in the future which calculates their probability and the severity (usually as the financial cost) of their effect. Indeed, risk has been technically defined elsewhere as the product of the probability and the severity of the event in question (Adams, 1995). Such calculations, as we all know, are fundamental to processes of insurance. Insurance-based thinking is an accommodation to risk. It neutralizes negative events by prescribing monetary compensation (for human life as well as loss of property) and it naturalizes those events by attributing to 'mere chance' the process whereby they befall one victim rather than another. Chance is beyond human control; attribution of events to chance is fundamentally fatalistic, and fundamentally amoral, being an abdication of personal or collective responsibility. It is a small step from arguing that chance determines who suffers to assuming that it is only chance that determines that anyone suffers.

In this sense, the common discourse of risk brings the future into a calculative relation to the present. Normality is the luck of avoiding victim-hood, or being well-compensated; dystopia is finding your insurance premiums have lapsed. A transformed future, especially one which is, as it must be, substantially unknown, and which stands in a very uncertain relation to the present, is unthinkable within the discourse of risk, which quite clearly operates as a legitimation of the existing system. It is, in fact, the standard discourse of capitalism, in which it is a matter of luck and market forces who are winners and who are losers (but we are all winners in the end). It promotes the pinning of utopian hopes on winning the lottery; pure luck, no skill, no responsibility, no guilt. This very primitive form of utopian dreaming depends on changing one's position within the system, rather than changing the system – and doing so in a way attributable only to luck and chance. As Bloch (1986: 33) put it, most people in the street look as if they are thinking about something else. That something else is usually money, and the things that can be bought with it. In terms of transformative utopianism, this discourse is profoundly anti-utopian. Indeed, the propensity of people (or, prior to the lottery, chiefly men) to gamble can be used, as by Milton Friedman in the early 1980s, to argue that people 'like risk'. A more sophisticated argument to that effect has been advanced by John Adams, who claims the existence of a 'risk compensation effect', whereby safety measures cause people to take greater risks until the accident level rises to its previous level, and argues that 'the safety literature almost universally ignores the potential loss of reward consequent on behaviour which is too safe' (Adams, 1995: 20).

Both Beck and Giddens are arguing that this discourse is no longer appropriate or adequate. In *Beyond Left and Right* (1995) Giddens argues that the processes of legitimation of hazard in 'risk' society are different from those of class society. He distinguishes between external risk and manufactured uncertainty. The latter is different in that it escapes or confounds insurance, partly because of the high consequence risks that we now face, but also because of the source of risk. The welfare state is/was, he argues, designed to cope with the consequences of risk; so, by extension, are all systems of insurance. Risk is essentially external. By contrast, manufactured uncertainty, which is 'risk actively confronted within frames of action organized in a reflexive way' (Giddens, 1995:152), deals with the causes of risk. It is not absolutely clear whether Giddens is arguing that the risks really are external or are perceived as such, nor is it wholly clear what they are deemed to be external to. The argument makes most sense if it is the perception of risk that is at issue; if risks are perceived as external, only the consequences will be addressed, whereas if they are perceived as manufactured, the causes will be called into question. Much political struggle is, and has been at least since the early industrial revolution, precisely between those who wish to reveal the fact that many negative events are products of social and economic processes, and those who have sought to either deny the reality of the events or to present them as external by attributing them to chance or to the operation of a naturalized market. Of course part of Beck's argument is that the risks are in another sense manufactured in the production of scientific knowledge; but again, this was true in nineteenth-century debates over whether child labour in the mines was harmful and stunted and deformed children's growth, or whether it was good for them and they enjoyed it. 'Experts' were found prepared to argue the latter.

Insurance is not just a way of dealing with consequences of risks perceived as external; it is a way of helping create that perception. Ideologically, whether the insurance is through the welfare state or private companies, it is highly ambiguous. State-run insurance does not need to deny wholly that negative consequences are the outcome of the system, only to argue that such consequences are unavoidable and outweighed by positive ones. In so far as it is state insurance rather than state charity (non-means tested versus means-tested benefits) the implicit principle is that who happens to suffer the negative consequence – of ill health or unemployment – is accidental, subject only to the laws of chance. On the other hand the negative consequences are so great that a system of no-fault compensation falls down, and it becomes preferable (for whom?) to push the costs of private insurance onto individuals and/or shift to a means-tested system and stigmatize recipients of both means-tested and non-means-tested benefits. (Of course, ideas of insurability and affordability in relation to the British Welfare State are undermined by the fact that there never was an insurance fund, but only a system of redistribution from current taxation.) In private insurance, the assumption is again that, within actuarially defined groups, the 'chance' of needing to claim is equal. The risks are external to the system of insurance, but there is no need to argue that they are external to society itself. What is interesting is that the idea of externality is actually diminished by making separate actuarial calculations for different groups, not just in terms of ascribed characteristics of age and sex, but also on the basis of lifestyle attributes such as weight, sexual orientation and smoking. The risks are not seen as external, but as produced by individual behaviour rather than by social processes. The consequent delineation of increasingly specific 'risk communities' has been commented on by Rose (1996) as part of a general process of the 'death of the social', which can itself be seen as a particular mode of governance.

Thinking in terms of insurance does, however, have the general tendency of externalizing risk. It is part of a system of arguing that since the risks cannot be removed, they must be compensated for. Both Beck and Giddens argue that the hazards now confronting us are such that they are not open to compensation. This is absolutely true, and a major flaw in 'polluter pays' attitudes to environmental damage. However, many risks have always been impervious to monetary compensation, particularly those involving human life. The real difference is not that risks were measurable and are now immeasurable in financial terms, but that the costs would be too high and the (highly profitable) insurance industry will not take them on. In extreme cases, particularly the risk of nuclear war, the idea of insurance is absurd because the institutions of insurance and the web of social processes on which the insurance industry depends would themselves be destroyed. The struggle between those who see the risks as manufactured in the sense of systemically generated and who want the causes removed, and those who wish to deny the risks, represent them external, and contain them through insurance-based compensation does not strike me as particularly new.

The central argument made by Beck in *Risk Society* is that we have moved or are moving into a new era, when the negative consequences of 'modernity' and industrialization cease to be inflicted on specific groups, but affect everyone. Not necessarily equally, but the key issue becomes the distribution of risk positions, rather than the distribution of class positions. The significant differences in people's social experience become their position as *consumers* (albeit of 'illth' to adapt John Ruskin's term, rather than wealth), rather than as *producers*. The problematic of scarcity, with its concomitant (positive) utopia of equality, gives way to one of risk, with its accompanying (negative) utopia of safety. Empirically, there is some truth in the claim that such a shift in utopian thinking has taken place. Every year, the first task I ask of my final year students is that they produce a short account of 'The World That I'd Like'. The question of safety (and hence the sense of risk) has been increasingly present in these accounts, and the question of economic equality less so. Moreover, in 1995 I followed this with an exposition of Beck's argument and its consequences for utopian thinking; this was met with a real sense of recognition. Indeed, it is exactly the shift that would be expected in dystopian times. If things are getting worse and there is no clear way out, utopia becomes a warding-off of danger. On the other hand, while the sense of risk in these accounts did refer to ecological and environmental issues, it referred also to questions of personal safety – especially, but not only, for the women. Their actual sense of danger was far more acutely focused on this than on long-term, invisible, socially inclusive hazards. Even for this social group who are not on the whole concerned about the economic security of their futures because they expect to be reasonably successful, the sense of risk is focused on routine daily life, although of course it is not read off in any simple way from routine daily experience.

For Beck, the shift from class society to risk society, from questions of the production and distribution of wealth to the production, definition and distribution of risks, depends on two conditions. Firstly, 'the change ... occurs ... where and to the extent that *genuine material need* can be objectively reduced and socially isolated through the development of human and technological productivity, as well as through legal and welfare-state protections and regulations'. Secondly, it occurs because 'in the course of the exponentially growing productive forces in the modernization process, hazards and potential threats have been unleashed to an extent previously unknown', although the sense that this is so is recognized as socially constructed (Beck, 1992: 19). The shift from class society to risk society is incomplete; but the central political issues are becoming the reduction or legitimation of risks, rather than the reduction or legitimation of inequality; there is a major distinction between the 'conflict field' of wealth production and the 'conflict field' of hazard production (Beck, 1995a: 28). Elsewhere, risk society is described as 'an epoch in which the dark sides of progress increasingly come to dominate social debate' (Beck, 1995a: 2).

What is posited here is both a structural change and a discursive change. Risk society is used to refer *both* to a change in real conditions, and to the modes of thinking about hazards which contest their legitimacy. While this captures the complexity of a situation in which we know there are dangers but we are constantly uncertain about their extent and the status of our knowledge, it also elides changes in social processes with representations of those changes and with changes in those representations. (Postmodernists would claim these are the same, but mercifully this is not a post-modern discourse.) The claim, then, is that the qualitative shift from class to risk society occurs not just because the hazards are greater, but because the pre-occupying issues are the legitimation of risks, rather than the legitimation of inequality, although this political change cannot be simply read off from material conditions.

However, one cannot define a society in terms of its discursive strategy for dealing with the negative consequences of its material practices. Beck has been criticized, in my view wrongly, for the realist element in his analysis, and much subsequent discussion seems to have been about the social construction of risk. This reflects the state of sociology, whereby there is a marked division of labour between those mapping material practices, including in the field of political economy, and those engaged in an increasingly idealist theorizing, predominantly concerned with discursive practices. The general lack of integration between these is a major weakness in sociology, and a major obstacle to its usefulness in transformative utopian thinking.

The whole thrust of the arguments advanced by Beck and Giddens is that the problems are real: the stakes are higher, this cannot go on, transformation is essential. If fatalism can be avoided, it is an argument which is potentially far more conducive to transformative utopianism than the discourse of risk and insurance. Unhappily, the analyses do not live up to this potential, and there are three reasons for this. One is the utopian nature of the analysis of actually existing society; the second is the related insufficiently utopian nature of the proposed alternatives; the third is the inadequate and deeply idealist proposals for transition from one to the other.

One of the great strengths of Beck's argument lies in the simultaneous assertion and questioning of his second condition, the production and (unequal) distribution of unprecedented, relatively socially indiscriminate, hazards. Because of the invisibility of so many sources of hazard, consciousness of risk is subject to political manipulability, and scientific arguments themselves not only politicized but perceived as such. It is a pity he does not apply the same analysis to the first condition, the removal or containment of material want and insecurity. Rather than supposing that we are progressing to a state where economic security prevails and have simply not fully arrived there, so that we are poised between class and risk society, should we not recognize that the problem of representation applies to both? The question then becomes how and why, at this particular historical moment, the undoubtedly still fundamental questions of economic inequality appear to be less important as loci of social protest and social legitimation. It is a situation which may be less true than we are led to believe, and in any case one which is quite volatile. Beck claims that German citizens (notably not including Turkish migrant workers) rate environmental issues as more important than unemployment (1995a: 5). Such claims are usually based on poll evidence: but as opinion pollsters we know that such priorities may change very quickly, and as sociologists we know that we must ask very searching questions about what such responses can possibly mean.

In Britain, the first condition of risk society has not been met. Genuine material need has increased with the rise in not just relative but absolute poverty since 1979, and the *removal* of welfare-state protections (reduced eligibility for benefits, near-collapse of the National Health Service, abolition of state provision for the elderly) and regulations (abolition of wages councils; refusal to accept the social chapter and working time directive). The sense of insecurity under these conditions derives from economic insecurity as well as from environmental hazards. Across Europe, unemployment, significantly described as social exclusion, is portrayed as a major threat to social cohesion. The term social exclusion is crucial because it is an attempt to *represent* material need as socially isolated, while simultaneously obliterating from view the income and class differentials among the socially 'included' (Levitas, 1996, 1998).

First, therefore, there is a utopia embedded in these analyses, which sees the issues of class society as resolved or in process of resolution – although Beck also says that 'no-one can seriously claim' that 'class society has been overcome' (1995a: 135). In common with dominant political discourse, there is an assumption that capitalism is the only game in town, and there is neither analysis of, nor challenge to, it. For example, in *Risk, Environment and Modernity* (Lash et al., 1996) the term capitalism appears in passing about five times; the capitalist character of 'industrial society' or 'modernity' has been naturalized. I am not arguing that nothing has changed, and that all we need to do is overthrow capitalism and everything else will follow; I am arguing that we need a sociological analysis which places at the centre of its interrogation the relationship between the accumulation of capital and the accumulation of danger, and which focuses on the real, as well as the discursive, production and distribution of risk. The collapsing of utopia into an analysis of the present in this way, by ignoring its capitalist character, is profoundly anti-utopian. It contradicts the need for radical, imaginative thought about the 'what' of utopia.

Secondly, this utopianizing of the present and glossing over of capitalist relations takes place even where, for example, Giddens does try to posit an alternative: the society characterized by a post-scarcity economy, humanized nature, dialogic democracy and negotiated power in place of economic polarization, ecological threats, denial of democratic rights and threats of large-scale war. Giddens' utopian alternative is reminiscent of Marcuse's 'pacification of existence' resulting from the replacement of the performance principle by a new reality principle. It is similarly unspecific about the fundamental institutional character of the new society. For Marcuse, the utopia that was no longer utopian was made possible by the enormous productive potential of technology, and was predicated on abundance – although Marcuse was very clear that global limits meant abundance could not be equated with unlimited consumption, and argued that the rich world would have to give up its manipulated comforts in order that poverty might be abolished; Marcuse thought that once we were in touch with our real needs, we would consume less. It is a mode of closing the 'scarcity gap' which is referred to in the utopian literature as 'arcadian', while the ethic of self-restraint, when successful, produces a 'perfect moral commonwealth' (Davis, 1981; see also Leiss, 1978; Levitas, 1990).

For Giddens, the post-scarcity economy is predicated on the adoption of non-material values: 'happiness and its opposite bear no particular relation to either wealth or the possession of power' (1995: 181). 'The culture of the excluded may be richer than consumerism in everything save material benefits ... it may be the "prefiguration of another society" on the other side of the modern' (1995: 167). Reading this, I was reminded of the old song written by John Bruce Glasier in the 1890s:

> Plain living may be wholesome and wondrous virtues may
> Abound beneath ribs scant of flesh and pockets scant of pay,
> And it may be poverty is best if rightly understood,
> But we'll turn things upside down because we don't want all the good.

The transition to a society in which economic growth is not paramount is equated with a society in which individuals value non-commodity satisfactions above consumption, and which is brought about by that preference. The actual relationship between non-commodity satisfactions and material goods is not addressed: when I decided that self-actualization meant doing something about the fact that I'd always wanted to play the saxophone, I went out and bought one (£500 second-hand) and took lessons (£9 a week for 6 months, or £234). Besides, it is incontrovertible that both absolute *and relative* poverty affect health, life expectancy and infant mortality; self-actualization is difficult when you are dead, and it is hard to see what non-commodity satisfaction can be derived from the death of a child. More crucially, the question of whether a *society* not based on economic growth is compatible with capitalism is not addressed; this is not the same as a society in which individuals have low aspirations for consumption. Nor, indeed, is there any consideration of what this might mean for the tiny percentage of even the British population that owns the bulk of its land, wealth and productive property. The absence of an analysis of capitalism and the crashing silence about property relations in the good society serve to naturalize capitalism and to ignore a major and intractable problem for utopia in the name of realism, by implying that the problems can be solved within the framework of capitalism itself.

Beck too is insufficiently utopian, and indeed tends occasionally to fatalism despite declaring himself against it. The line between serious dystopianism and fatalism is easily crossed, however. In dystopian mode, Beck talks about 'sliding into a new society', a 'new society with no awareness of an underlying plan' (1995a: 41), and about the blindness of reflexive modernity. Helplessness, he declares 'is the real revelation of our time' (1995a: 47). But his own tendency to see technology as having a trajectory of its own, rather than addressing the context of technological development and the production of hazard, has fatalistic (and potentially fatal) consequences. Take, for example, the discussion of the new eugenics in Beck's *Ecological Politics in an Age of Risk* (1995b). We are presented with a picture in which the possibilities of genetic manipulation and assisted conception techniques will (if this goes on) lead inexorably to a eugenic dystopia for human society, as well as the broader reduction of bio-diversity. Of course these issues are of crucial and urgent importance both practically and morally. Interestingly, the issues are presented in a very similar way to discussions about nuclear weapons in the early 1980s, when it was asserted that you could not 'ban the bomb' because you cannot undo knowledge; the fall is irreversible. But it is not just a question of unbridled technology versus its political containment, but one of recognizing the political and economic context in which the technology is developed.

As a sociologist of utopia rather than of science, there appear to me to be several reasons why such a eugenic dystopia is improbable. One is that the irrationality of human sexual behaviour means a very high proportion of conceptions are likely to be accidental, rather than planned. Another is the differential access (which will continue to exist) to interventionist procedures. In Britain, it is becoming more, not less, difficult to obtain fertility treatment on the NHS, although the private market is increasing. But even if this were not so, the assumption that women who do not have fertility problems will opt en masse for donor insemination and/or in vitro fertilization in order to have super-babies ignores the unpleasantness of these procedures. It runs counter to the actual trends of pressures from women to limit the medicalization of childbirth. The most fundamental reason why this fatalism is misplaced is that it assumes that the socio-biological claim of a near-perfect association between genes and the attributes of adult humans is correct, and forgets that except in very specific instances this is almost certainly wrong; eugenics will not work on human beings other than in limited cases. And the motive for its development on non-humans is profit-driven; hence the recent marketing of tomato purée made from genetically engineered tomatoes that do not rot.

I argued earlier that the dystopian argument 'if this goes on' can only posit a future utopia by prescribing or predicting a radical break. Marx predicted a radical break in the relations, but not the forces, of production. Beck seeks a radical break in the relations of production of knowledge. In utopian terms, I would argue that this is not radical enough. The 'how' of utopia is as weak as the 'what'. Indeed, both Beck and Giddens can be seen as exemplars of Habermas' argument about utopia, in which Habermas (1990) claimed that the shift from modernity to late modernity had brought about the end of utopias conceived in terms of content, and specifically utopias focusing on labour, and replaced them with one of process: we cannot agree about what the good society will be like, but we can (perhaps) agree on the processes by which we might get there. Habermas' utopian process, the ideal speech situation, actually carries an implicit content, in terms of the social conditions in which such a dialogue might be possible; it echoes Mannheim's hopes for a potential synthetic truth produced by a (relatively) socially unattached intelligentsia. Habermas also disintegrates the concept of social labour, so that utopia and the social are discussed in terms of communication, severed from the social production of material life.

What is important here is that both Beck and Giddens see the changes which must be wrought in social relations as primarily dialogic. Giddens prescribes dialogic democracy. Beck suggests, among other things, a change in the burden of proof, whereby it would be necessary to prove processes are safe, rather than, as at present, that they are dangerous. It is likely that any equitable and sustainable society in the future will need to operate just such a policy. Yet we must also ask under what conditions would such a change be possible? In theory, the licensing of drugs already depends on 'proof' that they are safe. I would contend that though necessary, such a policy would not provide an effective lever where the balance of economic interests remains unchanged. The point is not that I am opposed to dialogic processes, nor to attempts to imagine better democratic institutions, both nationally and globally – all this is necessary – but it is one of the weaknesses of the majority of utopias that they presume that in utopia the political process has to deal with differences of opinion, different perceptions of interest, rather than profound conflicts of interest. Or rather, there may be differences of interest, but they are minor by comparison with the overriding shared interest of all members of the society. Within sociology, this was true of liberal-pluralist views of the state dominant in the 1960s; the state existed to balance different interests, but everyone had a similar interest in the stability of the system, in social cohesion; this appears to be the dominant ideology once again. The problem is that in terms of environmental hazard, it is in the long term true that we are all in the same boat; but it is an argument that does not go down well with galley-slaves when someone is standing over them with a whip. The short- and medium-term conflicts, and the crucial split between those who profit enormously from capitalist relations of production and those who do not, render dialogic transitions to utopia implausible – unless you believe, like Robert Owen did, that the rich and powerful will on a global scale choose to give up their wealth and power as a result of rational discussion. The weight of historical evidence is against this.

Giddens asks, for example, for pacts between men and women. Rather, we should ask, as Beck and Beck-Gernsheim (1995) begin to do when they ask how may we love each other, what are the conditions under which our interests may cease to be opposed, and how may such conditions be brought about? The utopian vision of Marge Piercy (1979) is interesting in this respect, as it involves a model of separate attachment similar to that proposed as an ideal by some psychotherapists. But Piercy explores – as many utopian writers have done – the conditions of material equality and abolition of personal economic dependency on which such relationships depend. As always, this leaves the question, what about the children? And again, this is a subject on which utopian literature is rich, and not solely given to recommending communal child-rearing. Asking for pacts where there is a conflict of interests is ideological rather than transformatively utopian. The European Commission (1994) document, *Growth, Competitiveness, Employment*, similarly asks for solidarity between men and women, between those who have jobs and those who do not, and 'between those who earn their income from work and those who earn [*sic*] their income from investments' (European Commission, 1994: 139). Just because existing political discourses have successfully defined the risks of capitalism as inevitable, natural or external, does not mean that sociologists should do so; and certainly utopians, all of whom always believe themselves to be utopian realists, must take a more radical view.

What is to be done? Many important issues are placed on the agenda by current discussions. But a discourse of risk or risk society can only help towards a utopian transformation if it is allied to a rigorous analysis of capitalism; yet the term risk itself is so closely bound to the dynamics of capitalism that such an alliance may be difficult to sustain. We need to be both more and less utopian. More utopian, in that the exercise of imagining what might be done needs to be undertaken more radically by more people: H.G. Wells once said that the proper and distinctive method of sociology is the creation and exhaustive critique of utopias. Such a project cannot take place within the confines of a supposition that capitalism is the only game in town. Less utopian, in that, as Fredric Jameson argued (1984), we need new cognitive maps which do not simply represent to us the surface appearance of the world in which we live, but which render that appearance intelligible. Jameson was observing that the interesting, and then unasked question about postmodernism, was not why was the world fragmentary and contradictory, but why it appeared to be so. What is it about the nature of late capitalism that renders it so opaque? What is the relationship between appearances and what is actually going on? What are the levers, who is pulling them, how can they be stopped? Or, as Bloch said, the hinge in human history is its producer: these are very mechanical metaphors. Such an analysis cannot be undertaken without a critical analysis of capitalism – aimed not (just) at saying isn't it awful, but at identifying potential points of intervention which might lead to transformation, and potential agents of that transformation. Jameson didn't have the answers either, later saying he was talking about the international proletariat in hitherto undreamed of forms (Jameson, 1991). It was the wrong answer to the right questions.

And in a way, that too must be the verdict on the projects of Beck and Giddens as ventures in transformative utopia. The (partly) wrong answers to (partly) right questions. It's a start. Next year in utopia!

References

Adams, J. (1995) *Risk*. London: UCL Press.
Beck, U. (1992) *Risk Society: Towards a New Modernity*. London: Sage.
Beck, U. (1995a) *Ecological Enlightenment*. NJ: Humanities Press International.
Beck, U. (1995b) *Ecological Politics in an Age of Risk*. Cambridge: Polity.
Beck, U. and Beck-Gernsheim, E. (1995) *The Normal Chaos of Love*. Cambridge: Polity.
Bloch, E. (1986) *The Principle of Hope*. Oxford: Basil Blackwell.
Davis, J.C. (1981) *Utopia and the Ideal Society: A study of English Utopian Writing*. Cambridge: Cambridge University Press.
European Commission (1994) *Growth, Competitiveness, Employment: The Challenges and Ways Forward into the 21st Century*. Luxembourg: European Commission.
Giddens, A. (1995) *Beyond Left and Right*. Cambridge: Polity.
Habermas, J. (1990) 'The New Conservatism: and the Historians' Debate', *Cultural Criticism*. Boston, MA: MIT Press.
Jameson, F. (1984) 'Postmodernism: The Cultural Logic of Late Capitalism', *New Left Review*, 146: 53–93.
Jameson, F. (1991) *Postmodernism: The Cultural Logic of Late Capitalism*. London: Verso.

Lash, S., Szerszynski, B. and Wynne, B. (eds) (1996) *Risk, Environment and Modernity: Towards a New Ecology*. London: Sage.

Leiss, W. (1978) *The Limits to Satisfaction: on Needs and Commodities*. London: Marion Boyars.

Lenin, V.I. (1975) *What is to be Done*. Peking: Foreign Languages Press.

Levitas, R. (1981) 'Dystopian Times', *Theory, Culture & Society*, 1: 53–64.

Levitas, R. (1990) *The Concept of Utopia*. London: Philip Allan.

Levitas, R. (1996) 'The Concept of Social Exclusion and the New Durkheimian Hegemony', *Critical Social Policy*, 46 (1): 5–20.

Levitas, R. (1998) *The Inclusive Society: Social Exclusion and New Labour*. London: Macmillan.

Marcuse, H. (1968) *One Dimensional Man*. London: Sphere Books.

Morris, W. (1981[1890]) *News From Nowhere*. London: Longman Green.

Piercy, M. (1979) *Woman on the Edge of Time*. London: Women's Press.

Rose, N. (1996) 'The Death of the Social', *Economy and Society*, 25 (3): 327–56.

Thompson, E. (1977) *William Morris: Romantic to Revolutionary*. London: Merlin Press.

Williams, R. (1980) *Problems in Materialism and Culture: Selected Essays*. London: Verso.

12

Risk Society Revisited: Theory, Politics and Research Programmes

Ulrich Beck

Living in an age of constructivism, the attempt to draw a line between modernity (or as I would prefer to say first industrial modernity) and world risk society (or second reflexive modernity) seems to be naive or even contradictory. Within a constructivist framework no one is able to define or declare what really 'is' or 'is not'. Yet, this does not square with my experience. I cannot understand how anyone can make use of the frameworks of reference developed in the eighteenth and nineteenth centuries in order to understand the transformation into the post-traditional cosmopolitan world we live in today. Max Weber's 'iron cage' – in which he thought humanity was condemned to live for the foreseeable future – is to me a prison of *categories and basic assumptions* of classical social, cultural and political sciences. It is the case that we have to free ourselves from these categories in order to find out about the unknown post-Cold-War-world. Do not get me wrong. I do not consider most of the philosophies and theories (sociologies) of so-called postmodernity to fare any better since they cannot answer very basic questions about how and in what ways everyday lives and professional fields are being transformed. Conventional social sciences, I therefore want to argue, even if they are conducting highly sophisticated theoretical and empirical research programmes, are caught up in a circular argument. By using the old categories (like class, family, gender roles, industry, technology, science, nation state and so on) they take for granted what they actually try to demonstrate: that we still live, act and die in the normal world of nation-state modernity.

Some of the discussions in this volume, which accuse me of being a 'realist', therefore, are the result of a misinterpretation of my arguments. What strikes me about them is the inability of constructivist thinking to criticize and renew the frameworks of modern and post-modern sociology. Let me explain. I consider realism and constructivism to be neither an either-or option nor a mere matter of belief. We should not have to swear allegiance to any particular view or theoretical perspective. The decision whether to take a realist or a constructivist approach is for me a rather *pragmatic* one, a matter of choosing the appropriate means for a desired goal. If I have to be a realist (for the moment) in order to open up the social sciences to the new and contradictory experiences of the global age of global risks, then I have no qualms to adopt the guise and language of a ('reflexive') 'realist'. If constructivism makes a positive problem shift possible and if it allows us to raise important questions that realists do not ask, then I am content (for that moment at least) to be a constructivist. Having grown up with the constructivist philosophies of thinkers such as Kant, Fichte and Hegel, I find today, especially in the area of sociology of risk, that I do not restrict my analysis to one perspective or conceptual dogma: I am both a realist and constructivist, using realism *and* constructivism as far as those meta-narratives are useful for the purpose of understanding the complex and ambivalent 'nature' of risk in the world risk society we live in.[1]

Let us consider for a moment the current state of European intellectual thought. In 1989 a whole world order disintegrated. What an opportunity for venturing into uncharted terrain, exploring new intellectual horizons. Yet, this opportunity has not been seized. Instead, the vast majority of theorists are still holding on to the same old concepts. Reversal rather than revision seems to be the order of the day: radical socialism, Giddens (1995) suggests, has become conservative and conservatism has become radical. Little has changed: the script of modernity is yet be rewritten, redefined, reinvented. This is what the theory of the world risk society is all about.

At this point, I should emphasize that I do not believe that 'anything goes'. Instead, I argue that we have to be imaginative yet disciplined if we are to break out of the iron cage of conventional and orthodox social science and politics. We need a new sociological imagination, one that is sensitive to the concrete paradoxes and challenges of reflexive modernity and which, at the same time, is thoughtful and strong enough to open up the walls of abstraction in which academic routines are captured.

In this chapter I would like to accomplish three main tasks. First, I wish briefly to reiterate my argument of why the notion of risk society can be introduced as a new conception of a 'non-industrial' society, to ask, what are 'risks'? and to enquire about the reality status of risks using 'constructivism' and 'realism' as a matter of pragmatic choice. Secondly, I want to address the views of some of my critics and in the process offer the reader a discussion of what I see as the theoretical issues which now limit the development of my ideas on risk. Finally, I will highlight some of the theoretical and political avenues I would like to see explored in the near future and identify some issues for comparative study at a European level and beyond.

On the sociological concepts of risk and risk society

In the first part of this chapter I would like to gather up into a coherent whole arguments that are dispersed throughout my work on the sociological concepts of risk and risk society. In so doing, I also hope to illustrate, indirectly, what I have learned from the existing criticisms of my earlier work.[2] I have structured these issues into eight major points.

1. Risks are not the same as destruction. They do not refer to damages incurred. If they were, all insurance companies would be made bankrupt. However, risks

do threaten destruction. The discourse of risk begins where trust in our security and belief in progress end. It ceases to apply when the potential catastrophe actually occurs. The concept of risk thus characterizes a peculiar, intermediate state between security and destruction, where the *perception* of threatening risks determines thought and action. As a result, I have difficulty recognizing the difference discussed by Scott Lash (Chapter 2 this volume) between the 'risk culture' and my concept of 'risk society'. I do, however, find Lash's discussion valuable in that it highlights the radicalization of the cultural framework of risk by cultural theory and cultural studies. Yet, it seems to me that 'relations of definition' (analogous to Marx' relations of production, see below) in the age of culturally defined risks still make the notion of 'risk society' necessary (see discussion below). So ultimately: *it is cultural perception and definition that constitutes risk*. 'Risk' and the '(public) definition of risk' are one and the same.

This peculiar reality status of 'no-longer-but-not-yet' – no longer trust/ security, not yet destruction/disaster – is what the concept of risk expresses and what makes it a public frame of reference. The sociology of risk is a science of potentialities and judgements about probabilities – what Max Weber (1991) called *Möglichkeitsurteile* (trans. as *judgements about probabilities)*. Risks, then, 'are' a type of *virtual reality*, real virtuality. Risks are only a small step away from what Joost van Loon calls 'Virtual Risks in an Age of Cybernetic Reproduction' (Chapter 9 this volume) and I wholeheartedly agree with his assessment when he writes: 'Only by thinking of risk in terms of reality, or better, a *becoming-real* (a virtuality) its social materialization can be understood. Only by thinking risk in terms of a construction can we understand its indefinitely deferred 'essence'. Risks cannot be understood outside their materialization in particular mediations, be it scientific, political, economic or popular.' (Van Loon, see p. 176). I believe this is the way in which the notions of constructivism and realism, although seemingly incompatible, can complement each other:

> [The] electronic media involved in the BSE crisis connect science, politics and popular consumer culture. In so doing, they render the invisibility of risk, for example, the mutating prions of BSE, visible. They bring them into being through digitalized imagery. We, the consumers of such images, have no means to test the adequacy of such representations, nor do we have to. Their origin is fabricated, manufactured, in laboratories, under microscopes, and further enhanced by computer simulations. Their sources are truly cybertechnological, connecting chemistry, molecular biology, medicine with computer graphics and television broadcasting. Rendering the prion visible as a computer simulation allowed news broadcasts to begin to interpret the uninterpretable (to tell us what BSE and CJD actually 'are') and to explain the unexplainable (how a normal piece of protein – whatever that might be – could become a pathological prion). The mere possibility that the pathogenesis might be linked to the banal practice of consuming beef, ... further illustrates the force of Benjamin's[3] claim that in an age of mechanical reproduction, all aesthetic experiences may become politicized. (Van Loon, see p. 176)

Van Loon continues:

> The 'becoming-real' of the risk of BSE is directly related to its mediation. Now that 'we' know that there 'are' possible risks, 'we' face a responsibility. This responsibility takes the form of a *decision* whether to eat beef and other bovine products or not.

Therefore, CJD is no longer exclusively a hazard, as a strain has been identified that can be linked to BSE. Although the calculability of this risk has remained problematic, as a virtuality, it operates in exactly the same way. (see p. 176)

Indeed, 'the sudden accessibility of the "knowledge" of the possible relationship between BSE and CJD has thus transformed a hazard into a risk' (Van Loon, p. 176): we now have a decision to make with consequences for ourselves, our loved ones and possibly the rest of our world.[4]

The sociology of risk reconstructs techno-social praxis, both as abstract potential and in a very concrete sense. Where risks are believed to be real, the foundations of business, politics, science and everyday life are in flux. Accordingly, the concept of risk when considered scientifically (risk = accident X probability) takes the form of the calculus of probability, which we know can never rule out the worst case.[5] This becomes significant in view of the socially very relevant distinction between risk *decision-makers* and those who have to deal with the consequences of the decisions of *others*. In this respect, Niklas Luhmann's (1995) differentiation between risk and danger pointed to the sociologically crucial problem of the acceptance of risk decisions. However, this leaves the central question unanswered: What do the calculus of probability and the social difference between decision-makers (risks) and the affected parties, encompassing ever larger social groups (dangers), mean for dealing with disasters? Who has the legitimate right to make decisions in such cases? Or, more generally, how will decisions on hazardous technologies become capable of legitimation in the future?

Closely associated with this issue is the question of what the 'objectivity' and 'subjectivity' of risks would mean in the first place in the context of 'virtual risk realities'. What is 'rational' and what is 'irrational'? This is certainly one point where a sociology of risk and risk society differs fundamentally from technical and scientific risk assessment (more on this later).

2. The concept of risk reverses the relationship of past, present and future. The past loses its power to determine the present. Its place as the cause of present-day experience and action is taken by the future, that is to say, something non-existent, constructed and fictitious. We are discussing and arguing about something which is *not* the case, but *could* happen if we were not to change course.

Believed risks are the whip used to keep the present-day moving along at a gallop. The more threatening the shadows that fall on the present day from a terrible future looming in the distance, the more compelling the shock that can be provoked by dramatizing risk today. This can be demonstrated not only with the discourse on the environmental crisis, but also and perhaps even more emphatically, with the example of the discourse on globalization. For instance, as yet, the globalization of paid labour does not exist to a large extent. Rather, it looms as a threat or, more accurately, transnational management threatens us with it. After all, in Germany for example the exchange of expensive European labour for cheap Asian labour so far only amounts to at most 10% of the labour market and primarily affects the lower wage and skilled groups.[6] The brilliantly staged *risk* of globalization, however, has already become an instrument for re-opening the issue of power in society. By invoking the horrors of globalization, everything can be called into question: trade unions, of course, but also the welfare state, maxims of national policy and, it goes without saying, welfare assistance. Moreover, all of this is done with an expression of regret that it is – unfortunately – necessary to terminate Christian compassion for the sake of Christian compassion.

Established risk definitions are thus a magic wand with which a stagnant society can terrify itself and thereby activate its political centres and become politicized from within. The public (mass media) dramatization of risk is in this sense an antidote to current narrow-minded 'more-of-the-same' attitudes. A society that conceives of itself as a risk society is, to use a Catholic metaphor, in the position of the sinner who confesses his or her sins in order to be able to contemplate the possibility and desirability of a 'better' life in harmony with nature and the world's conscience. However, few sinners actually want to repent and instigate change. Most prefer the status quo while complaining about that very fact, because then everything is possible. Confession of sins and identification with the risk society allow us to simultaneously enjoy the bad good life and the threats to it.

3. Are risks factual statements? Are risks value statements? Risk statements are neither purely factual claims nor exclusively value claims. Instead, they are either both at the same time or something in between, a 'mathematicized morality' as it were. As mathematical calculations (probability computations or accident scenarios) risks are related directly and indirectly to cultural definitions and standards of a tolerable or intolerable life. So in a risk society the question we must ask ourselves is: How do we want to live? This means, among other things, that risk statements are by nature statements that can be deciphered only in an interdisciplinary (competitive) relationship, because they assume in equal measure insight into technical know-how and familiarity with cultural perceptions and norms.[7]

What then is the source of the peculiarity in our political dynamics that allows risk statements to develop as a hybrid of evaluations in the intermediate realm of real virtuality and non-existent future which nonetheless activates present action? This political explosiveness derives, primarily, from two sources: the first one relates to the cultural importance of the universal value of survival. Thus Thomas Hobbes, the conservative theorist of the state and society, recognized as a citizen right the right to resist where the state threatens the life or survival of its citizens (characteristically enough, he uses phrases such as 'poisoned air and poisoned foodstuffs' which seem to anticipate ecological issues). The second source is tied to the attribution of dangers to the producers and guarantors of the social order (business, politics, law, science), that is to the suspicion that those who endanger the public well-being and those charged with its protection may well be identical.

4. In their (difficult-to-localize) early stage, risks and risk perception are 'unintended consequences' of the *logic of control* which dominates modernity. Politically and sociologically, modernity is a project of social and technological control by the nation state. Above all others, it was Talcott Parsons who conceptualized modern society as an enterprise for constructing order and control. In this

way, consequences – risks – are generated that call this very assertion of control by the nation state into question, not only because of the globality of the risks (climatic disasters or the ozone hole) but also through the inherent indeterminacies and uncertainties of risk diagnosis. It is interesting to note that Weber (1956) does indeed discuss the concept of 'unintended consequences' in a crucial context, and not least of all because that concept remains related in structure to the dominance of instrumental rationality. However, Weber does *not* recognize or discuss the concept of 'risk', one of whose peculiarities is to have lost precisely this relationship between intention and outcome, instrumental rationality and control.

The construction of security and control of the type that dominated (social) thought and (political) action in the first stage of modernity is becoming fictitious in the global risk society. The more we attempt to 'colonize' the future with the aid of the category of risk, the more it slips out of our control. It is no longer possible to externalize risks in the world risk society. That is what makes the issue of risk so 'political' (in a subversive meaning). In this paradox lies an essential basis for an important distinction between two stages or forms of the concept of risk (which, I feel, should answer some of the questions Scott Lash raises with his concept of 'determinate judgement' in opposition to 'reflexive judgement'). In the first stage of modernity (essentially the period from the beginning of industrial modernity in the seventeenth and eighteenth centuries to the early twentieth century) risk essentially signifies a way of calculating unpredictable consequences (industrial decisions). As Ewald (1987) argues, the calculus of risk develops forms and methods for making the *unpredictable predictable*. This is what Lash means by 'determinate judgement'. The corresponding repertoire of methods includes statistical representations, accident probabilities and scenarios, actuarial calculations, as well as standards and organizations for anticipatory care. This meaning of the concept of risk refers to a world in which most things, including external nature and the ways of life as determined and co-ordinated by tradition, continue to be considered preordained (fate).

To the extent that nature becomes industrialized and traditions become optional, new types of uncertainties arise which, following Giddens (1990, 1995), I shall refer to as '*manufactured* uncertainties'. These types of internal risks and dangers presume a threefold participation of scientific experts, in the roles of producers, analysts and profiteers from risk definitions. Under these conditions, many attempts to confine and control risks turn into a broadening of the uncertainties and dangers.

5. Hence, the contemporary concept of risk associated with the risk society and manufactured uncertainty refers to a peculiar *synthesis of knowledge and unawareness*. To be precise, two meanings, namely risk assessment based on empirical knowledge (automobile accidents, for instance) on the one hand, and making decisions and acting on risk in indefinite uncertainty, that is, indeterminacy, on the other, are being conflated here. In this sense the concept of 'manufactured uncertainties' has a double reference. First, more and better knowledge, which most people assess in unreservedly positive terms, is becoming the source of new risks. Because we know more and more about the brain functions, we now

know that a person who is 'brain-dead' may very well be alive in some other sense (because the heart is still beating , for instance). By opening more and more new spheres of action, science creates new types of risks as well. The current examples are advances in human genetics, which make it possible to blur the boundary between ill people and healthy people because more and more congenital diseases can be diagnosed, even those affecting people who consider themselves healthy based on their own experience (Beck-Gernsheim, 1993, 1995). Secondly, the opposite is equally true: risks come from and consist of unawareness (non-knowledge). What are we to understand by 'unawareness'? In the unbroken security of a life-world, unawareness is often understood as being *not yet* aware or no longer aware, that is to say, as *potential* knowledge. The problems of unawareness are understood here from its opposite, from knowledge and the (unspoken) certainty in which the life-world resides. In contrast to that, the inability to know is becoming ever more important in this second phase of modernity. I am not referring here to the expression of selective viewpoints, momentary forgetting or underdeveloped expertise, but on the contrary, to highly developed expert rationality. Thus, for instance, the calculus of probability can never rule out a given event, or risk specialists may call each other's detailed results into question because they quite sensibly start from different assumptions.[8]

Against the background of this *growing* unawareness and non-knowledge in the wake of the modernization of knowledge, the question of *deciding in a context of uncertainty* arises in a radical way. If we cannot know the effects of industrial research, action and production – as is already generally the case in the fields of genetic engineering and human genetics – if neither the optimism of the protagonists nor the pessimism of their critics is based on certain knowledge, then is there a green light or a red light for techno-industrial development and mass utilization? Is inability to know a license for action or basis for *decelerating* action, for moratoria, perhaps even inaction? How can maxims of action or of being obliged not to act be justified, given the inability to know?

This is how a society based on knowledge and risk opens up a threatening sphere of possibilities. Everything falls under an imperative of avoidance. Everyday life thus becomes an involuntary lottery of misfortune. The probability of a 'winner' here is probably no higher than in the weekly lottery, but it has become almost impossible *not* to take part in this raffle of evils where the 'winner' gets sick and may even die as a result of it. Politicians such as the British ex-prime minister John Major, who complained about the 'hysteria' of consumers in reaction to the debate over BSE in Europe and the resulting collapse in the beef market, while, at the same time, encouraging people to take part in the national lottery, rendered a particular service to the credibility of politics. At the extreme end of the spectrum two strategies for dealing with 'manufactured uncertainties' are conceivable: if one embraces the view of John Major that only certain knowledge can compel us to act, then one must accept that the denial of risks causes them to grow immeasurably and uncontrollably. There is no better breeding ground for risks than denying them. If one selects the opposite strategy and makes presumed (lack of) knowledge the foundation of action against risks, then this opens the flood gates of fear and everything becomes risky.

Risks only suggest what should *not* be done, not what *should* be done. To the extent that risks become the all-embracing background for perceiving the world, the alarm they provoke creates an atmosphere of powerlessness and paralysis. Doing nothing and demanding too much both transform the world into a series of indomitable risks. This could be called the *risk trap*, which is what the world can turn into in the perceptual form of risk. There is no prescription for how to act in the risk trap, but there are very antithetical cultural reactions (within and outside Europe). Within different boundaries and times, indifference and alarmed agitation often alternate abruptly and radically.[9]

One thing is clear: how one acts in this situation is no longer something that can be decided by experts. Risks pointed out (or obscured) by experts at the same time disarm these experts, because they force everyone to decide for themselves: What is still tolerable and what no longer? They require decisions about whether or not, when, and where to protest even if this only takes the form of an organized, intercultural consumer boycott. These issues raise questions about the authority of the public, cultural definitions, the citizenry, parliaments, politicians, ethics and self-organization.

6. Even the antithesis of globality and locality is short-circuited by risks. The new types of risks are simultaneously local and global, or 'glocal' (Robertson, 1992). Thus it was the fundamental experience that environmental dangers 'know no boundaries' that they are universalized by the air, the wind, the water and food chains, which justified the global environmental movement everywhere and brought up gobal risks for discussion.

This 'time-space compression' (Harvey, 1989) of the hazards of choices between local and global risks confirms the diagnosis of the global risk society. The global threats have led to a world in which the foundations of the established risk logic are undermined and invalidated, in which there are only difficult-to-control dangers instead of calculable risks. The new dangers destroy the pillars of the conventional calculus of security: damages can scarcely still be attributed to definite perpetrators, so that the polluter-pays principle loses acuity; damages can no longer be financially compensated – it makes no sense to insure oneself against the worst-case ramifications of the global spiral of threat. Accordingly, there are no plans for follow-up care should the worst case scenario occur. In the world of risk society the logic of control collapses from within. So, risk society is a (latent) *political* society.

World risk society theory does not plead for or encourage (as some assume) a return to a logic of control in an age of risk and manufactured uncertainties – that was the solution of the first and simple modernity. On the contrary, in the world risk society the logic of control is questioned fundamentally, not only from a sociological point of view but by ongoing modernization itself. Here is one of the reasons why risk societies can become *self-critical* societies. Different agencies and actors, for example, managers of chemical industries and insurance experts contradict each other. Technicians argue that: 'there is no risk', while the insurers refuse insurance because the risks are too high. A similar debate is currently taking place within the realm of genetically engineered food.

In order to speak of the world risk *society*, it is also necessary for the global hazards to begin to shape *actions* and facilitate the creation of *international institutions*. That there are indeed such impulses can be seen from the fact that the majority of the international environmental agreements were concluded during the past two decades. This border-transcending dynamism of the new risks does not only apply internationally, but also exists inside nation states, implying that system boundaries no longer function properly either. This can be seen from the fact that risks are a kind of 'involuntary, negative currency'. No one wants to accept them or admit them, but they are present and active everywhere, resistant against all attempts to repress them. A characteristic of the global risk society is a metamorphosis of danger which is difficult to delineate or monitor: markets collapse and there is shortage in the midst of surplus. Medical treatments fail. Constructs of economic rationality wobble. Governments are forced to resign. The taken-for-granted rules of everyday life are turned upside-down. Almost everyone is defenceless against the threats of nature as recreated by industry. Dangers are integral to normal consumption habits. And yet they are and remain essentially knowledge-dependent and tied to cultural perception, be they as alarm, tolerance or cynicism.

7. Let us now return to the realism-constructivism debate and concentrate on the distinction between *knowledge*, latent *impact* and symptomatic effect, as suggested by Adam (1998, Chapter 1).[10] This distinction is important for understanding the second degree of 'uncertain global risks' faced by the world risk society, because the point of impact is not obviously tied to the point of origin. At the same time the transmissions and movements of hazards are often latent and immanent, that is, invisible and untrackable to everyday perceptions. This social invisibility means that, unlike many other political issues, risks must clearly be brought to consciousness, only then can it be said that they constitute an actual threat, and this includes cultural values and symbols ('*Le Waldsterben*') as well as scientific arguments. At the same time we know at least in principle, that the *impacts* of risks grow precisely *because* nobody knows or wants to know about them. A case in point is the environmental devastation of Eastern Europe under the communist regime.

So, once again, risks are at the same time 'real' *and* constituted by social perception and construction. Their reality springs from '*impacts*' that are rooted in the ongoing industrial and scientific production and research routines. Knowledge about the risks, in contrast, is tied to the history and symbols of one's culture (the understanding of nature, for example) and the social fabric of knowledge. This is one of the reasons why the same risk is perceived and handled politically so differently throughout Europe and other parts of the globe. Moreover, there are interesting relations between those two dimensions of risk. Thus, the enormous spatial disjuncture between knowledge and impact: perception is always and necessarily contextual and locally constituted. This local contextuality is only extendible in the imagination and with the aid of such technologies as television, computers, and the mass media. As Adam argues:

> the impact of the industrial way of life, in contrast, is spatially and temporally open and tends to extend across the globe on the one hand and to the stratosphere and the universe

on the other. Radiation, synthetic chemicals and genetically engineered organisms are pertinent cases in point. (1998: 34)

Many other examples can be used to highlight the unbridgeable spatio-temporal gap between actions and their impacts. 'Contemporary environmental hazards such as ozone depletion, damage to the reproductive and immune system of species or BSE have not arisen as symptoms until years after they began their impact as invisible effects of specific actions' (Adam, 1998: 34). Thus, for example, some of the Britons who died from the new variant of CJD (Creutzfeldt-Jakob Disease) had been vegetarians for the last ten years or so, which suggests a latent impact-period of ten or more years. Other hazards externalize as symptoms only after they have combined to form a critical mass. That is to say, the impact is temporarily open-ended and becomes perceivable as symptom and thus knowable only after it materializes into a visible 'cultural' phenomenon at some time and some place. This gap between source and perceivable symptom is one of the main conflict matters of social and expert construction: pesticides in foods, radiation and chemical damage to the unborn, and global warming are just a few illustrations of this temporal disjuncture.

This in turn links back to an issue I raised before and to the recognition that *the less risks are publicly recognized, the more risks are produced* (not only because of high industrialization but because of functional differentiation too). This might be an interesting 'law' of the risk society with particular relevance to the insurance business. The neglect of risk, in the first instance, would seem to serve the interests of the insurer, not those of the potential victims. Basic to the risk society is the self-transformation of risk from technical to economic risks, market risk, health risk, political risk and so on. Important to the insurer is the *time gap* between the insurance contract and the emergence of the risk through nature and culture. So the insurer (or the insurer of the insurer) has to pay up when this time bomb explodes. The problems that befell Lloyd's of London illustrate this case well. Several elements of this case are worthy of additional attention:

- Insurers are not in the same boat as manufacturers. Instead, insurers find themselves in a 'natural coalition' with the potential victims. This means that in order to act in their business' interest, they have to trust socio-scientific risk definitions, even rumours, and they have to find out about them during early stages of technological and industrial development.
- The neglect of risk information facilitates the growth and spread of risks. Asbestos is a case in point. During the Second World War the use of this material was expanding fast because it was seen as effective, durable, and above all, cheap, while the attendant risks were ignored.
- Commercial success and freedom from litigation result in complacency. Even worse, the manufacturers turn their back on medical evidence of the link between their products and ill health. Just as the tobacco manufacturers did not – and still do not – want to know the health consequences of smoking, so the asbestos industries preferred to ignore warnings.
- This way risk industries and insurance businesses get captured in the 'time cage' between ignored impact and growing risk on the one hand and between

risk knowledge and cultural sensitivity on the other. This is the very normal way the manufactured uncertainties of hazards are becoming internalized by industries and are transformed into potential *economic* disasters.

8. Finally, the notion of world risk society is pertinent to a world which can be characterized by the *loss of clear distinction between nature and culture*. When we talk about nature today, we talk about culture. Equally, when we talk about culture we talk about nature. Our persistent conception of a separation of worlds into nature and culture/society, which is intimately bound to modernist thought, fails to recognize that we are building, acting and living in a constructed artificial world of civilization whose characteristics are beyond these distinctions. The loss of boundaries between these realms is not only brought about by the industrialization of nature and culture but also by the hazards that endanger humans, animals and plants alike. Whether we think of the ozone hole, pollution or food scares, nature is inescapably contaminated by human activity. That is to say, the common danger has a levelling effect that whittles away some of the carefully erected boundaries between classes, nations, humans and the rest of nature, between creators of culture and creatures of instinct, or to use an earlier distinction between beings with and those without a soul (Adam, 1998: 24).

> In the threat people have the experience that they breathe like the plants, and live *from* water as the fish live *in* water. The toxic threat makes them sense that they participate with their bodies in things – 'a metabolic process with consciousness and morality' – and consequently, that they can be eroded like the stones and the trees in the acid rain. (Schütz (1984), quoted in Beck (1992a: 74)

That we live in a *hybrid* world which transcends our dichotomic framework of thought has convincingly been argued by Latour (1993). I totally agree with him. Both of us see that the hybrid world we live in and constantly produce is, at the same time, a matter of cultural perception, moral judgement, politics, and technology, which have been constructed in actor-networks and have been made hard facts by 'black boxing'. Yet the notion of a 'hybrid' world is necessary but insufficient to understand the new. 'Hybrid' is more of a negative than a positive concept. It somehow says what it is not – *not* nature and *not* society etc. – but it does not really say what it is. I want to suggest that we have to overcome the 'nots', 'beyonds' and 'posts' which dominate our thinking. But if you ask what begins where the ends end? my answer is: the notion of risk and risk society. Risks are *man-made hybrids*. They include and combine politics, ethics, mathematics, mass media, technologies, cultural definitions and perception; and, most important of all, you cannot separate these aspects and 'realities', if you want to understand the cultural and political dynamics of the world risk society. Hence, 'risk' is not only a notion which is used in a central matter by very different disciplines, it is also the way the 'hybrid society' watches, describes, values and criticizes its own hybridity.

This complex 'and', which resists thinking in either-or categories, is what constitutes the cultural and political dynamism of global risk society and makes it so difficult to comprehend.[11] A society that perceives itself as a risk society becomes *reflexive*, that is to say, the foundations of its activity and its objectives become the object of public scientific and political controversies. One could say that there is a naively realistic misapprehension in the talk of risk society and this can culminate in a type of 'neo-Spenglerism'. Equally possible and rational, however, is a reflexive understanding of risks, as developed here in the eight theses above. The concept of risk and the concept of world risk society are concepts of ambivalence, meaning that they destroy distinctions and reconnect antitheses. Accordingly, as stated above, the concept of (world) risk (society) means:

1   neither destruction nor trust/security but real virtuality;
2   a threatening future, (still) contrary to fact, becomes the parameter of influence for current action;
3   both a factual and a value statement, it combines in mathematicized morality;
4   control and lack of control as expressed in manufactured uncertainty;
5   knowledge or unawareness realized in conflicts of (re)cognition;
6   simultaneously the global and local are reconstituted as the 'glocality' of risks;
7   the distinction between knowledge, latent impact and symptomatic consequences;
8   a man-made hybrid world which lost its dualism between nature and culture.

Many social theories (including those of Michel Foucault and those of the Frankfurt School of Max Horkheimer and Theodor Adorno) paint modern society as a technocratic prison of bureaucratic institutions and expert knowledge in which people are mere wheels in the giant machine of technocratic and bureaucratic rationality. The picture of modernity drawn by the theory of world risk society contrasts sharply with these images. After all, one of the most important characteristics of the theory of risk society, so far scarcely understood in science or politics, is to unfreeze – at least intellectually – the seemingly rigid circumstances and to set them in motion. Unlike most theories of modern societies, the theory of risk society develops an image that makes the circumstances of modernity contingent, ambivalent and (involuntarily) susceptible to political rearrangement (Beck, 1992b, 1994, 1995, 1996a).

Due to this often unseen and undesired self-discreditation ('reflexive modernization') which is provoked everywhere by the discourse of risk, something ultimately happens which sociologists loyal to Weber would consider impossible: *institutions begin to change.* As we know, Weber's diagnosis is that modernity transforms into an iron cage in which people must sacrifice to the altar of rationality like the fellaheen of ancient Egypt. The theory of world risk society elaborates the antithesis: *the door of the iron cage of modernity is openening up.*[12] So I disagree with Ruth Levitas (this volume): there is a utopia built into risk society and risk society theory – the utopia of a *responsible* modernity, the utopia of *another* modernity, *many* modernities to be invented and experienced in different cultures and parts of the globe (see below). Anyone who is simply focused on the risk potential of industrial society fails to understand that risks are not only a matter of unintended consequences – the 'toxin of the week' – but also of the unintended consequences of unintended consequences *in* the institutions. Using the case of BSE, one could say that it is not just cows, but also governing parties, agencies, markets for meat and consumers who are affected and thus implicated in the madness.

A reply to criticisms of the risk society thesis

In the second part of this chapter I want to engage with some of the critiques formulated in this book and elsewhere: That there is a German, even a 'Bavariacentrism' (Alan Scott, Chapter 1 this volume) to my vision that risk society is identical with the 'Le Waldsterben-society'. If this were the case, would it mean that Great Britain, even after BSE, is *not* part of world risk society?

Maybe there is a German background to risk society theory. Being 'green' is undoubtedly part of the German national identity. Many Germans want Germany to be a greater, greener Switzerland. Testing atomic weapons may be part of the French national identity – I don't know. And the cultural significance of 'British (Sunday lunch) beef' may be an important backdrop to the BSE crisis. Yet the conflicts that arise from these national issues cannot be confined within national boundaries. People, expert groups, cultures, nations are getting involved involuntarily at every level of social organizations: a European public is born unintentionally and involuntarily from the conflict over British beef. If you, for example, visit a *Wirtshaus* (a small local restaurant) in southern Bavaria and look at the menu you will find a photograph of the local farmer with family; the intention being to build up trust in the restaurant's local 'good' beef which is to be differentiated from the 'bad' British beef.

Again the distinction between knowledge and latent impact is important as it enables us to differentiate between two phases of risk society. The first phase is dominated by identification with the 'goods' of industrial and technological progress, which simultaneously both intensifies and 'legitimates' as 'residual risks', hazards resulting from decisions ('residual risk society'). The first impacts are systematically produced but *not yet* the subject of public knowledge, scrutiny and debate and not yet at the centre of political conflict. A different situation arises when the hazards of industrial society begin to dominate public and private debates. Now the institutions of industrial society produce and legitimate hazards which they cannot control. During this transition, property and power relationships remain *constant*. Industrial society sees and criticizes itself *as* risk society. On the one hand, the society *still* makes decisions and acts on the pattern of the old industrial society; on the other, debates and conflicts which originate in the dynamic of risk society are being superimposed on interest organizations, the legal system and politics.

Throughout my work, I have sought to demonstrate that the return to the theoretical and political philosophy of industrial modernity in the age of global risk is doomed to failure. Those orthodox theories and politics remain tied to notions of progress and valorization of technological change. As such, they perpetuate the belief that the environmental hazards we face today can still be captured by nineteenth-century scientific models of risk assessment and industrial assumptions about danger and safety. Simultaneously, they maintain the illusion that the disintegrating institutions of industrial modernity – nuclear families, stable labour markets, segregated gender roles, social classes, nation state – can be shored up and buttressed against the waves of reflexive modernization sweeping across the West. This attempt to apply nineteenth-century ideas to the twenty-first century is the pervasive *category mistake* of social theory, social sciences and politics I am addressing in my writings. In risk society theory 'environmental' problems are no longer conceived as external problems. Instead they are theorized at the centre of institutions. This immanence has been recognized by the legal science in Germany (with a debate on manufactured risks and uncertainties in public law), but has not been as clearly and fully acknowledged by the sociology of risk either in Great Britain or Germany.

At this point it is pertinent to briefly outline some of the core notions of the hazards of risk society – *organized irresponsibility, relations of definition, social explosiveness of hazards* – and to summarize the arguments surrounding the *provident state*. These concepts, I want to argue, combine arguments why it is necessary not only to talk in terms of 'risk *culture*' (Scott and Lash, Chapters 1 and 2 this volume), which lacks the institutional dimension of risk and power, but also to theorize risk society with its cultural focus on the institutional base of contemporary globalized industrial society.

The concept of 'organized irresponsibility' helps to explain how and why the institutions of modern society must unavoidably acknowledge the reality of catastrophe while simultaneously denying its existence, hiding its origins and precluding compensation or control. To put it in another way, risk societies are characterized by the paradox of more and more environmental degradation – perceived and potential – coupled with an expansion of environmental law and regulation. Yet at the same time, no individual or institution seems to be held specifically accountable for anything. How can this be? The key to explaining this state of affairs, I suggest, is the mismatch that exists in the risk society between the character of hazards or manufactured uncertainties produced by late-industrialism and the prevalent *relations of definition* whose construction and content are rooted in an earlier and qualitatively different epoch.

In risk society *relations of definition* are to be conceived analogous to Marx' *relations of production*. Risk society's relations of definition include the specific rules, institutions and capacities that structure the identification and assessment of risk in a specific cultural context. They are the legal, epistemological and cultural power-matrix in which risk politics is conducted. The relations of definition I focus on can be identified with reference to four clusters of questions (also see Beck, 1996d; Goldblatt, 1996):

1 Who is to define and determine the harmfulness of products, the danger, the risks? Where does the responsibility lie: with those who generate the risks, those who benefit from them, those who are potentially affected by them, or with public agencies?
2 What kind of knowledge or non-knowledge about the causes, dimensions, actors, etc. is involved? To whom have evidence and 'proof' to be submitted?

3 What is to count as sufficient proof in a world where knowledge about environmental risks is necessarily contested and probabilistic?

4 Who is to decide on compensation for the afflicted and on what constitutes appropriate forms of future damage-limitation control and regulation?

In relation to each of these questions, risk societies are currently trapped in a vocabulary that is singularly inappropriate not only for modern catastrophes, but also for the challenges constituted by manufactured insecurities. Consequently, we face the paradox that at the very time when threats and hazards are seen to become more dangerous and more obvious, they become increasingly inaccessible to attempts to establish proof, attributions and compensation by scientific, legal and political means.

Of course, there is the question about the identity of the political subject of the risk society. Despite my extensive workings on this subject, however, my answer to this question eludes critics as long as they read my texts from within the dualistic frames of Enlightenment thought: to argue that nobody and everybody is the subject. So it should not surprise us that this answer gets lost. But there is more to it, and my argument here is close to Bruno Latour's theory of quasi-objects. In my work, hazards are quasi-subjects, whose acting-active quality is produced by risk societies' institutional contradictions. Moreover, risk society is *not* about a 'dystopian warning' (Ruth Levitas, Chapter 11 this volume). I use the metaphor of the *social explosiveness of hazard* to explain the politicizing effects of risk (definition) conflicts. I explore the ways in which the virtuality, the 'becoming real' (Joost van Loon, Chapter 9 this volume) of large-scale hazards, risks and manufactured uncertainties set off a dynamic of cultural and political change that undermines state bureaucracies, challenges the dominance of science and redraws the boundaries and battle lines of contemporary politics. So hazards, understood as socially constructed and produced 'quasi-subjects', are a powerful, uncontrollable 'actor' that delegitimates and destabilizes state institutions with responsibilities for pollution control, in particular, and public safety in general.

Hazards themselves sweep away the attempts of institutional elites and experts to control them. The 'risk assessment bureaucracies', of course, have well-worn routines of denial. By utilizing the gap between latent impact and knowledge, data can be hidden, denied and distorted. Counter-arguments can be mobilized. Maximum permissible levels of acceptance can be raised. Human error rather than system risk can be cast as villain of the piece. However, these are battles where victories are temporary and defeat is probable or at least possible because they are fought with nineteenth-century pledges of security in a world risk society where such promises are hollow and have lost their purchase. No longer the preserve of scientists and experts, the nature of hazards is demonstrated everywhere and for everyone willing and interested to see.

My political description and vision is close to François Ewald's idea of *safety* and the *provident state*. Ewald's theory marks a significant shift in the interpretation of the welfare state. While the majority of social scientists have sought to explain the origins and constructions of the welfare state in terms of class interests, the maintenance of social order or the enhancement of national productivity and military power, Ewald's argument underlines the provision of services (health care), the creation of insurance schemes (pensions and unemployment insurance) as well as the regulation of the economy and the environment in terms of the *creation of security*. In relation to industries and technologies, of course, technical experts play a central role in answering the question, 'how safe is safe enough?'. We need to appreciate, however, that this model of the provident state is most closely correlated with the institutions and procedures of continental Western European and much less with those of either Anglo-American capitalism or the social democratic states of Scandinavia.

Implications for the future of social theory

What follows from this for the future of a sociology of risk and risk society? In this final section of the chapter I will consider two possible implications.

First, as I said earlier, I admire the work of Bruno Latour, but with respect to the global risk society I disagree with his idea that 'we have never been modern'. Of course, the sun is rising as it has done always since ancient times. But – and this is a substantial proviso – this similarity is only a surface one. If you take the issue of risk beyond its cultural definition and explore instead the details of the management of risks in modern *institutions*, the contemporary paradoxes and dilemmas come to the fore and it becomes apparent that the global risk society and its cultural and political contradictions cannot be understood and explained in terms of pre-modern management of dangers and threats. This is not to deny, of course, that politicians as well as technical and legal experts could learn from the high priests of previous ages how to handle the demons of socially explosive hazards.

Second, risk society theory is *not* about exploding nuclear submarines, it is *not*, as Alan Scott (Chapter 1, this volume) suggests, one more expression of 'German Angst' at the millennium. On the contrary, I am working on a new and optimistic model for understanding our times. My argument interprets what others see as the development of a post-modern order in terms of a stage of *radicalized* (second phase) modernity, a stage where the dynamics of individualization, globalization and risk undermine the first phase of industrial nation-state modernity and its foundations. Modernity becomes *reflexive*, which means, concerned with its unintended consequences, risks and their implications on its foundations. Where most post-modern theorists are critical of grand narratives, general theory and humanity, I remain committed to all of these, but in a new sense. To me the enlightenment is *not* a historical notion and set of ideas but a process and dynamics where criticism, self-criticism, irony, and humanity play a central role. Where for many philosophers and sociologists 'rationality' means 'discourse' and 'cultural relativism', my notion of 'second reflexive modernity' implies that we do not have *enough* reason (*Vernunft*) to live and act in a global age of manufactured uncertainties.

Many theories and theorists do not recognize the *opportunities* of the risk society, the opportunities of the 'bads'. I argue for the opening up to democratic scrutiny of the previous depoliticized realms of decision-making and for the need to recognize the ways in which contemporary debates of this sort are constrained by the epistemological and legal systems within which they are conducted. This, then, is one of the themes I would like to see explored further, preferably on a comparative transnational, transcultural, potentially global level. It would entail that we reconstruct social definition of risks and risk management in different cultural framings, that we find out about the (negative) power of risk conflicts and definition where people who do not want to communicate with each other are forced together into a 'community' of shared (global) risks, and that we therefore combine it with the questions of *organized irresponsibility* and *relations of definition* in different cultural-political settings. This , it seems to me, would be a worthwhile new conceptual and political social science.

Notes

1   For the realism-constructivism-debate see Beck (1998a).

2   In addition to authors in this book, I owe a number of suggestions to Giddens (1990, 1995); Goldblatt (1996); Franklin (1997); Lash et al. (1996); Bonß (1991, 1995).

3   Benjamin (1973).

4   This position clearly gives us a different perspective on Alan Scott's (Chapter 1 this volume) very sophisticated distinction between Mary Douglas' and my version on 'constructed' and 'real risks'.

5   See Lindsay Prior, Chapter 5 this volume.

6   Kommission für Zukunftsfragen, Arbeitsmarktentwicklungen, Bericht Teil II, Bonn July 1997, chapter on globalization.

7   There may be one difference to the cultural theory concept of risk as advocated in the chapters by Alan Scott and Scott Lash. I sympathize very much with their (different) radical cultural approaches, but I do think 'risks' have to be understood and analysed from an inter- and trans-disciplinary perspective. Another way of operationalizing 'realism', I want to suggest, is to connect cultural, legal, and scientific approaches (besides all their differences and contradictionary background assumptions) to public perceptions of risk definitions, conflicts and politics. I am opposed to an *exclusive* view on 'risk culture' monopolized by cultural studies, but I am not sure that Scott Lash and Alan Scott would want to pursue such an exclusive status either.

8   Beck (1997) *Democracy Without Enemies*, see the chapter on 'Unawareness/non-knowledge'.

9   Maybe there is a 'Bavariacentrism' (Alan Scott, Chapter 1 this volume) and a 'taste of German security and wealth' (Hilary Rose, Chapter 3 this volume) to my risk society theory. There is no doubt, that the more Europe is becoming real, the more the differences in national cultural policies are becoming obvious. This means we have to study and concentrate on those cultural differences in risk perception and definition for example between Britain, France, Germany and Eastern European countries like Poland, Hungary or Russia in the future. But – and this BUT has to be written in big letters – is there, after the mad cow disease conflict and debate in Britain (Germany, France, etc.) any way of saying (as Hilary Rose seems to believe) that *only* Germany and *not* Britain is some kind of a risk society? Of course, we have to distinguish and develop theoretically different frameworks, *realizations* of risk societies. No doubt there is an amazing *pluralism* of risk societies – not only in Europe, but all over the world. But arguing that Britain is *not* a society trapped by the paradoxes of risk definitions and conflicts is to me like arguing that BSE in Europe is not of any (cultural) significance and (political) importance.

10   I am using Barbara Adam's (1998) arguments here.

11   For more detail on this, cf. Beck (1998b).
12   See also Beck (1996b), Beck et al., (1994).

References

Adam, B. (1998) *Timescapes of Modernity: the Environment and Invisible Hazards*. London: Routledge.

Bauman, Z. (1991) *Modernity and Ambivalence*. Cambridge: Polity.

Beck, U. (1992a) *Risk Society: Towards a New Modernity*. London: Sage.

Beck, U. (1992b) 'From Industrial to Risk Society', *Theory, Culture & Society*, 9 (1): 97–123.

Beck, U. (1994) *Ecological Enlightenment*. NJ: Humanities Press.

Beck, U. (1995) *Ecological Politics in an Age of Risk*. Cambridge: Polity.

Beck, U. (1996a) *The Reinvention of Politics*. Cambridge: Polity.

Beck, U. (1996b) 'World Risk Society as Cosmopolitan Society?', *Theory, Culture & Society*, 13 (4) : 1–32.

Beck, U. (1996c) 'Risk Society and the Provident State', in S. Lash, B. Szerszynski and B. Wynne (eds), *Risk, Environment and Modernity*. London: Sage. pp. 27–43.

Beck, U. (1996d) 'The Sociology of Risk', in D. Goldblatt (ed.), *Social Theory and the Environment*. Cambridge: Polity. pp. 154–87.

Beck, U. (1997) *Democracy Without Enemies*. Cambridge: Polity.

Beck, U. (1998a) *World Risk Society*. Cambridge: Polity.

Beck, U. (1998b) *Was ist Globalisierung?* Frankfurt am Main: Suhrkamp Verlag.

Beck, U. and Beck-Gernsheim, E. (1996) 'Individualization and Precarious Freedoms: Perspectives and Controversies of a Subject-oriented Sociology', in P. Heelas, S. Lash and P. Morris (eds), *Detraditionalisation*. Oxford: Blackwell, pp. 23–48.

Beck, U., Giddens, A., Lash, S. (1994) *Reflexive Modernization: Politics, Tradition and Aesthetics in the Modern Social Order*. Cambridge: Polity.

Beck-Gernsheim, E. (ed.) (1993) *Welche Gesundheit wollen wir?* Frankfurt am Main: Suhrkamp Verlag.

Beck-Gernsheim, E. (1995) *The Social Implications of Bioengineering*. NJ: Humanities Press.

Benjamin, W. (1973) *Illuminations*. Trans. H. Zohn. London: Fontana.

Bonß, W. (1991) 'Unsicherheit und Gesellschaft – Argumente für eine soziologische Risikoforschung', *Soziale Welt*, (42): 258–77.

Bonß, W. (1995) *Vom Risiko: Unsicherheit und Ungewißheit in der Moderne*. Hamburg: Bund.

Ewald, F. (1987) *L'Etat Providence*. Paris: Editions Grasser and Fasquell.

Franklin, J. (1997) *Politics of Risk Society*. Cambridge: Polity.

Giddens, A. (1990) *The Consequences of Modernity*. Cambridge: Polity.

Giddens, A. (1995) *Beyond Left and Right*. Cambridge: Polity.

Goldblatt, D. (ed.) (1996) *Social Theory and the Environment*. Cambridge: Polity.

Hajer, M. (1996) *The Politics of Environmental Discourse: Ecological Modernization and the Policy Process*. Oxford: Clarendon Press.

Harvey, D. (1989) *The Conditions of Postmodernity*. Oxford: Basil Blackwell.

Lash, S., Szerszynski, B. and Wynne, B. (eds) (1996) *Risk, Environment and Modernity*. London: Sage.

Latour, B. (1993) *We have never been Modern*. Trans. C. Porter. Hemel Hempstead: Harvester Wheatsheaf.

Latour, B. (1996) *Aramis or the Love of Technology*. Cambridge, MA: Harvard University Press.

Lau, C. (1989) 'Risikodiskurse', *Soziale Welt*, 3: 271–92.

Luhmann, N. (1995) *Die Soziologie des Risikos*. Berlin: De Gruyter.

Robertson, R. (1992) *Globalization: Social Theory and Global Culture*. London: Sage.

Schütz, R. (1984) *Ökologische Aspekte einer Naturphilosophischen Ethik.* Bamberg: Unpublished manuscript.

Weber, M. (1956) *Wirtschaft und Gesellschaft.* Tübingen: Mohr.

Weber, M. (1991) 'Objektive Möglichkeit und Adäquate Verursachung in der Historischen Kausalbetrachtung', in M. Weber, *Schriften zur Wissenschaftslehre.* Stuttgart: Reclam, pp. 102–31.

Wynne, B. (1996) 'May the Sheep Safely Graze?', in S. Lash, B. Szerszynski and B. Wynne (eds), *Risk, Environment and Modernity.* London: Sage. pp. 44–83.

Index

actor network theory, 115–18
actor networks: new genetics, 70, 110; nuclear energy, 98–9
aesthetic judgement, 52–5, 56–7
aesthetic reflexivity, 55–7
AIDS, 33, 53–4, 72, 169
allegories of everyday life, 165, 166
Amnesty International, 151–2
anxiety, 36, 67, 158, 200: attempts to counter, 155, 160–1;
    German, 39, 155
assemblage, 167, 168, 170, 80
atomic bombs, 78–9, 91–3: development, 96–7; tests, 94, 99
Austria, 64

'bads', 52, 53–4, 57, 166: opportunities of, 226–7
Barings Bank, 185
BBC see British Broadcasting Corporation
BBSRC see Biotechnology and Biological Sciences
    Research Council
Beck, U., 4, 5, 6, 7, 8, 12, 34–7, 38, 39, 42, 47, 49–50, 51, 53,
    54, 59, 60, 63–5, 67, 81, 93, 111, 112, 123, 129, 138, 166,
    168, 171, 174, 175–6, 198, 200, 201, 202, 203, 204, 205,
    206–8, 209
becoming-real, 176, 213–14
Benjamin, W., 165–7, 170, 176
Bhopal, 64
Big Science, 65–6, 67, 82, 109
biochemistry, 105
biotechnology: and discourses of desire, 100–1; medical
    perspective, 158–61, 162, 163; performance art perspective,
    161–3; religious perspective, 156–8, 159, 160, 161, 163;
    UK Consensus Conference, 112
Biotechnology and Biological Sciences Research Council
    (BBSRC), 71
biotechnology companies, 67
'black box', 82
blame, 40, 42, 51–2: responsibility and, 131–2
BMA see British Medical Association
body: economization of, 149–50; Fractal Flesh, 161–3;
    Instinktarmut, 57
body parts see child organ stealing stories
border sectarians, 48–9, 50, 51, 52
boundaries: disciplinary, porosity of, 5–6; of risk,
    expert-defined, 112
bovine spongiform encephalopathy (BSE), 12, 63, 71, 72, 169,
    174–8, 217, 222–3
breast cancer, 69, 70: screening, 111–12
Britain, 63–4, 205: atomic bomb project, 96; fertility treatment,
    207; Human Genome Project, 110; individualistic culture, 41,
    42; MAFF, 115–16; nuclear industry, 97–8; public
    attitudes to, 98–100; risk perception, 39; science; public
    attitudes to, 71, 72–3; public participation in decision-making,
    111–12; UK Consensus Conference on Biotechnology, 112;
    welfare state, 64, 74, 202, 205; Windscale Inquiry, 83
British Broadcasting Corporation (BBC), 140
British Medical Association (BMA), 158, 162, 163
BSE see Bovine Spongiform Encephalopathy

capitalism, 188, 205, 206, 208, 209; discourse of, 201; and
    nuclear power, 83–4
'catastrophic society', 90
category mistake, 223–4
chance, 200–1
Chernobyl, 3, 12, 33, 64, 72, 82, 84
Chicago futures exchange, 184, 185, 188, 191, 194
child organ stealing stories, 136–8: see also rumour
choices, 68, 69, 70: dualistic, 6
genetic, 127–8: see also freedom of choice

Church: Catholic, 49, 156–8, 159, 160, 161, 163; as institution,
    55–6; political impact in Germany, 41
CJD see Creutzfeldt-Jakob disease
class society versus risk society, 34–6, 203–4
class-bound expertise, 99
cognition see determinate judgement
Cold War, 66, 79, 88, 89
collectivism, 41, 42: versus individualism, 43
Committee for the Public Understanding of Science (COPUS), 71
common sense of nucleonism 87, 93
community (group/grid) typology, 39–42, 48–52
computer viruses, 169
conspiracy against life see culture of death
constructivism, 2–3, 51, 57, 176: science and technology, 84–7;
    versus realism, 168, 177–8, 211–12, 213–14, 219–21
consumer eugenics, 70
consumers, 203: BSE crisis, 177, 178
contextual nature of expert knowledge, 111
COPUS see Committee for the Public Understanding of Science
Creutzfeldt-Jakob disease (CJD), 63, 174–5, 176, 177, 178, 220
cultural politics, 157–8
cultural relativization, 38–9
cultural resources, 42
cultural shift, 68–9
cultural strategies, 16–1, 157–8
culture of death, 156–7, 158
culture of life, 156, 157, 158
culture and nature, 221
Cumbria see Sellafield
cybernetic reproduction, 167–72, 177–8

decision-makers, 214
decision-making: public participation, 110–12; risks versus
    hazards, 166
Denmark, 63, 71, 73
'derivatives' contracts, 191–2
desire for control, 171–2
desiring risk, 94–101
determinate judgements, 52, 53, 54–5, 56, 57; expert systems, 58
dialogical democracy, 207–8
discourses: of capitalism, 201; of globalization, 214–15; of
    molecular biology, 74; of risk, implications, 42–3; of risk
    society, 200–1; see also language of risk; military language
discursive strategies, 4, 204; nuclear power, 87–93
DNA, 69, 74, 105
Douglas, M., 38–41, 42, 43, 48–9, 51, 52–3, 54, 55–6, 59: and
    Wildavsky, A., 34, 47, 48, 50–2, 56
dramatization of risk, 215
Dunblane, 63

Ebola epidemic, 169
ecological utopia, 42, 43
economic change, 50–1
economic risks, 50
economy, post-scarcity, 205–6
electronic communications/media, 167, 168–9, 173, 174–8,
    184–5
enframing, 8
environmental damage, 33, 36, 40, 83
environmental disasters, 64
environmental groups, 40–1, 48, 49, 85
environmental (natural) risks, 49–51, 208
epidemics, 169: see also AIDS
'epistemic drift', 73
epistemologies, 3, 12, 67, 170: constructivist, 168, 177, 178
ethics: biotechnology, 158–9, 160; in cybernetic age, 171, 172;
    Human Genome Project, 110; medical, 158–9; social theory,
    179–80

eugenics, 67–8, 70, 110, 206–7
Europe: attitudes to new genetics, 67, 69, 125; Eastern, 70; economic problems, 64–5; health care, 70, 74; public participation in decision-making, 110–11; *see also* rabies eradication programme
European Commission, 114, 115, 116–17, 118, 175, 208
Evangelium vitae, 156–8, 159, 160, 161, 163
everyday life, 53, 87–93: allegories of, 165, 166
expert systems, 56, 58
experts/expertise, 99, 111, 112

face-to-face contact, 193
fertility treatment, 207
flows, 168–9, 173–4, 179–80, 184–5
Foetal Flash, 161]
France, 64, 85
freedom of choice, 125, 129: versus responsibility, 131
futures, 8–9, 58–61
futures markets, 185–7, 194–5: time value of future, 188–9; time value of money, 189–93; trading around the clock, 187–8; trust, risk and technology in, 193–4

gender relations, 208
gene therapy, 67, 68, 126, 160
genetic counselling, 74, 125
genetic diagnostics, 67, 68, 69–70, 126: *see also* prenatal diagnosis
genetically-engineered viruses *see* rabies eradication programme
genetics, 3, 67–71, 73–4, 206–7: genome analysis and health, 125–7; and probability theory, 106–9; *see also* Human Genome Project
germ line cell therapy, 160, 161
Germany, 34–5: anxiety, 39; collectivist/hierarchical culture, 41, 42; Gene Technology Commission, 127; Green movement, 69; neo-Nazism, 70; new genetics, 125, 130; risk perception, 39, 41–2, 204–5; science and society, 71; standard employment relation, 37; welfare state, 37, 42
Gesamtkunstwerk, 162
Giddens, A., 6, 49–50, 53, 54, 56, 59, 63–4, 67, 111, 184, 189, 198, 199, 201, 202, 204, 205, 206, 207–8, 209, 212, 216
global information economy, 58
'global media mix', 169, 173
global trading, 187–8
global/local logic, 184–5
global/local risks, 218
globalization: of nuclear power, 83; risk of, 214–15; of rumours, 144–7
globalized markets, 51
globalized nature of contemporary risks, 36
globalizing information flows, 168–9
Guatemala, 139–43, 145, 150, 151–2

hazards versus risks, 166, 176
health: expansion of concept of, 127–30; and genome analysis, 125–7; as individual task, 123–4, 129; and responsibility, 130–2
HGP *see* Human Genome Project
hierarchical-institutional cultures, 50, 51, 55–6
Hiroshima, 65–6, 78, 79, 91
Holland, 71
Human Genome Project (HGP), 67, 68, 69, 72, 73, 106, **110**, 111
human rights, suppression of, 139–40
humanism versus technocracy, 171–2, 175, 178–9
Huntingdon's disease, 68
hybrids, 72, 221

identity risks, 49–50
indeterminancy, 6, 216
individualism: market cultures, 39–42, 50, 51–2; risk and blame, 40; versus collectivism, 43; *see also* health, as individual task
individualization, 37–8

inequality *see* social exclusion
information technologies *see* electronic communications/media
insecurity *see* anxiety; safety
Instinktarmut, 55–6, 57
institutions, 55–6, 219, 226: reflexive, democratically structured, 50; and sects, 48–52, 59
insurance, 69–70, 202–3
interaction, 184
interconnectivity, 183–5
international institutions, 219
'iron cage', 211, 222

Japan, 39, 42
journalism see mass media
judgements: about probabilities, 213, 214; aesthetic/reflexive versus determinate, 52–9

Kant, E., 47, 52, 53, 56–7
knowledge: and latent impact, 219–21, 223; models of, 9–12, 55; new production system of, 73; scientific and medical, 68, 159–61; situated, 4–5; and unawareness, 216–17; *see also* expert systems; experts/expertise

language of risk, 6–8, 12
late modernity, 64, 183, 184–5, 194, 207
latent impact, 219–21, 223
Leventhal, T., 136–7, 138, 143–5, 146, 150
Lloyds of London, 220–1
'local logic', 184, 185
logic of control, 215–16
London futures exchange, 184, 185, 187

'mad cow disease' *see* bovine spongiform encephalopathy
Manhattan Project, 78, 82, 96
manufactured uncertainty, 6, 201, 216–17
marginalized groups *see* border sectarians; social exclusion
Marx, K., 4, 183, 189, 190, 199, 207, 224
Marxism, 66
mass media: globalization of rumours, 139–44, 145–6, 147; new genetics, 127–8; nuclear discourse, 79–80, 88–9, 90, 92; social theory focus, 64
mathematics see probability
'media event', 169–70, 172
mediation *see* electronic communications/media
Milford Haven, 63
militarism versus techno-economism, 65–6
military desires, 97–8
military language, 88
military power, 140–1
military use of rumour, 141
Mills, C.W., 106, 109, 112
modernity, 81–7, 198, 205, 222: and nuclear power, 82; shift to late modernity, 207; and technology, 81
M"glichkeitsurteile, 213
money, time value of, 189–93
myth: Guatemalan, 142–4; Oedipus complex, 171; *see also* rumour

Nagasaki, 65–6, 78
natural risks, 49–51
nature and culture, 221
nature versus technology debate, 132–3
'network society', 58
norms versus values, 59–60
nuclear deterrence, 88
nuclear industry, 83, 85–6: Britain, 72–3, 97; Eastern Europe, 70
nuclear myths, 94–101
nuclear power: dual use, 95, 97; and modernity, 82; public opinion, 80; re-positioning sociological analysis, 3, 81–7
nuclear protests, 35, 85
nuclear weapons, 66, 90–1
nuclearism, common sense of, 87–93
'nukespeak', 89–93

opportunities, 226–7

organized irresponsibility, 224, 227
Our Genetic Future (BMA), 158–61
ozone depletion, 220

perfectibility of man, 129
physicists' desires, 95, 96–7, 99
Polaris, 88–9, 92
political desires, 97–8
political manipulability of risk consciousness, 204
political mobilization, 4, 9
politicization of BSE, 174–5
politics in cybernetic age, 171, 178–9
pollution, 36, 72–3: ritual, 51, 52
Pope John Paul II, 156
post-scarcity economy, 205–6
postmodernism, 204, 209, 211
prenatal diagnosis, 129, 130–2, 159
preventative health care, 129–30
prions, 169, 176, 177
probability, 106–9, 213, 214
proximity, 193
public anxiety see anxiety
public desires, 98–100
public issues and personal troubles, 105–6
public participation in decision-making, 110–12
public perception of risk, 39, 90–1
public understanding of science, 71–2

rabies eradication programme, 112–18, 139
race, concept of, 70
realism, 51, 168, 174, 176, 177: science as, 67; utopian, 199;
    versus constructivism, 168, 177–8, 211–12, 213–14, 219–21
reality versus representation, 169–70, 177–8
reflexive communities, 47
reflexive judgement, 52–5, 58–9
reflexive modernity/modernization, 1–2, 37, 48, 54, 60, 206,
    221–2, 226
reflexivity, 37, 38, 173, 175–6
relations of (risk) definition, 224–5, 227
religion see Church
representations versus reality, 169–70, 177–8
reproductive technologies, 137–8, 149–50
responsibility, 130–2
risk: definitions, 3–5, 112, 138–9, 166, 200; language of, 6–8, 12;
    sociological concept of, 212–23; criticisms addressed, 223–6
'risk compensation effect', 201
risk consciousness, 38–9, 204
risk culture, 47, 48–52, 59, 60–1: recasting, 12–16; versus risk
    societies, 5, 50
risk perception, 3, 7, 8, 38–9, 201–2; categories of, 10;
    community (group/grid) typology, 39–42, 48–52
risk society: concept of, 222; versus class society, 34–6, 203–4;
    versus risk culture, 5, 50
risk trap, 218
risk-averse society, 39, 42–3
rumour: localized, 139–44; as 'modern urban legend', 144–7;
    and risk, 148–51, 152
Russia (Soviet Union), 33, 79

safety, 203, 208, 225–6
salmonella, 72
satellite technology, 188, 194
scarcity versus risk, 34, 35–7
scepticism, 64, 100: bridgehead strategy to allay, 126–7; and
    trust, 71–4
science fiction, 91–2, 179
science, social standing of, 64, 66, 71
science and technology, sociological study of, 65–6
sects and institutions, 48–52, 59
security, declining, 34
Sellafield (Windscale), 73, 83, 86, 100
sense-making, 9, 10, 11
signification, 170–1

Simmel, G., 37–8, 185, 189–93
simulacrum, 167, 172, 177
situated knowledge, 4–5
social change, 168–9
social engineering, 9
social exclusion, 205, 206
social explosiveness of hazards, 224, 225
social risks, 50
social theory: in Britain, 63–4; risk concept, 212–23; criticisms
    addressed, 223–6; role in cybernetic age, 179–80; role in risk
    society/culture, 9–12; science and technology, 65–6
socio-political risks, 50
somatic cell gene therapy, 160, 161
space/time, compression of, 171, 183–5, 186–7, 218
Stelarc, 161–4
sub-politics, 49, 59, 61: medicine as, 132, 133; of risk
    definition, 4
subjectivity, 52, 54–5, 58–9, 65: and probability, 107–8
sublime judgements, 57

techno-economism: birth of, 66–7; versus militarism, 65–6
technocracy versus humanism, 171–2, 175, 178–9
technological futures, 59, 60–1
technological risks, 50, 52
technologically-induced hazards, 3, 4, 8–9
technology: and modernity, 81; precursors and 'pedigree', 85;
    as spiral-shaped process, 122–3, 127; versus nature debate,
    132–3; see also electronic communications/media
Three Mile Island, 82, 94
time value of future, 188–9
time value of money, 189–93
time/space, compression of, 171, 183–5, 186–7, 218
Tokyo futures exchange, 185, 187–8
Torrey Canyon disaster, 64
trading around the clock, 187–8
transformative utopianism, 199–200, 201, 204
transnational adoption, 137–8, 147
trust, 51, 56, 64: futures markets, 193–4; and scepticism, 71–4

unawareness, 216–17
uncertainty, 68, 175–6, 194, 200: manufactured, 6, 201, 216–17
unemployment, 34, 64–5, 204–5
UNESCO statement on race (1946), 70
United Kingdom Atomic Energy Authority (UKAEA), 97, 98
United Kingdon see Britain
United States (US): atomic bombs, 78–9, 94; Department of
    Agriculture, 113; health care system, 69–70; individualism,
    41, 42; liberal market model, 125; nuclear technology
    funding, 101; public participation in decision-making,
    111–12; public perception of nuclear energy, 98–9; risk
    perception, 41; US Information Agency (USIA), 136–7, 144
urban myth/legend see rumour, as 'modern urban legend'
utopia: definitions, 198–9; ecological, 42, 43
utopianism, transformative, 199–200, 201, 204

values: detraditionalization of, 37; health, 123–4, 127;
    non-material, 206; technology versus nature, 132–3;
    versus norms, 59–60
Vatican, 156, 161
violence, 140–1, 151–2: as efficiency, 156–7
virtual reality see cybernetic reproduction
virtual risks, 172–4
viruses, 169: genetically-engineered see rabies eradication
    programme
voluntary compulsion, 129–30
vulnerability, 34, 172, 179

Weber, M., 38, 54, 211, 213, 216
welfare state, 201, 202, 203: Britain, 64, 74, 202, 205;
    Germany, 37, 42; Scandanavia, 64
Wildavsky, A., 34, 47, 48, 50–2, 56
Windscale see Sellafield
witchcraft, 148, 150